The Koreans

Contemporary Politics and Society

Satellite view of the Korean Peninsula (photo courtesy of Korea Overseas Information Service)

The Koreans

Contemporary Politics and Society

Donald Stone Macdonald

Westview Press
BOULDER & LONDON

Copyright © 1988 by Westview Press, Inc.

Published in 1988 in the United States of America by Westview Press, Inc.; Frederick A. Praeger, Publisher; 5500 Central Avenue, Boulder, Colorado 80301

Library of Congress Cataloging-in-Publication Data
Macdonald, Donald Stone.
  The Koreans, contemporary politics and society
  Bibliography: p.
  Includes index.
  1. Korea—History. 2. Korea (South)—Politics and government. 3. Korea (North)—Politics and government. 4. Korean reunification question (1945–). I. Title.
DS907.18.M33 1988   951.9′04   86-32613
ISBN 0-8133-0515-2

Printed and bound in the United States of America

⬡ The paper used in this publication meets the requirements of the American National Standard for Permanence of Paper for Printed Library Materials Z39.48-1984.

6   5   4   3   2   1

CONTENTS

TABLES AND FIGURES

PREFACE

Among its foreign residents, Korea is known as "the best-kept secret" because living there is so much better than they had expected. This gap between expectation and reality is only one of many indications that the West—particularly the United States—does not know Korea. Such ignorance is grossly out of proportion to the real importance of Korea to the rest of the world. It also overlooks the fascinating history of the Korean people, who have preserved their own distinctive identity and culture despite hundreds of invasions over the centuries by their neighbors.

Since World War II, Korea has undergone a dramatic transformation from a sleepy and poverty-stricken nation of landlord-ridden peasants to become a vital, expanding modern economy. Tragically divided since 1945 by ideology, superpower rivalry, and civil war, both Koreas have nevertheless led the developing world in economic progress. In fierce competition with each other, the two Korean states have become major factors in the security, stability, and progress of East Asia.

This book is intended as an attack upon Western ignorance about Korea. In brief summary form, it endeavors to explain why Korea is important—strategically, economically, and culturally. It traces the historical roots of the Korean people, the development of their culture as a blend of native heritage and foreign influence, and the problems of national development under the conflicting pressures of Confucian tradition, U.S. democratic capitalism, and Soviet communism. It tries to convey something of the fascination that Korea has for people who, like the author, have studied its problems and sought to understand its delightful but fractious people.

Korea should be understood as a single nation, even though it was divided into two states by superpower rivalry and ideological differences. (To emphasize the point, *north* and *south* are not capitalized in this book when referring to the two halves of Korea.) The Democratic People's Republic of Korea (north Korea) deserves full attention, along with the Republic of Korea (south Korea). Yet I have given north Korea far less space than south Korea. The reason is that reliable detailed information about the north is exceedingly difficult to obtain because of the self-isolation and secretiveness of its government and the virtual absence of relations between that government

xi

and the United States. In the future, perhaps, the doors to the north may be further opened to outside inquiry and knowledge.

It is my hope that this introductory survey will help to stimulate much-needed general awareness and understanding of Korea. One test of its usefulness will be the interest it creates in reading the growing number of English-language books available on various aspects of Korean affairs. Appendix C has suggestions for further reading.

Most Western readers have difficulty with East Asian names and terms. This is due partly to the strangeness of the foreign words. A glossary (Appendix A) is provided to assist the reader in dealing with Korean terms. In addition, it is difficult to write the East Asian languages phonetically in Latin letters (a difficulty that applies to Korean, Chinese, and Vietnamese words, but not Japanese). The Koreans have one of the world's best alphabets for their own language, but few non-Koreans can read it.

There is no really satisfactory way of writing Korean words in the Latin alphabet. The best available system, devised in 1939 by George M. McCune and Edwin O. Reischauer along the lines of the Wade-Giles system for romanizing Chinese, has been adopted by the U.S. government and most English-speaking scholars. It recently became the official romanization system of the Republic of Korea (south Korea). North Korea uses a somewhat different system, apparently modeled after the pinyin romanization system for Chinese, which was developed by the People's Republic of China.

The McCune-Reischauer system is used in this book for all pre-1945 Korean names, places, and terms and for those of post-1945 south Korea (except that the diacritical marks over "o" and "u" that distinguish certain vowel sounds are omitted to facilitate printing). However, where other spellings are preferred by individuals or in common use, they have been used here (the city of Seoul, for example would be *Soul* in McCune-Reischauer spelling). The north Korean spellings, insofar as known, are used for post-1945 north Korean names, places, and terms. A few facts about the Korean language and the McCune-Reischauer system are presented in Appendix B.

Donald S. Macdonald

ACKNOWLEDGMENTS

In preparing the manuscript, I have had the advice and support of many friends, colleagues, and associates. Their names appear alphabetically below. Literally dozens of them have read all or a portion of the draft manuscript and made valuable criticisms and suggestions. (Some family names come first, in the East Asian order; in such cases a comma is inserted after the family name. Romanization of Korean names is according to the individuals' preference, where this is known; otherwise, according to the McCune-Reischauer system.) The list does not include many other people who shared their knowledge and insights with me in the course of conversation and whose ideas are reflected, explicitly or implicitly, in these pages. The final product is my responsibility, but whatever merit it may have comes in greater part from these many contributions.

- Chung Shil Adams, Seoul International Publishing House, Seoul
- Dr. Ahn, Young Sop, Director for Political Studies, Korea Institute for Policy Studies
- Dr. Vincent S.R. Brandt, Center for East Asian Studies, Harvard University
- Dr. Ardath W. Burks, Professor Emeritus of Asian Studies, Rutgers University
- Dr. Choi Jang Jip, Professor of Political Science, Korea University
- Dr. Choi Young, Director, Division of National Security and Strategy Affairs, Institute of Foreign Affairs and National Security, Ministry of Foreign Affairs, Republic of Korea
- Dr. Paul S. Crane, M.D., Director, Health Ministries, Presbyterian Church (U.S.A.)
- Sophie Montgomery Crane, former missionary and writer
- Thomas P.H. Dunlop, Counselor for Political Affairs, U.S. Embassy, Seoul
- Col. Kerry G. Herron, Office of the Assistant Chief of Staff, J-3, ROK-U.S. Combined Forces Command
- Dr. Hong, Sung-Chick, Director, Asiatic Research Center, and Professor of Sociology, Korea University
- Dr. Dong Joon Hwang, Research Director, Korea Institute for Defense Analysis

- Dr. Im Hoe-sop, Professor of Sociology, Korea University
- H.E. Kim, Chung Yul, former Minister of National Defense and presently Prime Minister of the Republic of Korea
- Kim Jin-Hyun, Chief Editorial Writer, *Dong A Ilbo,* Seoul
- Gen. Frederick C. Krause, U.S. Army, retired, former Executive Vice President, American Chamber of Commerce in Korea
- Dr. Ku Young Nok, Professor of Political Science, Seoul National University
- Dr. Paul Kuznets, Professor of Economics, Indiana University
- Kwak So Jin, United States Information Service, U.S. Embassy, Seoul (retired)
- Dr. Yung-hwan Jo, Professor of Economics, Arizona State College
- Dr. Lee Hahn Been, former Deputy Prime Minister, Republic of Korea
- Dr. Lee On-Jook, Visiting Professor of Sociology, The Johns Hopkins University
- Dr. Dennis McNamara, S.J., Professor of Sociology, Georgetown University
- Paik Syeung Gil, Director, Dept. of Culture and Information, Korean National Commission for UNESCO
- Dr. Eul Y. Park, International Bank for Reconstruction and Development
- Park Kwon Sang, former Editor, *Dong A Ilbo,* and Visiting Fellow, Institute of Sino-Soviet Studies, The George Washington University
- Hon. Park Sang Yong, Vice Minister and former Director, Institute of Foreign Affairs and National Security, Ministry of Foreign Affairs, Republic of Korea
- Fr. Basil M. Price, S.J., Chairman of the Board, Institute for Labor and Management, Sogang University, Seoul
- Hon. Shin Byung Hyun, former Deputy Prime Minister, Republic of Korea
- Dr. Dae Sook Suh, Director, Institute of Korean Studies, University of Hawaii
- Sul Kuk-hwan, Chairman of the Board, Korea Tourist Bureau, Ltd.
- Dr. George Viksnins, Professor of Economics, Georgetown University
- Dr. Yi Myong-yong, Professor of Political Science, Songgyun'gwan University, Seoul

Apart from the foregoing contributions, my efforts would have come to naught without the support I received from many institutions and individuals. A generous grant from the U.S. Department of Education provided time and opportunity to complete the manuscript in Korea during the first half of 1986. Gratitude is particularly due to Georgetown University's Asian Studies Program and its director, Professor Matthew M. Gardner, Jr.; to the Asiatic Research Center of Korea University and its then director, Professor Sungjoo

Han; and the Yongsan Library of United States Forces, Korea, directed by Sunny Murphy and Arlene Hahn.

About seventy participants at a Yongsan Library lecture series based on the manuscript provided helpful criticism of style and substance. The Korea Research Foundation provided support for Korean courses at Georgetown University that provided the testing ground for the material presented here. Kim Chin-ki, in Seoul, and Gregory O'Connor, in Washington, provided valuable research assistance.

Wongi Sul, a New York artist, created the illustrations for the chapter headings. Dr. Paul S. Crane provided the photograph of his ancient screen depicting the sixteenth-century Battle of Pyongyang, which appears in Figure 1.3. Edward B. Adams, headmaster of Seoul International School, and the Korea Overseas Information Service of the Republic of Korea's Ministry of Culture and Information kindly provided several of the illustrations. Park Shinil, Cultural Service director in New York, Park Young-Gil, Information Office director in Washington, and Clyde Hess, consultant to the Cultural Office, were particularly helpful.

I wish to acknowledge with profound gratitude my debt to the many scholars and associates who have helped me over the years to understand something of Korea's fascinating nature and spirit. Among them are the late Professor George M. McCune, the late Shin Chung Kiun, Sul Kuk-hwan, Professor Suh Doo Soo, Dr. Min Kwan-sik, Dr. Lee Hahn-Been, Suh Kwang-soon, Key P. Yang, Kim Yong-song, Hong In-pyo, Kwak So-jin, and many members of the Republic of Korea diplomatic service, including ambassadors Hahn Pil Wook, Park Sang Yong, Oh Jay Hee, and Minister Lee Sang-kon. Finally, no words can convey adequate recognition of the contribution to this and many other projects by my wife, Jean Carroll Macdonald, in time, energy, and loving support.

D.S.M.

1 INTRODUCTION: LAND, PEOPLE, PROBLEMS

Storm Center of East Asia

Korea is fated by geography and history to be the storm center of East Asia. For centuries, it has been both bridge and battleground among its neighbors. Three of the world's greatest nations—the Soviet Union, China, and Japan—surround Korea. Each of them considers the country to be of major importance to its own security and each, in the past century, has sought to dominate it. Since 1945, the United States has also developed a major security interest in Korea. Thus, far more than most of the U.S. and European public realize, Korea is of vital importance to the peace and progress of this dynamic region.

The Korean people have virtually no record of aggressive ambition outside their peninsula. More than a thousand years ago, Korea was a major, but wholly peaceful, influence on the growth of Japanese culture. Yet the peninsula has endured nine hundred invasions, great and small, in its two thousand years of recorded history.[1] It has suffered five major occupations by foreign powers. Four wars in the past hundred years were fought in and around Korea.

Despite these trials, Korea had a history of well over a millennium as a unified, autonomous nation until Japan took it as a colony in 1910. The victors in World War II, who drove out the Japanese, divided the country for military convenience in 1945. The Soviet and U.S. occupiers, withdrawing three years later, left two hostile states in the peninsula, reflecting the Cold War confrontation of their sponsors. The resulting three-year Korean War, with its enormous human and material toll, has never formally ended. Today one and one-half million soldiers (including forty thousand from the United States) still face each other, armed to the teeth, along the 1953 armistice line, while an armistice commission—now approaching its five-hundredth meeting—offers a forum for endless repetition of charges and countercharges.

Traditional East Asian rivalries are thus eclipsed by the Soviet-U.S. confrontation, which has shaped the attitudes of the superpowers' respective Korean allies. The Koreans' own aspiration for reunification intensifies the confrontation and heightens the risk of renewed hostilities to achieve it. The stakes are high. If reunified, Korea would be among the twenty most populous countries in the world, as well as having one of the most talented and energetic peoples.

Even in their tense and divided conditions, both Korean states have made impressive progress toward the realization of a modern industrial society. However, there is another confrontation in Korea: the clash between modernity and tradition, between a new urban industrialized society and an old rural agrarian one, between the new demands for political participation and social justice and the old hierarchical, authoritarian order. To understand this problem in all its complexity, as well as to appreciate Korea's progress, requires some knowledge of Korean history and social and political background.

This introductory chapter briefly reviews the geography, resources, and people of the Korean peninsula. It then touches upon the problems arising out of Korean history, culture, politics, economics, and international relations—topics that are examined in greater detail in the rest of the book.

Basic Geographic Facts

The Korean peninsula juts southward from the Eurasian land mass between Soviet Siberia and Chinese Manchuria. As nineteenth-century strategists used to say, it points "like a dagger at the heart of Japan" (Fig. 1.1). The national territory, now as for many centuries past, includes a slice of the

FIGURE 1.1 Korea and its Northeast Asian setting (reprinted with permission from the American Map Corporation, New York)

Asian mainland—a reminder of ancient Korean domains in parts of Manchuria (see Frontispiece).[2]

Korea's shape has been compared by Korean scholars to a rabbit, whose ears touch Siberia at the 43d parallel in the northeast; whose legs paddle in the Yellow Sea on the west, and whose backbone is the great T'aebaek mountain range along the east coast (Fig. 1.2). The semitropical, volcanic Cheju Island, which is just above the 33d parallel south of the peninsula, could be regarded as the rabbit's slightly misplaced cottontail.

The 1,025-kilometer (636-mile) Korean boundary with China is formed by two rivers, the Yalu to the west and Tumen to the east; they rise near the fabled Paektusan (White Head Mountain, 2,744 meters or 9,000 feet), highest point in Korea, and flow through rugged mountains into the Pacific on either side of the peninsula. The last 16 kilometers (about 11 miles) of the Tumen's course separate Korea from the Soviet Union's Maritime Province. Japan, to the east, is separated from Korea by the East Sea (Sea of Japan) and by the 100-kilometer (60-mile) width of the Korea Strait (Strait of Tsushima). The Japanese island of Tsushima, in the middle of the strait, is about 35 kilometers (20 miles) from the nearest point in Korea.

The de facto boundary between the two Korean states is the Military Demarcation Line established by the Armistice Agreement of 1953, which replaced the division at the 38th parallel agreed to by the United States and the Soviet Union in 1945. The boundary lies in the middle of a so-called Demilitarized Zone, 4 kilometers (2.4 miles) wide.[3] The line begins on the west in the Han River estuary on the west coast, runs just south of the city of Kaesong (ancient capital of the Koryo Dynasty), and then extends generally east-northeast to the East Sea. The narrow triangular area above the 38th parallel thus added to the south by the Armistice Agreement is technically under United Nations Command jurisdiction, but in fact has become part of south Korea.

The total area of north and south Korea is 220,847 square kilometers (about 85,300 square miles). The Democratic People's Republic of Korea (DPRK) in the north has 122,370 square kilometers (47,300 square miles), or 55 percent of the total, and the Republic of Korea (ROK) in the south has 98,477 square kilometers (38,000 square miles). The whole of Korea is about as large as the U.S. state of Minnesota and slightly smaller than the United Kingdom.

Korea is very mountainous; the Koreans themselves speak of their "three thousand *ri*[4] of beautiful rivers and mountains" in song and story and often go to the mountains for meditation or enjoyment. The dominant T'aebaek Range (the "rabbit's" backbone) has a series of spurs, mostly running southwestward, that cut the peninsula into narrow valleys and alluvial plains. In the northeast, the picture is more complicated; it includes a range of extinct volcanoes from Paektusan southeastward to the East Sea (Sea of

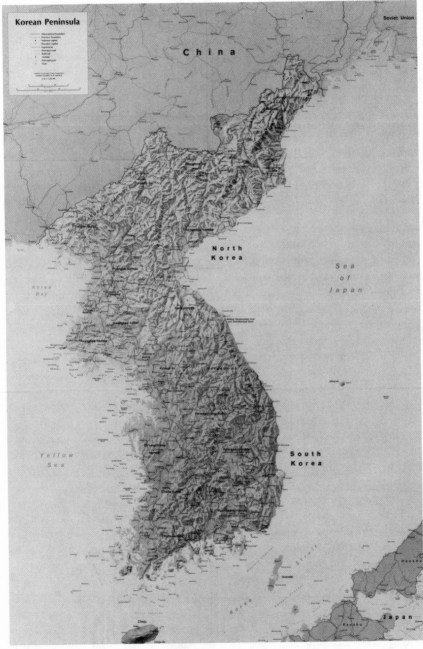

FIGURE 1.2 Physical-political map of Korea (U.S. government map; photo by Dunn Photographic Associates)

Japan). About 16 percent of the land in the north and 20 percent in the south is flat enough for grain and vegetable crops.

The mountains of Korea are not very high for the most part, but they are quite steep and form a dominant feature of the landscape almost everywhere in the country. The so-called Diamond Mountains in southeastern north Korea, a very striking area of sharp, rocky pinnacles, have long been a tourist attraction. For the most part, Korean mountains are non-volcanic granite of great age, but two of the three highest peaks in the country—Paektu on the Manchurian border in the extreme north and Mount Halla on Cheju Island in the extreme south—are extinct volcanoes with lakes in their craters. There are a few other volcanic peaks in the north, none of them active. Korea, unlike Japan, does not lie on a major fault line in the earth's crust; consequently, earthquakes are not a problem.

Like the rest of East Asia, Korea has a monsoon climate characterized by cold, dry winters and warm, humid summers. The Korean spring and autumn are very pleasant, with generally fair weather and moderate, gradually changing temperatures. Rainfall varies between 76 and 102 centimeters (30 and 40 inches) per year in the south (somewhat less in the north) of which about half comes in June, July, and August. For comparison, in the continental United States, annual rainfall is 107 centimeters (42 inches) in New York City, 79 centimeters (31 inches) in Oklahoma City, and 51 centimeters (20 inches) in San Francisco.

Southern Korea is warmed by the Japan Current, somewhat as the eastern U.S. seaboard is warmed by the Gulf Stream; for this and other reasons, southwestern Korea and the adjacent island-province of Cheju are semitropical and have more rainfall. Mean daily temperatures in the extreme north range between −18° Celsius (0° Fahrenheit) in January and +20°C (68°F) in August; in the extreme south (Cheju Island), between +3°C (34°F) in January and +27°C (81°F) in August. In Seoul, near the center of the peninsula, the range is from −6°C (21°F) to +26°C (79°F). Considerably higher and lower temperatures are not uncommon. For comparison, average New York City temperature in January is 0°C (32°F); in July, +25°C (76°F).

Korea's rivers—except for the Yalu on the border with China and the Taedong River near Pyongyang, capital of north Korea—are generally too small, silted, and variable in flow to be practical for navigation. Some of them—particularly in north Korea—have hydroelectric potential; but for this purpose, too, their variation in flow, because of the concentration of rainfall in the summer months, reduces their utility. Most of them rise in the eastern mountain chain and flow west to the Yellow Sea or south to the Korea Strait. The Yalu, with a length of 790 kilometers (490 miles), is Korea's longest and is navigable for most of its length. Other north Korean rivers are the Tumen (exceptional in flowing northeast and southeast), 521 kilometers (323 miles) long, of which only the seaward one-sixth is navigable; and the

Taedong, 397 kilometers (246 miles), which flows through the capital city of Pyongyang and is navigable for about three-fifths of its length.

South Korean rivers include the Naktong (defense line of the beleaguered UN forces in the summer of 1950), 521 kilometers (323 miles) long, and the Somjin, both of which flow south to the Korea Strait; the Han, 514 kilometers (319 miles), which flows past Seoul; and the Kum, 401 kilometers (249 miles). Other, shorter rivers are the Yongsan, flowing southwest into the Yellow Sea at the southwestern port of Mokp'o; a tributary of the Han, the Pukhan, which rises in north Korea; and the Imjin, also rising in north Korea, which flows for part of its length along the Demilitarized Zone separating the two Korean states.

On Korea's east coast, the mountains rise almost directly from the sea. There is a narrow coastal strip in some areas, and there are a few harbors at north Korean cities such as Chongjin, Kimchaek, Hamhung, and Wonsan and south Korean cities like Kangnung and Ulsan. Pusan, perhaps the best port on the peninsula, marks the eastern beginning of the southern coastline along the Korea Strait. On the west, the coastline is deeply indented, with hundreds of islands and islets; a nine-meter (thirty-foot) differential between high and low tide causes mud flats, treacherous currents, and other navigational problems. The ports of Sinuiju and Nampo, in north Korea, and Inch'on, Kunsan, and Mokp'o, in south Korea, are at or near the mouths of rivers (the Yalu, Taedong, Han, Kum, and Yongsan, respectively); at Nampo, in north Korea, and Inch'on, in south Korea, giant locks maintain a constant water level within the port area. Along the south coast there are ports at Yosu, Chinju, and Masan.

From the strategic point of view, Korean geography offers something of the same defensive advantage against ground forces as does Switzerland. The majority of the boundary is seacoast, much of which is not practical for landing large ships. The land boundary with China is mostly in difficult, mountainous terrain, and the flatter coastal approaches are cut by the wide Yalu River. A similar coastal approach from the Soviet Union is cut by the somewhat narrower Tumen River. Roads within Korea wind between mountains and over passes, where defensive action is relatively easy. However, there are three major invasion corridors across central Korea: one near Ch'orwon in the middle of the peninsula, the other two in the west, where the bulk of the south Korean defense is concentrated.

From the air, Korea is as vulnerable as any country, and its internal communication lines, concentrated as they are in narrow valleys and often bounded (in summer) by soggy rice fields, could be readily interdicted by bombardment. South Korea's greatest geographical vulnerability is the difficulty of supply from any source other than the two hostile neighboring continental powers, China and the Soviet Union. The sea lanes are open to attack from either air or water.

Resources

Although Korea was essentially self-sufficient as an agrarian subsistence economy until the twentieth century, its development prospects as an independent state depend upon world trade. This is even more true of the two present divided states—particularly south Korea. The peninsula as a whole is only moderately endowed with natural resources; in both north and south, the principal asset is an educated, motivated, and able work force. The north has far more natural resources than the south; the rugged northern mountains contain coal (chiefly a poor grade of anthracite), iron ore, and a variety of non-ferrous minerals, including tungsten, lead, copper, zinc, gold, silver, and manganese. Other ores include graphite, apatite, fluorite, barite, limestone, and talc. There are extensive hydroelectric power resources, particularly along the Yalu, Tumen, and Taedong rivers, as well as smaller streams. (Since the Yalu and Tumen rivers are on Korea's northern border, their resources must be shared with China.) Only about one-sixth of the mountainous north Korean terrain is suitable for cultivated crops, and the climate is relatively harsh. Nevertheless, coastal lowlands, particularly in the west, produce rice as well as other grains; elsewhere, corn, wheat, millet, and soybeans are grown. There are rich timber reserves and extensive orchards. Livestock grazing is also possible in the upland areas.

The south is the traditional rice bowl of Korea, with somewhat greater rainfall, warmer climate, and a slightly larger expanse of flat terrain than the north. These same factors make for higher population density in the south—much increased by in-migration since World War II—which offsets the agricultural advantage. There are some of the same kinds of minerals as the north, but in less desirable deposits and smaller quantities, coming nowhere near the requirements of an industrial economy. The only significant reserves are tungsten, graphite, and limestone. Offshore oil possibilities in the Yellow Sea, and on the continental shelf between Korea and Japan, have so far yielded nothing but are being explored by south Korea, to the extent that the competing interests of Japan and China permit. By the 1950's, south Korea was virtually deforested; a vigorous reforestation program has brought a surprising recovery, but indigenous timber resources can never approach consumption requirements.

People

According to the 1985 census, south Korea's population was announced as 40,466,577, an increase of 8.1 percent since the previous census in 1980.[5] The Republic of Korea was thus the fourth most densely populated country in the world, with 408 persons per square kilometer (1,060 per square mile). The capital city, Seoul, accounted for almost a quarter of this number (9,646,000), with a staggering density of 15,933 per square kilometer (41,500 per square mile, equivalent to a square of land 8 meters [25 feet] on a side per person). In addition to Seoul, there were three other cities with over 1 million people: Pusan, the major southeastern port, with 3,160,000; Taegu, in the southeastern agricultural region, with 1,773,000; and Inch'on, the major west-coast port near Seoul, with 1,084,000. Cities of more than 50,000 people accounted for 65.4 percent of the total population.

North Korea's population, according to United Nations statistics, was 18,747,000 in 1982. The UN projection of that year was that the 1985 population would be 20,032,000, corresponding to a population density of 167 persons per square kilometer (434 per square mile), about two-fifths that of the south. (However, south Korean sources reported that the official Chinese Radio Beijing in August, 1987 had given the population of north Korea as 18 million.)[6] The capital city is Pyongyang, with a population of 1.3 million in 1980; the second largest urban center is the twin-city area of Hamhung-Hungnam, on the east coast, with 775,000. Other major cities are Chongjin (490,000) and Wonsan (240,000) on the east coast and Kaesong (240,000), Haeju, Nampo, and Sinuiju (200,000), on the west. In 1980, 60 percent of the north Korean people were urban; this was projected to rise to 64 percent in 1985.

Although the Koreans physically resemble the Chinese, their language is totally unlike Chinese; it has similarities with Turkish, Mongolian, Japanese, and other Central Asian languages, which are sometimes considered to be related to Hungarian and Finnish. (However, both the Koreans and the Japanese borrowed the Chinese writing system and many Chinese words; about half the words in a standard Korean dictionary are of Chinese derivation.)[7] The Koreans, then, may trace their ancient origin to the Central Asian area whose tribes burst out of their steppe and desert habitat from time to time to conquer much of the known world—the Golden Horde of the Mongols, the Seljuk and Ottoman Turks, and to a much more limited degree the Jurchen, or Manchu.

The south Koreans enjoy an average life expectancy of sixty-three years for males and sixty-nine years for females. Literacy is close to 100 percent. Education is a high priority for all Koreans. Elementary education has been universal and compulsory for more than twenty years; over four-fifths of the school-age population complete high school, and over a quarter of the corresponding age group get some post-secondary education. Vigorous efforts have been made to provide supplementary schooling through military training, adult and night classes, and literacy programs. North Korea has a similar record.

The Korean people today are culturally and biologically homogeneous (although differences may grow over time if the political division of the peninsula persists). They are taller, on the average, than most other East

Asians and are sufficiently distinctive in appearance so that a trained observer can often identify them—as one can sometimes distinguish between French and Germans, for example. Nevertheless, there are readily visible differences in physiognomy among Koreans. Distinctive provincial dialects, stereotypes, and prejudices have been strong and still persist. There are few permanent foreign residents in Korea; the largest minority are the Chinese, of whom there are forty thousand in the south.

The total number of ethnic Koreans in the world today is probably around 65 million. In addition to the 60 million in south and north Korea, there are perhaps 5 million in other countries: 1.8 million in China, 1 million in the United States, 0.7 million in Japan, 0.4 million in the Soviet Union, and the remainder in many other countries in Asia, Europe, and the Americas.[8]

History

Since their ancestors entered the peninsula five or more thousand years ago, the Koreans have been influenced by their own indigenous tradition, by their close contact with China, and by the impact of Japan and the West. The first recorded Korean state was exterminated in 108 B.C. by the Chinese, who established an imperial outpost under direct Chinese rule. Three Korean kingdoms emerged—one of them taking over the Chinese domain. By A.D. 668 Silla, one of the three kingdoms, had conquered the other two, with Chinese support. An autonomous, united Korea and a special relationship with China endured for over a millennium thereafter.

United Korea was ruled by three royal dynasties, each of them long-lived by world standards. Silla gave way to Koryo in 936, and Koryo to Choson (reviving the ancient kingdom's name) in 1392. Choson endured for over 500 years, until the rapidly modernizing Japanese occupied Korea in 1905 and annexed it to their empire in 1910. Each of the three dynasties in turn had its days of glory and decline and of invasion from outside.

Buddhism flourished in the Silla and Koryo dynasties; Confucianism became the state philosophy of Choson, which evolved a political and social structure transcending in some respects its Chinese model. Each dynasty brought forth cultural and aesthetic accomplishments: Silla, for example, had its distinctive pottery, gold and silver ornamentation, and architecture; Koryo, the beautiful celadon ware that has never been fully reproduced; Choson, a scientifically correct phonetic alphabet to replace the ill-fitting Chinese ideographs.

Khitan[9] and Japanese raiders menaced Silla and Koryo; the Mongols invaded Korea and maintained hegemony over it for a hundred years in Koryo times; the Japanese ravaged Korea for six years in the middle of the Choson dynasty and were followed hardly over a generation later by a Manchu invasion (see Fig. 1.3). Weakening of the rulers' ability to rule, and propensity of aristocratic landholders to resist central control and taxation, brought troubles to the people and eventual dynastic collapse.

As this cycle was repeating itself in the decaying Choson dynasty of the nineteenth century, Western influence made itself felt. Rivalry among reawakening China, modernizing Japan, and expanding Russia for hegemony over Korea led to two wars fought in and around the peninsula. Japan, having beaten both China in 1895 and Russia in 1905, became Korea's master with the blessing of the Western powers. The Japanese brought modern industry, transportation, communications, and government administration to Korea and improved Korean agricultural productivity. The world was impressed, but the Koreans benefited little from the process. The people resisted Japanese attempts to assimilate them into the Japanese culture. They rose up in nationwide unarmed protest in 1919, responding to President Wilson's ideas of national self-determination, but to no avail. However, the identity of Korea was maintained by nationalists in exile, and the Allies in World War II pledged to restore the country's independence.

Japan's defeat in World War II ended its control of Korea, but Korean independence was deferred by three years of U.S. and Soviet military occupation, during which no agreement was reached as to how independence would be arranged. In the end, two independent states emerged out of the respective occupation zones, each reflecting the political complexion of the occupier, and each committed to reunification by any means. The Korean War was the result. The Koreans, their entry into the modern world delayed first by their own policy of isolation, then by Japanese domination, now had to deal with the complex problems of modernization in a telescoped time frame. It is against this background that Korea's recent development and its problems must be viewed.

The Cultural Heritage

Korea, in contrast to many developing countries and even some developed ones, has a well-established national tradition reaching back for at least two thousand years. For two-thirds of that time, the Koreans have lived in a unified, autonomous state. They share a sense of ethnic identity, a language intelligible everywhere in the country, and a common culture. The culture (not the language or the sense of identity) has been strongly influenced over the centuries by China and the philosophy of Confucius, somewhat as the culture of the United States has been strongly influenced by Greece, Rome, and Europe; but Korean culture is no more identical with Chinese culture than U.S. culture is with that of England, France, or Germany. In recent decades, Western influence, industrialization, and urbanization have induced changes. Korean values and behavior patterns—for better or worse—are moving in the direction of the world's industrialized societies. Yet the Korean

FIGURE 1.3 Depiction of the Battle of Pyongyang, 1592, between the Chinese and the Japanese, showing the muskets of the Japanese, the bows and arrows of the

mix of old and new, native and foreign, remains distinctive, as it has always been. An understanding of the tradition helps one to appreciate the present.[10]

In the Confucian-oriented Korean society, people have thought of themselves as part of an organic whole that included human society and the world around it, hierarchically arranged, related in a family-like pattern with eternally ordained responsibilities for everyone. Individuals found their identity not so much in themselves as in their relationships and mutual obligations within their extended families (out to the eighth degree of relationship) and, above all, in their relationships with their parents. Families have been a key element of society. Order and harmony, rather than competition and adversarial relations, have been supreme values, to be upheld by the conduct and example of superior men. Government officials were expected to be such men, with superior benevolence and wisdom derived from study of the classics and tested by state examinations. The king, at the pinnacle of

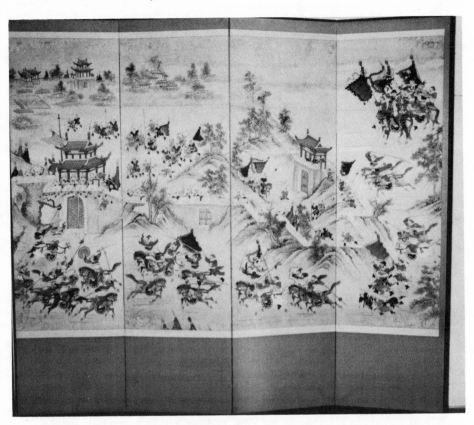

Chinese, and the Chinese three-barrel cannon (photo of eight-panel screen loaned by Dr. Paul S. Crane to the Hannam University Museum, Taejon, Republic of Korea)

government, ruled by authority of the Mandate of Heaven, which he might forfeit if he failed to rule correctly. These attitudes toward government have carried over to some extent into the present day.

Human affairs being part of a larger whole, a person's capacity to control his or her fate was traditionally seen as small. Social change was cyclical within limits that forever remained the same. An idealized past, rather than a golden future, was the goal and norm. The model of conduct and behavior laid down by the sages of old was to be studied, understood, and emulated. Form was of importance equal to substance. Right interpersonal relations were more important than contractual or legal obligations. Family duty and obedience took preference over personal aspirations or the interests of the nation. Political contention and faction, though common in practice, were considered unseemly or heretical. Government and scholarship were the highest callings; industry and commerce were looked down upon. Yet at the same time, Koreans had an individualistic, ambitious element that clashed with the Confucian norms.

In the Chinese international system, the Chinese Emperor was at the center of the universe. Neighboring civilized people had a subordinate status, like younger brothers; they acknowledged their status by sending periodic tribute missions to the Chinese Emperor. Peoples who did not acknowledge Chinese supremacy or accept Chinese values were barbarians—a category that included the Europeans—to be dealt with by exclusion, by playing one against another, and if need be, by force. The Koreans, close as they were to China, evolved an attitude of acquiescence in the Chinese-centered social order. In recent times, the Koreans have condemned themselves for this attitude, which they call *sadaejuui*—respect for, or subservience to, greater status.

Korean culture thus evolved along very different lines from that of Europe and the United States. The West valued mastery over nature, not blending with it; equality of men, rather than hierarchy; individual dignity and freedom, rather than a web of reciprocal duties and responsibilities; subordination of rulers to the will of the ruled and subordination of all to an impersonal law, rather than benevolent personal rule by superior men; sovereignty deriving from the people, not from Heaven; change and progress, rather than a static, past-oriented order; supremacy of rational thought, rather than feeling and intuition; dignity of labor and commerce, rather than scholarship. The West extolled, in theory, the virtue of struggling for the right, rather than acquiescence to superior power; yet at the same time it saw virtue in compromise, in contrast to the Asian priority for loyalty and steadfastness. Only in matters of religion did the West compel uniformity and exclusivity, as opposed to East Asian eclecticism and tolerance; but the West saw political, economic, and social aspects of life as separate, whereas Confucianism saw them all as part of a whole.

As we shall see in subsequent chapters, Western philosophy and thought patterns have nonetheless had a tremendous effect in Korea and East Asia in the century and a half since the Opium War between Great Britain and China demonstrated Western power. Yet the Western impact irreparably tore the Confucian fabric and left Korea—like other East Asian nations—groping in the dark for values to guide society and politics. Korea is engaged in a search for new directions, to which Christianity has made an important contribution. However, Western values are not uncritically accepted; indeed, there is something of a backlash against them in some quarters. In south Korea, the Chinese and indigenous tradition is being given renewed attention, but only in the context of an industrializing society and the new imperatives that industrial organization imposes.

The process of accommodation has taken very different directions in north and south Korea. The whole body of classical philosophy has been explicitly rejected in the north by Kim Il Sung, its leader since 1945. The philosophy of Marxism-Leninism has been imposed on the people since the Soviet occupation of 1945–1948 through education, propaganda, and "agitation." In recent years, Marxist-Leninist principles have been included within Kim's own philosophy of *juche* (self-reliance), which is represented as a higher stage of thought to deal with the problems of national development. There are indications, however, that Confucian elements persist beneath the surface.

In the south, the United States endeavored to encourage Western social, educational, economic, and political ideas during its three-year occupation and in the formative years of the Republic, building upon foundations laid by missionaries and Korean modernizers; but the democratic belief system, by its own nature, prevented its imposition in the way that the Soviet Union and Kim Il Sung could impose Marxism-Leninism in the north. Instead, there has been an ongoing search for a system of indigenous values that will provide answers to the problems of a modern industrializing state.

Politics

Like other developing countries, Korea (both north and south) has serious political growing pains—more evident in the relatively open south than in the closed north. Its problems arise from the clash between the deep-rooted attitudes and values of a traditional agricultural society, on the one hand, and the requirements of an urban industrial economy, on the other.

There was a deep gulf in political thinking between the Koreans and the Western world on the eve of their liberation from Japanese rule in 1945. Notwithstanding some exposure to Western ideas in the brief and traumatic period from 1876 (when the Japanese concluded the first Western-style treaty with Korea) to the Japanese annexation in 1910, most Koreans had had little opportunity for political or social change under Japanese control. David Apter has pointed to a similar contrast between his "sacred collectivity" model and his "secular-libertarian" model. Regarding the applicability of the latter model to the developing countries, he commented: "Since this model does not set up authority easily, what are the conditions favorable to it . . . ? If a libertarian system is proposed for a new state in which the odds are that it will fail to establish authority, should the attempt be made?"[11]

Since 1945, the two halves of Korea have followed different paths of political development, separated by the gulf between competing Western political ideologies of liberal democracy and communism. The Republic of Korea, in the south, was legitimized by elections under United Nations observation in 1948, followed by adoption of a Western-style constitution. Since then, the Republic has been experimenting with a succession of constitutional forms (the present 1980 constitution is the fifth version since

1948, not counting several other amendments, and as this book goes to press, the Republic is about to implement a sixth form). At the same time, south Korea's political system has showed remarkable continuity and durability, as well as increasing effectiveness; but it has functioned more nearly in accord with traditional political norms than with the Western concepts expressed in the successive constitutions.

As already noted, the Confucian ethic—still accepted in south Korea and probably surviving under the surface in north Korea—makes the individual a part of a family collectivity, whose collective goals and interests are his or her own. Family responsibility has traditionally taken precedence over all other responsibilities, including duty to the ruler and the state. Interpersonal responsibilities within other non-family groupings, such as relations between a scholar and his disciples, have also been important. In today's Korea, alumni associations are one modern equivalent of such groups. Political communication still flows largely through informal family and group connections.

The Confucian ethic also imposes a hierarchical pattern of relationships, in which people are superior or inferior to one another but rarely equal. It calls for modesty and restraint and for behavior motivated by principle, not by hope of material gain. Governmental position has traditionally been high in the hierarchy, while business and industry have been low. Moreover, harmony and consensus, rather than competition, are valued; Western-style adversary relations in courts, legislatures, political campaigns—even elections—have been uncomfortable or absent.

Nevertheless, despite the outward Confucian discipline, all Koreans seem to contain within themselves a second person who is assertive, eager for material gain and for recognition, impatient with family and group restraints on individual freedom of action. This duality has undoubtedly been encouraged by Western contact, but it is not new. It may help to explain the success of some Koreans as entrepreneurs. It also makes Koreans somewhat fractious and contentious in their political behavior. Together with the long tradition of factional rivalry and external influence, it contributes to a suspicious and conspiratorial approach to politics.

Western political ideas followed Western military, technical, and economic ideas into Korea. The present south Korean constitution, like its four preceding versions, nominally sets up a modern Western system of government under popular sovereignty, with separate executive, legislative, and judicial branches and a bill of rights. The north Korean constitution is similarly modern in Communist terms. Despite the attractiveness of Western concepts of individual liberty, equality, and basic rights, however, Western institutions (except in such areas as administrative organization and industrial production) have thus far been respected more in form than in substance. The part played in Korean politics by the large military establishment since the Korean War (including the conditioning of millions of young draftees over the years) has reinforced the authoritarian strain in Korean political behavior.

Growth and adjustment difficulties have an external dimension as well. Since foreigners tend to judge Korea by their own standards of political behavior, there is a propensity for foreign governments to criticize Korean political performance. Moreover, there is a temptation for opposition politicians to curry Western favor and support through similar criticism, whatever their personal convictions. At the same time, south Korean contact with the West has reinforced the other aspect of Korean character—individualism and competitiveness. The conflict between the two sets of attitudes, and the resultant change and confusion, help to explain current south Korean political tensions.

Such difficulties have kept Korea's political progress from keeping pace with economic development and, in north Korea, have begun to interfere with economic progress as well. In the south, the continuation of authoritarian, paternalistic policies and behavior is increasingly out of phase with the expectations of a literate and sophisticated population, exposed to the outside world. In the closed society of the north, where the population has been conditioned over a forty-year period to the totalitarian philosophy of Communist rule, no mass dissatisfaction has shown itself to foreign observers; yet the north's political system is hardly a model for the future.

The political systems of both south and north have maintained, in their separate ways, a high degree of stability and continuity. In the non-Communist south, income distribution is more equitable than in most developing countries; tax collection is efficient and reaches both rich and poor; and despite headlines in the Western press, violence and loss of life have been relatively small.[12] No facts are available to make such judgments about the north, especially regarding the costs of several political purges, although the system appears to function as well as any among Communist nations.

Charges continue to be made, by both foreign and domestic critics, of press controls, imprisonment for political dissent, overly coercive action against dissidents—particularly college students—and use of torture by security agencies. Such charges are easier to document against the south, because of its relative openness, than against the north, where such abuses may well be far more widespread and repression more severe. Yet, in the south, except for direct criticism of the government or support for Marxist ideas, personal liberty of speech, action, and movement is not seriously restricted (group political activity in opposition to government policies, however, is quite circumscribed).

The principal south Korean political problems in the mid-1980s are all the result of Korea's historical experience and developing status. They include the weak legitimacy of the present government in the public eye; the dislike of what the people see as a disproportionate military influence in politics;

the lack of a legitimate channel for expressing critical political views; the uncertainty of orderly succession to political power when President Chun Doo Hwan's constitutional term ends in early 1988; the lack of key cultural elements necessary for representative government to function, including a sense of responsibility to the nation and a willingness to compromise; and the growing demands of the south Korean population, with students and intellectuals in the forefront, for more freedom, equity, and voice in political decisions.

North Korea also faces problems, particularly the transfer of power from the septuagenarian Great Leader, Kim Il Sung, to his successor (presumably his son, Kim Jong Il) and the sluggishness of the economy, which has left the north Korean people's living standard far below that of the south. Overhanging both the Koreas are the threat each poses to the other and the intractability of the reunification problem.

Economics

In recent years, south Korea has been universally acclaimed as an economic success story. It has one of the longest-sustained and highest national economic growth rates in history; in 1987 it had one of the lowest inflation rates in the world; it has successfully coped with international economic crises, such as the "oil shocks" of 1973 and 1979 (although it suffered a serious recession in 1980). It has achieved, by the standards of developing countries generally, a reasonably equitable distribution of the benefits of economic growth; and it expects, not without reason, to sustain an annual real economic growth rate of around 7 percent or more until the year 2000, with exports of increasingly sophisticated technology including automobiles, computer chips, and electronic products. Its principal economic problems stem from its very success: Expanding Korean exports are exciting protectionist reactions in the United States and Europe; growing income levels at home are making Korea vulnerable to competition from other developing countries; and its more affluent workers can turn from former worries about their next meal to new concerns about distribution of wealth and political freedom.

It is easy to forget that twenty-five years ago north Korea was the success story, impressing the newly independent Third World countries of Asia and Africa with its burgeoning economic growth, while south Korea was viewed as an economic "basket case"—a rat-hole down which large quantities of U.S. grant aid were being wastefully and perpetually poured. In their very different ways, both north and south Korea have made impressive economic gains. In recent years, however, the north's inflexible central planning and lack of incentive, together with its inward-looking stance of self-reliance, seem to have seriously damped its growth curve, while the south's outward-looking, export-oriented economy, driven by an effective relationship between government and private enterprise, is ever more outdistancing its northern rival.[13]

Until the end of World War II, Korea was essentially a traditional agrarian economy, based primarily on rice and other grains. During their forty-year occupation, the Japanese installed an industrial superstructure geared to their own imperial needs, but this was of little benefit to most Koreans, whose standard of living did not improve and whose dietary intake actually fell. Koreans had little role in managing the modern sector, economic or administrative. However, the beginnings of a trained labor force emerged, a few Koreans established themselves as entrepreneurs, and a transport and communication infrastructure was put in place.

Liberation in 1945 left to the Koreans the shell of the economy built by the Japanese. The plant they inherited was heavily depreciated from wartime over-exploitation and partly irrelevant to their own needs. The Japanese market was cut off, and division of the country separated the mineral resources and heavy industry of the north from the light industry and agricultural surplus of the south. Moreover, the Koreans lacked the necessary managerial and technical skills, as well as the capital, for an industrial economy.

Development after liberation proceeded in very different ways in north and south. South Korea, under U.S. guidance, had the semblance of capitalism and private enterprise. It did, however, complete a thoroughgoing land reform, which subsequently meant that the farming population would support the political regime. After a slow start, economic progress began to be visible in 1950, but the war destroyed most of what had been accomplished. In the north, land had been redistributed to the tillers more promptly than in the south, and all large industry was nationalized. The single-minded zeal of the northern leaders under Soviet guidance and their centralized direction of the economy made up for lack of experience, and the north achieved more rapid progress than the south. War damage, however, was even greater in the north, obliterating almost all the industrial plant.

By mid-1951 the fighting was chiefly limited to the line between the two halves. South Korea could then begin its reconstruction effort, assisted by the United States, the United Nations, and private American relief donations; but the economy was plagued by inflation, mismanagement, and the costs of the positional warfare that continued for another two years. Prewar consumption levels were not reestablished until the late 1950s. In north Korea, U.S. saturation bombing continued until the armistice; the years from 1953 to 1955 were devoted to reconstruction, followed by multi-year economic plans that at first resulted in truly extraordinary rates of growth. Well-publicized north Korean economic progress probably added to the growing popular discontent in the south, based on both political repression and lack of economic progress, that led to the overthrow of the Syngman Rhee government in 1960. Continued economic stagnation was also a factor in the military seizure of power in 1961.

Rapid development in the south began under military leadership. General Park Chung Hee, later elected President, recognized that rapid economic improvement would justify a regime that had been established by force and therefore lacked legitimacy. Applying discipline and managerial skill, the military leaders utilized the human abilities and economic infrastructure that had been accumulating in earlier years. Continued external economic aid from the United States, and new aid from Japan after normalization of relations in 1965, provided capital investment and technology. Emphasis was shifted from import substitution to export-led growth, beginning with traditional labor-intensive consumer goods (south Korea has never had significant exportable raw materials except for graphite and tungsten).

Despite some early mistakes, the new south Korean leadership achieved an economic takeoff by 1965. For the next twenty years, annual real growth of gross national product ranged from a high of over 15 percent (1975) to a low of 5 percent (1983), with one year of unaccustomed negative growth (1980) resulting from the second oil crisis and internal problems. From the 1970s on, south Korean export moved increasingly into shipbuilding, iron and steel, machinery, electronics, and most recently, highly technical items like computers and computer chips. Automobile export began in the 1980s. In 1982, inflation was brought to single digits for almost the first time since liberation; in the mid-1980s it was below 5 percent. In 1986, with a real growth of 12.2 percent in gross national product, the Republic showed a surplus on its balance-of-payments account and began paying off its foreign debt.

However, south Korea in the mid-1980s faces serious problems of adjustment. The United States, Japan, and other principal export markets are increasingly erecting protectionist barriers, while demanding more access to protected Korean markets. Other developing countries are entering into competition with Korean textiles and other traditional exports. Falling oil prices reduced south Korea's import bill, but they ended the Middle East construction boom that had carried the economy through two oil crises and brought both companies and workers back home in search of employment. Domestically, the growing concentration of economic power in a few giant combines (the *chaebol*) and disparities in earnings between rich and poor, as well as the failure of some highly leveraged and overly ambitious corporations, have aroused concern. Labor unrest in the freer political environment of 1987 resulted in wage increases of over 17 percent, causing worry about future competitiveness. Nonetheless, economic projections remain guardedly optimistic, sustained by south Korea's twenty-year record of sustained performance and flexible, pragmatic response to changing circumstances.

In north Korea, for the first twenty years after the Korean War, the centrally planned Communist economy progressed very well, continuing to grow faster than that of the south. At first, the north benefited from considerable sums of Soviet and Chinese aid. This aid dried up in the 1960s, however, accounting in part for failure to fulfill the first seven-year plan on schedule in 1967. In the early 1970s, the north tried to hasten progress by importing entire industrial plants from Western European nations and Japan, but because of the 1973 oil crisis and perhaps faulty planning, north Korea could not repay the massive foreign-currency bills for the equipment it bought. This debt remains, despite several attempts at renegotiation, and has complicated subsequent attempts to deal with the outside world. For over a decade, north Korean official statements have implied problems with bottlenecks in transportation, electric power, and mining, as well as lack of technology and problems with worker productivity.

Annual north Korean economic growth in the mid-1980s is apparently respectable, at an estimated 5–6 percent per year; but it must sustain massive military expenditures amounting to around 20 percent of the gross national product. Substantial improvement in agricultural production is claimed. A joint venture law was passed in 1985, and the regime has professed openness toward economic relations with non-hostile countries outside the Communist bloc. However, north Korea continues to emphasize self-reliance. Its foreign trade is largely with other Communist countries, and non-Communist response to the joint venture law has been minimal.

International Relations and Security

Korean international relations since 1948 have been overshadowed by the hostility between the two Korean states—a hostility hugely magnified by the war. Each state has regarded itself as properly sovereign over all Korea, and the other as illegitimate. Since hostilities ended with the Armistice Agreement of 1953 (which south Korea never signed), the two Korean states have been in competition with each other for international recognition and support, while beefing up their huge armed forces along the so-called Demilitarized Zone that separates them. The continuing presence of forty thousand U.S. soldiers close to the front line, and a Combined Forces Command headed by a U.S. general, serve as a deterrent to the renewal of hostilities by either state.

Security has been the dominant foreign-policy concern of both Koreas since their establishment. South Korea looks primarily to the United States as its protector under the Mutual Defense Treaty of 1953. It faces over 800,000 heavily armed and offensively deployed north Korean forces, many of them within fifty kilometers (thirty miles) of the south's capital city, potentially supported by huge Chinese and Soviet forces nearby. Recalling that the withdrawal of U.S. forces in 1949 was followed by a north Korean invasion, the Republic has opposed all subsequent U.S. withdrawal initiatives, particularly that of President Jimmy Carter in 1977. North Korea, which since 1961 has had defense treaties with the Soviet Union and China, insists on the withdrawal of U.S. forces, often as a precondition for any other step toward reduction of tensions on the peninsula. Its fear of U.S.-Korean invasion, voiced constantly but particularly at times of annual joint south Korean–U.S. maneuvers, may well be genuine. At the same time as it professes peaceful intentions, the north talks of popular revolution in the south, which it would support, and repeatedly attempts infiltration of the south by armed special warfare teams and agents. A vague United Nations umbrella over the armistice still exists, in the form of a skeleton United Nations Command that staffs the south side of the Military Armistice Commission; there is also a vestigial four-country Neutral Nations Supervisory Commission.

Economic relations are a growing part of south Korea's foreign-policy concerns, since exports account for nearly a third of its national product and it must import most of its industrial raw materials. For many years, the south's largest markets have been the United States and Japan, each of them accounting for roughly a third; but increasing protectionism in both countries and in other industrial nations and competition from other developing countries are making third-country markets an important target, particularly those of Southeast Asia. Mainland China has become a significant market, largely but not wholly through Hong Kong. The United States and Japan have also been south Korea's principal sources of capital investment, in both loan and equity form, and of technology; capital induction from abroad will be needed for some years to come, but technology will be even more needed.

North Korea, with greater natural resources and a policy of self-reliance, is less concerned with economic relations outside the Communist bloc; yet it apparently wants Western technology to stimulate its own economic growth and cultivates relations with Japan for economic as well as prestige reasons—this despite the large role that the anti-Japanese struggle plays in north Korean mythology about its recent past.

Both Koreas cultivate the Third World for reasons of prestige, ideology, and economics. North Korea has supported its policies by export of weapons and military aid, including training in unconventional warfare, to a number of left-oriented developing countries. North Korea gained considerable Third World support in the 1950s and 1960s by its economic success and its strong anti-Americanism, playing a leading role in the Non-Aligned Movement with such other radical nations as Cuba. At that time, south Korea suffered in its Third World relations both from an indifferent economic performance and from its conservatism and close alliance with the United States. This picture began to change in the 1970s. North Korea no longer appeared as an economic leader; its shrill radicalism started to backfire; and its initiatives in the Non-Aligned Movement no longer gained majority support. The north's attempt to blow up the south Korean president and his party in Rangoon in 1983 was costly in international-relations terms.

Reunification of Korea remains a supreme desire of all the Korean people, both north and south. No Korean government could avoid doing something about it. Both states have repeatedly advanced proposals for reunification since 1960, but little real progress has been made because of the hostility and distrust between the two sides. In 1972, driven by the uncertainty that followed the U.S. withdrawal from Vietnam and opening toward Mainland China, the two states issued a joint declaration pledging peaceful negotiations on a basis of grand national unity without outside interference; but attempted negotiations soon fell apart. In 1985, fifty citizens of each Korean state were admitted to the other state for meetings with separated family members. Several sets of preliminary talks on north-south relations broke down soon thereafter and up to mid-1987 had not been meaningfully renewed. Given the deep ideological gulf between the two regimes, no early progress seems possible except in peripheral areas. The 1988 Olympic Games will be a test of north-south willingness to compromise. If that test is passed, then possibly some reduction of tensions on the peninsula may lie ahead.

Notes

1. The figure of nine hundred invasions has been cited by such Korean authorities as Dr. Hahm, Pyung Choon, although I have never seen a precise list to justify it. There can be little doubt that the total of incursions across Korea's northern border, Japanese pirate raids, and Chinese border actions over the centuries could add up to some such number. The five major occupations (as distinguished from raids or incursions) referred to in the text are the Chinese extinction of ancient Choson in 108 B.C. and establishment of four commanderies under Chinese rule (one of which, Nangnang, lasted four centuries); the Mongol domination of Korea in the thirteenth and fourteenth centuries; the Japanese invasion of 1592–1598; the Japanese control of Korea, 1905–1945; and the Soviet and U.S. occupation, 1945–1948.

2. For detailed discussion of Korean geography, see Patricia Bartz, *South Korea* (Oxford: Oxford University Press, 1972); Shannon B. McCune, *Korea's Heritage: A Regional and Social Geography* (Rutland, Vt.: C. E. Tuttle Co., 1956); *North Korea: A Country Study* (Washington: U.S. Government Printing Office, 1981); *South Korea: A Country Study* (Washington: U.S. Government Printing Office, 1982).

3. The Demilitarized Zone has in fact been heavily militarized on both sides. See Chapter 7.

4. A *ri* (also romanized as *li*) is a traditional Korean unit of distance, equivalent to about one-half kilometer (one-third of a mile). The initial consonant is one of the most confusing Korean sounds for foreigners, pronounced like "l," "n," or "r," depending upon its location in a phrase or word. The sounds of the Korean language are briefly discussed in Appendix B.

5. This is a preliminary figure, subject to correction.

6. The report appeared in *North Korea News* No. 390, September 14, 1987, p. 6. The same report stated that *Chosun Shinbo*, newspaper of the north Korean-controlled federation of Korean residents in Japan, had said on July 9 that north Korea's population was expected to grow to 19.7 million by 1993, the year scheduled for completion of the third seven-year economic plan.

7. The Korean language is discussed in Appendix B.

8. For a discussion of Korean minorities overseas, see Chapter 7.

9. The Khitan were a nomadic people of East Central Asia, contending with other peoples such as the Jurchen (Manchu) and Mongols for control in the region. As the Liao Dynasty, they ruled part of China in the tenth to twelfth centuries. They may be related to the Koreans; their language (like Mongolian and Japanese) is structurally similar.

10. An excellent brief discussion of the modern change in Korean society is contained in a pamphlet by Vincent S.R. Brandt, *South Korean Society In Transition* (Elkins Park, Pa.: Philip Jaisohn Memorial Foundation, 1983).

11. David Apter, *The Politics of Modernization* (Chicago: The University of Chicago Press, 1965), p. 36.

12. The most serious incidents of political violence in south Korea since 1945 (excluding the Korean War period, 1950–1953) include the October 1946 riots in the Taegu area during the American occupation, in which perhaps 100 people were killed; the "student revolution" of April 1960, in which 203 students were killed or subsequently died; and the Kwangju uprising of May 1980, for which the official report shows 193 deaths, but critics claim considerably more. In the military seizure of power on May 16, 1961, one person was shot; there was virtually no other damage or casualty. There were several suicides and accidental deaths of students, workers, and riot police in the demonstrations of 1986 and 1987. These deaths are lamentable, but by Third World standards they are on a very small scale.

13. Figures from south Korean sources indicate that the current gross national product (GNP) of the Republic of Korea (south Korea) is approximately five times that of the Democratic People's Republic of Korea (north Korea); the south, with twice the population of the north, therefore has a per capita GNP about two and a half times that of the north. Since there is no satisfactory means of comparing north and south Korean monetary statistics, the comparison is uncertain, but leading non-Communist sources (e.g., U.S. government, The Economist Intelligence Unit data, World Bank statistics) agree that the south is substantially ahead of the north.

2 HISTORICAL BACKGROUND

Westerners have a tendency to view all East Asians alike and to think of East Asian nations as having similar backgrounds. It is important to counteract this tendency by considering the countries' ethnic and cultural diversity and the variety of their historical experiences, which far exceed those of Europe. Far from being similar, each nation is the product of its own experience over many thousand years.

Understanding Koreans, therefore, comes from looking at their historical and cultural roots. The Koreans began as small tribes entering the peninsula eons ago from the north. They gradually came together—first into small collections of villages; then into three good-sized states; and finally into a single homogeneous nation that has kept its identity despite repeated invasions from surrounding peoples.

In this process, Korea has been shaped by four main influences:

- the tradition of its own people, reaching back into the Siberian steppes of five thousand or more years ago;
- the power and culture of neighboring China;
- the impact of Japan, particularly since the late nineteenth century;
- the economic and cultural inroads of the West.

It is important to note that the Western influence has come to Korea in two conflicting forms: the capitalist, liberal-democratic tradition of Western Europe and the United States, and the Marxism-Leninism of the Soviet Union. This conflict between Western influences contributed to the separation of Korea into two states.

Although Korea up to now has been classified as a developing country (or two developing countries), it differs from most other developing nations in three important ways. It was an autonomous, unified state with a sophisticated central government for over thirteen hundred years. Its people all speak the same language and share the same culture (the largest minority in a population of sixty million is about forty thousand Chinese). The Korean colonial experience was under an Asian power (Japan), not a Western one. As we shall see, all three factors help to explain Korea's condition today.

In one short chapter, it is impossible to do justice to Korea's long, rich history. The best that can be done is a gallop through thousands of years, in which the passing scenery is blurred—particularly in the earlier periods. Many readers will undoubtedly want to know more; they are encouraged to consult the English-language histories in the list of suggested readings in Appendix C.[1] A chronological summary of Korean history appears at the end of this chapter in Table 2.1A.

Origins

People have lived in the Korean peninsula since the Paleolithic period (about sixty thousand years ago), but the origins of the first settlers have not been clearly established. Around the fifth millenium B.C., a Neolithic people entered the peninsula or nearby Manchuria. Korean tradition calls them Yemaek and regards them as the ancestors of present-day Korea. They must have come from the north and west, in small tribal groups, probably from the Yenisei river valley of Siberia. Such movement of related peoples continued into historic times. Links with Central Asia are suggested by the structural similarity of the Korean language to those spoken by Turkic, Mongolian, Tungusic, and other peoples who originated in East Asia north of China.[2] There are also similarities between Neolithic Korean pottery and other remains, such as stone dolmens, and those found in Central Asia.

The stylized fir-tree and reindeer motifs on ancient gold crowns found in Korean royal burial mounds also point to Central Asian origins.

The most popular Korean origin myth states that the founder of the nation was Tan'gun, a man born of a bear at the bidding of a god. A tiger, also offered the opportunity, lacked the patience to wait the prescribed gestation period. The animals probably represented ancient tribal totem symbols. This event is dated 2333 B.C., and is celebrated in south Korea as Foundation Day (kaech'onjol) on October 3. Another myth, with some basis in Chinese records, holds that Kija, a Chinese prince (Chinese: Qize), established Ancient Choson in 1122 B.C. In both myths, people are already present when the founder arrives.

By Neolithic times, the Koreans lived in small communities both by the sea and inland, fishing, hunting, and gathering fruits for their livelihood. Rice cultivation entered from China in the first millenium B.C. Chinese records establish that by the third century B.C., as China itself was becoming a unified empire under the Qin (232–208 B.C.) and Han (208 B.C.–A.D. 220) dynasties, tribes were moving from Siberia and Manchuria into Korea, bringing knowledge of bronze and iron. At the same time, Chinese influence expanded into the northwestern part of the peninsula, bringing with it new agricultural techniques and the use of metal. Partly in response to these pressures, the state known as Ancient Choson (Chinese: Chaoxian) emerged.

The nomadic peoples of Central Asia were a constant challenge to the Chinese Empire from earliest times. Determined to crush their threat, the Han Emperor Wu-ti in 109 B.C. undertook a campaign to outflank them by conquering Ancient Choson. (This was about the time that Rome was demolishing Carthage in the West.) By the following year, he had destroyed Choson and replaced it with four military commands over large territories in the northern half of the Korean peninsula and southern Manchuria. However, the Chinese could not long maintain their hold on so much distant alien territory. A generation later, only one of the commanderies remained, known as Nangnang (Chinese: Lolang), with its capital at Pyongyang (now the capital of north Korea).

Controlling the northwestern part of the Korean peninsula, Nangnang endured four centuries, outlasting by a hundred years its parent Han Dynasty. Its ruling class was Chinese, and its culture was a replica of that at the Chinese capital; some of the finest remains of Han Dynasty culture have been found near Pyongyang. Nangnang was finally overwhelmed by the resurgent Koreans in A.D. 313 (roughly at the same time the Roman Emperor Constantine established Constantinople as his capital). By that time, it had assured a permanent place for Chinese cultural influence in the Korean peninsula.

Three Kingdoms Period

Outside the Chinese commanderies, the Koreans gradually came together into three kingdoms, Koguryo, Silla, and Paekche—a process doubtless helped by the influence of Nangnang. The Koguryo people were a hunting tribe that had settled the mountainous regions of Manchuria and northern Korea. They asserted their independence as the Chinese relinquished three of their four Korean commanderies and drew back into Nangnang in the first century B.C. Three hundred years later, Koguryo conquered Nangnang to complete its control of the northern part of the peninsula and part of Manchuria as well.

In the southern part of the peninsula, where conditions were more favorable for settled agriculture, the process of nationbuilding took longer. The tribal people there, called Han (not to be confused with the Han Dynasty), belonged to three broad groups, Mahan, Chinhan, and Pyonhan, which had no central authority. The divisions among the Han may have been the result of geography: A rugged mountain range, the Sobaek, isolates the southeast.

By the middle of the fourth century A.D., however, two states had arisen in the south: Silla on the east, and Paekche on the west. Paekche was probably dominated by a branch of the Puyo tribe that, like other peoples entering Korea, had come from the area of the Yenisei River in Siberia.[3] The fluctuating division between Koguryo, on the north, and Silla and Paekche, on the south, was in the general vicinity of the 38th parallel— the line along which Korea was divided in 1945.

The Three Kingdoms period is traditionally dated from about the time of Christ to A.D. 668 (roughly contemporaneous with the rise and fall of the Roman Empire), but in actuality it probably covered no more than three to four centuries. It was characterized at first by Koguryo ascendency and by repeated wars between a militant Koguryo and its less warlike and less well organized southern neighbors. Nevertheless, Paekche was a prosperous and cultured state in the fourth century, trading with both China and Japan and calling upon Japan as an ally against Koguryo. Influenced extensively by Chinese culture, Paekche first encountered Buddhism, brought by a Chinese monk, in A.D. 384 (Koguryo was probably ahead of Paekche, both in Chinese influence and the adoption of Buddhism). Later, Paekche transmitted Buddhism, as well as Chinese scholarship, to Japan—which was then just beginning its own national development.

Silla, less affected by Chinese culture or outside conquest because of its geographic isolation, was at first weak and backward in comparison to the other two Korean states. It had a confederal rather than autocratic political structure. The six major constituent tribes had an elite leadership strictly separated into hereditary classes known as "bone ranks." Silla also had groups of young warriors, known as *hwarang*; accounts of their training and esprit de corps are reminiscent of feudal Japanese or European fighting men. Their tradition, *hwarangdo,* is a source of patriotic inspiration for the modern Republic of Korea, as well as a school of martial art.[4]

As Silla matured in political organization, Chinese influence increased and may have been a factor in Silla's growing power. In the mid-sixth century, Silla and Paekche together crushed a smaller confederation of Han tribes in the south, known as Kaya (called Mimana by the Japanese, with whom Kaya had close relations); then Silla extended its territory at Paekche's expense. Meanwhile, China was reunited under the Sui Dynasty after three hundred years of internal division. As in previous periods of Chinese strength, the Sui emperors undertook campaigns to control the northern barbarians and again threatened Korea. This time, however, the Koreans were a match for the Chinese. Koguryo's defeat of the second Sui Emperor's invasion attempt contributed to his overthrow by the succeeding Tang Dynasty in China. The hero of this campaign was General Ulchi Mundok, who is still acclaimed as a Korean national hero.

China, however, tried to take advantage of the rivalries among the three Korean kingdoms as they sought allies in their struggles for hegemony. In 660, allied with Silla, a Chinese naval assault crushed Paekche. The victors then turned on Koguryo, and by 668 Silla alone remained to rule a united Korea; but it took eight years to push the Chinese out of the territories they had conquered and intended to hold.

Unified Korea

By the end of the seventh century, most of the Korean peninsula was thus brought under a single government.[5] The leaders in the unification effort, Silla Prince Kim Ch'un-ch'u (later King Muyol) and General Kim Yu-sin, brought many of the Koguryo and Paekche leaders into their ruling elite. Once it had rid the peninsula of Chinese power, Silla accepted a tributary relationship to China and utilized the Chinese political model in consolidating its own control. This was a brilliant period for East Asia, with China flourishing under the Tang Dynasty and Japan becoming a nation-state—while Europe was in the depths of the Dark Ages.

Notwithstanding Chinese influence on Silla, distinctive Korean characteristics endured. Notable among these were the "bone-rank" system of inheritance of political power, in preference to the Chinese merit examinations, and the survival of rigid class distinctions, with virtual serfdom among the peasants; some were slaves. Buddhism had more influence than Confucianism. Great Buddhist temples and shrines were erected with official patronage. One of the finer examples of the Buddhist art and architecture of the time is an artificial stone grotto on a mountaintop near the Silla capital of Kyongju, with a magnificent stone image of the Buddha (see Fig. 3.2 in the next chapter).

The Silla Dynasty fell in 936. Internal decay, encouraged by the tension between the indigenous culture and transplanted Chinese institutions, had set in by the late eighth century. The cohesiveness of the ruling groups broke down; a king was killed, and members of collateral lines succeeded to the throne in rapid succession as various factions gained ascendency by force or guile. The peasantry rose in revolt or retreated into banditry. Inevitably rival leaders rose, carving out domains for themselves called "latter Koguryo" and "latter Paekche." A latter-Paekche general named Wang Kon, from a trader family in the west-central port city of Kaesong, emerged supreme. Overthrowing the Silla Dynasty, but treating the fallen ruling class kindly, he proclaimed himself founder of the Koryo Dynasty, moving the capital to Kaesong (then called Songdo). Wang Kon's accession to the Korean throne thus followed Charlemagne's in the West by a little more than a century.

The new dynasty again drew from the Chinese model in organizing its political institutions, even modelling its capital city after the Chinese capital of Changan. However, it still differed from the Chinese in its aristocratic distinctions and in its patronage of Buddhism as a state religion. The status of women appears to have been higher in Koryo than in China. The Chinese examination system for entry into the bureaucracy existed, but in practice it was open only to members of the aristocracy. The extended family system was even stronger than in China. As time went on, the aristocracy gained more and more independent control over its land holdings, thus weakening the central government.

During its first century, Koryo successfully repelled invasion by a Tungusic Khitan tribe from the north and then pushed the northern frontier to approximately its present location (along the Amnok [Yalu] and Tumen rivers).[6] Peace came a decade later, to be followed by thriving commercial, intellectual, and artistic activity. Then, like Chinese dynasties and like Silla before it, Koryo began to decay internally through weakness at the top, rivalry among court factions, growth of tax-exempt aristocratic landholdings, and indifference to the problems of the masses.

Koryo military officials, perceiving themselves discriminated against by civil officials, seized power in 1170, Korea's first military coup d'état.[7] Three following decades of civil war and revolt ended with assertion of power by a self-proclaimed administrator, Ch'oe Ch'ung-hon, reminiscent of the shoguns of Japan.[8] His family held power for sixty years under impotent kings.

In addition to its internal troubles, the dynasty was constantly under external military threat from northern tribes. One of these, the Khitan, captured the Koryo capital in 1011 before being expelled. Such threats were climaxed by the Mongol invasion of 1231—Korea's share of the Mongol sweep through most of the known world. After a quarter-century of struggle, the Koreans submitted; their kings, with titles and privileges reduced, were married off to Mongol princesses, and the sons were held hostage at the Mongol court at what is now Beijing. Mongol officials watched over the Korean administration, and Mongol culture strongly influenced the ruling class. Survivals of this influence can be seen in Korean cuisine and traditional military costume. The Koreans were mobilized to support the Mongols' unsuccessful attempts to invade Japan; meanwhile, the Koreans suffered repeated attacks by Japanese pirates.

The Koryo period was the zenith of Buddhism in Korea but also saw the growth of Confucian influence. Buddhism was, in effect, the state religion. The temples and clergy were powerful and often wealthy; some temples had large landholdings and private armies. The oldest remaining wooden temple buildings in Korea date from the thirteenth century; many stone pagodas also survive from the Koryo period. The entire Buddhist scripture was codified and carved on wooden blocks early in the dynasty. The blocks were destroyed by the Mongols. A second set of 80,000 blocks, prepared as a penance early in the period of struggle against the Mongols, is still preserved at Haeinsa, a temple in southeastern Korea.

Graphic art and poetry flourished, particularly among the emerging Confucian literati, who often expressed themselves in Chinese-language poetry. The peasantry, also, had their *changga* (long poems) with accompanying song. Two important historical works date from Koryo: the *Samguk Sagi* (History of the Three Kingdoms), by Kim Yu-sin, and *Samguk Yusa* (Records of the Three Kingdoms), a more anecdotal writing by the Buddhist monk Iryon. Internationally best known of Koryo's cultural achievements are the beautiful celadon bowls and vases.

With all its political and economic problems, the Koryo Dynasty could not long survive the collapse of the Mongol Empire in the mid-fourteenth century. The final blow came when a Korean general, sent by the Koryo court against the advancing armies of the new Ming Dynasty in China, realized the folly of the mission. Making his peace with the Ming, General Yi Song-gye turned on his own government, seized control of it, and in 1392 proclaimed a new dynasty. He moved the capital to its present location, Seoul, and readopted the old name of Choson for the dynasty and the nation.

Medieval Korea: The Choson (Yi) Dynasty

The new Yi monarch (known by the posthumous title T'aejo, "Great Progenitor") promptly sought confirmation of his status by the Chinese court and eventually received it. T'aejo consolidated his power with great skill. He granted extensive privileges to his supporters ("merit subjects") but nonetheless established a governmental system closely modelled after the Chinese, including merit examinations for public service. He redistributed the land to ease the lot of the peasants. To dispose of the heavy Buddhist hand on the court, he banished the Buddhist priests to the hills, confiscated much Buddhist property, and established the neo-Confucianism of Ming China as a state philosophy. He made Choson a far more perfect embodiment of Chinese philosophy and politics than any previous Korean regime, adopting, among other Chinese institutions, the Ming administrative code. After six years on the throne, he wearied of the power struggles in his family, and abdicated in favor of one of his eight sons. Another son seized the throne four months later, setting the stage for the constant power struggles that characterized the dynasty thereafter.

The Korean adoption of the Chinese political system extended to society and culture. Within one to two centuries, Korea became recognized as a more perfect Confucian state than China itself. Court records were kept in Chinese; scholars composed excellent Chinese prose and poetry and were learned in the Chinese classics. The behavior of even the common people was governed by Confucian ethics.

Yet differences from China persisted. These differences included the strong aristocratic tradition, which limited examination takers to sons of the aristocracy; a marked tendency toward collective power at the expense of the king's authority; and a high incidence of factionalism, in which family, clan, and regional connections were factors. The Chinese institution of the Censorate, intended as a check on official misconduct and inefficiency, became in Korea an instrument for attack on the administration. The Korean state, smaller and less secure, was more strongly centralized than China. Moreover, the Korean king was not the Son of Heaven, but the vassal or licensee of the Chinese Emperor.[9]

The first century of Choson was one of notable cultural as well as political achievement. The fourth king, the great Sejong (1418–1450) (Fig. 2.1) and his scholars created a phonetic alphabet, han'gul, which is considered to be one of the best writing systems ever devised (see Appendix B on the Korean language). Printing with movable metal type was developed a century before Gutenberg's invention in Europe. Rain and wind gauges were devised, as well as clocks, sundials, and surveying instruments.

Toward the end of the fifteenth century, however, the leadership talent of the succeeding kings declined. There were struggles for power and position among cliques of yangban (scholar-officials) at court. Factional rivalries, which often took precedence over the general welfare, were partly responsible for the weakness of Korea in the face of the Japanese and Manchu invasions. King Yonsan'gun (1494–1506) condemned numbers of literati to death and exile in his attempts to control factional strife.[10]

FIGURE 2.1 Statue in Seoul of Sejong, fourth king of the Choson Dynasty (reigned A.D. 1418–1450) (photo by Edward Adams)

The aristocratic factions gradually came to have distinct family, regional, economic, even educational roots of their own. By the late seventeenth century, the *yangban* were divided among four hereditary groupings, which endured through the rest of the dynasty. Their adherents had their own economic base in agricultural estates, lived in separate areas of the capital, and schemed to gain power.[11]

In 1592, Hideyoshi, second of three great leaders who reunified Japan after a century of civil war, decided to invade the Asian continent through Korea. (This was fifteen years before the first permanent English settlement was established at Jamestown in the United States.) He was initially successful against weak and faction-ridden government forces. However, he suffered a severe naval defeat at the hands of the Korean Admiral Yi Sun-sin, who invented an armored ship (the famed "turtle ship") and used a flotilla of them to devastating effect. Volunteer bands called *uibyongdae* (Righteous Armies), and even armed Buddhist monks, offered significant resistance.

In the end, the Japanese were made to abandon their adventure in 1598 by Chinese intervention and the death of Hideyoshi. Six years of devastation, however, had dealt Korea a blow from which it never fully recovered. Adding insult to injury, the retreating Japanese took with them many of Korea's best artisans and craftsmen. The Japanese ceramic and lacquer industries, for instance, owe their start in large part to the imported Koreans. The resentment of the Korean people that resulted from the war has never ceased. Nevertheless, peaceful relations were established with the leaders who succeeded Hideyoshi.[12] The Japanese were given limited access and residence rights in a small area near the southeastern port city of Pusan, an arrangement that continued into the nineteenth century.

The strain of countering the Japanese invasion of Korea weakened China, as well as Korea, and facilitated the Manchu conquest. The Jurchen, or Manchus, one of the northern barbarian tribes, had established their own empire before taking over China. They invaded Korea in 1636, thirty years before they usurped the Chinese throne, and forced the Koreans to transfer their allegiance to the Manchu Emperor from the Ming. The Korean reaction was to establish a rigid exclusion policy against all foreigners, except for the Chinese and for the Japanese enclave near Pusan.

The Japanese and Manchu assaults, together with continuing factional strife, weakened the Korean political and economic structure. The familiar cycle of dynastic decay asserted itself: The aristocratic class entrenched themselves in privileged political and economic positions at the expense of the throne and the common people, upholding the rigid neo-Confucian order inherited from China against all attempts at change.

There were significant efforts at reform. One of these was the philosophical movement now referred to as *sirhak* (Practical Learning), which arose among aristocrats out of power in the seventeenth century. It was inspired in part by deteriorating social conditions and in part by new currents of thought in China, including Christian ideas, brought by young members of the official tribute missions to China. At the same time, new agricultural techniques brought about the growth and concentration of wealth and the beginnings of a commercial economy, despite continuing aristocratic disdain for such activity. During the reigns of kings Yongjo and Chongjo (1724–1800), factional strife was brought under control by a policy of equal distribution of posts.

However, decline resumed in the nineteenth century. Rival families jockeyed for power through their women relatives (reigning and previous queens, subsidiary wives, concubines) in the court, while a succession of boy-kings were put on the throne. Mid-century reform efforts by the regent T'aewon'gun (father of the boy-king Kojong, who ascended the throne in 1863) failed to meet the country's needs. On the contrary, the T'aewon'gun's rigid enforcement of the long-standing policy of excluding all foreigners made Korea all the more vulnerable when the nineteenth-century imperialists commenced their penetration of Korea. The ensuing struggle for hegemony ended with Japanese annexation in 1910.

The Choson Dynasty thus perished, but its long rule of 518 years had left a deep impression upon national attitudes and behavior that is still important. Chinese philosophy, ethics, and politics had become accepted as part of Korean culture. The process was similar to the European assimilation of Greek and Roman culture, but perhaps even more complete. A brief summary of the traditional political and social order, which endured into the late nineteenth century, will show the foundation upon which modern Korea has been built.

At the apex stood the king, with theoretically absolute power within Korea, although acknowledging the overlordship of the Chinese Emperor. A bureaucracy of scholar-officials controlled the central government functions and extended into the eight provinces (increased to thirteen in 1895 by subdivision) down to the county level. There was a large royal household, not clearly differentiated from the government until the 1880s. A censorate was charged with criticizing malfeasance and error, even by the king himself. A distinct but subordinate military hierarchy staffed the Five Commands into which the country was divided; the military also performed police functions. Officials were named on the basis of examination, inheritance, or otherwise demonstrated merit (such as supporting the king against rivals). The *yangban,* together with the royal family, were the social aristocracy of the country. They preferred to live in the capital city but also lived in provincial towns and country estates. Many *yangban* were not in government office, either because they were out of favor or because there were no vacancies. Those without government position lived as scholars (often critical of the administration), teachers, or agrarian landlords; many of them hoped to resume office, individually or through factional struggle.[13]

The *yangban* were both artists and art patrons (but not artisans or manual workers); their taste set the standard for artifacts such as ceramics and lacquerware, produced during the first part of the dynasty by government-employed artisans. Because of the Confucian emphasis on proper form in social activity, rites and ceremonies were as important for the *yangban* as was the substance of government. In Korea, as in China, one of the six major government ministries specialized on Rites (which in the Confucian view included relations with foreign states).

The common people lived in their own separate world of agricultural villages, clustered in the midst of the fields they tilled. (Only social or economic outcasts lived outside villages.) The villages were largely self-governing and self-sustaining. Political and social authority rested in a council of elders of the leading local families. One or more of the elders were recognized by the government as titular leaders and served as the linkage to higher governmental levels. County magistrates had advisory councils of local dignitaries. Decisions were reached through discussion and consensus, rather than Western-style voting. Families were expected to provide for themselves and settle their own quarrels; those that could not be contained within the family were settled by the village elders and only in exceptional cases referred to county magistrates. If things got out of hand, the provincial police and military units might be called in.

The central government protected the villagers from foreign invasion and domestic disorder. It provided the critically important agricultural calendar, received annually from Beijing.[14] It sometimes afforded relief from natural calamities. It levied taxes in money and kind on grain crops and on individuals and mandated labor on public works and military service (exemption from which amounted to a kind of tax). The central government was accepted by the people—with fear and awe, rather than love, sometimes mingled with contempt—as part of the natural universe, along with the heavens, the spirits, the winds, and natural calamities. Since county magistrates and other officials were reassigned frequently to prevent corruption, essential linkage and continuity were provided by locally appointed functionaries, called *ajon*. Not included in the civil service structure, these men often inherited their posts and served for life. They played an important liaison role in dealing with the agricultural villages where the bulk of the population lived.

In the latter nineteenth century, the picture of Korean government commonly drawn by Western observers, and largely corroborated by Korean folklore, is one of a tremendously swollen bureaucracy, preoccupied with ceremonial and status and jockeying for power. The office-holders were supported by constantly growing taxes and rents exacted from those of the peasantry who could not evade them. Tenants or laborers on the estates of absentee landlords made up a growing proportion of the farming population.

Many of the landlords had managed to assure themselves tax-exempt status, thus adding to the people's burden. The resulting poverty, discontent, and injustice, coupled with a conservative and unyielding aristocracy, made Korea a tinderbox for social upheaval. The Western impact provided the spark.

The Imperialist and Colonial Period

The period from 1876 (when Japan forced the signing of Korea's first modern treaty) to 1945 (the end of World War II) marked a great divide in the history of Korea. Prior to 1876, Korea had been wholly within a China-centered international order.[15] Then began a transition, as Western diplomacy and culture upset the traditional order. In Korea—unlike most Asian countries—much of this influence was indirect, through Japan. It was Japan, itself rapidly modernizing in response to Western influence, that emerged as the winner among imperialist contenders for control of Korea and that monopolized control until the end of World War II. Other significant external influence on Korea came from the United States and the Soviet Union. China, after coming to the support of north Korea in 1950, affected events and ideas there.

European countries began their march to the East in the late fifteenth century. By the nineteenth century, they had reduced much of Asia and Africa to colonial possessions and were rapidly penetrating and manipulating the countries that had remained independent (except Japan and Thailand, which managed to hold their own). Until the 1860s, however, Korea was virtually untouched because it was not perceived as important enough, and little was known about it.[16] French missionaries had been martyred, and the crew of a U.S. trading ship had been killed on the Taedong River near P'yongyang because of a misunderstanding. Both France and the United States sent small punitive naval expeditions in retribution, but their small scale and quick withdrawal left the Koreans with the illusion that they had defeated the West.

It fell to Japan, as the newest member of the imperialist club, to open Korea to the modern world. Following the example of Commodore Matthew Perry's opening of Japan in 1853, the Japanese sent a naval force to Korea and in 1876 forced the signing of Korea's first Western-style treaty as an independent sovereign state. A Japanese legation was set up in Seoul. The Chinese, fearful of Japanese penetration on their borders, dispatched a resident to Korea, who sought to extend Chinese political influence; the Chinese also encouraged the Koreans to sign treaties of friendship, commerce, and navigation with a number of Western states, beginning with the United States in 1882.

The Western nations were hoping for trade opportunities; but what little trade Korea could offer had already been monopolized by the Chinese and

Japanese. Finding that not much opportunity remained for them, most Westerners soon lost interest. Japan aspired to hegemony in Korea for reasons of economics and national pride; Russia had designs on both Korea and Manchuria as part of its eastern expansion; Great Britain was interested in preventing any Russian advance. Korea, suddenly exposed to Western political, economic, and cultural influence, became a cockpit of contention both among external powers and between traditionalists and modernizers at home.

In 1884, young, aristocratic would-be Korean modernizers attempted a coup d'état with the support of the Japanese. The modernizers' bid for power failed; the traditionalists, backed by China, retained control; the Japanese minister, who had supported the coup, fled the capital to escape angry crowds. War between China and Japan over the incident was averted with an agreement that each nation would withdraw its troops from Korea and give advance notice to the other before sending troops in. [17]

Ten years later, a major popular rebellion in southwestern Korea against deteriorating economic and social conditions brought a new crisis. Some years previously, in 1860, a frustrated local *yangban* named Ch'oe Che-u had founded a new religion known as *tonghak* (Eastern Learning). The *tonghak* movement was a product of both the frustrations of the era (which had led to other rebellions in various parts of Korea) and a hostile reaction to Western and Christian influence; it was somewhat similar to the *taiping* movement in China at roughly the same time. *Tonghak* gained growing support from the oppressed peasantry. On their behalf, the movement's leaders demanded reforms from the central government, which temporized and then ignored them. Rebuffed, the growing *tonghak* movement became a rebellion in 1894, gaining control of considerable territory.[18]

The Korean court, under Chinese influence, asked for help in suppressing the rebellion. The Chinese sent troops without prior notification to Japan, although the rebellion was suppressed by Korean forces before the Chinese went into action. Japan also sent troops; the Japanese and Chinese forces engaged each other, and Japan declared war on China. To the world's surprise, Japan emerged victorious. The 1885 Treaty of Shimonoseki, which ended the war, declared Korea an independent sovereign state. Korea was thus separated from her centuries-old political link with China and entered an uneasy decade of nominal independence while Russia and Japan jockeyed for preeminence.[19]

After their victory over China, the Japanese overplayed their hand in Korea by forcing reforms against the still-conservative opinions of the people and by murdering the Korean Queen, whom they viewed as an enemy of their interests. As a result, the Russians temporarily gained a dominant position. The Korean King fled from Japanese confinement in his palace, took refuge in the Russian legation, and ruled the country from there for a year (1896–1897). However, the Russians in their turn went too far. The Russo-Japanese contest for hegemony continued for a decade, with the Western powers playing minor roles. Korea, militarily and economically weak, was almost helpless; Korean factions sought advantage from one great power or the other.[20]

Emboldened by the Anglo-Japanese alliance of 1903, Japan went to war with Russia in 1904, driving it out of Korea and Manchuria and establishing a protectorate over Korea. (The Treaty of Portsmouth, which ended the war in 1905, was mediated by U.S. President Theodore Roosevelt.) Five years later, with the acquiescence of the Western powers—including the United States—Japan annexed Korea. The Korean people, except for a small opportunistic minority, were deeply resentful of Japanese control, but the nation was totally unequipped to resist. A number of guerrilla bands (called Righteous Armies, like those that had resisted Hideyoshi's forces three centuries before) nevertheless fought the Japanese forces for several years.

As colonial masters of Korea, the Japanese had the advantage over Western colonizers: They shared much of the same Chinese tradition and utilized the same Chinese writing system. However, Korean hostility toward Japan was traditional; memories of the devastation wreaked by Hideyoshi's forces in the sixteenth century were still vivid. Moreover, the Koreans did not consider the Japanese to be superior, as some colonial peoples had considered their foreign rulers. On the contrary, the Koreans thought of themselves as culturally superior. Furthermore, the legitimacy of imperialism itself was beginning to be challenged. For these reasons, as well as from sheer assertiveness, the Japanese relied extensively on force to maintain their control; and their regime was never regarded as legitimate by the Korean people.

Mindful of world opinion, the Japanese made much of their alleged successes in modernizing Korea and improving the conditions of life. Many books and reports were published in English to persuade foreigners of the virtue of Japanese progress. A good deal of Western opinion subscribed to it. But the objective of the Japanese administration was primarily to serve Japanese interests and preserve order. The traditional Confucian-ordered agrarian society was preserved, but a modern administration and economic system replaced the political structure of the Choson Dynasty.

Heading the Japanese colonial administration was a Governor-General, always a senior military leader, who reported directly to the Emperor of Japan. Virtually all key positions both in government and in major business and financial enterprises were staffed by Japanese. Landholding was drastically reformed, and the Japanese appropriated large agricultural tracts for themselves; yet the old gentry were largely confirmed in their landholdings, so long as they did not obstruct the new order. Both agricultural and industrial production were directed to serve the needs of Japan, while the Korean standard of living—except for those who were coopted by the Japanese or acquiesced in their rule—was actually reduced.[21]

Under these circumstances, business, education, and above all, the rapidly growing Christian churches offered the only opportunities for most Koreans to rise to responsible positions in the modern sector. In 1942, Koreans accounted for 18 percent of the 442 senior government officials, 32 percent of the 15,479 junior officials, and 57 percent of the 30,000 in lower ranks. There was an advisory council of 65 Korean members, but they were little more than window dressing.[22]

Elections for provincial, city, and town councils were held at intervals beginning in 1921, but Japanese candidates and voters had the advantage (property requirements for voter eligibility gave disproportionate weight to Japanese). Villages and towns were more closely linked to government than in pre-annexation times, and police were omnipresent. Nevertheless, most village and town chiefs were Korean. As in the Choson Dynasty, the lowest career official was the county magistrate.

Nine years after annexation, the Koreans rose up in a remarkable nationwide non-violent demonstration for independence, known as the March First Movement (*samil undong*) after the month and day of the event—March 1, 1919. This action, an expression of the deep Korean resentment at Japanese overlordship, followed the death of the former King and Emperor Kojong (reigned 1863–1907), who had been forced by the Japanese to abdicate because he sought international support for Korean independence. His approaching funeral had drawn thousands of Koreans from the countryside to Seoul. The uprising was stimulated by Woodrow Wilson's doctrine of self-determination, which had been put forward at the Versailles Peace Conference then in session to end World War I. Wilson himself, however, refused to support the Koreans against the Japanese, who were World War I allies.

The harsh suppression of the uprising—reported abroad primarily through Western missionary channels—caused strong international criticism, and the Japanese did moderate their rule somewhat in the 1920s, among other things permitting some Korean groups to meet and to publish in their own language. Nevertheless, passive Korean resistance continued, with the March First Movement as a major symbol of Korean nationalist aspirations. Within Korea, nationalists constantly sought expression through the media and the few Korean groups the Japanese permitted, only to have the leaders arrested and the groups or media suppressed. One example was the Seoul newspaper photograph of Son Ki-jong, who won a gold medal as a member of the Japanese track team at the 1936 Berlin Olympics. The newspaper staff retouched the photograph to erase the Japanese Rising Sun on the runner's uniform. The newspaper was suppressed.

Many nationalist leaders left Korea after 1919 and continued their activities in China, the United States, and the Soviet Union. Foremost among exile groups was the Provisional Government established in Shanghai, China, by prominent nationalist leaders following the Japanese suppression of the March First Movement of 1919 in Korea. It was headed first by Dr. Syngman Rhee, but Dr. Rhee soon returned to his activities in Hawaii as teacher, preacher, and propagandist. He and his Korean Commission in the United States maintained a tenuous link with the Provisional Government, which, for most of the time thereafter, was headed by Kim Koo. The Provisional Government, however, was weakened by the difficulty of maintaining contact with the homeland, by the lack of significant international support, and above all by the ideological left-right split among nationalists that had been fueled by the Bolshevik Revolution of 1917 in Russia (see below).[23]

As Japan moved toward domestic autocracy and external aggression in the mid-1930s, liberal policy toward Korea was reversed, and a policy of assimilation took its place. In 1938, exclusive use of the Japanese language was ordered. Koreans were "encouraged" to take Japanese names; schoolchildren had to make ritual obeisance to the Japanese Emperor. Korean versions of Japanese patriotic associations were organized. Pressures intensified as war in China expanded into world war. Koreans were mobilized on a large scale as both civilians and soldiers for labor in Japan and throughout the Pacific. Large numbers of Koreans, mainly from the southern provinces, were encouraged or forced to move into Manchuria as laborers or farmers (these people and their descendants constitute an autonomous region in China today). By the end of World War II, more than 2.5 million Koreans had been sent abroad. As a token palliative, the Governor General was put under the authority of the Japanese Home Minister in 1942, and two representatives were elected from Korea to the Japanese Diet.

Although the Japanese regime benefited the Japanese disproportionately, and diminished rather than improved Korean living standards, it nonetheless played some role in Korea's modernization. It gave the Koreans greater expectations, as they observed the affluent Japanese community in their midst. Industrialization led to urbanization and the beginning of a modern labor force. Japanese education, limited as it was for Koreans, increased literacy and put Korean intellectuals in touch with international currents of thought. Some young Koreans, principally the children of those who worked with the Japanese, went on to Japanese universities. However, few Koreans gained experience or competence at high management levels. Those who did enter the Japanese system, or conducted successful business under it, were branded by their compatriots as collaborators.

The Western Impact

Western religious and philosophical ideas had seeped into Korea since the seventeenth century, by way of the tribute missions to Peking. These ideas played a role in the *sirhak* reform movement. At the end of the eighteenth century, Catholic converts clandestinely entered the country. They were followed by a few French priests and even a Scottish Protestant missionary. The government swung from toleration to persecution of the converts, but virtually wiped them out in 1866 when it discovered a Korean priest's letter asking for French military intervention to protect the Christians. It was not until 1885 that missionary activity resumed, although the Presbyterian medical missionary Dr. Horace Allen entered in the guise of a U.S. legation physician in 1884. The attempt by young Korean progressives to modernize by coup d'état was inspired, in the immediate sense, by Japanese influence, but that influence was ultimately traceable to the West. The *tonghak* movement was also, in part, a result of Western influence (even though it was anti-Western).

From 1884 to 1905, several Westerners occupied influential advisory and even administrative roles in the Korean government. Trade expanded; although it was still dominated by Chinese and Japanese, there was some European and U.S. investment (U.S. citizens owned and operated a profitable gold mine in north Korea from the 1890s until 1940 and built the first streetcar line, electric plant, and railroad). Korean officials travelled in Europe and the United States. The King confided in U.S. diplomatic representatives, particularly the first naval attaché, Lieutenant George Foulk, and Dr. Allen, who later became U.S. Minister. Missionaries were freely admitted from 1885. Led by Presbyterians and Methodists from the United States, they not only established churches but also started Western-style schools and hospitals all over the country. A retired U.S. general (William Dye) became the first modern Western military adviser. But the old Confucian patterns still held fast.

Although Western powers maintained diplomatic and consular establishments in Korea until 1905, and consulates thereafter, they played peripheral roles in Korean affairs. Attempts by U.S. diplomats to help Korea in dealings with Russia and Japan were vetoed by Washington. (Minister Allen and General Dye were involved in attempts to break the Japanese house arrest of the King in 1895.) By the time of the Russo-Japanese War, Westerners were disenchanted with the decadent and backward Korean scene and were content—except for the missionaries—to leave the country to Japan.

After 1905, the Japanese themselves became the chief instruments of modernization in Korea. Even after annexation, the Japanese permitted Western missionary, educational, and business activity as long as it did not involve politics. Young people continued to study in Western countries, and many of the students returned to Korea to spread new ideas. Some of these ideas (including Marxism) also entered by way of the Japanese educational system. Thus a small but growing number of Korean intellectuals learned something about Western ideas of government and society.

Until the end of the Japanese occupation, the great majority of the Korean people were still only superficially touched by Western ideas; their attitudes were basically shaped by the long Confucian tradition and by antipathy toward their Japanese overlords. Nevertheless, the growth of industry and a money economy and the spread of Western ideas—especially through the growing Christian community—were gradually planting the seeds of social change.

The clearest manifestation of Western influence was the nationwide Korean uprising of 1919. The Western concept of self-determination, as enunciated by U.S. President Wilson, encouraged the Korean will to resist. The language of the Korean Declaration of Independence—proclaimed in a public park in Seoul as the Japanese police arrested the thirty-three signers—was reminiscent of the U.S. declaration and the French Declaration of the Rights of Man and Citizen. The Provisional Government in Exile, established in China following the uprising, adopted a Western-style parliamentary constitution and the form of an elective legislature. The Provisional Government, despite its weakness and its infighting, was regarded by the Koreans as the principal legitimate expression of their aspirations for freedom.

By the end of World War I, the Russian Revolution was stirring attention throughout East Asia, with its dramatic overthrow of the old despotic order and its appeal to the impoverished and oppressed workers and peasants of the world. Many nationalists, especially intellectuals, were drawn to socialist and communist ideas as a better solution to political and economic oppression than the conservative capitalist doctrines that had failed to bring desired improvement in quality of life for the masses. Moreover, geography as well as ideology enabled the Soviet Union to help East Asian nationalists in organizing their struggle.

In contrast, conservative and propertied people and many Christians (some of whom had been educated in Western Europe and the United States), though their nationalist feelings might have been equally strong, could not accept radical programs for social change and economic and social levelling; they feared communism as their Western counterparts did.

Thus, both in exile and within the country, Korean nationalists were divided by the influence of two antithetical Western doctrines, as well as by their own factional rivalries and personal differences, into left and right camps. Korean communist groups were organized in Manchuria and in the Soviet Union and generally competed rather than cooperated with the Provisional Government in Exile. Elements in both camps resisted the Japanese by terror and guerrilla action, sometimes in association with the Chinese Nationalists or Communists, but they were rarely united. Both camps received a modicum of external support: from the Soviet Union for the Communists, from Chiang Kai-shek's Nationalist China for the non-communists (with some tacit moral support from the churches and foreign missionaries), but no U.S. or Western European backing or endorsement.

Liberation and Divided Independence

The United States and the Soviet Union, after forty years of near indifference to Korean affairs, renewed their involvement through the Cairo Declaration of November 1943, as a part of the plan for post–World War II dismembering of the Japanese empire. President Franklin D. Roosevelt, Chinese Generalissimo Chiang Kai-shek, and British Prime Minister Winston Churchill pledged that ". . . mindful of the enslavement of the people of Korea, [the Allies] are determined that in due course Korea shall become free and independent." Marshal Joseph Stalin associated himself with the declaration soon afterward at a conference in Tehran.

Little specific thought was given to the implementation of these ringing phrases until after the end of the war. Roosevelt proposed a forty-year international trusteeship (based on the U.S. experience in the Philippines), which at Soviet insistence was shortened to five years. He paid no attention to detailed planning documents. It would seem that the Soviets, also, gave Korea low priority in their plans.

The end of the war came sooner than expected, on August 15, 1945, without the anticipated U.S. invasion of the Japanese home islands. The United States hastily proposed a temporary military occupation of Korea in zones divided at the 38th parallel. The Soviets (who had advanced into the peninsula upon their declaration of war against Japan in early August) agreed. The division, by U.S. design, put the national capital on the American side.[24]

Word of the Cairo Declaration filtered into Korea, and as it became evident that the Japanese would lose the war, clandestine nationalist activity within the country intensified. At war's end, the Japanese felt obliged to turn to a Korean leader to maintain order, pending arrival of Allied forces. Spurned by conservatives, who feared being typed as collaborators, the Governor General finally called on a left-leaning nationalist leader—Lyuh Woon Hyung, a missionary-educated journalist and middle school teacher.[25] Lyuh posed five stiff conditions, including release of political prisoners. The Japanese accepted and designated him to head an organization to maintain public order. Promptly exceeding his mandate, Lyuh organized a Preparatory Committee for Korean Independence. With its encouragement, local notables organized people's committees throughout the country, with associated volunteer police forces, and in many places displaced the Japanese in de facto functions of government. However, the arrangement did maintain order; there was no serious violence against the Japanese, notwithstanding their forty years of oppression.

The Preparatory Committee called a national convention, which included delegates representing the local People's Committees and claimed to be elected by them. On September 7, 1945, two days before U.S. occupation forces arrived, the convention proclaimed a People's Republic of Korea, with a cabinet that included distinguished nationalist names of all political persuasions, right and left. Syngman Rhee, conservative nationalist leader in exile in the United States and probably the best known among Koreans, was named President without his consent; but the whole was clearly dominated by the left, with Communists playing important roles.[26]

The U.S. occupation forces had to be brought from Okinawa, because General Douglas MacArthur did not want to weaken his relatively thin force for the occupation of Japan. Upon the arrival of the U.S. forces, three representatives of the nascent People's Republic went to Inch'on to greet the U.S. commander, Lieutenant General John R. Hodge, but were refused access. Disillusioned by the naive and faction-ridden clamorings of Korean nationalist exiles before and during World War II, the United States had adopted a policy of refusing to recognize the governmental claims of any Korean group until the Korean people themselves could make a choice.

In ignorance of Korean conditions, and without any plan of action, the U.S. command at first directed the Japanese Government-General to govern the country until other arrangements could be made. The Korean outcry forced hasty abandonment of this tactic. The only remaining option was direct U.S. military government of the zone south of the 38th parallel. The story is told that a community group in one provincial city approached the U.S. military mayor, a major, with a nomination for civilian mayor. The major drew himself up to his full 162 centimeters (65 inches) and exclaimed, "Mayor! We came here to kill all you people."[27] Not all of the U.S. command had such prejudices, but the story illustrates the ignorance in which the United States and its representatives undertook the administration of a proud and cultured nation.

U.S. authorities nevertheless tried to stimulate dialogue with representative Koreans and began to recruit into the government those they considered qualified—qualifications usually including conservative political views and knowledge of English, which gave the landed gentry and the business community a leading role. The U.S. authorities also brought Syngman Rhee from the United States and the leaders of the Provisional Government in Exile (as individuals) from China. Rhee and the Provisional Government leaders were given preferential treatment and promptly set about building a political base.

Meanwhile, the Soviets in the northern zone assembled an administration based on the indigenous people's committees and established a central Five Provinces People's Committee at Pyongyang, ancient Koguryo capital and largest north Korean city.[28] To head this administration, they called upon a highly respected Christian leader, Cho Man Sik—the only noted nationalist figure who had remained within the country throughout the Japanese regime. For administrative skills, they relied on several thousand ethnic Koreans brought from the Soviet Union.

In December 1945, the foreign ministers of the United States, the Soviet Union, and Great Britain met in Moscow. They reaffirmed the proposal for a five-year trusteeship by their three states plus China, renewable if necessary for an additional five years. The United States and the Soviet Union were to establish a joint commission for establishment of an interim Korean administration, in consultation with the Korean people. Although rumors of such a policy had already circulated, its publication profoundly shocked the Korean people. They saw in the trusteeship proposal a renewal of the foreign interference that liberation was supposed to end. Demonstrations began all over Korea but were immediately suppressed in the Soviet zone. Communist and sympathetic leftist groups in the south, as well, were ordered to support trusteeship. In the U.S. zone, Provisional Government leaders seized upon the issue as a means of increasing their political power and called a general strike (which the U.S. command hastily converted into a New Year holiday). Uninformed of the background, General Hodge blamed the Russians for the trusteeship proposal, only to be corrected publicly by the Soviet newspaper *Izvestia* and privately by the U.S. State Department.

Preliminary talks between the two commands began in January 1946. Each side was deeply suspicious of the other, and apart from agreement on supply of electricity by the north to the south, only minor matters were settled, such as the exchange of mail. By March, both sides had named delegates to a Joint Commission, which met alternately in Seoul and Pyongyang over several months in 1946 and 1947. However, the Commission never got beyond the preparatory question of whom to consult among the Koreans. The Soviets demanded that only those accepting trusteeship be consulted, while the United States (which had allowed many groups to form) insisted that all credible groups should have a hearing.

In August 1947, the Commission adjourned for the last time, and the United States referred the Korean question to the United Nations. The Soviets, on valid legal grounds, objected that the UN had no jurisdiction, but the United States in those days had overwhelming majority support. A UN commission was established to oversee elections for a constituent assembly. When the Soviets, acting through their north Korean surrogates, refused to admit the commission, elections were held "in the areas where the Commission was able to observe and report," resulting in the establishment of an independent Republic of Korea south of the 38th parallel on August 15, 1948.[29] Syngman Rhee was duly elected President, under a Western-style constitution that mixed parliamentary and presidential forms. The north Koreans held their own election in Communist style, resulting in the proclamation of the Democratic People's Republic of Korea the following month, headed by Kim Il Sung under a Soviet-style constitution. Neither side recognized the other, and both states claimed exclusive sovereignty over all of Korea.

Within south Korea, the U.S. Army Military Government in Korea (or USAMGIK) during its three-year existence (1945–1948) displayed to the Koreans a confused picture. The U.S. command set up an administration based on the former Japanese colonial structure, installing locally recruited conservatives and moderates in senior posts and retaining many Korean former civil servants of the Japanese, including many of the Japanese-trained police. Although a Korean administration was thus promptly rees-tablished, it was criticized by many Koreans as a government by collaborators and interpreters. USAMGIK rescinded all Japanese economic controls, an act that led to maldistribution of food and to hunger in the cities despite a bumper 1945 harvest. The controls were, of course, reimposed. Economic problems were complicated by the repatriation of one and one-half million Koreans from former Japanese territories, as well as a growing flow of refugees from north Korea. Industries were paralyzed by lack of electricity, raw materials, markets, and managerial skills. Inflation was rampant.

The conservative landlord and business class, which had organized its own political party in opposition to the People'sRepublic, dominated senior positions under USAMGIK. Their Han'guk Democratic party became a sort of pro-government political force. Both this group and the U.S. command were opposed to any moves against private property or anything else that smacked of socialism or, worse, communism. The local people's committees, regarded (not always with cause) as Communist-dominated, were system-atically disbanded.[30]

Since U.S. policy until 1948 was to promote formation of a unified regime in cooperation with the Soviets, the State Department opposed any reforms in the south that might hinder unification prospects. Even the universally desired land reform was delayed. The Military Governor's initiative to establish a Department of National Defense in January 1946 was rescinded at State Department direction, although a Philippine-style constabulary was inau-gurated in 1947. Moreover, no U.S. funds were available for economic development, and the departure of the Japanese had removed most indigenous capital.

The south Korean populace grew increasingly restive, urged on by the South Korean Workers' (Communist) party and agents from the north.[31] Political activity was increasingly polarized between left and right. A Wash-ington-inspired attempt to build a moderate centrist coalition failed. There were demonstrations, serious strikes, and a major uprising in Taegu in October 1946, which was put down with considerable loss of life. Two leaders of the moderate coalition, Chang Duk Soo and Lyuh Woon Hyung, were assassinated. Syngman Rhee—to the discomfiture of the U.S. authorities—campaigned for immediate independence of south Korea while the U.S.-USSR Joint Commission negotiations were still in progress. In doing so, he lost some of his former allies, including Kim Koo, president of the Provisional Government in Exile (who with other Provisional Government leaders had come back to Korea after liberation).

In an effort to allay popular unrest, the United States organized a South Korean Interim Government (SKIG) and held elections in late 1946 for an interim legislative assembly. The election, held mostly under Japanese rules, resulted in a wholly conservative body, which was offset through the Military Governor's appointment of an equal number of moderates. The U.S. Military Governor retained final authority and made no bones about it. By 1947, however, the United States wanted to get out of south Korea as gracefully as possible, both to redeploy scarce troops to Europe and to avoid the unpopularity of being a foreign occupier. To the Koreans, the United States seemed to lack a central philosophy or overall plan. In their eyes, this drift contrasted unfavorably with the purposeful reforms in the north.

Despite all its mistakes, and its conservative bias, the Military Government generally acted with diligence and fairness, pragmatically working within very limited resources to meet basic human needs, revive the economy and infrastructure, and expand education. In 1948, as the UN-observed elections approached, the Military Government distributed all former Japanese agricultural lands to tenants, while leaving the disposition of Korean estates to the future Korean government. Some last-minute reforms of the legal and educational systems were also made. USAMGIK brought the economy under control, with the aid of $300 million in "disease and unrest" funds (spent chiefly for food and clothing). The United States was able to turn over a reasonably stable if poverty-level economy and a debt-free administration to the newborn Republic of Korea in 1948, with a surplus in the treasury. On the whole, the display of U.S. goodwill outweighed the mistakes of the administration and the individual sins of the foreign occupiers; Koreans continued to admire and respect the United States.

Korean nationalist feeling nonetheless required that President Rhee display his independence and break continuity with the previous U.S. administration of south Korea. On acceding to power, Rhee discharged all but one of the senior Korean officials of USAMGIK, replacing them with his own supporters. The Han'guk Democratic party got only one Cabinet post, despite its support for Rhee's election, and went into opposition. The new government leaders were inexperienced in administration or economics; under their management, budgetary deficits, inflation, maldistribution, and corruption grew.

As the United States commenced its military withdrawal, two regiments of the fledgling constabulary mutinied, inspired by Communist agents. The mutiny was put down, and a thousand mutineers were executed, but the ensuing guerrilla war took more than a year to bring under control. There were political crises centering on Rhee's suppression of the Left, his unwillingness to allow punishment of alleged collaborators (because he depended upon many of them to support him and run the government), and an opposition attempt to gain power through constitutional amendment.

Nevertheless, by the spring of 1950, an era of progress seemed to have begun. Finances were stabilized (in part because of strong U.S. pressure). The economy picked up, with modest U.S. economic development aid and technical assistance and improved government performance. A land reform law was finally passed, over bitter conservative opposition. Korean estates began to be distributed to the tillers, while landlords were compensated by government bonds. When Rhee endeavored to postpone the scheduled May 1950 parliamentary election, U.S. pressure forced it to be held (under observation of a UN Commission). All but a score of the 200 former legislators were replaced with independents who were not necessarily supporters of the President.

During the same three years (1945–1948) of Soviet occupation, north Korea moved promptly toward popular reforms. The Soviet-sponsored regime confiscated large agricultural holdings, distributed land to the peasants without cost, and nationalized all large industry (the Japanese had concentrated heavy industry in the north, where most of the nations's coal and mineral resources were located).The Korean People's Army was born in 1946, under Soviet tutelage. The Communist party, known as the North Korean Workers' party (later renamed Korean Workers' party when it took in the remnants of its counterpart in the south), became the central organ of control, and the Five Provinces People's Committee became the central government.

The first Committee chairman, as already noted, was the distinguished Korean nationalist and Christian lay leader, Cho Man Sik. He refused to accept trusteeship (and probably other Communist dictates as well); the authorities placed him under house arrest in December, 1945, after which he disappeared and was never heard from again. Kim Il Sung, a guerrilla leader active against the Japanese in Manchuria who had joined the Soviet Army, was imported and established as a leader by the Soviet authorities. With their blessing he displaced not only Cho but other leaders as well (such as Kim Tu-bong, who had returned to Korea from service with the Chinese Communists) and became chief of state and party when the Democratic People's Republic of Korea (DPRK) was proclaimed.

Soviet troops were withdrawn from the north by December 1948. Under apparently firm control of Kim Il Sung and the Korean Workers' party (the division between northern and southern Communist parties having been abolished), Communist-style collectivization and economic development were under way. Christianity, which had previously been stronger in the north than in the south, was suppressed, as were other religions. The results

apparently pleased many peasants and workers, as living standards improved
and the traditional status and economic privilege were abolished; but well
over a million property owners, Christians, and professional and technical
people fled to the south. At the same time, with Soviet assistance, the
north vigorously built up its military forces. Both north and south castigated
each other, and with their respective allies cancelled out each other's bid
for United Nations membership. Each side talked of military action against
the other, although the United States took pains to ensure that the south
Koreans had no offensive capability (they were denied an air force, for
example). Unification, although universally desired, was perceived on both
sides as a zero-sum game.

The Korean War

In January 1950, Secretary of State Dean Acheson made a speech at
the National Press Club in Washington. Although it reaffirmed existing U.S.
policy on defense of the Pacific area, it could be interpreted as a signal
that Korea would not be defended by the United States—a signal also
conveyed by other U.S. actions and statements, including a comment the
following May by Senator Tom Connally, chairman of the Foreign Relations
Committee, that if the north should invade, the United States could not do
anything about it.[32]

The south Koreans warned the United States of an offensive north Korean
military buildup. Although U.S. intelligence had picked up similar indications,
the south Korean claims were dismissed as more border probes of the kind
that had been going on for a year and as typical belligerent Rhee rhetoric.
It was considered unlikely that the Soviets would permit a north Korean
attack. The north Koreans opened a peaceful unification offensive, offering
to return Cho Man Sik in exchange for three of their agents held in the
south and proposing a unification conference.

In the midst of this propaganda campaign, north Korea attacked the
south without warning at dawn on June 25, 1950, all along the 38th parallel,
with a well-trained and tank-equipped force of 100,000. At the time, the
attack was viewed as a Soviet challenge to the free world; in recent years,
scholars have tended to agree with Nikita Khrushchev's statement in his
memoirs that the invasion was a north Korean initiative, although it could
not have been undertaken without Soviet agreement. The south Koreans,
with light World War II weapons inherited from the departed U.S. forces,
and without training in maneuver above the battalion level, could not stand
against such an onslaught. Notwithstanding some brave fighting, they were
forced south of Seoul in three days and were badly disorganized.[33]

The United States immediately reversed its policy of withdrawal, not only
because of the prospect of Communist forces close to Japan, but also

because the aggression challenged the new United Nations framework. Moreover, the attack appeared to be part of an aggressive Soviet pattern similar to Germany's in the 1930s, that, if not stopped, would lead to another world war. (Additionally, the U.S. administration was under domestic attack for "losing" China and lacking resolution in its policy toward Asia.) Because the Soviet representative on the United Nations Security Council was absent in protest against exclusion of the People's Republic of China, the Council was able to adopt a series of resolutions leading to the establishment of a United Nations Command, with the United States as executive agent, to repel the north Korean aggression. President Rhee placed his forces under General MacArthur as UN Commander. Eventually seven U.S. divisions, a British Commonwealth Division (comprising a British brigade and forces of Australia, Canada, and New Zealand), and troops from eleven other countries joined the south Koreans in a campaign that held a small perimeter around the southeastern port of Pusan against the north Koreans and then cut them off in a masterful amphibious landing at Inch'on, west of Seoul.

Following the north Korean defeat, the United Nations General Assembly acquiesced in an American proposal to occupy north Korea pending elections for a unified government. However, an overly rapid UN advance to the north Korean border brought Communist China to north Korea's support; up to a million "volunteers"—many of them impressed former Nationalist troops—pushed back the UN forces south of Seoul. A UN counteroffensive begun in March 1951 returned the lines to the 38th parallel and pushed to more defensible terrain slightly north of it.

At this point, in June 1951, the Soviet representative to the United Nations proposed discussions for a cease-fire. While bitter fighting continued for small changes in the battle line, truce negotiations went on for two years. Most issues were settled in the first few months, but the talks then bogged down—principally over the issue of voluntary repatriation of prisoners of war. The United Nations side insisted on this point because of humanitarian concerns and the World War II experience and because, as it maintained, the great majority of the 100,000 prisoners it held did not want to return to north Korea or China and thus represented a propaganda triumph.[34]

In July 1953, an armistice agreement was finally worked out between the United Nations Commander, on one side, and the commanders of the (north) Korean People's Army and the Chinese People's Volunteers, on the other. A last-minute threat to the agreement was President Rhee's unilateral release of 28,000 prisoners, in a deliberate attempt to torpedo the armistice and compel a fight for UN victory over the entire peninsula. To gain his acquiescence in the armistice—which south Korea has never signed—the United States promised and delivered a mutual defense treaty, $1 billion in economic aid over three years, and equipment for an army of twenty divisions (about 700,000 soldiers).

Under the 1953 Armistice Agreement, there has been no significant military action for over thirty years, although the so-called Demilitarized Zone has been heavily militarized, most sessions of the Military Armistice Commission have been propaganda exercises, and a number of provocations have occurred (such as the north Korean murder, with axes, of two U.S. officers in the Joint Security Area in 1976 and the digging of large tunnels from north to south under the Demilitarized Zone, of which three have so far been found). The U.S. presence was reduced to two divisions plus supporting units, then in 1970 to one, which still remains just behind the frontline. All except token representatives of other nations have withdrawn. The bulk of the Korean combat units remains under U.S. operational control; current command arrangements are discussed in Chapter 7.

The Korean War devastated both halves of the country, but particularly the north, where repeated strategic bombing flattened the industrial plant. Up to 4 million lives were lost on both sides (including 33,729 from U.S. units), and millions more were disabled or made refugees.[35] Around 1 million more north Koreans came south with the retreating UN forces. Damage in the south amounted to one year's gross national product. Only the strength of the Korean family and community system and massive American and foreign aid (both governmental and private) permitted south Korea to survive; similarly, north Korea received substantial aid from the Soviet Union and China, although the Soviet Union provided no military support once the north Koreans were defeated.

Korea from the War to 1970

In south Korea, economic reconstruction and development were handicapped by U.S. and UN controversy over priorities, methods, and responsibilities and by economic ignorance and even indifference on the part of President Rhee and his associates. Inflation again grew beyond 100 percent per year. By 1957, the economy had once more been stabilized, and living standards had returned to prewar levels. After 1957, however, politics got in the way of economics. Economic stagnation was a large factor in the fall of the Rhee regime in 1960.

Political infighting in south Korea resumed as soon as the fighting lines stabilized in 1951. In the heat of conflict, Rhee had accepted some capable opposition leaders in a unity cabinet, but unity dissolved in the face of Rhee's determination to succeed himself in office. The National Assembly, which was to elect the President under the 1948 Constitution, was clearly opposed to Rhee. In a crisis period from January to July 1952, Rhee and his lieutenants forced through an amendment for popular election of the

President, which he easily won. The decision of the United States not to intervene in this crisis, despite its enormous wartime power and influence in Korea and despite Rhee's autocratic and coercive tactics, was a watershed in the history of Korean-U.S. relations.

Two years later, his Liberal party having gained a majority in the National Assembly, Rhee forced through another amendment allowing him a third term. This move unified opposition forces, and in the 1956 election the opposition Democratic party vice-presidential candidate, Chang Myon, won the vice-presidential contest (the Democratic party's presidential candidate had died of natural causes two weeks before the election). When in 1958 the opposition increased its representation in the National Assembly, supporters of the rapidly aging President Rhee resorted to naked coercion in their effort to stay in power. Their tactics included a grossly rigged presidential election in March, 1960, which was accompanied by riots and police brutality.

On April 19, 1960, students marched on the presidential palace to present their grievances. Guards opened fire; in the ensuing violence, 200 students were killed. In the nationwide demonstrations that followed, the United States played a catalyzing role by publicly acknowledging the "legitimate grievances" of the people. Rhee was persuaded to resign and go into exile in Hawaii, where he died in 1965.

Under an interim government led by Huh Chung, a respected senior statesman, the Constitution was again amended to provide for a European-style parliamentary government. New elections in July 1960 swept the opposition Democratic party into power. The new two-house legislature elected Chang Myon (John M. Chang) Prime Minister and Yun Po-son President. A ten-month period of unprecedented political freedom ensued, in which the governing party split into two nearly equal factions, respectively headed by the Prime Minister and the President.

The new regime, weakened by inexperience and political infighting, faced massive challenges. In the absence of firm central control and with an atmosphere of unprecedented freedom among a people accustomed to strong leadership, politics approached anarchy. Economic problems could not be remedied overnight, but they aggravated popular discontent. The north Koreans proposed unification discussions, to which some south Koreans responded positively, leading to fear of subversion. Chang Myon's overtures for relations with Japan, though overdue, were unpopular. Unlike Rhee, who had made a political asset out of resisting U.S. advice, Chang Myon was perceived as too compliant. When he proposed a reduction of 100,000 in the armed forces, and when students took it upon themselves to propose unification talks with north Korean counterparts, a group of military officers moved in.

In a few early hours on May 16, 1961, a force of about 3,600 men led by Major General Park Chung Hee and former Lieutenant Colonel Kim Jong

Pil seized control of the government. Despite the unconstitutionality of the action, the people accepted it—not with enthusiasm, but with something like relief. Restoration of strong control, after the confusion of the experiment in parliamentary democracy, was a return to Korean political normalcy. Moreover, the armed forces, which were not only the symbol of national security but had also refused to support the unpopular Rhee regime in the crisis of 1960, were favorably regarded by the public. The apparent setback to democracy was, however, a problem for the new American administration of John F. Kennedy.

The military leaders established a ruling group of thirty-two military men (the Supreme Council for National Reconstruction), abolished the legislature, suspended the Constitution, and ruled by decree for two years (at first leaving the elected president in place as a cloak of legitimacy). The military leaders enforced law and order vigorously and harshly, sweeping hoodlums and petty criminals from the streets. Hundreds of former civilian political leaders were forbidden political activity for several years. Despite initial mistakes, the military administration moved to revitalize the economy. They coopted trained civilian economists and administrators and placed military officers in civil government positions both to improve operations and to reward supporters.

Reluctantly at first, but then on a businesslike basis, the U.S. authorities worked with the military government to stabilize the economy and then to help finance the first five-year development plan (1962–1966). When the military showed unwillingness to return to civilian government, as they had pledged at the beginning, the United States brought its economic and military leverage to bear. A new constitution was put to popular referendum in 1963 and approved by a wide majority. It was generally an improvement over the 1948 document, with extensive guarantees of civil rights. Park Chung Hee (who had resigned his military rank) was elected president. An elected civil government took office in January 1964, with a respected senior journalist and scholar, Choi Doo Sun, as prime minister.

President Park's political control in the new order was effective enough to bring about acceptance of normalized relations with Japan—a badly needed source of economic support—in 1965, despite widespread demonstrations of popular anti-Japanese sentiment, fanned by opposition politicians. Over token objections by the political opposition, Park also acceded to the U.S. request for support of its military forces in Vietnam; two south Korean divisions eventually served there in the period from 1965 to 1971. In contrast to its opposition to the normalization treaty with Japan, the public generally supported the dispatch of forces to Vietnam, even though it was the first Korean expeditionary force since the fourteenth century,[36] because they saw it as repayment for U.S. support in the Korean War. (The actual south

Korean government motives for sending forces were more complex, involving economic advantage and maintenance of U.S. strategic support.)

To ensure continued control of the fractious Korean body politic, the military government as one of its first actions had set up a large Central Intelligence Agency (KCIA), whose powers transcended those of the U.S. Central Intelligence Agency and Federal Bureau of Investigation combined. This organization remained after 1963, ensuring autocratic management of the south Korean political scene, in which the legislature and political parties had little real power. Nevertheless, there was some semblance of democracy, which gradually increased. Park Chung Hee was reelected in 1967, by a wider margin than in 1963.

Remarkable economic progress began in the mid-1960s. The gross national product increased by 10 percent or more per year, and population growth was slowed from over 2.5 percent to under 2 percent annually. The consequence was rapidly improving material conditions and social stability for a populace that had long suffered from poverty, inflation, stagnation, and uncertainty. This progress, which far outweighed the burden of autocratic control in the popular mind, gave this regime, called the "Third Republic," something of the legitimacy it sought.

North Korea also faced massive postwar political and economic challenges. Kim Il Sung, his position weakened by failure to achieve his war aims, faced challenges from the factions that had been brought together in the Korean Workers' party: the "domestic faction" of Communists from within Korea, headed by the ex-southerner Pak Heun Yung; the "Yenan faction" of people who had been associated with the Chinese Communists during the civil war, headed by Kim Tu-bong; and the "Soviet faction" of people who had entered Korea with the Soviet forces, headed by Ho Ka I. Pak was disgraced, then executed; the other leaders were purged and disciplined. By the end of the decade, Kim Il Sung and the "Kapsan faction" of loyalists who had been associated with him in Manchurian guerrilla campaigns had consolidated their political control. They have maintained it ever since.

The wartime experience greatly diluted Soviet influence in north Korea because it was the Chinese who saved the state from extinction. Moreover, Kim Il Sung, who followed Stalin's example in encouraging a personality cult to bolster his power, was estranged by Khrushchev's policies. For a time, the Soviets sharply reduced their economic support. In these circumstances, Kim elevated the concept of self-reliance, *juche*, to a philosophical dogma. *Juche*, as elaborated by Kim, was eventually represented as a higher form of communism for the Third World, transcending Marxism-Leninism. Kim also performed a balancing act between the Soviet Union and China to reinforce his own independence (a feat that south Korea, with a meager natural resource base and no viable alternative to the United States as a support for its security, could not duplicate).

Collectivization of agriculture, which moved through three successive stages, was completed by 1959; all farmers participated in cooperatives, theoretically owned in common, and shared in the product in proportion to their labor input. North Korea's *chollima* (Thousand-League Horse) movement, more or less contemporary with China's Great Leap Forward, brought the cooperatives to village size and made them political as well as economic units, administered from county centers. In 1969, in the course of one of his famous "on-the-spot guidances," Kim Il Sung inaugurated the Chongsan-ni work method for agriculture, under which the manager of each cooperative shared policy control with a committee representing the farmers. This system was extended to industry by another "on-the-spot guidance" at the Taean steel works the following year. (The use of the Chongsan-ni and Taean models somewhat parallels the roughly contemporaneous use by the Chinese of the model Dazhai commune and Daqing oil complex.)

After an initial two-year reconstruction period from 1953 to 1955, north Korea undertook a Six-Year Plan for economic development and completed it ahead of schedule. This was followed by other multi-year plans; the Second Seven-Year Plan was supposed to be completed in 1985. Annual economic growth was as high as 20 percent in the first few years but declined thereafter; this is partly explainable by the very small base from which recovery started, given the enormous wartime destruction.

Internationally, north Korea assumed a militant anti-American posture and, in competition with south Korea, successfully cultivated the Third World. North Korea encouraged celebration of the month from June 25 (outbreak of the Korean War) to July 27 (date of the Armistice) each year as Anti-American Month, both at home and abroad, and promoted visits from Third World leaders. It also sought to foment revolution in south Korea through propaganda and the clandestine dispatch of subversive agents, establishing a People's Revolutionary Party for Unification for this purpose. In 1968 it both attempted to assassinate the south Korean President (by means of a hit squad that infiltrated to within 500 yards of the presidential residence) and sought to take advantage of perceived U.S. weakness by capturing the intelligence interception vessel *Pueblo* and holding its crew captive for nearly a year. (North Korea also shot down a U.S. intelligence reconnaissance aircraft in 1969.) By 1970 it was at the height of its Third World influence, having been admitted as member of the non-aligned movement and named to the movement's steering group. It gained observer status at the United Nations (a status held by south Korea since 1949).

Developments Since 1970

International developments in the late 1960s and early 1970s had a profound impact on Korea, both north and south. The U.S. quagmire in

Vietnam and President Richard Nixon's move to extricate the U.S. forces, created the appearance of weakness and withdrawal. This appearance worried south Korea and encouraged the north, which for years had sought to get U.S. forces out of Korea. Nixon's Guam Doctrine of 1969, ruling out direct involvement by U.S. forces in other countries' wars, put in question the role of the U.S. divisions in Korea—one of which was withdrawn soon afterward. Above all, Nixon's opening to China created profound uncertainty in both Korean states.

In consequence, there were changes both in relations between north and south and within the two states. South Korea in 1971 initiated discussions between the Red Cross societies of the two states regarding separated families. Then a secret south Korean feeler in late 1971 led to the Joint North-South Declaration of July 4, 1972, in which both Koreas pledged peaceful unification, independence of outside forces, and "grand national unity" (since referred to by north Korea as the "three great principles of unification"). The two sides also promised cessation of mutual vilification, but it soon resumed. There has been virtually no movement toward unification, although there have been intermittent contacts between the two sides since 1972 and one token visit by members of separated families.

Within south Korea, President Park first imposed a state of emergency, then conducted a "coup d'état from within," leading to a new and much more authoritarian regime, the Fourth Republic, under the so-called *Yusin* (Revitalization) Constitution. Some observers believe that Park was genuinely frightened by the power and discipline his representatives had seen in north Korea, as well as worried about diminution of U.S. support. In addition, however, he had nearly lost the 1971 presidential election to a charismatic opposition figure, Kim Dae-Jung, whose capacity to govern the country under such circumstances was distrusted by the military. The election was preceded by amendment of the constitution to permit Park a third term— evoking memories of Rhee's controversial 1954 amendment for the same purpose.

Under the *Yusin* regime, the President had sweeping powers to rule by decree and used them aggressively to control political activity. For example, criticism of the Constitution itself was made a punishable offense. The legislature and the political parties that centered on it were narrowly circumscribed, and although debate within the legislative hall was supposedly protected, it often was not reported to the public. Kim Dae-Jung, the opposition challenger of 1971, was abducted from a Tokyo hotel in 1973 and imprisoned. The press was self-censored within guidelines provided by the government. A critical declaration by opposition leaders, read from the pulpit of the Catholic cathedral in Seoul on March 1, 1976 (fifty-seventh anniversary of the independence uprising) with foreign reporters present, resulted in prison terms for those who signed it.

Although south Korea rode out the oil crisis of 1973 with relatively little difficulty, the 1979 crisis was more serious. Its effects were compounded by overinvestment in heavy and defense industry, another result of the new international uncertainty, and by rising demands for better industrial wages. A leading opposition Assemblyman, Kim Young-Sam, was expelled from the legislature for his criticism of Yusin regime policies. As Park's hard-line advisers clamped down on growing unrest, labor disputes and student demonstrations erupted into street riots. In October 1979, the Director of Korea's Central Intelligence Agency, as a final protest against overly harsh controls, shot and killed the President.

The civilian Prime Minister, Choi Kyu-Hah, constitutionally succeeded to the presidency, and was shortly thereafter confirmed in office by the electoral college. Martial law was declared to ensure order. Investigation of the assassination began; but key military officers led by Major General Chun Doo Hwan, loyal to the dead President, perceived the investigation as a whitewash. In December, they took over the martial law command.

A new civilian cabinet of technocrats named by President Choi undertook to stabilize the economy, commenced political liberalization, and with the legislature set up a forum for developing a new constitution. In the liberalized atmosphere, leading political figures—particularly Kim Dae-Jung (1971 presidential candidate), Kim Young-Sam (head of the main opposition party), and Kim Jong-Pil (known as architect of the 1961 military coup and as Prime Minister for a time under Park)—jockeyed for position in anticipation of the coming presidential election. Progress on a new Constitution was slow and beset with political rivalries. The economy was in recession, both because of political uncertainty and in response to belt-tightening policies; the gross national product fell by over 5 percent in 1980, the first downturn since the early 1950s. Students demonstrated for more freedom, and workers struck in several locations for better wages and working conditions. The north Koreans, as they had in previous times of south Korean political tension, made overtures for unification talks.

As in 1961, senior military leaders grew impatient with civilian political wrangling, feared for the country's security, and saw an opportunity to further their own prospects. On May 17, 1980, as student demonstrations marked the military coup d'état of 1961, General Chun followed in the late President Park's footsteps of nineteen years before. He tightened martial law, dismissed the legislature, and directed the government, although the President and a civilian cabinet continued to hold office. The martial law authorities dispersed the student demonstrators.

In the large southwestern city of Kwangju, however, students at Chosun University refused to disperse. Army Special Forces troops were mobilized against them; the townspeople rose up in their support; and the troops used brutal force against the crowds. The resulting public fury was such that the army had to evacuate the city, which ran itself for over a week within the encircling army forces. After futile negotiations, a new group of regular army troops (from the 20th Infantry Division) seized control of the city in a pre-dawn and relatively bloodless maneuver.[37] The uprising cost at least 193 lives (the official government count) and very possibly more—although not the 2,000 claimed by emotional students and opposition leaders. The Kwangju uprising shocked the entire nation and left a bitter memory that damaged General Chun's public image and that of the armed forces.

In deference to both foreign and domestic opinion, General Chun convened a new commission to draw up a new Constitution, for a Fifth Republic; it was adopted by referendum in October 1980. Martial law was withdrawn, new political parties were allowed to organize, and elections in January 1981 reconstituted the legislature. An electoral college of over 5,000 elected local representatives named Chun, now a civilian, to a single seven-year term as President.

The Fifth Republic, roughly similar in law and fact to the Third, was a significant step toward more liberal politics. This liberalization permitted an opposition political party to win more than a third of the legislative seats in the 1985 election and to mount an aggressive challenge to the administration, including demands for constitutional amendment. The President has repeatedly pledged to leave office in 1988 and ensure a peaceful change of power. Such change, in the face of the political challenges that liberalization has permitted, together with the economic problems posed by a stagnant and protection-minded world environment and workers' demands for better wages and working conditions, will be a critical test of south Korea's political maturity.

Increasingly militant and violent student demonstrations, a bolder opposition party, and popular resentment at the slow pace of change led in 1987 to a political about-face by President Chun and extensive amendment of the Constitution, providing for direct popular election of the President's successor. The election of December 16, 1987, gave the government party's candidate a plurality, and he was scheduled to assume office the following February, as the new Constitution went into effect. The opposition voiced some objections to the election and its result. However, the basic political and economic structure of the Republic remained in place and seemed likely to weather the crisis.

In north Korea, there were also changes after 1970. Apparently the north was concerned about the south's rapid economic progress, the evidence of which the northern representatives saw for themselves in 1971 and 1972, and decided to seek Western technology. The 1971 oil crisis upset their plans for paying the costs of importing production facilities from Europe and Japan. As a result of the crisis, and perhaps also of faulty planning, the north Koreans have been in default on their payments to Western and Japanese creditors for over a decade.

In 1972, the north Korean Constitution was changed to emphasize indigenous authority for political philosophy and administration, although the Communist structure was little modified. Minor cosmetic changes reflected the spirit of the July 4 north-south Declaration. The new office of President was established for Kim Il Sung, who by his seventieth birthday in 1982 had been chief of state and government longer than any contemporary national leader.

North Korea's rapid postwar economic progress met increasing obstacles as the economy became more complex and less amenable to centralized planning and direction, and as external aid declined. The south's growth rate exceeded the north's by the mid-1970s. Partly for this reason, and partly by reason of its radical militancy on the international scene, the north has lost much of its former international advantage over the south. These adverse factors may contribute to north Korea's recently increased willingness to engage in dialogue with the south and its attempts to open discussions with its declared archenemy, the United States.

The Sixth Korean Workers' Party Congress in 1980 set the stage for the transfer of Kim Il Sung's power to his son, Kim Jong Il—a process that now seems far advanced, although the senior Kim in mid-1987 remained the chief of both state and party. Kim Il Sung visited the Soviet Union (for the first time in many years) and Eastern European countries in 1984. This visit was followed by increased Soviet military support for north Korea, including long-desired high-performance MiG-23 fighter planes, and by closer relations between the two countries after some years of coolness. North Korea thus continued its policy of balancing its relations with its two giant allies.

Conclusion

Korea's long history (see Table 2.1A) has been characterized both by persistent assertion of a distinctive Korean identity and by military, political, and cultural assaults from external sources. Given Korea's strategic location and the much greater power, first of China, then of Japan and Russia, it is remarkable that the Korean nation has survived. Its weakness at the time of European and U.S. penetration into East Asia and Japan's success at building strength from this penetration led to forty years of subjugation. No sooner was it liberated than ideology and great-power rivalry split it in two. Notwithstanding thirteen hundred years as an autonomous, unified country, Korea is now deeply divided into two hostile states backed by rival external camps. This hostility shows few present signs of receding and deprives the

Korean people of the strength they would have as a single state of sixty million in a good-sized homeland with clear and defensible borders.

Nevertheless, both Koreas have done better than the vast majority of states in the developing world in terms of total economic development and distribution of wealth and income. The north, with its strong ideology and centralized control, economically outdistanced the south in the first twenty years of its separate existence. But from the 1970s on, the south forged ahead with a more flexible, market-oriented system developed out of the confused experimentation of earlier years. In both Koreas, the material welfare of the average citizen has dramatically improved, but the north now lags behind.

The autocratic Korean political tradition, reinforced by north-south hostility and the associated military threat, has retarded political development in south Korea. However, recent events suggest that political development is in progress there, even at the cost of some trauma. In the north, the authoritarianism of Marx, Lenin, and Kim Il-Sung seems to intensify the old Confucian restraints. Even in the succession of Kim Jong Il to the leadership role of his father, Kim Il Sung, north Korea has so far shown little outward evidence of basic political change.

TABLE 2.1A Chronological Summary of Korean History

2333 B.C.	Legendary Founding of Korea by Tan'gun
1122 B.C.	Legendary Arrival of Kija from China to Establish Ancient Choson
108 B.C.	Fall of Ancient Choson to Chinese; establishment of Chinese commanderies in Korea
313 A.D.	Fall of Nangnang (Chinese Commandery) to Korean Kingdom of Koguryo
4th-7th centuries	Three Kingdoms period (Koguryo, Paekche, Silla)
668	Unification of Korea by Silla
936	Establishment of Koryo Dynasty by Wang Kon
1231	Mongol invasion, leading to Mongol domination
1392	Establishment of Choson Dynasty by Gen. Yi Song-gye
1446	Korean alphabet (han'gul) devised by King Sejong
1592-98	Japanese invasion of Korea
1627-37	Manchu invasions
1783	First Christian convert; philosophical reform movement (sirhak) at its height
1876	First Western-style treaty signed with Japan
1882	Treaty of friendship and commerce with U.S.
1884	Failure of modernizers' attempt to seize power
1894	Tonghak Rebellion, starting Sino-Japanese War
1905	Protectorate over Korea after Russo-Japanese War
1910	Annexation of Korea by Japan
1919	Korean independence uprising
1945	Occupation by US and USSR; division at 38th parallel
1948	North and south Korea become independent states
1950-53	Korean War
1960	Ousting of south Korean President Rhee by "student revolution"; establishment of Second Republic
1961	Coup d'état led by south Korean Gen. Park Chung Hee
1963	Civilian government reestablished as Third Republic
1965	Normalization of relations with Japan
1971	Kim Dae Jung narrowly defeated in south Korean presidential election
1972	North-south Joint Declaration on peaceful unification; establishment of autocratic Fourth (yusin) Republic in south Korea; north Korean constitution revised
1979	South Korean President Park assassinated
1980	Seizure of political control in south Korea by Gen. Chun Doo Hwan; Kwangju uprising; Fifth Republic
1983	Attempted assassination of south Korean President by north Korean agents in Rangoon; 17 Koreans killed

Notes

1. In a short historical summary, it is impossible to note the variations in interpretation by individual historians, among whom there are considerable differences. Such differences are greatest in the earliest and most recent periods of Korean history. The author is indebted to Dr. Suh Dae Sook of the University of Hawaii for making this important point. The account in this book is intended to reflect, as nearly as possible, a coherent consensus of varying schools. Material in this chapter on the pre-Japanese era is based primarily on Ki-baik Lee, *A New History of Korea*, translated by Edward Wagner (Cambridge, Mass.: Harvard University Press, 1985); Professor Lee is generally considered the foremost Korean historian of the postwar era.

2. Cf. Kim, Jung-hak, "Ethnological Origins of Korean Nation," *Korea Journal* 3 (No. 6, June 1963):5–8. Some scholars identify these peoples as members of an Altaic family. The term "Tungusic" refers to the basin of the Tunguska rivers in central Siberia (tributaries of the Yenisei River) from which these peoples are believed to have come. The Turkic and Mongol peoples are also considered Altaic.

3. The traditional dates for the founding of the Three Kingdoms are 37 B.C. for Koguryo, 18 B.C. for Paekche, and 57 B.C. for Silla; but if Paekche and Silla existed at that time, they were far smaller and less inclusive than in the Three Kingdoms period. (One still unproven theory holds that the same Puyo people who dominated Paekche, skilled horse-riding warriors, swept on into Japan to become an important component in its national development.)

4. South Korea tends to stress the role of Silla in the formation of the Korean nation, while the Democratic People's Republic of Korea in the north emphasizes the role of Koguryo.

5. A separate Korean-Khitan state called P'arhae (Chinese: Pohai) existed in the harsh and rugged northeast, part of old Koguryo, until the tenth century.

6. The Khitan are a Tungusic people like the Koreans. Under the name Jurchen, one part of this people established a kingdom in present Manchuria that in 1644 conquered China and ruled it as the Manchu or Ching Dynasty until 1911.

7. The civil and military bureaucracies were parallel but separate in both Koryo and the ensuing Choson (Yi) Dynasty and were collectively termed the *yangban* (literally meaning "both classes"), which became a term for the aristocracy generally.

8. The Japanese *shogun* were men who seized political power and passed it on to their descendants, but left the powerless emperors on the throne. There were three successive shogunates, extending from the eleventh to the nineteenth centuries. In form, they resembled European feudalism. Korea's brief experience under the Ch'oe family was at most a rudimentary and faint parallel; Korea never had a similar feudalistic system of government.

9. North Korean scholars' research on the seventeenth- and eighteenth-century literati of the *sirhak* school (see Appendix A) also notes the difference between Korean and Chinese culture.Cf. *Progressive Scholars at the Close of the Feudal Age in Korea* (Pyongyang: Ministry of Culture and Propaganda, DPRK, 1955. 142 pp.).

10. The other Choson Dynasty king without a posthumous title is Kwanghaegun (1608–1623). The dynasty had a total of twenty-four reigning monarchs.

11. Edward W. Wagner, *The Literati Purges; Political Conflict in Early Yi Korea.* Harvard East Asian Monographs: 58 (Cambridge, Mass.: East Asian Research Center, distributed by Harvard University Press, 1974).

12. Tokugawa Ieyasu succeeded Hideyoshi as leader of Japan under the nominal but powerless emperor. He and his descendants ruled Japan as *shogun* (in effect, regents or chief ministers) from 1600 to 1868, when the emperor's power was restored by a group of rebellious young aristocrats.

13. William Henry Wilkinson, *The Corean Government; Constitutional Changes, July, 1894, to October, 1895.* (Shanghai: Statistical Department of the Inspectorate General of Customs, 1897).

14. The agricultural cycle of planting and harvest, essential to the people's livelihood, depended upon knowledge of when the various tasks should be done to take best advantage of the weather. Preparation of the calendar called for sophisticated mathematics and astronomical observations that were completely beyond a largely illiterate population.

15. For a description of the traditional Chinese international order and the place of Korea in it, see M. Frederick Nelson, *Korea and the Old Orders in Eastern Asia* (Baton Rouge: Louisiana State University Press, 1945).

16. Cf. W. E. Griffis, *Corea; The Hermit Nation* (New York: AMS Press, 1971; reprint of 9th, or 1911, edition), the earliest English-language book on Korea of the nineteenth century and one of a very few.

17. Harold F. Cook, *Korea's 1884 Incident; Its Background and Kim Ok-kyun's Elusive Dream* (Seoul: Royal Asiatic Society, Korea Branch, 1972). See also In K. Hwang, *The Korean Reform Movement of the 1880s; A Study of Transition in Intra-Asian Relations.* (Cambridge, Mass.: Schenkman Publishing Co., 1978).

18. Benjamin Weems describes the *tonghak* movement in his book, *Reform, Rebellion, and the Heavenly Way* (Tucson: University of Arizona Press for Association for Asian Studies, 1964).

19. To symbolize Korea's new sovereignty and equality, the Korean king proclaimed himself Emperor in 1897.

20. See Hilary Conroy, *The Japanese Seizure of Korea, 1868–1910; A Study of Realism and Idealism in International Relations* (Philadelphia: University of Pennsylvania Press, 1960), and C.I. Eugene Kim and Han-Kyo Kim, *Korea and the Politics of Imperialism, 1876–1910* (Berkeley: University of California Press, 1967).

21. Regarding the Japanese occupation of Korea, see Andrew Grajdanzev, *Modern Korea* (New York: Institute of Pacific Relations; distributed by the John Day Co., 1944); and *Korea Under Japanese Colonial Rule; Studies of the Policy and Techniques of Japanese Colonialism,* Andrew H. Nahm, editor, Korea Study Series 2: Proceedings of the Conference on Korea, November 12–14, 1970 (Kalamazoo, Mich.: Center for Korean Studies, Western Michigan University, 1973).

22. Kim, Han-Kyo, "The Japanese Colonial Administration in Korea—An Opinion," in *Korea Under Japanese Colonial Rule,* pp. 45, 51–52.

23. See Chong-Sik Lee, *The Politics of Korean Nationalism* (Berkeley: University of California Press, 1963.

24. An excellent discussion of the origins of the 38th parallel division is Michael Sandusky's book, *America's Parallel* (Alexandria, VA: Old Dominion Press, 1983). I have discussed this problem in more detail in Chapter 8.

25. Brief biographies of Lyuh Woon Hyung (Yo Un-hyong) and most other Korean leaders mentioned in this book can be found in the Encyclopedia of Asian History, Ainslie T. Embree, Editor in Chief (New York: Charles Scribner's Sons, 1985).

26. For a discussion of the People's Republic and its background, see Bruce Cumings, The Origins of the Korean War; Liberation and the Emergence of Separate Regimes 1945–1947 (Princeton: Princeton University Press, 1981), pp. 68-100.

27. This incident occurred during my duty in Korea in 1945–46, in the city where I was stationed.

28. The northern occupation zone comprised all or most of five Korean provinces: North and South Hamgyong, North and South Pyongan, and Hwanghae. A portion of the thinly populated and mountainous Kangwon Province also lay north of the 38th parallel. (The provincial boundaries were subsequently redefined by the northern government to add Yanggang and Chagang provinces along the border with China, and Hwanghae has been divided into North and South Hwanghae, thus bringing the total number of provinces, including Kangwon, to nine—the same as in the south.) The southern zone in 1945 included eight provinces: Kyonggi (in which Seoul, the capital, was situated), much of Kangwon, North and South Ch'ungch'ong, North and South Kyongsang, and North and South Cholla. In 1946, Cheju Island was separated from South Cholla and became a ninth province. A small strip of Hwanghae Province lay south of the 38th parallel and was administered as part of the southern zone until the Korean War, although it could be reached by land from the rest of the zone only by passing through the northern zone.

29. First Report of the United Nations Temporary Commission on Korea, United Nations General Assembly Official Records, Supp. No. 9, 3d Session (Lake Success, 1948); Second Part of the Report (Paris, 1949).

30. Bruce Cumings, The Origins of the Korean War: Liberation and the Emergence of Separate Regimes (Princeton, N.J.: Princeton University Press, 1981).

31. See, for example, reports by the Political Advisers to the Commanding General, USAFIK (Benninghoff and Langdon) in 1946; Foreign Relations of the United States, 1946, Vol. 8, The Far East, pp. 615–16, 662, 704–05.

32. Acheson listed the areas that were considered within the U.S. Pacific defense perimeter (not including Korea) and said that other nations should look to the United Nations for their defense. At the time, the failure of the collective-security provisions of the UN Charter was not so clear as it has become since. For the text of his speech, see U.S. Department of State Bulletin 22 (No. 551, January 23, 1950), pp. 111–18.

33. For accounts of the Korean War, see (among others) Carl Berger, The Korea Knot; A Military-Political History (Philadelphia: University of Pennsylvania Press, 1957); Joseph C. Goulden, Korea: The Untold Story of the War (New York: Times Books, 1982); Kim, Chum-kon, The Korean War; The First Comprehensive Account of the Historical Background and Development of the Korean War (1950–1953) (Seoul: Kwangmyong Publishing Co., 1973); Robert Leckie, Conflict: The History of the Korean War (New York: G. P. Putnam Sons, 1962).

34. Cf. Callum A. MacDonald, Korea; The War Before Vietnam (New York: The Free Press, 1986), pp. 249–256.

35. The Encyclopaedia Britannica lists U.S.casualties in the Korean war as 33,729 killed, 103,284 wounded, and 10,218 captured. The corresponding figures for south

Korean forces were 70,000, 150,000, and 80,000; for other nations, 4,786, 11,297, and 2,769. North Korean and Chinese battle casualties were estimated at 1.6 million, plus 400,000 deaths from disease; around 500,000 south Koreans and 3 million north Koreans are believed to have died from causes related to the war. *Encyclopaedia Britannica*, Fourteenth Edition, Volume 13, 1973, p. 475.

36. Korean troops were pressed into service by the Mongols in 1274 and 1281 for their unsuccessful attempts to invade Japan. In the late fourteenth century, King Kongmin sent an expeditionary force into Manchuria against the then-weakened Mongols. William E. Henthorn, *A History of Korea* (New York: The Free Press, 1971), pp. 121-22, 129.

37. Some critics of U.S. policy toward Korea maintain that the United States should have exercised its operational control of the Korean armed forces to prevent despatch of military units to Kwangju. This view is based upon misunderstanding of the concept of operational control, which is discussed in Chapter 7.

3 KOREAN SOCIETY AND CULTURE

Introduction

The people of the United States, like people of all countries, are very proud of their national culture and identity. Most of that culture really came from elsewhere. Cultural values, legal traditions, and ideas of democracy from Greece and Rome; religious traditions from Palestine; myths and legends from northern Europe; language from England and France; and art and music from Europe and Africa are examples. In fact, the United States has no indigenous tradition except that of the Native Americans. Any culture that can be uniquely attributed to the United States is recent and peripheral: baseball, rock-and-roll, blue jeans, fast food. The particular blend of borrowings, and what has been made of them, is what ultimately establishes the U.S. cultural identity.

In somewhat the same way, the modern society and culture of Korea are a blend of historical influences.[1] But this blend is no mere copy, and its roots are ancient. The individuality of the Korean people, and their sense of ethnic identity, have both survived and accommodated Chinese, Japanese, and Western impact. Despite its thorough integration of Chinese culture over many centuries and despite the traumatic inroads of Japan and the West, Korea keeps its own distinct culture.

Fitting Western values and behavior patterns into Korean tradition is an ongoing process, which began only a hundred years ago (although elements of Western thought had attracted Korean scholars by the eighteenth century). This process, often painful, is an unavoidable part of Korean modernization and industrialization. The Koreans must therefore be understood in terms of both a relatively fixed tradition and a rapidly changing present. Because English-speaking readers are already familiar with Western culture, the emphasis in this chapter is placed upon Korean tradition; but it must be understood that the Koreans themselves are moving away from tradition toward a new cultural synthesis.

The Western cultural impact has been all the stronger because it came at a time when both Chinese and Korean traditional orders were already weakened from internal causes. The consequent rapid change in values and customs has led to uncertainty regarding the basic guidelines of behavior and aspiration, and consequent personal trauma and social unrest. For a time after World War II, this cultural uncertainty, coupled with Japanese distortions, misled the Koreans into disparaging their own heritage. Among the most poignant memories of U.S. military government officials in the post–World War II years were the expressions of shame and inferiority by many Koreans in speaking of their own past history.

Since then, the work of both Korean and foreign scholars has rediscovered Korea's proud indigenous tradition and the Korean contribution to the Chinese heritage. For example, the writings of great Korean scholars, such as Yi Yulkok and Yi T'oegye in the seventeenth century, are now recognized in Japan and China as contributions to the Confucian literature.[2] Contemporary Korean culture is assimilating Western culture as it did the Chinese, and Korean authors and artists are gaining recognition in the West.

Korea's own adaptations to the needs of a modern industrial society—notwithstanding the dramatic differences between traditional and industrialized values and ways of life—are a renewed demonstration of the nation's vitality; although uneven, they have thus far been fairly successful in spite of the enormous problems involved. Korea's economic and military achievements since the Korean War have given both leaders and public a renewed sense of their own worth. Koreans are now reasserting their identity in both parts of Korea. Cultural borrowings are being critically reexamined for their relevance to current Korean needs and aspirations.

Nevertheless, despite their dramatic progress since 1945, the people in both parts of Korea still have an underlying sense of insecurity. This feeling is engendered not only by their historical experience and the present military confrontation, but also by the uncertainties of cultural change. New economic problems have recently added to this insecurity. In reacting to it, Koreans are voicing criticism of the behavior of other nations. The United States, for example, is being blamed for its effect on Korean culture (as well as for its other sins, including the division of the country), although it is the Koreans themselves who have accepted U.S. movies, jazz, blue jeans, English vocabulary, and the rest. All this is part of the painful process of cultural accommodation.

Family

The family is basic to the life of every Korean. Its importance has for centuries been greatly reinforced by the Confucian philosophy, received from China, and fully accepted into Korean culture by the fifteenth century. This philosophy emphasizes family relationships as fundamental to the entire social fabric and includes relatives far beyond the simple parent-children household. Although the nuclear family (father, mother, children) as a living unit is becoming the norm in the big cities, the traditional Confucian view of family relationships and responsibilities continues as a strong influence on individual attitudes and behavior.

In the Confucian view, the family has the central role in society. Three of the traditional five Confucian social relationships deal with family: father to son, husband to wife, and elder brother to younger brother (senior to junior). The fourth relationship, of ruler and minister, extends a family analogy to the entire polity. Moreover, all but the fifth—the relation between friend and friend—are based on relations of superior to inferior, not of equals.

Accordingly, most social relationships are conceived in terms of hierarchical order between unequal pairs. The senior has responsibility for wise and benevolent direction of behavior, and for the welfare of those in his charge; the junior has the duty of respect and obedience. Filial piety—children's obedience and respect toward their parents—is a cardinal Confucian virtue, which the literature extols even to the point of caricature, as when grown men and women are portrayed as acting like children before their elderly parents to amuse them. Although the traditional relationships are changing in both north and south Korea, and obedience within the family is less strict and formalized, respect of juniors for seniors is still strong, as is the seniors' expectation of obedience and decorum.

The Confucian family unit is not only based on junior-senior relations; it is also a collective in both space and time. In the Confucian ethic, individuals consider themselves as part of this collective, which extends (in diminishing intensity) to eight degrees of relationship (illustrated in the

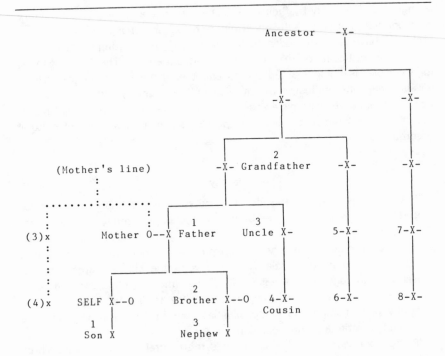

In the above chart, (X) denotes males in patrilineal line; (o) denotes females. The dashed lines are patrilineal relationships (ch'injok), the dotted lines are matrilineal relationships (oejok). Numbers represent degrees (ch'on) of relationship to self. Relationships by marriage (ch'ojok), other than wife (o), are not shown. The same degrees of relationship apply to all three kinds of relatives, but the patrilineal relations are the important ones.

Source: Pak, Ki-hyuk and Sidney D. Gamble, *The Changing Korean Village* (Seoul: Shin-hung Press for the Royal Asiatic Society, Korea Branch, 1975), pp. 58-59 (adapted).

FIGURE 3.1 Chart of family relationships

diagram, Fig. 3.1) and links the living with deceased ancestors. The personal satisfactions of family members are linked with the fortunes and status of their family and relatives (notwithstanding rivalries and tensions within the family group). So-called ancestor worship is simply a continuing relationship with family members who have died.

Feelings of mutual responsibility among family members have traditionally been very strong. They outweigh responsibilities of neighborliness, which in turn outweigh those of citizenship. Providing jobs for one's relatives, condemned as nepotism in Western societies, was—and to a limited extent still is—both a virtue and a matter of course in Korea. In the old days, officials promoted to high office were expected to look after their less fortunate relatives, to the point where the burden made such appointments mixed blessings for their recipients. Family geneologies are carefully maintained and preserved.

It is important to recognize that family responsibility is still the main basis for the individual's social security. Governmental and private responsibility for the welfare of the unrelated individual is a very new idea and only beginning to develop. (According to north Korean claims, social welfare is further advanced in the north than in the south, and loyalty to leader and Party has officially displaced family loyalty.) There is a school of thought in south Korea that holds family responsibility for the welfare of its members to be better, because it is cheaper and more responsive to individual need, than governmental welfare programs. Current south Korean emphasis on the family and on the virtue of filial piety is consistent with this outlook.

The Confucian ideal of family life was "five generations under one roof." This ideal was not often fulfilled, because of the cost and because the traditional life expectancy was not much over thirty years (it is now in the high sixties, in both parts of Korea). Moreover, in Korea it was normal for married children other than the oldest son to set up their own households. This process led in former times to whole villages of close relatives. However, three generations (parents, children, and children's children) were, and often still are, frequently under one roof.

In modern cities, the Western-style nuclear family is increasingly common because of the small space and high cost of high-rise apartments, as well as the growing desire of young people to form and raise their own families, independent of their parents. Nevertheless, it is still considered normal for parents to live with their eldest son in their old age, and the American practice of packing parents off to nursing homes is abhorrent to Koreans. Reunions of extended families, particularly on three traditional occasions, New Year's and the spring and fall holidays, are common; these may include ceremonies to honor ancestors, who are often buried in a separate family cemetery. Intercity buses and trains are crammed at these times.

Family relationship in Korea exists on four levels. The basic family group comprises the nuclear family and (to a diminishing extent) people within five degrees of relationship (see Fig. 3.1), among whom the senior active male member formerly had authority over the whole. The mourning group includes eight degrees of relationship; this is the group that honors deceased ancestors at funerals and subsequent formal occasions. Larger and less well defined is the common descent group, recognizing a noted individual as common ancestor. Finally, there is the clan, comprising all persons descended from an actual or mythical ancient progenitor. Many mourning groups, and even common-ancestor groups, still maintain geneological records and ceremonial properties.

Marriage, crucial to the continuity of the family, was traditionally too important to be left to the man and woman concerned. It was arranged between the families of the prospective bride and groom for mutual advantage, usually through a go-between who assisted in assuring compatibility by means of a mixture of common sense and astrology. The bride and groom, in theory, had no contact until the wedding; after the wedding, the bride cut her ties with her own family and entered her husband's—there often to be mercilessly exploited until she, in her turn, could exploit her own daughter-in-law. A married woman continued to use her own family name for legal purposes and was entered by that name in her husband's family register (to honor her father's family, rather than to recognize her separate identity; her own given name was traditionally not recorded).

From the family's point of view, selection of a wife did not necessarily involve education or talent, so long as she was of good background, could be a good mother, and could perform her assigned household duties. It was perhaps natural, therefore, that men often sought female companionship outside the home. If a man was wealthy enough to support a concubine, there was only weak social opposition to it; the children of the concubine might suffer social disadvantage, but not moral opprobrium. Social gatherings of men outside the home often included the services of professional entertainers, *kisaeng*, who could make intelligent conversation, recite and even compose poetry, sing, dance, and play musical instruments. Sexual services might or might not be involved, although solicitous behavior and physical contact usually were.

Today, many marriages are made by men and women themselves on the basis of emotional attraction and perceived compatibility; but the approval of both families remains important. Marriages are still arranged, but no longer in disregard of the couple's wishes or preferences. There is now more social disapproval of concubinage; it still exists, particularly for the wealthy, but it is increasingly rare.

Until recently, it was both immoral and illegal for a man to marry a woman within the same clan. There are only a few hundred family names in Korea (all but about ten of them monosyllabic, written with one Chinese character),[3] and for many of these names there is only one clan, meaning that persons of the same surname could not marry. However, there are thirty-two Kim clans, and some other surnames also have multiple clans. Since the mid-1950's, easing of the law has been under discussion, but marriage within a clan is still frowned upon by traditionalists.

For centuries it has been the custom to give all children of the same generation within a common-ancestor group a common generation name.

This name is selected by a recognized senior relative. Part of the Chinese character used for the generation name usually represents one of five traditional elements—wood, fire, earth, metal, and water, in that order—used in succeeding generations. Thus, each individual has a name composed of three characters (each of one syllable): family name first, then personal and generation names (usually linked by a hyphen when Romanized). However, some families give only one personal name, and in families with two-syllable surnames, there may be four characters. This practice became general only during the Choson Dynasty, so that older names (such as Ulchi Mundok, defender of Koguryo) do not necessarily follow the rule. (Foreigners should note that among adults there is a strong tabu against addressing people by their personal names, except among very close friends; titles or "pen-names" are used instead.)

In north Korea, Communist social and economic norms have been systematically inculcated for forty years. It is hard to say how much real change in the people's attitude and behavior has resulted, but personal observations by visitors to the north, and some of the official ideology, suggest that there is considerable continuity with the past. The personality cult of Kim Il Sung is rooted in the old familism (for example, he is called *oboi*, meaning parent, both father and mother). His father, mother, and grandfather are held up as models in official publications, and his son, Kim Jong Il, has been designated his successor. Filial piety is still a virtue. Within each family, and to some extent in the wider circle of close relatives, the old hierarchical relationships still exist. The collectivism of the Korean political and economic order is akin to the collectivism inherent in the traditional family system.[4]

However, many aspects of north Korean life obviously weaken traditional family solidarity. Decisions affecting people's lives, including place of residence, education, employment, and even marriage are controlled by party and state authorities rather than by families or individuals. Since private property, other than modest personal possessions, has been eliminated, inheritance is impossible. The cult of Kim Il Sung has transferred to the Great Leader at least some of the loyalty and affection traditionally given to parents.

Family is important in north Korean social standing, but the traditional status ranking is reversed. Descendants and relatives of former landlords and capitalists are officially discriminated against in education and employment, whereas families of outstanding workers and revolutionaries are favored. Honor is therefore least, under the current ideology, for the ancestors of families who would be most likely to follow the old custom. The traditional extended-family ceremonies would also be made difficult because of family dispersal, expense, and official suspicion of assemblies.

Community Life

The rural community was the center of social activity for most Koreans for thousands of years. By the first century of the Choson Dynasty, the community also was guided by Confucian principles; a sixteenth-century scholar, Cho Kwang-cho (1482–1519) institutionalized them in the form of a "village code."[5] Except for taxes, labor on public works, military service, and occasionally the control of major disputes, the villages managed their own affairs. They were largely self-sufficient, with a simple barter economy. Markets held every five days in local centers and itinerant peddlers supplemented village handicrafts. As late as 1960, over 70 percent of the south Korean population lived in centers of less than 50,000 people.

Village affairs, including maintenance of social order and propriety, were traditionally governed by an informal council of elders from the constituent families; one of them might be recognized by the central government as village chief, but his authority (except in actions ordered by the state) was subject to the elders' consensus. The process did not originally involve elections or voting.

Industrialization and urbanization began to affect Korean community life in a significant way only in the twentieth century. The Japanese occupation, World War II, the division of Korea, and the Korean War all combined with the industrialization process to uproot traditional agrarian communities. Yet traditions persist to a considerable extent in the shrinking agricultural population and even in the urban consciousness. The continuing strength of family and community bonds was demonstrated by the capacity of refugees during and after the Korean War to move as groups to places of safety and to look out for one another's welfare.

Although attempts were made even during the Japanese period to reform village life, they were resisted as exploitation. In south Korea there was relatively little economic or social change until nearly a generation after liberation. The U.S. military authorities brought in the 4-H movement (an agricultural youth movement sponsored by the Department of Agriculture in the United States), but its impact was limited. However, one dramatic reform in this period, begun by the military government and pushed to completion by the new south Korean government even in wartime, was universal land reform. This program gave ownership of all agricultural land to the tillers, limiting holdings to three hectares (about 7.5 acres), with an average of less than one hectare (2.5 acres). Although criticized for causing some inefficiency of scale, this measure won the hearts of the farmers as nothing else ever had, and helped, at least in the earlier years of the republic, to maintain consistent rural support for the regime.

In 1971, the New Community Movement (*saemaul undong*) was launched on a nationwide basis to mobilize villagers in their own service. Thatched roofs gave place to sheet iron and then tile; irrigation was improved; feeder roads and community halls were built; wells were dug; cash crops were planted (some in new plastic hothouses); boundaries among tiny plots were rationalized; techniques were improved, including planting of "green revolution" rice varieties and mechanization. These projects were generally carried out with local labor and resources, the government providing some materials, such as cement, and small amounts of start-up money.[6]

Coupled with other government programs, such as electrification, road construction, grain price supports, subsidized fertilizer, and an agricultural extension program, the movement had dramatic impact. Rural family incomes were brought up to a par with urban incomes by the mid-1970s for the first time in Korean history, while all incomes shared in the rapid national growth. There has been some deterioration in the rural position since then, but income distribution in south Korea is still relatively even by developing-country standards.

Unlike their U.S. counterparts, Korean farmers live together in hamlets, surrounded by the fields to which they go daily to plant, till, and reap. Farming is a family enterprise; but the major tasks of transplanting and harvesting are shared by the community. Hamlets are made up of one to three dozen families each in its own home, perhaps with one or two small shops. Several hamlets may make up an administrative village unit. Virtually all villages are connected to main highways by all-weather feeder roads; the villages have electricity and radios, and many households have television. All children receive at least an elementary education. As a result of wartime dislocation and other factors, villages are often no longer dominated by a few families. Village heads are still named from the local population, but the central government enters into local affairs far more than under the Yi Dynasty. Most villages have their own New Community Movement councils and representatives, in addition to traditional mutual-assistance groups for various purposes, called *kye*. Thus, the traditional decision-making processes are changing, with less automatic authority going with status and seniority, and with less reliance on Confucian tradition. However, there have been no elective local government councils since 1961. Their re-establishment was being discussed in 1987.

In north Korea, after an initial distribution of farmland to individual families in the late 1940s, the traditional villages have been incorporated into collectives of township size, each with its Party committee and administration linking it to the county and thence to the central government. In theory, the farmers collectively own their enterprise, sharing the fruits on the basis of their labor input and supplementing their income with small private plots. Since individuals are frequently moved from one collective to another, community solidarity is probably much less than in pre-Communist days.

The center of gravity of Korean community life has shifted from the rural villages to towns and cities—more so in the south than in the north. According to the 1985 census, 65 percent of the south Korean population lives in cities of over 50,000—nearly 10 million, as already noted, in the capital city, and a total of almost that number in three other major cities. Thus the old village life, with its close-knit relationships, its festivals and ceremonies, its folk music, its barter economy and handicrafts—and its grinding poverty—are only a memory for urban Koreans, like the Westerners' illusion of Grandmother's house in the country, "over the river and through the woods." Nevertheless, ties with relatives in native villages persist. For those still living in rural areas, the same cohesive, kinship-centered life continues, and cooperation and barter remain important social features, along with TV viewing and some modern conveniences (virtually all villages have electricity, but nearly half do not have central water systems and fewer have sewer systems).

Traditional house styles vary in Korea by province and by socioeconomic status, but in many areas the floor plan of the average home has been an L-shape, with the kitchen forming the base, or a U-shape—in either case around a small central courtyard, the whole enclosed by a high wall. (Many new homes have recently been constructed in rectangular designs.) Walls were constructed of clay and straw; the roof, supported by poles and crosspieces, was of straw thatch, replaced every year or two. Windows were small and covered with a special strong paper. A narrow open porch along the front of the house connected the two or three living rooms, which also served for sleeping.

A unique feature of Korean house design was the heating system, called *ondol*: The hot gases from the kitchen fire passed through a serpentine channel, built with large flat stones, beneath the floors of the rooms, to a chimney at the end of the house. (Sometimes there was one wooden-floored living room without *ondol*, for summer use and entertaining.) The stones retained the heat after the fire died down, and the warm floors (the stones sealed with clay and covered with a special heavy oiled paper) provided efficient radiant heating.

In all but the smallest houses, it was traditional for men and women to sleep in separate rooms, young children with the women. Meals were eaten by the men on small individual tables brought to their rooms; women ate what was left over in the kitchen. Affluent houses had a special room (*sarangbang*) where men met and entertained; women were not supposed to be visible. The toilet was in an outhouse; if bathing was done at home (rather than at a bathhouse or in a local stream) a large tub was used, washing oneself from a bucket before entering. Such homes had little furniture, except for chests to store bedding and clothing. People lived on the floor, sleeping with a pad (*yo*) below and a quilt (*ibul*) above, eating and studying on low tables. There were no chairs, except in Western-style rooms that were added to homes of the rich in the nineteenth century. Pets and other animals were never allowed in the living rooms.

By the mid-1980s, rapid economic progress had forced many of the traits of industrialized social life on Seoul, and to a considerable extent on other large cities as well: fixed-hour employment, commuting long hours to and from work, the pressure for constant rapid movement and upward striving, heavy use of mass transport and motor vehicles, traffic jams, pollution, noise, mass advertising, and many hours of TV viewing.

For about a quarter of the population of Seoul and to a lesser but growing extent in other cities of south Korea, apartments (many of them in large high-rise buildings) have replaced single houses, although most people still prefer a freestanding home. There has been an acute urban housing shortage since the Korean War, because of war damage, urban in-migration, and the change in family living patterns. According to the 1985 census, the ratio of households to housing units rose from 1.49 in 1980 to 1.53 in 1985 (meaning that there were over three families for each two houses or apartments, although the multiple families might be related). Over the same five years, the number of households grew 20.2 percent, compared with a population growth of 8.1 percent—meaning that the old big families were breaking down into more and smaller families.[7]

The same trend seems to be true in north Korea as well, although statistics are lacking. The difference in housing between north and south is that in south Korea most housing is obtained through the free market by individual families for whatever price they can afford, but in north Korea housing is assigned and subsidized by the state, according to the political and other qualifications of the families.

Family life in south Korea still shows some of the traditional patterns, but social modernization, growing affluence, and scarcity of space in a densely populated country have brought much change. Some families have adopted Western furniture and life styles. For the majority who have not, the most significant change is in the position of women in the home. Women move as freely as men around and outside the home, and modern kitchens and streamlined menus have lessened their burden. Husband and wife of the younger generation usually sleep in the same room, as in the West.

The *ondol* heating system is still preferred, in apartments as in private homes. However, the old wood kitchen fires have been replaced with coal briquettes, or with oil or natural gas. In many homes, hot water circulating in pipes does the work of the traditional serpentine flues (there are many deaths each winter from leaks of flue gas from burning of coal briquettes). Linoleum is replacing oiled paper as floor covering. Windows are of glass, not paper; roofs are tiled. For most people, sitting and sleeping on the floor continues to be the norm, both by custom and for economy of space. Shoes are removed before entering a home, as both tradition and cleanliness demand. Apartments cannot preserve the traditional floor plan; the entrance court, for example, is reduced to a small entryway.

School and workplace have partially displaced the family as social centers in the cities; fast-food restaurants are multiplying, along with high-priced restaurants and bars for business contacts. Nevertheless, traditional family relations continue to be more important than in the West, even among the most urbanized (the extent to which this remains true in north Korea, with its emphasis on Party-oriented loyalty, is unknown). Moreover, in the south, the myriad traditional small enterprises—both along streets and alleys and within vast market areas—manage to hold their own against proliferating modern department stores. In both south and north, the state has promoted the organization of "block' groups of residents, somewhat equivalent in size to rural villages.[8] Heads of these groups are expected to maintain local order and provide information to the authorities on local conditions, including suspicious behavior of residents. (There is a tradition for this arrangement reaching back to Tang Dynasty China of the seventh century, where five-family groups were organized for the same purpose.)

The Individual and Interpersonal Relations

The Korean individual's view of himself and his place in society traditionally centered on his family, of which he considered himself a part. In the Confucian tradition, the dominance of men was unquestioned in form, although not infrequently the facts were otherwise. The henpecked husband is very much a part of Korean folklore. Male children were preferred because only they could carry on the family line.

It was the man's duty before his parents and his ancestors to assure continuity and prosperity of the family; his success was their success, his failure their failure, his shame their shame. Social responsibility beyond the family extended to the community, and in some measure to the person of the ruler and his officials, but not to society as a whole. Anyone outside the established circles and lines of relationship was viewed as a "non-person," to whom only the universal courtesy for strangers was due.

In today's Korea, although family ties remain a far more important component of attitudes and behavior than in most Western countries, the sense of family responsibility is diminishing as nuclear family living becomes common. In urban areas, moreover, there is not a strong sense of community responsibility; rather, there is the usual anonymity and isolation of industrialized city life. The hurrying people on the streets of Seoul appear to the foreign visitor to be rude in their pushing and shoving, as though others were inanimate objects; such behavior contrasts sharply with Korean decorum in more controlled situations. In a sense, this is the way Koreans still feel about people, such as casual passersby, with whom they have no established social relationship. The sense of universalized civic responsibility and civility is still weak.

In south Korea, at least, part of the role of family and community has been taken over by groupings based on common local origin, common school experience, and common workplace. People within such groups have a strong sense of shared identity and mutual responsibility. Business firms operate on the same autocratic and somewhat family-style lines found in Japan (and in an earlier era in the United States), although there is more movement among firms than in Japan. Many formal organizations bring together people of common origin and alumni of schools at all levels. These associations function to some extent as mutual-aid institutions, looking out for less fortunate members through the use of influence and connections. In north Korea, the main visible groupings—other than among the men of Kim Il Sung's age group who were purportedly associated with him in Manchurian guerrilla activity—are those based on Party, state, workplace, and place of residence.

The status of women in Korean society has greatly advanced since the Choson Dynasty and is still rapidly evolving in both south and north Korea. Christianity from its beginnings in Korea emphasized the equality of all persons under God (although early congregations still seated men and women separately). A U.S. missionary founded the first girls' school in Korea in 1886—the nucleus for the noted Ewha Woman's University. This influence, together with the example of modernized societies elsewhere, has had great effect. Women's access to education is virtually the same as for men. Women in considerable numbers pursue high-prestige occupations; there have been women cabinet members, women members of the legislature, and women presidents of universities. Many women leaders are interested in advancing the status of their sex.

Despite women's progress, male dominance continues. Male babies are still preferred; women workers largely fill low-paid factory and household jobs—often to earn a dowry for marriage—and women still do most of the household work. The family law is still based on male superiority in marriage, divorce, household administration, and inheritance. However, revision of the law is under discussion. An increasingly strong women's movement in south Korea is applying pressure for this and other reforms. A government-supported Women's Development Institute encourages further progress.[9] Two-worker families are becoming increasingly common in the cities. (Labor-short north Korea has gone further than the south in this respect. The north has also promoted a high birthrate.)

Children in Korea were traditionally reared by women until, by Confucian precept, boys and girls were separated at the age of seven years (in traditional East Asia, a child was counted one year old at birth). Their early environment was loving and permissive; when outside the house, children were strapped to their mothers' backs, and mothers nursed them for as much as two years, or even longer.[10] The father and male relatives were remote authority figures until the age when sexes were separated. For boys, the transition from a sheltered infancy to the stern discipline of subsequent youth was traumatic.

Much has been made of this tradition in trying to explain the high level of the average Korean's self-confidence, on the one hand, and his underlying rebelliousness, on the other. In any event, these child-rearing patterns are changing, particularly in the cities: Fathers are sharing in the raising of children, the sexes are no longer separated to the same extent, and all children get the same schooling. Observers differ on how much change in attitudes and values has occurred as a consequence of this and other modern trends; but all agree that in many respects Koreans do not think or react like Westerners.

In interpersonal relations, age and relative status still carry some of their traditional importance: The junior owes respect to the senior, and the senior carries the obligation to look out for the junior. It is still impolite to smoke or cross one's legs before a senior without permission. Koreans bow to superiors; they also shake hands with acquaintances. Calling cards are usually exchanged when introductions are made, partly to establish social relationship. It is still customary for people to call upon their parents, senior relatives, and office or factory superiors, at New Year's and at other occasions, such as a death in the family. It is usual in such calls to bring a present— a pleasant custom, but one that has sometimes deteriorated into bribery. Koreans are alert to one another's state of mind, and respect for others' personal dignity and social status ("face") has high priority in social intercourse. Outspokenness, therefore, is not ordinarily a Korean virtue.[11]

Attitudes and World View

Korean behavior is the result of three main factors: the traditional Confucian ethic; an underlying individualism that is somewhat at odds with that ethic; and an overlay of Western ideas.[12]

In the traditional Confucian order, harmony among men was the supreme goal. Lack of harmony might disrupt the order of nature; thus a linkage was perceived between social disorder and natural calamities, such as floods or earthquakes. It was the ruler's duty to maintain social order by his benevolence and superior wisdom and that of his ministers. It was the people's duty to obey the benevolent ruler's commands. Similar relationships applied to each family.

The standard for just rule was an ancient Golden Age, described in the Confucian classics; the emphasis was on understanding the wisdom of the ancient sages (although interpretations of that wisdom might differ). Violation of the rules of right conduct resulted in a sense of personal and family shame before one's superiors or fellows. It was shame before others, rather than a feeling of guilt from an inner conscience, that regulated behavior. In a relatively static agrarian society, this past-oriented and situation-oriented approach worked well; indeed, it sustained both China and Korea for over two thousand years.

Two basic characteristics of traditional Korean society followed from these attitudes. First, the whole of human activity was viewed as a seamless web of interpersonal relations; no distinction needed to be made between political, economic, social, religious, and artistic endeavors. All were within the ruler's responsibility to control. (Confucius gave low status to manufacture and commerce; the only respectable economic activity was farming, although commercial and industrial activity were evident in Korea, on a small scale at least, since the mid-seventeenth century.[13]) There was no such thing as free private enterprise, except to the extent that the ruler chose to permit it.

Second, there was no legitimate room for differing opinions concerning policy decisions between opposing groups, except for the narrow area of interpretation of the classics. The ruler gave his command, or discussion among ministers led to decisions by consensus, which then had total authority. (The same pattern prevailed in families and communities.) Contending factions existed, nonetheless, but they were not sanctioned by the culture, and usually all but one of them was excluded from power at any one time.

Human nature was also perceived as a continuous whole. The Western separation of body, mind, and spirit did not exist. Western observers have suggested that in East Asia, for this reason, the region of the navel was traditionally considered the center of the body rather than the head. A person's feelings, as well as mental processes, were an essential part of decision and action. Thus the Western priority for cold logic had no Korean counterpart. Moreover, contemplation—drawing upon one's whole being for guidance—rather than Western-style reasoning was a basis for decision and action. This difference is evident in comparing Korean martial arts with Western-style boxing or wrestling: Contemplation is even more important than physical action and takes more time. Contemporary Koreans have proven themselves in all lines of Western intellectual and scientific endeavor— they lack nothing in intellectual skills—but their thought processes are nonetheless still influenced by this tradition.

Within the tradition, the individual's attitude toward the self and the self's future was in terms of cultivation rather than improvement: that is, realizing one's innate capacities, rather than transcending them. The ideal to be achieved was true wisdom or sageness. Mastery of the classics, and self-discipline and right conduct, could bring full realization of one's inherent capabilities. For some, self-cultivation might include solitary contemplation and esoteric practices of various kinds, such as breathing exercises—akin to the ideas of Zen Buddhism, but not inherently religious. In seeking to fulfill oneself, of course, each person was conscious of responsibility to the family collective.

Although this Confucian world view is changing in Korea, it still strongly conditions Korean attitudes and behavior. However, now as in previous times, it coexists with a strong, aggressive underlying sense of individual asser- tiveness and ambition. Often, therefore, men's burning desire for wealth, power, and social recognition tears through the network of Confucian harmony and propriety. Koreans are gamblers for high stakes; they take extraordinary risks to further their ambitions. Success, wealth, and status are flaunted for all to admire. This tendency makes the distribution of wealth in south Korea seem more unequal than it really is.

In viewing the world outside them, the Koreans have seen themselves as "shrimps among whales." China was the principal whale until the latter nineteenth century, but generally a benevolent one. The Koreans accom- modated themselves to Chinese cultural and military superiority, accepting younger-brother status in China's world family. The collapse of China, source of so much of their culture and political institutions, had a traumatic effect, adding to Korea's own internal difficulties and external challenges.

Although the Koreans have not accepted the cultural superiority of any other nation in the way they did China's, the relationship of south Korea to the United States after liberation in 1945, or of north Korea to the Soviet Union, was a transference from China of the older-brother–younger-brother relationship. Koreans, both north and south, criticize themselves for their sadaejuui—obeisance to power, or over-respect for greatness. This view is, of course, reinforced by Western ideas of individual and national independence. These two attitudes—a perception of themselves as a small and weak nation, coupled with rising feelings of independence—confront Koreans with a basic dilemma. As the economic and military power of both Koreas grows, the dilemma becomes less painful; but to some extent it will continue to plague them, at least until reunification can be achieved. This mixture of dependence and independence still complicates the conduct of relations between south Korea and the United States. For example, Korean negotiators have played on their weaknesses in economic discussions concerning protected markets or the need for better Foreign Military Sales credit terms but then argued that U.S. policies do not reflect the new Korean status in the international community.

Today's south Koreans have discarded some of their traditional Confucian intellectual baggage because as a whole it has not shown itself capable of guiding the nation into the modern world. Nevertheless, many of the traditional attitudes continue to influence Korean individual and social behavior, even while alternate values and systems are being borrowed and adapted. In south Korea, there has been renewed recent attention to the positive elements of the Confucian tradition, along with growing nationalist sentiment. The survival of Confucian values makes Korean behavior sometimes incomprehensible and frustrating to Americans.

The continuing influence of Confucianism can be attributed not only to inertia—people don't like to change their basic values—but also to the inherent magnificence of the Confucian philosophical system and the deep roots it established in the Korean consciousness. The ideas of Confucius and of his various disciples in succeeding centuries—notably Mencius and Chu Shi—emerged in China and spread to all of East Asia, somewhat as the ideas of Plato, Aristotle, and Jesus spread to Europe. Partly because of this heritage, some scholars (including myself) believe that China had ideals, culture, refinement, and power far beyond any other part of the world until the nineteenth century. Future Korea is far more likely to arrive at a synthesis of Confucian and other ideas than to abandon its tradition.

Evolution of new values and ideas in south Korea, unlike north Korea, has been a relatively free process, notwithstanding authoritarian controls. Basic cultural values have been allowed to work themselves out in free interaction with all outside ideas except those of communism (although communism has been the excuse for suppression of a wider spectrum of "progressive" ideas). There have been official attempts to instill patriotism and virtue, particularly through the schools, the New Community Movement, and military training; but such programs lack the coerciveness and single-mindedness of north Korean ideological training. Criticism of south Korean official ideology has focused on governmental repression of subversive ideas through press and media controls and court action. The definition of subversive ideas has fluctuated in scope and at some times has been wide enough to include almost all criticism of government. In recent years, however, there has been a trend, despite periodic retrogressive moves, toward greater intellectual freedom.

In north Korea, Confucianism has been officially thrown on the scrapheap, along with all other isms except communism and Kim-Il-Sung-ism. Yet Confucian influence probably persists in north Korea also, under the surface. As noted above, the cultivation of a father-image for Kim Il Sung, the emphasis on the importance of family in north Korean statements, even the apparent transfer of political power from father to son, all point toward continuity with the past. Kim Il Sung and his associates, with initial guidance from the Soviet Union, have been deliberately engineering a cultural revolution in attitudes and values according to blueprints imposed from above. This approach, with its emphasis on the ruler's authority and its reference to the classics (communist, rather than Confucian) continues the Confucian tradition.

Since the mid-1960s, the official ideology is no longer pure Marxism-Leninism, but a new interpretation of communist thought called the *juche sasang* (self-reliance idea). Beginning in the 1960s, at a time when badly needed support from both China and the Soviet Union was diminishing, Kim Il Sung's writings began to emphasize the idea of self-reliance as a guiding social principle. This concept has been elaborated to include much of the basic doctrine that guides north Korean affairs and is represented as a higher form of Marxism-Leninism, shaped to reflect the needs of a developing nation. A basic aspect of *juche* is the idea that man is the master of all things and can accomplish all things, given the necessary will and training. "Bourgeois" ideas demeaning the dignity and power of the individual are condemned. Other basic ideas include love and obedience for the Leader; loyalty to the Party; the Three Revolutions (ideological, cultural, and technical) for the transformation of the nation; and devotion to practical service, as contrasted with bureaucratic dogmatism and quest for status.

Although, like other Communist states, north Korea has had to modify somewhat its opposition to private profit, the ideal remains unselfish service to society for its own sake, rather than capitalist money grubbing. Thus, some material incentives have been incorporated in industrial and agricultural operations, but heavy reliance continues to be placed on exhortation of Party, state, and workers on the basis of ideology and duty. Collectivism, "one for all and all for one," is a constant theme of north Korean leaders' exhortations to the people. This concept derives from the Confucian tradition as well as from communist theory. A quotation from Kim Jong Il's explanation of *juche* is included in a discussion of north Korean political culture, in Chapter 5.

Education and Students

The enormous importance attached to education in Korea is a principal reason for the nation's rapid development. This attitude, however, is only partly motivated by current realities; it springs from the Confucian tradition, in which entry into government service was by superior merit obtained through years of study of the Confucian classics, proven by examination. Governmental position and scholarship were intimately related; the social ideal was the scholar-official, and scholarship in effect served the state. At a time when government positions were the only way to rise in the world, education thus was the key to fame and fortune.

Education for the masses did not begin in Korea until the end of the nineteenth century. However, schools for the children of the aristocracy to learn the Confucian classics were established in the Koryo Dynasty (936–1392), and the Buddhist temples were also centers of learning. In the Choson Dynasty (1392–1910), with the official adoption of Confucian philosophy and the examination system, education became a major social activity. State schools were established in the capital and the provinces, highest of which was the *songgyun'gwan*, the Confucian university. Individual scholars and ex-officials out of favor organized academies of their own, called *sowon*, for the instruction of young people. By the nineteenth century, there were around 300 such academies. They were centers of factional political activity as well as education, and for this reason most of them were abolished a generation before Western influence generated interest in modern schools.

Western missionaries (especially U.S. Protestants), entering Korea in the 1880s, opened elementary and secondary schools and eventually three colleges. These institutions were open to anyone with the requisite ability. They continued to operate during most of the Japanese colonial period, although constrained by Japanese regulation. The Japanese authorities extended primary education through "common schools" throughout the country, which eventually enrolled about half the eligible age group. Secondary schools and the Keijo (Seoul) Imperial University were primarily for the children of Japanese expatriates, but admitted some Korean students. During their three-year administration of south Korea, the U.S. military authorities encouraged education and sought to introduce U.S. educational principles. However, the traditional and Japanese influence remained strong, with its emphasis on discipline, veneration for ruler and state, and rote learning. It is still strong today.

Education is still regarded by Koreans as the key to success. Until recently, law and government were the preferred college courses in south Korea, because they led to government position. Recent south Korean polls and career choices of college graduates in south Korea show that a significant change is taking place: Business and some of the professions are beginning to be preferred over a career in government.

South Korea: Elementary and Secondary Education

The south Korean educational system outwardly parallels those of the states in the United States, in providing six-year compulsory primary education, three years of middle school, and three of high school, followed by two to four or more years of college or technical school. One-fifth of the national budget, as well as some local government revenue, is devoted to education. There are both public and private schools on all levels; curricula are closely controlled by the Ministry of Education and its provincial counterparts. Private schools charge substantial tuition and are both profit and non-profit enterprises (some such schools have made substantial profits for their founders).

Overall educational policy is set forth in a 1968 Charter of National Education. The Ministry of Education exercises close control over both public and private schools, approves all textbooks, and prescribes many of them. Curriculum is essentially uniform throughout the country. Appointive educational committees of local citizens exist at provincial and local level; their functions were purely advisory in 1987, but there was discussion about broadening their role. Schools have parent-teacher associations for support. Private schools have legally incorporated foundations but generally have to meet their expenses from students' tuition and fees.

The first six years of school are free and compulsory. Although even state-operated middle schools charge a fee, over 90 percent of children in the eligible ages attend, and 90 percent of those go on to high school.[14] The school year, which begins in March, must have at least 220 school days, or 34 weeks (32 weeks for education above secondary level); school hours range from 782 per year for first grade to 1,088 in sixth grade and 1,224 for ninth grade (high school requirements are in units of 50 minutes' duration, and range from 204 to 216. Some schools operate on two shifts because of classroom shortages). Teachers must teach 25 hours a week and often do more.[15]

A typical high-school student's school day in Seoul starts at 7:30. He or she studies until 8:50, then attends classes until 5:00, with one hour for lunch. After 5:00, specially designated students have another four to five hours of study. Incoming third-year students get only two weeks of summer vacation, because they must take extra courses to prepare for the college entrance examination. Classes are also held on Saturday, although the day is somewhat shorter.

Any given subject of study in Korean schools is spread out over a longer time than in the United States, so that students study more subjects in a single term. Homework requirements are stringent. Students apply themselves diligently because of the emphasis placed on examinations as a measure of academic achievement—especially the crucially important government-administered examinations for admission to college. Instruction emphasizes factual learning, lectures, and memorization. Relatively large classes—averaging over 30 pupils at elementary (and often more), up to 65 at middle- and high-school level—require firm discipline, which is made easier by Korean attitudes toward authority, by respect for education, and by supportive family influence.

Elementary-school instruction, according to the Ministry of Education, has seven purposes: to teach the Korean language; to nurture morality, civic spirit, and social responsibility; to observe and analyze natural phenomena; to handle quantitative relationships necessary in life; to "nurture a spirit of industry, perseverance, and self-help"; to appreciate art; and to learn and practice hygiene and sanitation. The regular curriculum includes moral education (including anti-communism), Korean language, social studies, arithmetic, science, physical education, music, fine arts, and crafts. Extracurricular activities begin at third grade.

Middle-school objectives are a continuation of elementary education; occupational opportunities, development of a sense of justice, and physical and emotional development are included. The regular curriculum includes twelve courses: moral education, Korean language, Korean history, social studies, mathematics, sciences, physical education, music, fine arts, classical Chinese (from which the characters used with Korean phonetic script are derived), foreign languages, vocational skills and home economics. Students must pay tuition, but fees in public schools are moderate, and some poor families receive an education subsidy; thus, nearly all children get a middle-school education.

High schools are classified into general, vocational, and other (art, physical education, science) types. Their objective, continuing from middle school, is to

> impart the necessary qualifications and capabilities [of] a solid citizenry; to foster understanding and a sense of judgment regarding the Korean country and society; and to provide education in general education and specialized subjects in order to instill a correct understanding of the mission of the Korean nation, to upgrade physical standards, and to enable students to properly choose their future course and direction in life.[16]

The regular curriculum consists of thirteen general subjects and several specialized subjects, both divided between required and elective courses. General subjects are the same as for middle school, with the addition of military training. Specialized subjects include agriculture, engineering, commerce, fishery and marine industry, home economics, and other related subjects. Students pay tuition, except for those in agricultural schools; nevertheless, 88 percent of middle school graduates go on to high school. To equalize access to top-class schools, students in some areas have been assigned by lot on the basis of scores in an examination given to all middle-school students (high scorers being thus distributed over a number of schools).

South Korea: Higher Education

College and university education has been a major focus of social and political attention in south Korea since 1945 and remains so today. In 1985, there were 1,209,647 students at 456 institutions of higher education, representing roughly a quarter of high-school graduates (932,000 at 100 colleges and universities; the remainder at 201 graduate schools, 120 junior colleges, and various specialized schools). In 1984, 27 percent of students were enrolled in social science, 21.3 percent in engineering, 12.5 percent in linguistics and literature, 11.1 percent in education, 9.4 percent in natural sciences, and the remainder in arts, medical science, agriculture, and humanities.[17]

Admission to the four-year undergraduate course, in 1987, was based on scores in a state-administered examination, plus essay tests given by individual colleges, and high-school grade point averages. Entrance was fiercely competitive, since ceilings on student numbers were set by the government (even though freshman admissions were greatly increased in 1981 to reduce this pressure). Competition was especially keen to enter the "top five" in Seoul—the state-operated Seoul National University and privately-operated Yonsei, Korea, Ewha Woman's, and Sogang universities.

Completion of 140 credits (16 semester hours per credit) was required for the bachelor's degree in any of 25 fields; but by controversial government order, the bottom 30 percent of each class was not allowed to graduate. (This requirement was somewhat tempered in practice by exceptions and re-enrollment opportunities.) Both public and private institutions were closely controlled by the Ministry of Education. Over 90 percent of the hundred south Korean colleges and universities were privately operated, with virtually no government support; hence tuition was high at private institutions. It was no longer free at government schools, but was still relatively low.

North Korean Education

In north Korea, scholarship still serves the state, in ways reminiscent of the Confucian tradition, although Confucianism as such is proscribed. Academic institutions, from kindergartens to Kim Il Sung University, are part of the state and Party hierarchy. Major essays on many subjects are written by, or in the name of, President Kim Il Sung—and, in recent years, his son and successor, Kim Jong Il. These writings enjoy great authority, reading of them is enjoined upon the people, and they form a part of educational curricula. Although critical thought is not forbidden, it must be in conformity with the broad principles that govern the state and Party and must serve state and Party purposes.

North Korean education is administered by the state at national, provincial, and local levels, under the general supervision of parallel Party organizations. It is free, compulsory, and universal through middle school. There are also Party schools, and there are training institutes within large factories and some government ministries. Few facts are available on curriculum or on educational administration. Presumably, however, emphasis is placed on science and technology, as well as on the basic ideology of the Party and state, including the national history (undoubtedly giving major attention to anti-Japanese and anti-American themes). Judging from the large amount of visible organized athletic activity by school children, there must be emphasis on physical education. There are no precise recent figures on school enrollment, but in 1976, total school-age population was reported as 4,153,000, of which 98.5 percent were said to be in school.[18]

College Students: Life, Attitudes, Activities

The great majority of south Korean college students behave like their counterparts in other countries. They spend from 15 to 21 hours a week in 50-minute classes during the school term. Attendance now averages 80 to 90 percent, even during the periods of active political demonstrations; this is in contrast to earlier years, when class attendance was low.

Some clues to student life outside the classroom can be drawn from surveys of students made at Korea University in 1983 and 1985.[19] Nearly half the students said they spent their free time at school with fellow course members and classmates; a third spent it alone, mostly for study. Only 2 percent spent it with members of the opposite sex. A little more than a quarter of the students said they spent their after-school time with friends and classmates; nearly the same number studied in the library; about one in eight went home, and about the same number went to "circle" (equivalent to club or society) gatherings or activities on campus.

Among student worries, military service was highest for juniors and second-highest for sophomores. Problems of values and ideals were foremost worries among sophomores and freshmen. Almost half the students said they preferred to discuss their problems with friends, about a quarter with classmates, one-eighth with parents, a few with older brothers.

Students reported spending an average of 40 to 50 thousand won per month ($44 to $55, at 1986 exchange rates) for daily living. A fifth of this amount went for books; about a sixth each for travel, food, drink, and cigarettes; about a quarter for hobbies and amusements (including dates). A third of the students said they drank *soju* (a strong native ale) because it was cheap; a quarter drank *makkoli* (a weaker, cruder drink brewed from rice, traditional in the countryside) for fellowship; and about one in five drank beer "for its taste." About one in nine said they didn't drink.

Respondents reported they spent an average of 5 to 6 hours per week outside school in reading books (21 percent of the books were novels), and 50 minutes per day reading newspapers (6 percent said they didn't read newspapers). They watched television 1.4 hours a day (mostly news and sports), listened to radio nearly 2 hours. Seventy-one percent of students believed that not enough was being done to assure freedom of communication; 22 percent believed that nothing was being done. Three out of eight students believed that current events involving students were being unfairly reported, and another half believed the reporting was very unfair. They had similarly negative views on mass media in general, and nearly half felt that south Koreans were greatly intimidated in their freedom of speech.

These reactions are symptomatic of the critical view held by the majority of students. Although only a small proportion (most observers suggest around 5 percent) of south Korean college students are actively involved in planning and carrying out political demonstrations, students generally are much more conscious of their status as the nation's future leaders than are their U.S. counterparts. They consider themselves to be at the leading edge of political and social criticism and reform. In a time of rapid and painful social change, there is no lack of problems for them to criticize, and they do so with youthful idealism and rigid black-and-white moral standards. Moreover, students enjoy relatively high social status, deriving from the tradition of the Choson Dynasty (when scholarship and government were closely related). Students were a major factor in the 1919 independence movement against Japan, and led the uprising in 1960 that ended the Rhee regime. Since that time, they have been a significant factor in south Korean politics.

In addition to a traditional sense of political responsibility and a critical view of the Korean political scene, other factors have fostered student political activism. Universities operated until the mid-1960s on the European system: Class attendance was not required so long as students could pass the examinations. After years of intense concentration in secondary school to pass the college entrance examinations, students tended to treat much of their college as a sort of vacation between test periods. The didactic and authoritarian attitudes of some professors, whose offerings were often anachronistic and unstimulating, did little to promote attendance. Thus there was ample time to meditate on the evils of society and to listen to dissident intellectuals.

Moreover, in 1960, unemployment was high among college graduates. Demand caught up with supply in the 1970s; but then, as already noted, college enrollment nearly doubled in the early 1980s in response to popular pressure for improved access to higher education. Thus, intellectual employment again became a problem. Only slightly over half the university graduates of 1985 had found jobs by the end of the year (although some others continued into graduate school).[20] In recent years, students with no personal memory of the Korean War are less willing to interrupt their careers for compulsory military service. The week-long active service required of college sophomores has been a major recent target of protest.

The student problem has been magnified by the illegitimacy, in the students' eyes, of the south Korean governments since 1961, dominated by the military after seizures of power. In 1964 and 1965, masses of students took to the streets to protest the normalization treaty with Japan. Organized protest on most major Seoul university campuses has become a part of south Korean life, particularly in the spring, when the college year begins. Student protest in May, 1980, was partly responsible for the declaration of martial law and for the uprising in Kwangju that year. Kwangju has been a major theme of student criticism ever since. Together with other social and political themes, it motivated the massive demonstrations in the spring of 1987 that led to the major political policy changes of June and July (discussed in Chapter 4).

Extreme student activism of the shouting, rock-hurling variety became a way of life to a certain hard-core few, with encouragement from graduates or dropouts of like mind. Many demonstrations seemed to be charades in which both activists and police played out their parts: The students, usually fifty to two or three hundred, organized a march on the campus in quasi-military style, generally in mid-afternoon, carrying banners and shouting slogans; they proceeded to the main gate, attempting to exit; the police, in helmets, shields, and gas masks, barred the way; the students threw a barrage of rocks collected ahead of time for the purpose; the police eventually fired tear gas, and occasionally a choking gas; in an hour or two, all was over. Usually there were no serious casualties, but severe injury and occasional death occurred, particularly among the young riot police—draftees who volunteered in place of army service; they were under orders to avoid injury to students. Another form of demonstration involved the occupation of buildings on college campuses or in cities, and sometimes throwing of firebombs (all four U.S. cultural centers, for example, have been occupied in recent years, and one—in Pusan—was firebombed).[21]

The non-participating majority of students have mostly gone about their regular business during such demonstrations; a few watched them from a distance. Nevertheless, there is a body of fairly widespread student sentiment that focuses on substandard wages and working conditions, maldistribution of wealth, the authoritarian nature of the present government and its perceived military domination and lack of legitimacy, and, to some extent, the capitalist system generally. There is growing criticism of the United States, for its alleged imposition of political and economic dependency, paralleling the neo-Marxist ideas of Herbert Marcuse and Latin American dependency theory. It was these factors that motivated the massive demonstrations in the spring of 1987.

The Reaction: Control and Reform

The south Korean government has responded to the college student problem in a variety of ways, both academic and political. Academically, the government has moved to upgrade college standards by imposing government-administered examinations in addition to the schools' own entrance procedures; by promoting the growth of scientific and technical institutions on both college and high-school level, including schools of business administration, to ensure that the supply of college graduates better meets the changing social demand; by ending the lifetime tenure system of professors (a move attacked as a device for getting rid of politically unpalatable teachers, which was also a result); by requiring student attendance at classes as a condition for evaluation; and, most recently, by a requirement that colleges graduate only 70 percent of each admitted class (with growing exceptions for certain categories of students).

The pay of professors has been brought somewhat closer to parity with their high social status to promote excellence, and tuitions have increased as a result (although the most prestigious institution, Seoul National University, is state operated and charges low tuition). Public universities were established in all provinces to make education more accessible and to decrease the student concentration in Seoul.

The educational reform measures, although criticized as political control of education, have materially improved the quality of college education—at some considerable cost to freedom of social and political inquiry. Except in this respect, the curriculum and offerings of south Korean colleges and universities are similar to those in the United States; and the high proportion of faculty educated abroad ensures a continuing flow of ideas and information from the outside world. (In 1985, there were also 801 foreigners on south Korean university faculties, the majority of them from the United States.[22])

Successive south Korean governments have also applied political means to control student activism. Demonstrations outside college campuses, and sometimes inside them, have been suppressed by force—usually without major injury, clubs and tear gas being the principal weapons, as above noted. Student governments and campus organizations were disbanded, to be replaced by paramilitary organizations controlled by the Home Ministry through the college administrators. College presidents and administrators were required to suppress student activism—through suspension, expulsion, and otherwise—and were discharged if they failed to do so. Student activists themselves—mostly those involved in violence—were apprehended and given severe exemplary prison sentences; expelled students were, by prevailing practice, immediately subject to military draft.

Beginning in early 1984, government control of colleges was somewhat relaxed. The academic authorities regained a larger role in their own affairs. Student organizations were again permitted, the paramilitary organizations disbanded, and police withdrawn from campuses. Subsequently, however, government control has been reasserted in periods of severe student unrest. Police have again entered campuses to put down disturbances, and a number of students have been charged and sentenced for violating laws on national security, demonstrations, and the like. The level of violence has escalated; university buildings have been burned, several students have burned themselves to death, and the death under torture of a Seoul National University student in early 1987 became a major national political issue. Student activists are still a small minority of college students, but their visibility is increasing.

Art and Literature

Korean aesthetic expression has a tradition of thousands of years, as evidenced by paleolithic and neolithic remains. Most surviving evidence of artistic activity, however, dates from and after the Three Kingdoms period (roughly, fourth to seventh centuries A.D.). Tombs of royalty and nobility in each of the three kingdoms have been excavated to disclose remarkable wall paintings, ceremonial vessels of both metal and clay, tableware, gold crowns, weapons (many of them apparently ceremonial rather than for actual combat), costumes, and ornaments. The conception and workmanship of these objects is impressive.

Buddhism came to Korea in the fourth century A.D., bringing with it the rich inspiration of Indian and Chinese art forms depicting the Buddha and the many scenes and personages from Buddhist scripture. The Koreans adapted these forms to their own tastes—they preferred carving in stone, for example, to wood. Few examples of Buddhist graphic art survive from the Three Kingdoms period, but there are a number of extant sculptures and monuments, and the remains of temple foundations.

The oldest known Korean written work is a stone monument commemorating the victories of King Kwanggaet'o of Koguryo (A.D. 391–413), erected at his tomb north of the present Korean border in Manchuria. The inscription is in Chinese characters; the Koreans, as already noted, did not develop their own writing system until the fifteenth century, although earlier use was made of a phonetic adaptation of Chinese.

The earlier part of the United Silla period (668–936) saw a flowering of art forms. Buddhism was now in the ascendancy; great temples were built, although only the foundations survive (the great temple of Pulguksa, at the Silla capital, was burned by the Japanese in 1592). Perhaps the most impressive survival from this period is the heroic granite statue of the Buddha in an artificial stone grotto atop a hill near Pulguksa (Fig. 3.2); the statue is surrounded by a series of splendid stone reliefs depicting Buddhist scriptural figures. Some temples and palaces had immense bronze bells; among those surviving today the most notable is the so-called Emille Bell, now kept at the state museum in Kyongju.

The Silla kings were buried in huge and relatively theft-proof mounds in the vicinity of Kyongju; a few of them have been excavated, yielding a rich collection of gold, silver, bronze, and ceramic artifacts that show the grandeur of the period—rich and delicate, yet with an exuberant touch. Poetry, calligraphy, painting, and writing flourished. Only stone inscriptions and

FIGURE 3.2 Statue of the Buddha at the Kyongju stone grotto in Sokkuram (photo courtesy of Korean Information Office, Washington, D.C.)

secondary references remain today, but sung poems of the period, called *hyangga*, have survived in the oral tradition.[23]

The Koryo period (936–1392) is best remembered for its lovely celadon pottery—graceful in shape, with a blue-green glaze that has never been copied with total success. Another famous Koryo achievement is the carving of wood printing blocks for the entire Buddhist scripture. These were destroyed during the Mongol invasion, but were redone in 1251; all 81,258 of them are preserved at the Buddhist temple of Haeinsa.[24] Since Buddhism was the dominant religion, many temples were built, but only a few of them have survived the ravages of time and foreign invasion. (The oldest surviving wooden buildings in Korea are two at the Buddhist temple Pusoksa, dating from about 1350; a wooden image of the Buddha in the temple's main hall also survives.) Metal and stone images and stupas remain. The art of painting flourished and—like pottery—was influenced by Chinese Song Dynasty techniques; but few examples of the graphic arts from this period survive.

The earliest extant Korean literature dates from the Koryo period. Most notable is Kim Pu-sik's *Samguk Sagi* (Historical Account of the Three Kingdoms). This work, written in 1145 (in Chinese like all Koryo literature) is the earliest indigenous source of Korean history still in existence, although it quotes earlier documents. Two other histories also survive, adding insights on ancient folkways and traditions. New forms of poetry made their appearance, among both aristocrats and common people. Wood-block printing, of which the greatest example was the Buddhist scripture already mentioned, was also used for other works; and by 1234, a generation before Gutenberg in Germany, Korea had independently developed movable metal type. Korea's first medical treatise was published in 1236.

The Choson Dynasty (1392–1910) saw an early flowering of artistic and literary work. The creation of the Korean phonetic alphabet (*han'gul*) in 1446 has already been mentioned. Movable type was improved, making possible wide distribution of works on history, geography, medicine, and agricultural technique. Most books, however, continued to be written in Chinese because of the preference of the intellectuals, and *han'gul* was used chiefly in works by or for women or the common people—except for military treatises to be kept secret from foreigners. Most of the prose writing was on serious subjects until the latter part of the period, but there was some anecdotal material and poetry.

By the sixteenth century, two poetic forms had evolved, distinct from the Chinese-style poems of the late Koryo and early Choson literati: the *kasa*, a brief form of prose-poetry usually focused on the beauties of nature; and the more philosophical *sijo*, written in the Korean language (although often including Chinese characters), which became a major form of literary expression. (The origin of the *sijo* can be traced to the late Koryo period, but it came to full flower at this time.)

The *sirhak* reformist philosophical movement of the sixteenth to eighteenth centuries gave rise to new literary forms, including fiction. Authors of non-*yangban* status grew in number (many of them illegitimate sons of the aristocracy or of the intermediate *chungin* class). Some of these indirectly attacked the parasitic status and life-style of the *yangban*. Other materials

transcribed oral folklore. Much of the work from this time appeared in
han'gul[25] to appeal to the general public. Some of the fiction dealt with
historical or moral themes, but romantic love was uppermost in those most
widely read. *Sijo* poetry, also, came to be written by non-*yangban,* who—
like the professional painters—often did not sign their works.

The disestablishment and official discouragement of Buddhism led to its
decline as a cultural force, although its impoverished temples and monasteries
continued. Thus Confucianism governed social life, particularly among the
upper classes; Buddhist themes diminished in the art forms of the time,
and although the monks continued to produce works centered on these
themes, the quality diminished.

Graphic art became clearly divided between amateur "literati paintings"
of the aristocratic scholars, often exceedingly well done, and the paintings
of professionals, which were beneath the dignity of the *yangban.* Many were
done on commission by government artisans—both landscapes and portraits
of the status-conscious aristocrats. Calligraphy, in contrast,was a province
of the scholars. Korea's famed eighteenth-century calligrapher and painter,
Chusa (Kim Chong-hui), was hailed in China as well as at home for his
distinctive style. From the seventeenth century on, landscape painting became
more realistic and centered more on Korean scenery in preference to the
traditional Chinese scenes. Paintings of daily life—of workmen, peasants,
or partying *yangban*—also flourished.

Chinese models continued to exert their influence, but distinctive touches
in painting—a certain freedom and vitality—distinguish most Korean painting
from contemporary Chinese or Japanese work in the eyes of experts. Evelyn
McCune wrote:

A growing appreciation of Korean art has accorded it recognition for certain
qualities which have set it apart in the museums of the world. . . . Korean
artists were obliged, more often by their poverty than by their neighbors, to
rely upon beauty of line and shape rather than upon costly materials. The
resulting works of art were marked by elegance and refinement during periods
of political stability, but during periods of war they were rustic and careless.
In both extremes of refinement and rusticity, however, were to be found
strength and an attractive honesty that were much admired in China and
Japan—in particular by the Japanese, who imitated them.

She went on to say that Korean art reflected attachment to the land and
tradition, love of nature, adaptation of foreign influence, respect for learning,
and a "cult of weakness" deriving from Korea's vulnerable location.[26]

Dr. Kim Won-yong in a recent article on ancient Korean art said, "Anyone
who has some knowledge of Asian art can easily discern Korean art from
Japanese or Chinese art. But it is not easy to explain the difference. . . ."

He quoted Professor Seckel, who suggested two basic elements of "Koreanness": "(1) The decomposition of form-complexes into small elements like a mosaic work; (2) Flat in volume and graphically linear in surface design." The underlying characteristics are "vitality, spontaneity and unconcern for technical perfection (nonchalance)."[27]

Choson Dynasty Confucian literati tastes turned away from the celadons of the Koryo period—first to a cruder, but freer, brownish or grayish punch'ong ware (which is popular with Japanese today), then to white and blue-and-white true porcelains. Although these latter were similar in some ways to the porcelains of the Ming Dynasty in China, they were simpler and freer in expression.

A simple, uninhibited folk art emerged during this period in both graphic and performing fields. Paintings of tigers and other creatures, some of them illustrating shamanistic themes or ideas from Chinese folk Taoism, were popular among the people. The artists rarely signed their work, so they remain unknown. Until very recent times, these works were ignored by the ruling classes; their development may have been encouraged by the growth of a small commercial and manufacturing class from the mid-seventeenth century on. Their merit is now recognized, partly through the pioneering efforts of the privately sponsored Emillle folk-art museum of Zo Za-yong.

Traditional folk music (nongak) of the countryside, played by amateur farmer musician-dancers, has a spontaneity and gaiety lacking in the formal Confucian court music (a-ak); the folk music, too, has lately become recognized. A form of folk story with song, called p'ansori, emerged among the people; responding to the oppression of the ruling yangban; its often humorous repertoire ridicules the life of the aristocracy and priesthood and extols the traditional Confucian virtues. P'ansori also absorbed some of the shaman practitioners' ritual themes and techniques.

Western artistic and literary influence had no more than started to affect Korea when the Japanese established their rule. The colonial era inhibited Korean national self-expression, but nationalistic themes nonetheless appeared in novels and poetry, many of these works quite Western in form. Use of han'gul by the foreign missionaries in widely circulated Bible translations and religious tracts helped to overcome the traditional bias against it. A society for the study of the Korean language became a focus of nationalist sentiment under the Japanese, who eventually suppressed the group—and from 1938 on, endeavored to suppress the language. Before this happened, however, the society had developed a revised system of spelling that reflected the structure as well as the sound of the language. After substantial controversy in the early post-Japanese years, the new system became standard for both north and south Korea. (For a discussion of the Korean language, see Appendix B).

South Korea since 1945 has demonstrated enormous talent for Western art forms, particularly music. Both classical and modern Western music are extensively played and enjoyed; there are two national and several civic symphony orchestras, some of which have been acclaimed on international tours. Music appreciation is stressed in the schools. A recent survey showed that nine out of ten professors of music had studied abroad for two to seven years—40 percent of them in the United States. Korean instrumentalists have played with distinction in European and U.S. orchestras.

In the graphic arts, traditional styles continue in vogue, executed in black and colored ink on paper or silk, sometimes including modern themes. All Western schools of graphic art are represented among contemporary Korean artists, whose use of oil, acrylic, and water-color techniques is fully up to international standards. Some artists' works command exceedingly high prices. Modern Korean art has been said to display "dynamic tension" and "serial repetition" in both realist and abstract modes.[28]

Both fiction and non-fiction books and magazines abound, as do bookstores. A recent survey of the Economic Planning Board showed that 62 percent of the south Korean population read newspapers and 37 percent regularly read magazines. At the end of 1985, there were 2 news agencies, 30 daily newspapers, 158 weekly publications, and a total of 1,909 periodicals, of which 478 were sold by subscription or on newsstands; periodical readers numbered 35 million.[29] In 1985, 2,631 publishing houses printed 114 million volumes and published 33,743 new titles. Books include numerous translations from foreign languages (some of them without the permission of authors or publishers, although control over such pirating is increasing). Western plays are produced in Korea in both Korean and original languages. There is a thriving Korean movie and television industry, which has won international prizes. In addition, U.S. and other foreign movies are popular, both in theaters and on television.

As in most developing countries, south Korean news and literary media have been subject to government controls since the modern press began in the 1880s. At times, censorship has been quite severe, extending even to the blacking or scissoring out of objectionable sections of foreign publications. Controls have been somewhat relaxed in the past few years, particularly for scholarly and foreign-language publications. However, the government issues guidelines to govern press self-censorship, and in 1986 the security authorities began a crackdown on publications considered leftist or subversive of "liberal democracy." Since mid-1987, press and publishing controls have been greatly relaxed.

In north Korea, contemporary literature and other art forms reflect the same general quality of "socialist realism" as in the Soviet Union. All forms of art are expected to promote the goals of state and Party. Western influence is apparent, but it is more controlled—for example, modern popular

Western musical forms are apparently not tolerated, nor abstract graphic art. Architecture is heavy and grandiose. Nevertheless, north Korea has produced spectacular artistic performances, some of which have gone on foreign tour. There seems to be an active publishing industry. Many north Korean motion pictures are technically of high quality, although their themes are usually somewhat labored and circumscribed. Observers who compared north and south Korean performances during the exchange of September 1985 thought the south was in the lead in terms of artistic quality.

Religion

Four main streams of religious and philosophical experience have shaped Korean culture: the indigenous shamanism, with its roots in east-central Asia; Buddhism, which entered Korea in the fourth century A.D. and was firmly established by the eighth century; Confucianism, probably brought first to Korea through the Chinese colony of Lolang until the fourth century A.D., and thereafter through diplomatic and trade exchanges with China; and Christianity, which first entered Korea from China in the eighteenth century and was promoted by foreign missionaries from the late nineteenth century on until it became self-propagating, fifty years or so later. Chinese Taoism has had influence in Korea, mostly as a leitmotif in shamanism and the other main philosophies (except Christianity). There is also a native Korean church called ch'ondogyo, which inspired the tonghak revolt of 1894 and still endures, although it is diminishing.

It is important to recognize, in discussing these various religious and philosophical currents, that Koreans and other East Asians are not exclusive in their religious beliefs. Christians are a partial exception; but in general, the various religions are seen to complement rather than contradict one another. Moreover—with the exception of Christianity, and ch'ondogyo as well—the Asian religions are not congregational, but a matter of personal communion with the eternal. Temples, images, scriptures, clerics are means of attaining this communion at the option of the believer. Affiliation with a religion is a matter of attitude and faith, more than formal indoctrination and membership, unless one enters the priesthood.

In north Korea, as in most other Communist states, religion has been proscribed as "the opiate of the people." The proscription specifically includes Confucianism. Vestiges survive: After years of neglect, some historic Buddhist temples are being restored at state expense, and a Christian group is occasionally recognized. How much unacknowledged belief may continue is unknown; but it must struggle against the officially promoted Marxist-Leninist and juche philosophies, which in north Korea are supposed to respond to all people's spiritual as well as physical and social problems.

Shamanism

In south Korea, shamanism—earliest among Korean religions—continues to have a large number of believers, often in combination with other beliefs. Shamanism recognizes a myriad of spirits who can work for good or ill. They must be propitiated to avoid evil, cast out if need be, and solicited to ensure success and fortune. Families, houses, natural objects all have spirits. Many ancient customs have to do with winning the spirits' favor or averting their wrath. In Korea (unlike Japanese Shinto, which in some other ways is similar), there are few large shamanistic shrines or groups of practitioners. However, Buddhist temples typically have a small building dedicated to the "mountain god," implicitly a shaman deity, and some villages and families have modest shrines.

The adepts of shamanism are mostly women, known as *mudang*, who inherit their profession or otherwise demonstrate special communion with the spirits; they are retained by individuals or families in time of special fortune or special trouble. Often they perform a lengthy ceremony called *kut*, including costumes, song, and dance, to communicate with the spirits and sometimes to be possessed by them.

Buddhism

Buddhism claims the largest number of Korean believers among the five main religious groups (7.5 million, or 18.9 percent of south Korea's population, according to south Korean government figures). It is divided among eighteen sects, principally according to the priority given to meditation and inspiration, and to the priority given to various portions of the enormous volume of Buddhist scripture. More mundane issues in recent years have been the organization of the clergy, control of temples and temple property, and the question of whether priests should be married.

Korean Buddhism, like that of Japan and China, is mainly of the Mahayana school, emphasizing attainment of eternity through faith. The original Gautama Buddha, a historical north Indian figure of the sixth century B.C., taught that the pain of life is due to earthly desire, and that the attainment of Nirvana, or deliverance from life's bondage, is to be sought through the elimination of desire, through many reincarnations, followed by enlightenment. The three great foundations of the Buddhist faith are the Buddha himself, the body of scripture, and the clergy, whose conduct is guided by an Eightfold Path of right living and right thinking. Ordinary people are expected to live and improve themselves according to standards of righteous life, but cannot expect to attain Nirvana within their lifetimes. Salvation is an individual matter, and the emphasis is on withdrawal more than on social action. This does not mean, however, that Buddhism is not socially conscious; love and charity toward all sentient beings are a dominant part of it.

Over the years, Mahayana Buddhism has evolved a pantheon of luminaries. The Buddha himself is believed by some to exist in many forms and persons. Some sages, having attained enlightenment, restrain themselves from entering Nirvana in order to help enlighten others; these are called Bodhisattvas. Disciples and priests of eminent virtue are recognized. Temples contain images of the Buddha, Bodhisattvas, and sometimes many of the disciples. They also contain murals illustrating scenes from the Buddha's life and other scriptural messages, for the benefit of the faithful who go for prayer, meditation, and guidance.

Confucianism

Confucianism is a philosophy, rather than a religion. Confucius did not deny metaphysics, but rather took it for granted, on the basis that it was people's main business to run their own world in a way that would please Heaven. If human affairs were properly ordered, this would enhance the universal harmony; if they were not, nature might be disturbed, and the ruler might lose the Mandate of Heaven.

Although Confucius was the first and greatest thinker of the philosophy that bears his name, his ideas were shaped and modified by others after him, particularly Mencius, a century or so later, and Chu Xi around A.D. 1100. Chu Xi enhanced the metaphysical content of Confucianism and shaped it in such a way that it became a potent instrument of rule in both China and Korea. As interpreted over the centuries, Confucianism holds that man is basically good, but malleable; that human affairs should be ordered by those who earn authority through superior wisdom and benevolence, attained through study of the classics and of the ancient Golden Age they describe as a model. In addition to teaching principles of right social action—including a version of Jesus' Golden Rule, expressed negatively—Confucianism emphasizes the importance of doing things in the right way. Thus ceremony becomes important, as well as substance. Family plays a central role in social life, and its extent over space and time is emphasized.

It is clear from these brief descriptions that Confucianism and Buddhism complement each other. Buddhism fills the spiritual void of Confucianism; Confucianism puts its emphasis on interpersonal relations, rather than relations with the eternal. The Western advent, however, challenged the structure of both beliefs because they took for granted an essentially static world of suffering, ruled by specially qualified authority entitled to unquestioning respect and obedience from the common people. In the rapidly changing Western world, however, old relationships did not work, and new horizons of earthly progress and of equality among men were opened.

Christianity

For many Koreans, Christianity seems to have filled the void created by intellectual stagnation and peasant impoverishment, and by the impact of social change. It took hold among a few reform-minded aristocrats in the late eighteenth century and quickly spread, until it was suppressed by the royal authorities. The Pope's visit to Korea in 1985 celebrated the bicentennial of Catholicism. During his visit, 103 Korean and French martyrs—sacrifices to nineteenth-century pogroms against outsiders and foreign ideas—were canonized.

The treaties of the 1880s brought Western representatives to Korea. Horace Allen, a physician-missionary attached to the U.S. legation, opened the way for missionaries when he saved the life of Prince Min after an attempted coup d'état in 1884. U.S. and European missionaries arrived the next year, making 1985 also the centennial of Protestantism. Rev. Billy Graham's visit to Korea celebrated the anniversary. It was also marked by erection of a memorial statue of Rev. and Mrs. Henry Appenzeller and Horace Underwood, the first to engage in organized Protestant missionary work.

With its message of human salvation through faith and its programs of social action, including education, health, and welfare activities, Christianity has grown steadily and rapidly, until Christians now number over 1.5 million Catholics and 5.3 million Protestants—nearly a fifth of the south Korean population. Among these are many Christians from the north who fled from communism, and their descendants; north Korea originally was more Christian than the south.

Like the Buddhists, Christians—especially the Protestants—have proliferated in divisions as well as adherents. The early divisions were brought by the missionaries themselves, dividing the Koreans from the start into Catholics and several sects of Protestants. The Protestant sects, however, have divided and subdivided. Additionally, they have spawned new religions and new interpretations of Christianity, responding not only to doctrinal differences and the tensions of social change, but also to the individual ambitions of some clergymen. According to one 1985 tabulation by the Korean Religion Research Institute, there are now 112 Protestant denominations in south Korea. There is also a small Eastern Orthodox congregation in Seoul, which began in the days of Russian ascendency in the late nineteenth century and was given new impetus by the Greek forces in the United Nations Command during and after the Korean War.

Christianity brought modern social values of freedom, equality, and human rights to Korea and was associated with movements for independence and democracy. This history, added to the greater organization of the Christian churches, has impelled some clergy and lay leaders to play active roles in movements for social reform (such as the Urban Industrial Mission, to improve wages and working conditions among poor urban workers) and to speak out on political issues. Like student activists, such leaders do not necessarily represent the majority of Christians, but they do reflect, in extreme degree, attitudes that are more widely held. Also like the students, some Christian activists have been arrested, tried, and sentenced for alleged subversive activity under both President Park and President Chun. A recent example is Rev. Moon Ik-hwan, indicted in June 1986 and subsequently imprisoned for his alleged encouragement of student activists at Seoul National University and leadership in the protest riot at Inch'on in May of that year. (Rev. Moon was released in an amnesty for political prisoners in mid-1987.)

Ch'ondogyo

In 1860 a native Korean religion, known as *tonghak* (Eastern Learning), was founded in a rural part of central Korea, as a conscious reaction against the introduction of alien Christian doctrines. Its originator, Ch'oe Che-u, was executed three years later. Nevertheless, its appeal spread rapidly in response to economic and political oppression, and its adherents formed the core of the *tonghak* rebellion, which captured most of two Korean provinces in 1894. Although the rebellion was crushed, the religion survived under the name *ch'ondogyo* (Heavenly Way Doctrine).

The *tonghak,* or *ch'ondogyo* principles incorporate neo-Confucian and Buddhist ideas and reflect some Christian influence (such as congregational worship). A central *ch'ondogyo* theme is that every person has the eternal within him and is therefore equal to everyone else—a revolutionary idea in a Confucian society. Other elements of Ch'oe Che-u's doctrine include incantation, meditation, use of a talisman to cure sickness, and revelation of truth. "The teachings of Ch'ondogyo assert that through self-discipine and cultivation one can obtain the divine virtue of being able to influence everything without conscious effort or volition."[30] *Ch'ondogyo* was one of the chief forces in the 1919 independence uprising, along with Christianity and Buddhism. Greatly reduced in numbers over the years, *ch'ondogyo* had 52,530 followers in 1983, according to government statistics.

Since 1945, a variety of religious sects have sprouted, some of national extent, but most locally organized. These include *taejonggyo,* organized around the worship of Tan'gun, mythical founder of Korea; it had 325,000 adherents in 1983. The Unification (*t'ongil*) Church of Rev. Sun Myung Moon is now perhaps more influential in the United States than in Korea. A former Presbyterian elder organized the so-called Olive Tree Sect, shortly after Liberation; his adherents, concentrated in their own villages, operate a number of factories and collectives. Turkish troops in the Korean War brought Islam to Korea, and subsequent Korean contact with the Middle East reinforced it. A mosque now overlooks the south-central part of Seoul, along with innumerable Christian churches. The tabulation above cited states that there was a total of 538 sects of all religions in Korea in 1985.[31]

Social Welfare

In Korean tradition, the state is responsible for social regulation rather than social welfare, the latter being a family and community responsibility. (It is often forgotten that this was the tradition of all governments, including those in the West, until the mid-nineteenth century, although charity by religious and private institutions was perhaps more common in Europe.) Modern social welfare programs began in Korea with the Christian missionaries. During the Japanese period, relatively little was done for the Koreans, although such institutions as state-operated hospitals were established. However, the spread of Western social welfare ideas inspired their inclusion in the platforms of all groups aspiring to political power after 1945.

If state responsibility for individual needs is the basis for judgment, then north Korea has moved far ahead of south Korea in social welfare. Limited observation by foreigners suggests that there is no abject poverty. Although north Korean wages and living standards are believed to be considerably lower than those of the south, there appears to be a universal system of health care, subsidized housing, and food rations, as well as a system of worker vacation resorts. The state professes to ensure work for everyone, although not at the choice of the worker, and to provide for support of the aged. Education through the ninth grade is universal, free, and compulsory. Whether these programs truly meet popular aspirations, and whether they are actually carried out in accordance with the claims of the regime cannot be determined.

South Korea has had to cope with four times the population density of the north. Until the mid-1960s, its economic development was slow and its resources poor. Accordingly, it is only in recent years that state-sponsored social welfare programs have spread to large parts of the public. Although the concept of state responsibility for the needy was recognized in legislation, most action was left to individual families—the traditional source of welfare—and to private organizations. A separate Ministry for Health and Social Affairs was established in 1948, but less than two years later its efforts had to be directed wholly at wartime and postwar relief for refugees, widows, orphans, and disabled soldiers and civilians of the Korean War. Only massive U.S. government and private support—largely in food, clothing, and consumer goods—averted widespread starvation in the war and immediate postwar period.

Given the state of the south Korean economy and the pressure of population, there was little more the government could do in the ensuing decade, even had there been a tradition of state social responsibility. South Korea in the postwar period was supporting one and one-half million returnees from the Pacific, three to four million refugees from north Korea (before and during the Korean War), and a growth rate of nearly 3 percent a year, while the economy was growing at only a slightly higher rate (around 5 percent).

From the mid-1960s on, rapid south Korean economic progress has made more social welfare programs possible in response to continuing public demand. In the private sector, earlier foreign missionary enterprises in such areas as hospitals, leprosy colonies, and orphanages were supplemented and often taken over by indigenous Christian and other groups, whose activities broadened. The Government also increased its concern for social programs, particularly for disabled veterans and widows. A separate Ministry of Labor was established, taking the former Office of Labor from the Ministry of Health and Social Affairs. Most recently, a Ministry of Sports was created. The New Community Movement, launched in 1971 in the rural areas, had a welfare component. Provisions of existing laws, such as employers' payment, on dismissal, of one month's separation pay for each year of work, were better enforced.

The fourth and fifth five-year plans for the economy included emphasis on social welfare—particularly the extension of health insurance programs financed by employers, workers, and government. Such programs now cover approximately half of all workers and are scheduled for near-universal application by the end of the 1980s. More attention is being given to working conditions. The Government and some large firms now have pension plans, and a minimum wage is projected for 1988. Employment information centers were being set up in the mid-1980s to help workers find jobs.

South Korean government policy differs from north Korea, however, in putting emphasis on economic growth and a strong family system as the bases for social welfare, rather than centralized state allocation of the individual's economic share. The consequence for the individual is more opportunity but less security in south Korea than in north Korea. The comparative evidence of the last decade suggests that the south Korean formula is more conducive to economic growth. Nevertheless, intellectuals, students, and religious leaders have shown increasing concern for what they see as an unfairly skewed apportionment of wealth and income.

Although medical care in south Korea has improved, it still has not reached the level of industrialized societies. Official statistics in 1986 indicated that there was 1 doctor per 1,392 persons, compared with 1 to 400 or 500 in Europe or the United States. Statistics for nurses and dentists showed similar gaps. Yet a Korean newspaper reported in 1986 that 30 percent of south Korean doctors were unemployed, despite the need for them in rural areas and small cities, because of the preference of educated people for living in Seoul.[32]

Sports and Recreation

Koreans traditionally put less emphasis than Western societies on physically strenuous sports and games, and more on socializing, for recreation and amusement. Moreover, games tended to involve individuals and small groups, rather than team confrontations. (However, there were inter-village contests such as tugs-of-war and rock fights). Much of the recreational activity followed the holidays of the Chinese lunar calendar, with sports and games appropriate to certain holidays. Men and boys sought their group recreation separately from women, particularly in the upper social levels, although female entertainers were a standard feature of male parties. Weddings, funerals, and other celebrations of life-cycle events, such as a man's sixtieth birthday (*hwan'gap*) and a child's first year of life (counted as his second birthday), were great social occasions, offering entertainment and relaxation as well as expressions of joy or sorrow.

Forms of Recreation

Traditionally, men and women sought their recreation separately. Men relaxed with friends of the same approximate age, leaving children in the care of their wives. Men with enough money had a separate room in their houses (the *sarangbang*) for entertaining their friends. Among the upper classes, parties in eating and drinking houses or in outdoor pavilions might involve poetry reciting, singing, dancing, and listening to performances by trained women entertainers (*kisaeng*). Calligraphy, board games, or just conversation or strolling, might be the focus of male gatherings. Women, in the old days, were far more restricted. The phrase "gathering mulberry leaves" refers to the device for young women of getting out of the house to see a friend by pretending to gather leaves for the silkworms.

Today, the recreation picture is greatly changed. Young men and women frequently enjoy dates together; there is still some separation of sexes for relaxation, but women, at least in the cities, have the same access to entertainment as men. Television is almost universally available. Cities and good-sized towns have movie houses, featuring both foreign and Korean films. There are innumerable eating and drinking places; tea houses (which usually serve coffee today) are particularly popular and U.S.-style fast-food restaurants have made their appearance. Billiard halls, electronic game rooms, driving ranges, and other blessings of advanced civilization are everywhere. National parks have greatly developed in recent years. Koreans are very fond of nature and take full advantage of such facilities. In Seoul, the old royal palaces and other monuments to the past are open to the public; museums, art exhibits, concerts are available and quite well attended. Travel is a favorite Korean recreation and has become available throughout the country by means of local and intercity bus service, railroads, and—for a growing number of people—private automobiles.

Traditional Athletics

Until the nineteenth century, sports were primarily martial arts (including archery) and the Korean version of wrestling (*ssirum*). The martial arts were pursued for spiritual and physical training and military readiness, more than for relaxation or enjoyment. Physical exertion was considered beneath the aristocrats' dignity; they left it to the soldiers, the women, the peasants, and the children.

The Korean sport most widely recognized in other countries is *t'aegwondo* (Tae Kwon Do), a disciplined form of person-to-person combat without weapons. One book on the subject describes *t'aegwondo* as "essentially discipline: discipline of the mind, the body, and the spirit. The physical manifestations . . . simply provide a measure of progress. . . . The lethal aspects of Tae Kwon Do attack come about just because one hopes it will be there. . . . It must be developed. Also, the individual must have certain mental, physical, and spiritual resources in the first place. . . ."[33] Totally unlike boxing, *t'aegwondo* involves periods of waiting and inward preparation, followed by quick and brief physical contact in forms carefully planned and practiced in advance.

T'aegwondo participants go through stages of training and practice. Completion of each stage, as demonstrated to a master, is marked by award of a different-colored belt to be worn with the traditional fighting garment; black is the highest level. In training and exhibition, physical injury is neither contemplated nor allowed, but the techniques are intended to subdue and if necessary incapacitate or kill an adversary in real-life situations.

Hwarangdo, a less widely known combat form, is similar in basic concept to *t'aegwondo* but makes use of the sword and other weapons. Its origin is traced to the young *hwarang* warrior-aristocrats of the Silla dynasty. Its discipline incorporates Buddhist spiritual elements. *Yudo* (judo) is another similar art, weaponless like *t'aegwondo;* usually associated with Japan, it is believed to have a Korean origin. *Ssirum* is somewhat similar to Western wrestling and is primarily a spectator sport. The wrestlers are specialists, with large, heavy bodies. (Japanese *sumo* is similar.)

Archery and horsemanship were traditionally essential in Korean military readiness. Practice of both was encouraged, particularly among the military, until the end of the Choson Dynasty. Archery is still popular but is becoming increasingly Westernized.

A succession of festive and solemn days throughout the lunar year enriched the lives of traditional Koreans, and some of these celebrations survive today. On festive days, the people of agricultural villages had group competitions such as tug-of-war. There were also rock fights between the young men of competing villages. A major form of village relaxation was impromptu dancing, often to the *nongak* [music of a farmers' band. Swinging and seesawing are traditional women's games, engaged in particularly on festive days (New Year's, for seesawing;] *tano*, fifth day of the fifth lunar month, for swinging).[34] The famous romantic story of Ch'unhyang, a commoner woman loved by a young aristocrat, begins with a scene in which the hero spots Ch'unhyang swinging near the pavilion where he is relaxing. Kite-flying is a traditional and still-popular boys' sport, particularly at the New Year; there are national kite-flying contests. The traditional forms are still enjoyed in regional and national folk celebrations, and in some agricultural villages. They have had a recent comeback on college campuses, accompanying the growth of nationalist spirit.

Modern Sports

Team sports were brought to Korea by Europeans and Americans and were incorporated into the programs of modern schools and other institutions (such as the Young Men's Christian Association). Soccer, for example, the most popular team game in Korea, was introduced by the crew of a British warship in 1882. Until recently, team sports were mainly thought of as physical and mental training, rather than recreation. Such ideas as pick-up teams and sand-lot softball are very new. Nevertheless, as the world is coming to realize, Koreans—both north and south—are demonstrating high skill in the new sports forms. South Korea first entered a national team in the 1948 Olympics and has steadily improved the country's showing. North Korea has fielded its own teams in international competitions and scored significant victories: Its athletes won medals in boxing, wrestling, and weight-lifting in the 1976 and 1980 Summer Olympics (the latter boycotted by south Korea along with the United States). In the 1984 Olympics (boycotted by north Korea along with the Soviet Union), south Korea was tenth among competing nations in medals won (six gold, six silver, seven bronze). South Koreans will undoubtedly distinguish themselves in the 1988 Summer Olympics, to be held in their capital city of Seoul; whether the north Koreans would participate or would host some events was still under debate in 1987.[35]

South Korea has scored major international competition successes in soccer, wrestling, boxing, and basketball. As long ago as the 1936 Olympics at Berlin, Son Ki-chong won a gold medal in track as a member of the

Japanese team. A National Sports Festival, held each October in various major cities, includes twenty-seven categories of sports; there are also junior and winter meets. Professional or semi-professional leagues play soccer and baseball (baseball is second in popularity to soccer); leading professional players command very high salaries. There are a number of skilled amateur teams sponsored by Korean business enterprises. Volleyball is another popular team sport. Western-style boxing was introduced in 1912. Tennis and golf are widely played, as is table tennis. Swimming, skating, roller-skating, and mountaineering have their followers; a Korean mountain-climbing team reached the top of Mount Everest in 1977.

Traditional Games

Adults and children alike play a game of Korean origin called *yut*, which uses a set of four sticks tossed in the air by each of several players in turn. The sticks are semicircular on one side, flat on the other; the number that land flat side up determines the score. Players advance scoring markers around an impromptu board; the first to complete the circuit wins.

Far more intellectually serious are the games of *paduk*, a kind of checkers which is the same as Japanese *go*, and a form of chess called *changgi*. Both are board games for two people. International *paduk* competitions are held, featuring mostly Japanese and Korean players. Like their Western counterparts, these games call for intense mental concentration and may go on for hours.[36]

Traditional card games use decks of 40 to 60 cards of a different design from those in the West. They are very popular and are frequently the basis for gambling. Western poker has become a favorite activity among Koreans, who frequently play for very high stakes; an apocryphal story has it that a player once bet his entire business on a single hand and lost. Mahjong is also popular and is another means of gambling.

Notes

1. Material in this chapter is based chiefly upon the the author's experience and observations, as verified by Korean and U.S. colleagues. Relevant sources include Vincent S.R. Brandt, *South Korean Society in Transition* (Elkins Park, Pa.: Philip Jaisohn Memorial Foundation, 1983); Paul S. Crane, *Korean Patterns* (Seoul: Hollym Publishing Co., 1967); Hong, Sung Chick, *The Intellectual and Modernization: A Study of Korean Attitudes* (Seoul: Social Science Research Institute, Korea University, 1967); Park, Ki-Hyuk and Sidney D. Gamble, *The Changing Korean Village* (Seoul: Shin-hung Press for the Royal Asiatic Society, Korea Branch, 1975); Yi, Man-gap, *Sociology and Social Change in Korea* (Seoul: Seoul National University Press, 1982).

2. On the Korean contribution to Confucian philosophy, see *The Rise of Neo-Confucianism in Korea*, William T. deBary and JaHyun Kim Haboush, editors (New York: Columbia University Press, 1985), p. xvii.

3. The twelve most common family names in Korea, in McCune-Reischauer romanization (with variant spellings in parentheses) are Yi (Lee, Rhee), Kim, Pak (Park), Chong (Chung), Yun (Yoon), Ch'oe (Choi), Yu (Yoo, Ryu), Hong, Sin (Shin), Kwon, Cho (Joe), Han (Hahn), and O (Oh, Auh). Individuals adopt their own romanized spellings, which may vary considerably: For example, a former prominent political leader, Cho Pyong-ok, spelled his name P. O. Chough. See Bruce Grant, *A Guide to Korean Characters; Reading and Writing Hangul and Hanja*, Second revised edition (Elizabeth, N.J.: Hollym International Corp., 1982), p. 335.

4. I am indebted to Professor Lee, On-Jook for this and several other points in this chapter.

5. William E. Henthorn, *A History of Korea* (New York: Free Press, 1971), pp. 161–62.

6. On the New Community Movement, see Vincent S.R. Brandt and Ji Woon Cheong, *Planning from the Bottom up; Community-Based Integrated Rural Development in South Korea* (Essex, Ct.: International Council for Educational Development, 1979). I discuss the New Community Movement also in Chapter 4.

7. *Korea Times*, March 4, 1986.

8. The Western term, "block," does not precisely explain the equivalent Korean area but is the best approximation.

9. The Korea Women's Development Institute encourages and publishes an annual *Women's Studies Forum* and issues a newsletter. In 1987, its office address was CPO Box 2267, Seoul.

10. Women traditionally believed they could prevent pregnancy by nursing children. Moreover, few alternatives were available in an economy without milk-giving animals or refrigerators.

11. Koreans may seem outspoken to Westerners because of a different idea of privacy. A person's age, for example, is a normal thing for a Korean to ask, even of a stranger, because it helps to establish social precedence.

12. For a scholarly summation of Korean ethical values, see Michael Kalton, *Korean Ideas and Values* (Elkins Park, Pa.: Philip Jaisohn Memorial Foundation, 1979). See also Steven R. Brown, "Values, Development, and Character: Appraising Korean Experience," *Korea Fulbright Forum*, No. 1, Winter 1984, pp. 33–66.

13. Interestingly, a north Korean scholar noted the emergence of "capitalist" enterprise in Korea at this period in a paper delivered to the conference of the Mid-Atlantic Region, Association for Asian Studies, in October 1985: Ch'oe Chin-hyok, *"choson minjujui inmin konghwagukeso ui rijo sigi ui ryoksa wa munhwa yongue taehayo"* (Regarding Research on the History and Culture of the Yi Dynasty in the Democratic People's Republic of Korea), paper delivered at the annual conference of the Mid-Atlantic Region, Association for Asian Studies, October 1985.

14. The south Korean government's Sixth Five-Year Plan (1987–1991) envisages extension of free compulsory education through the ninth grade.

15. Republic of Korea, Ministry of Education, *Education in Korea 1985–1986* (Seoul, 1985), pp. 30 ff; conversations with Korean professors.

16. *Education in Korea 1985-1986*, pp. 41-42.

17. Enrollments from Ministry of Education annual report; distribution from *Social Indicators in Korea, 1985*.

18. *North Korea: A Country Study*, ed. Frederica M. Bunge (Washington, D.C.: U.S. Government Printing Office, 1981), p. 249.

19. *Kodae Sinmun* (Korea University News), June 21, 1983, pp. 6-7, and September 16, 1985, p. 6.

20. Figures from Korean newspaper reports.

21. The U.S. cultural center in Taegu was also bombed, but by two men suspected of being north Korean agents; there was no apparent organized student involvement.

22. *Korea Times*, April 5, 1986.

23. Evelyn McCune in *The Arts of Korea; An Illustrated History* (Rutland, VT: Tuttle, 1962), p. 90, has stated that a work of the great Silla scholar-official Ch'oe Chi-won (858-910) called "Pen Scratchings in a Cinnamon Garden" still exists. See also Henthorn, *A History of Korea*, p. 76.

24. Paik, Nak Choon, "Tripitaka Koreana; Library of Woodblocks at Haein Sa, Korea," *Transactions of the Royal Asiatic Society, Korea Branch* 32 (1953):62-78.

25. Appendix B on the Korean language includes examples of the *han'gul* phonetic script.

26. McCune, *The Arts of Korea*, pp. 19-20.

27. Kim, Won-yong, "Spontaneity Defines Korean Art," *Korea Newsreview*, March 14, 1987, p. 23. Cf. also the same author's "Philosophies and Styles in Korean Art," *Korea Journal* 19 (No. 4, April 1979):8.

28. *Contemporary Korean Painting*, Berkeley, California, 1979.

29. *Korea Times*, March 25, 1986.

30. Susan S. Shin, "Tonghak Thought: The Roots of Revolution," *Korea Journal* 19 (No. 9, Sept. 1979):11-20.

31. *Korea Annual 1985* (Seoul: Yonhap News Agency, 1986).

32. *Korea Herald*, May 18, 1986.

33. Duk Sung Son and Robert J. Clark, *Korean Karate; The Art of Tae Kwon Do* (Englewood Cliffs, N.J.: Prentice-Hall, 1968), p. 5.

34. A description of traditional holidays is in Choe, Sang-su, *Annual Customs of Korea* (Seoul: Seomun-dang Publishing Co., 1983. They are observed according to the lunar calendar, thus vary every year. The major ones are New Year's (observed for three days); the Spring and Fall Confucian shrine ceremonies; *hansik* (cold food day), the 105th day after the winter solstice, on which people visit their ancestors' graves; *yokpul-il*, Buddha's birthday, the 8th day of the fourth month; *tano*, 5th day of the fifth month; *chusok*, the 15th day of the eighth month, a harvest festival and a day for honoring ancestors' graves; *kaech'onjol*, 3rd day of the tenth month, birthday of T'angun, the legendary founder of Korea (now a modern holiday, celebrated as south Korea's national day on October 3 of the solar calendar). For each of these holidays and a number of additional ones, there are traditional foods, games, social activities, and ceremonies.

35. The political problems of the 1988 Summer Olympics, involving rivalry between north and south Korea, are discussed in Chapter 8.

36. *A Handbook of Korea*, 5th ed. (Seoul: Korea Overseas Information Service, 1985), pp. 747-771; *Facts on File*, vol. 44, #2283, Aug. 17, 1984, pp. 593-598.

4 POLITICS AND GOVERNMENT OF THE REPUBLIC OF KOREA (SOUTH KOREA)

Introduction

The political system of Korea is a fascinating study in the interplay of four different traditions. Strongest of the four, even yet, is the Chinese Confucian pattern of institutions and behavior, with its emphasis on hierarchy, virtue, and proper form. The Western European and U.S. political model of liberal democracy, although long admired by Korean intellectuals, is only beginning to penetrate below the surface (although Western organization and management techniques have had greater impact). The Marxist philosophy, as systematized by Lenin and Stalin, was transplanted and fostered in north Korea; the gentler socialist version colors political attitudes in the south as well. Beneath all these traditions lie Korea's own native ways, giving a distinctive Korean cast to political life.

A good way to approach the study of Korean politics (or any politics, for that matter) is to think of government, as well as related political institutions, as a kind of mechanism within society. This mechanism responds to basic needs and wants of the people for security, order, livelihood, fair sharing of resources, and national pride. The government does this by listening to popular demands, choosing those that are most important, making plans and policies for meeting the chosen demands (in the form of laws and programs), and applying national resources to carry out the plans and policies. The people support the system by providing taxes, military service, respect, obedience, and votes. This support provides the government with the authority and resources it needs to make and carry out decisions. It also enables the government to use force against those who do not follow its directions or obey its laws.

In a democratic system, when the people dislike the government, they vote the leaders and ruling party out of power in favor of a new group. In an autocratic system, the government tells the people what the limits of their demands are and gives the people what it thinks they should have. The political system can be stable under either democracy or autocracy— or some in-between arrangement—so long as the people accept it or the government has the necessary force and efficiency to make them accept it.

Although it may seem strange to people with a democratic tradition, many people in the world—including the Koreans, until recently—live without protest in an autocratic system as long as its leaders govern effectively and with reasonable concern for the public welfare. Most governments in the world throughout history have been autocratic. The rulers were perceived to have divine right to rule; in some cases, as in the Roman Empire, they themselves had the status of gods. Their actions were therefore beyond the control of ordinary mortals, like floods and earthquakes.

However, if massive discontent develops in an autocracy, it boils over in rebellion, which compels the rulers to change their policies, or (if it becomes a revolution) transforms the political system. Revolution and rebellion may or may not be good things, depending upon the evils rebelled against and the practical means of doing away with these evils. The problem is that most revolutionaries have little experience in running a government; yet the problems of government are most difficult in the conditions of disorder that accompany rebellion. The resultant process of trial and error can have terrible consequences, including aggression from outside.

It follows that political stability is generally preferred to the risks of rebellion. In the words of the U.S. Declaration of Independence, "Mankind are more disposed to suffer, while evils are sufferable." The genius of democracy, of course, is that it provides a built-in device for instant peaceful revolution by voting the rulers out of power. However, if democracy is to function, the complex rules and understandings of the democratic political game must be known, understood, and respected by leaders and people. Otherwise, it will fail, as many recent examples demonstrate.

In today's interdependent world, moreover, sovereign nations have demands and expectations of one another that also must be met. The smaller a nation is, the more important these outside expectations become, and the more they limit that nation's freedom of action. South Korea, particularly, faces such limitations: It has few natural resources, yet must support a dense population on an ever-higher level and defend them against a heavily armed adversary, north Korea, backed by two giant nations—China and the Soviet Union. Its international relations, both political and economic, are therefore of key importance in domestic stability and prosperity.

Politics involves more than the formal government structure, as laid down by the constitution and laws. It also involves all of the groups and categories of people who look to the political system to meet their needs and expectations. Some of these people, individually or in groups, have more influence than others, so they may get more benefit. The political system works according to a set of understandings shared by the population, most of them unwritten, that make up the political culture. The way the system really functions cannot be understood just by reading the constitution; rather, it must be learned by observing how people actually think and behave. To emphasize this point, the south Korean Constitution is summarized toward the end, rather than the beginning, of this chapter.

Political Culture

The political culture of the Republic of Korea is a blend of native, Chinese, and Western elements. The native element, as it existed prior to the Chinese impact, can only be guessed at. It seems to have had a strong element of aristocratic authority, based on birth and family, coupled with an equally strong spirit of individual independence. The Chinese input sank in very deep over nearly two thousand years of exposure—particularly after Confucianism was officially adopted by King T'aejo at the beginning of the Choson Dynasty (see Chapter 2). It became an integral and dominant part of Korean political culture.

The political aspects of this culture, as it existed down to the mid-nineteenth century, included the following elements:

- belief that human society was an integral part of the whole universe, interrelated with it in maintaining order and harmony;
- acceptance of harmony, order, and consensus as major political values and purposes;

- acceptance of duty toward family and associational group (such as the court factions) as more important than individual satisfaction;
- concurrently, a strong individual drive for power and position, often manifested as a struggle among factions of rival leaders and their supporters;
- loyalty of subject to the person of the ruler, rather than to the whole state as such;
- belief that the proper model for political behavior was the ideal kingdom of the ancients, the principles of which were to be found in the Chinese classics;
- a static view of the human condition, in which nations and dynasties and families rose and fell in cyclical fashion, but life's potentialities remained basically the same;
- acceptance of hierarchical relations among people within the society, and among nations, so that everyone was inferior or superior to everyone else except for friends of the same age;
- a view of the ruler as responsible to Heaven (through China) for the order and well-being of all aspects of his kingdom—political, economic, and social—and possessing the Mandate of Heaven to rule so long as he fulfilled this responsibility;
- disparagement of industrial and commercial activity, and encouragement of agriculture as the central activity;
- emphasis on form and procedure, as well as substantive performance, as key elements in maintaining order;
- preference for decision-making by consensus, rather than by majority vote or force of arms; yet at the same time, unwillingness to compromise on matters perceived to involve principle;
- respect and honor to scholar-officials, passers of the examinations, as a class possessing superior benevolence, wisdom, and administrative ability and therefore entitled to special status;
- self-governance of the agricultural majority of the population in their villages, except for governmental collection of taxes and labor and punishment of particularly heinous crimes;
- reluctance to involve governmental institutions in personal or family quarrels, which were settled wherever possible within families or communities.

These values were opposite in many respects to those of the West, which (at least from the latter eighteenth century, particularly in the United States) emphasized progress, change, individual freedom, equality of all persons, adversary relations, government by consent of the people, separation of political from economic and social affairs, and the importance of civic duty. However, as Korea—like China and Japan—was driven to modernize and industrialize, both for self-protection and to meet the rising expectations of the people, it had to accept the Western values that accompanied the process. Attempts to be selective failed; yet the traditional culture resisted change.

Since 1876 (the year of the first Western-style treaty with Japan), and even before that, Korean leaders and people have lived in a shifting cultural environment where the old values crumbled but the new ones were suspect. In the military and economic spheres, modern organizational values are accepted and applied (along with some traditional values). In north Korea, the political culture seems to have been drastically modified. Communist attitudes, beliefs, and values are accepted there as they are in other Communist nations, although with some Korean variations such as the *juche* principle discussed in Chapters 3 and 5.

In south Korea, however, an integrated political culture is still emerging, through a much freer process. Significant elements of the traditional pattern survive beneath an overlay of Western institutional forms. Family, associational group, and factional loyalties still outweigh civic consciousness. Informal group networks, such as school and college alumni associations (notably the successive graduating classes of the Korea Military Academy), or shared provincial origins, are powerful channels of communication and influence. The sense of abstract justice and universal human rights is weak in comparison to group loyalties and duties.

The right and duty of citizen participation in voting and other political acts is still imperfectly understood among the general public, although that understanding is growing. The concept of political parties is not clearly established; parties still carry something of the contempt attached to the old court factions. The concept of loyal opposition and open debate on policy still does not fit a culture emphasizing authority, hierarchy, and harmony. Political opponents tend to be viewed by those in power as heretics and subversives, just as they were in the Yi Dynasty court, and a conspiratorial element persists in opposition political activity. The relation between the economic and political sectors of the society is currently a matter of leadership debate, in which the old tradition that included all national life within the domain of political control seems still strong.

An anecdote may illustrate Korean political style. In 1956, a newly formed opposition party was preparing for the presidential election. At that time, the President and Vice President were both elected by separate popular votes. Public discontent with political and economic conditions was running high. President Rhee had angered the previously divided opposition forces into unity by forcing through the Assembly a constitutional amendment permitting him to run again. Three senior politicians, who led the main factions of the new Democratic party, gathered one afternoon in the home of a party supporter to decide which of them would be the party's presidential and vice presidential candidate.

It was relatively easy for the three men to agree that Shinicky (Sin Ikhui), former speaker of the National Assembly, would run for President; but Chough Pyong Ok, "old faction" leader, and Chang Myon, "new faction" leader, each wanted to be Vice President. Shinicky and Chough had been opposition leaders for years; Chang had only recently joined the party. The three men sat in solemn silence for hours: neither man would yield, but it was not seemly to covet the candidacy openly.

Finally, in the small hours of the morning, Dr. Chough—who had a reputation for impatience—said, "Dr. Chang, why don't you run?" Etiquette required that Chang should reciprocate by inviting Chough to do so. Instead, he quickly agreed.[1]

Shinicky died of a heart attack on his campaign train shortly before the presidential election, but Chang Myon, to the surprise of observers, defeated President Rhee's ailing running mate, and held the powerless office of Vice President for four years. Shortly after his election, he was the target of an assassination attempt, but suffered only a wound in his hand. He became Prime Minister after the 1960 student revolution overturned the Rhee regime.

A key test of political development in Korea will come in 1988 (which is also the year of the Seoul Olympic Games). The 1980 Constitution of south Korea limited the President to a single seven-year term. Previous constitutions also had limited presidential terms, only to be amended so that the incumbent could remain in power. President Chun Doo Hwan (Fig. 4.1), following his election in 1981, pledged that he would step down in 1988 and assure a peaceful transfer of power. He has repeatedly reaffirmed this pledge, and his successor was elected in late 1987.

If President Chun retires from office on February 26, 1988, and his elected successor is duly inaugurated, it will be the first such event in the Republic's history and will symbolize a new precedence for law and public opinion over personal ambition and autocratic tradition. (The election of Yun Po Sun by the legislature to succeed acting President Huh Chung in August 1960 was not comparable, because it simply confirmed a change that had already occurred.) The importance of this symbolism will be reduced, but not negated, by problems that are sure to arise following the presidential election of December 16, 1987.

The opposition New Korea Democratic party, which newly emerged at the time of the 1985 legislative elections and won a surprisingly large number of seats, had made amendment of the Constitution its major issue. This issue drew wide public support—manifested in large demonstrations and an opposition-sponsored petition campaign—because of general discontent with the current administration. The amendment controversy centered around two major points: whether the president should be elected by direct popular

FIGURE 4.1 Chun Doo Hwan, eleventh President of the Republic of Korea (1981–1988), presiding at a cabinet meeting (photo courtesy of Korea Overseas Information Service)

election, as the opposition wanted, or indirectly by an electoral college or the legislature, as the government wanted; and whether the structure of government should be presidential (like the United States), parliamentary (like Great Britain or Japan), or "dual-executive" (like France).

President Chun, who had previously opposed amendment before 1989, agreed to accept the idea of amendment before the 1988 elections. In June, 1986, the National Assembly created a committee to work out a draft; but in a year of sparring, neither government nor opposition departed from their opposite positions. Each side sought a formulation that would maximize its chance to retain or to gain power. On April 13, 1987, the President announced an end to discussion, thus returning to his earlier position that constitutional change should come after the next presidential election.[2] In June, the President's political party approved his choice of the party chairman, Roh Tae Woo (an ex-general who had supported Chun in his assumption of power in 1979 and 1980), as candidate to succeed him. Massive popular demonstrations manifested public displeasure at this apparent extension of military-dominated rule. In consequence Roh acceded to opposition demands, and President Chun agreed. Resumed discussions on a constitutional amendment in the National Assembly resulted in approval of a compromise that provided for direct presidential elections and for expanded guarantees of rights but otherwise continued the present form of government. The amendment was approved by popular referendum in October 1987.

Seven presidential candidates then registered, in addition to Roh. The differing ambitions of the two principal opposition leaders, Kim Young Sam and Kim Dae Jung, prevented the designation of a single major opposition candidate, as they had earlier pledged, and split the major opposition party. In the election on December 19, 1987, Roh won 36.6 percent of the popular vote, against 28 and 26 percent, respectively, for the two Kims—both of whom claimed large-scale fraud. It was therefore clear that President Chun's determination to step down would be sorely tested by the fact that the election winner would almost certainly have less than majority support and would have a difficult time in consolidating control of his administration by democratic means.

Underlying the dispute over constitutional amendment was the problem of devising a governmental system that takes account of both the people's democratic aspirations and their cultural experience and tradition. Aspirations relate to the future; experience is rooted in the past; the debate was constrained by both, as well as by the security threat overhanging the Republic. The immediate problem was—and still is—how to rid the civilian government of what many people perceive as military domination and how to give the people a voice in the choice of their President. At bottom are basic questions: how to maintain democracy and order at the same time; how to provide for human rights and political participation, on the one hand, and harness the personal ambitions of political leaders for power, on the other.

The Political Process in South Korea

Inputs: Popular Demands on Government

The demands that the Korean people make on their government are rapidly changing and growing. So are their expectations of response. Traditionally, the predominantly agrarian society asked little more than to be secure and left alone in their villages; the *yangban* sought power and prestige. If the *yangban* became too predatory, the people resorted to petitions and often to riots. During the period of Japanese rule, the prevailing popular mood was one of sullen, reluctant compliance with coercive authority. Those who learned to live with the colonial regime were condemned by the others as collaborators. The 1919 popular uprising demonstrated the demand for liberation.

In 1945, the Koreans' longing for liberation was fulfilled, but only by the action of outside forces—the United States and the Soviet Union. That action had little connection with the domestic nationalist movement, and it resulted in both foreign occupation and division. The original simple demand was therefore replaced, first, by a demand for immediate independence, and then for reunification. Independence in 1948, even though divided between two states, partially met one of these demands, but left the other unresolved. The Korean War added a demand for security, which was met in both north and south by defense alliances and massive military buildup.

In the first twenty years after liberation, security and social-economic demands took precedence over everything else. Food, clothing, shelter, education for children, economic opportunity, and equitable distribution of wealth were the primary wants. (The annual "spring hunger," when considerable numbers of Koreans ate grass and tree bark for want of grain, did not end until the mid-1960s.)

Until very recently, demands for political and civil rights were generally weak except at times of crisis or political provocation. Western concepts of personal liberty and civic rights were learned in school or from the media. While these concepts were attractive in the abstract, there was little native experience or cultural support for them. An often-cited public opinion poll conducted in Korea in the mid-1960s indicated that popular demands were for rapid economic development, national security, and democratic politics, in that order.

Now the "spring hunger" is only a memory; rapid economic development has brought a dramatic rise in the standard of living for many people, and at least some improvement for most. The number of people officially below the poverty line is claimed by the government to be roughly the same as in the United States (although the definition and absolute level are different), and the wealth distribution curve is similar, although much lower. Health insurance programs, pension plans, and other social benefits are expanding. Thus the economic imperative is being met in gross terms. Security continues as a major concern, although many observers believe it is overplayed by the government, and although thirty-five years without major hostilities have reduced the anxiety level. The attempted assassination of the President by north Korean agents in Rangoon in 1983 recalled the 1968 attempt in Seoul, and reports of captured spies come every few months.

Freed to some extent from economic want and the immediate threat of war, south Koreans are also becoming better educated and more politically aware. They have a greater stake in the political process, in a society where political decisions affect their hard-earned property as well as their personal freedom. It is therefore natural that a 1980 public opinion poll reversed the economic and political demand priorities of the 1960s.[3] Although the Korean people are not looking for U.S.-style politics, they are unlikely to accept indefinitely the authoritarian ruling patterns that have characterized Korea up to now. Radical students and intellectuals probably represent, in extreme form, a much broader but unorganized popular discontent, as the events of 1987 have demonstrated.

Moreover, as Korean society becomes more modern and more complex, political and social interest groups that have more complex and sophisticated needs are developing. Such matters as women's rights, environmental controls, financial policies, the special needs of medium and small business, which received little political attention in the past, are now coming to the fore. Foreign demands are also more sophisticated, as foreign business increasingly enters the Korean market, and Korea plays a larger international role.

The capability of the government of the Republic of Korea to meet its people's demands is determined by four factors: the people's support for it—including their acceptance of its legitimacy and authority; the competence of the government itself; the resources of the nation; and the ability of the government to influence the character and intensity of the demands made upon it. These factors are interrelated, but in the long run they determine the stability of the political order.

Acceptance of government authority is a function of two perceptions by the public: the government's legitimacy, in terms of tradition, law, or popular will; and its effectiveness in doing what the people want, or in forcing them to accept what they get. The Republic of Korea was first established in 1948 by general elections conducted by the U.S. military government under United Nations observation. Although up to 20 percent of the eligible voters may have withheld their support because the election (held in the south only) conflicted with the goal of reunification, the great majority accepted the legitimacy of the election.[4] They accepted the Constitution and government it produced. Syngman Rhee, probably the most noted Korean nationalist of the time, was accepted as the elected President.

Support for the legitimate political order was nonetheless weak because of traditional family and parochial loyalties, struggles for political power, and the blatant manipulation that accompanied them—especially in the fraudulent election of 1960. Poor government performance in economic development gave the regime poor marks for effectiveness (the best non-coercive substitute for legitimacy). The protests and violence that followed the 1960 election brought down the Rhee government. The ensuing experiment in open parliamentary democracy under Prime Minister Chang Myon suffered from leadership inexperience and factional infighting. It could not stand against the military coup d'état of 1961.

None of the three subsequent south Korean political regimes has enjoyed the legitimacy of the First Republic. However, the extraordinary economic progress achieved by President Park Chung Hee, and continued at a rapid though somewhat lower rate by the successor Fifth Republic of President Chun Doo Hwan, has maintained broad (though far from universal) popular acquiescence. In 1971, Kim Dae Jung, the opposition candidate for President, got 45 percent of the votes. Since then, presidential elections have been by electoral college and therefore—in many people's view—more susceptible to official pressure. In 1985, a new opposition party won more than one-third of the votes for National Assembly candidates—about as many as the government party received. These votes made clear that there was considerable popular disenchantment. The manner in which President Chun came to power, and the responsibility he is perceived to bear for the violent suppression of the 1980 Kwangju revolt, have created a reservoir of popular discontent. This is particularly true of younger people, who make up a large proportion of the electorate.

Up to now, the Republic's government has had ample authority and capability to carry out its functions, based upon a combination of legitimacy, effectiveness, and police power. It has greatly improved the efficiency of tax collection, which in all forms at both national and local levels yield about 20 percent of gross national product. Savings for investment have reached a marginal rate of nearly 25 percent. Universal military conscription for males has been effectively enforced, with a little less than 2 percent of the population on full-time active duty (more than any U.S. peacetime level), not counting the millions in reserve and civil defense activity. Voting turnout has remained high. Through efficient police and security forces and fairly sophisticated social controls—such as formal and informal pressures on the press and social and economic institutions—the government has generally been able to defuse or counter those pressures that it could not satisfy through responsive actions. The events of 1986 and 1987, however, suggest that the limits of the government's capacity to control the people had been reached.

Governmental Process

Korean government is still heavily conditioned by the Confucian tradition, in which the officials are expected to decide what the people should have and give it to them as the officials' superior wisdom indicates. To some extent, the people still accept this tradition, although with growing skepticism (rumors about incompetence and corruption in high places circulate quite freely, despite controls). Government coercion has been applied to modify attitudes on some matters. In the early stages of the rural New Community Movement, for example, there were charges that government representatives dictated what the farmers should want to do to benefit themselves, such as replacing their thatched roofs with sheet iron.[5] Constant government emphasis on the north Korean threat is another example. Press controls have been applied to prevent stirring up political demands in sensitive areas.

However, even during the Choson Dynasty, public demands could reach government policy-makers by way of politically influential groups and their family or other connections in government. This is still a primary channel for communicating demands. Its weakness is that it gives priority to the demands of those in influential positions and their supporters and families. Some of the kings recognized this problem and endeavored to meet it by a procedure for individual petitions, as well as a network of secret agents. These channels still function, in more modern form.

To a limited degree, popular demands also reach the government through more modern, Western-style channels, such as representatives in the National Assembly, local government leaders, the mass media, and elections. None of these channels can bring the pressure to bear on government that counterpart institutions in mature democracies have. An additional, but little-recognized, channel is the reports of security agencies on the state of public order. If the government ignores popular discontent, the result—as in Yi Dynasty times—is unrest, demonstrations, and riots. The most recent examples have been the labor and student unrest of 1979, which led to the assassination of President Park; the Kwangju uprising of May 1980, the harsh suppression of which left an enduring bitterness toward the administration of President Chun; and the demonstrations of June, 1987, which brought the government to compromise with opposition forces on constitutional amendment. The 1987 demonstrations had their beginnings in the opposition signature campaigns and rallies in the spring of 1986, and in increasingly violent student demonstrations, signalling public discontent over questions of political freedom and participation.

The Western institution that has had the most impact on Korea is the election system. Both north and south Korea have held elections at more or less regular intervals since 1946; but while those in the north have been a virtual 100 percent endorsement of decisions already made by the elite, those in the south have been important means of registering popular discontent. Turnout has been from around 60 to nearly 85 percent (the latter figure reached in the legislative elections of 1985); only once, in the local elections of 1960, did turnout fall below 50 percent.[6]

Up to 1986, there had been thirteen general legislative elections since 1946, and thirteen presidential elections since 1948. Each of the legislative elections has been wholly or largely by direct popular vote. Of the presidential elections, six have been by direct popular vote, two by the legislature, and five by electoral colleges. Each legislative election has offered a choice of candidates (often ten or more, in earlier days) and has resulted in at least some opposition showing. Presidential elections have also offered a choice of candidates, and in 1956 the opposition vice presidential candidate (Chang Myon) was put in office. There were also elections of local councils in 1952, 1956, and 1960, but elective offices have not existed below the national level since 1961 (they are scheduled to be reinstituted in 1988). In the legislative elections of 1977 and 1985, opposition parties together received more votes than the government party, although they did not achieve a majority in the Assembly. Since 1963, popular referenda have been used for ratification of constitutional amendments. Although their use is provided for in the 1980 Constitution, they have rarely been employed for other purposes. The referenda have generally approved government positions by margins of 60 percent or more; turnout has ranged from about 70 to nearly 80 percent. An unprecedented 85 percent of the voters turned out in the referendum of October 27, 1987, on the newest Constitutional amendment, and 93 percent of the voters approved it.

Response to election results has sometimes been increased repression, rather than changed policies. Large-scale rigging of the 1960 election, to prevent the defeat of President Rhee and his running mate, led to the fall of the Rhee government. The near-defeat of President Park in 1971 led to establishment of a more authoritarian government structure. Nevertheless, the process has provided a largely non-violent channel for public displeasure—which may help to explain the relatively low level, compared to many other developing countries, of major political violence.

In mature democracies, the individual needs and desires of citizens go through a process of combination, so that the resultant, aggregated demands of large groups will have more weight and meaning for political decision-makers. This aggregation is mostly done by a wide variety of interest groups, by political parties, and by the legislature. In Korea, interest groups are only beginning to develop such a role. The process is more informal, personal, and hierarchical; the legislature plays a relatively small part. Aggregation of popular demands is, as a practical matter, done chiefly by leading officials of the executive branch, responding to information they receive through both formal and informal channels.

In Korean terms, it has been considered a loss of face and dignity for high government officials to appear pressured into action by citizen demands. Accordingly, even when demands were responded to, the response might be delayed or indirect. Some demands were simply ignored, others damped down or suppressed by propaganda, official statements, or in some cases coercion. This attitude, however, is currently changing. For example, in a few cases courts have recently upheld civil suits against government agencies for injustice or malfeasance.

Decision-making

Basic decisions—choices between conflicting demands, and allocation of national resources—are strongly centralized in Korea. Although the President and his immediate staff do not literally make all decisions, they apparently make a very large proportion of them. The preeminence of the executive branch, and surviving traditions of deference to higher authority, reinforce the President's primary decision-making role and could even be said to force it upon him, irrespective of his own character or preferences.

The President's advisers and secretaries function as auditors of the performance of cabinet (State Council) ministers, ensuring that the President's will is executed. The President can call upon the State Council for advice in reaching decisions; the Constitution requires State Council deliberation upon eighteen specified matters. The President also has a National Security Council, amounting to a committee of the State Council, and other advisory bodies. Probably the most important of all is the Economic Planning Board (EPB), headed by a Deputy Prime Minister, which for over twenty years has had the major voice in formulating the country's overall economic policies and five-year development plans. The EPB, although nominally composed of State Council members heading economic ministries, has managerial functions and staff of its own, including budget, planning, evaluation, and statistics.

The centralization of decision-making authority also makes the President a prime target for would-be assassins and plotters; thus the President has his own separate security force, comparable to the US Secret Service.

Given the hierarchical nature of Korean politics, and the limits on the President's time, it follows that many policies, once laid down, must be carried out in the prescribed way despite changing circumstances or negative feedback from those affected. The decision latitude of Korean government officials is therefore narrow; referral to superiors of any doubtful point is commonplace.

Moreover, matters of personal dignity and status are involved. Juniors must be careful not to preempt the decision prerogatives of their seniors, or to appear disrespectful or disobedient. An added factor is the surviving Confucian emphasis on form, reinforced by the heritage of the Japanese colonial period. To carry out the procedures of government in the right way, using the right language, procedures, and paperwork, may be considered equally as important as the accomplishment of a substantive purpose. These characteristics—centralization of authority, personal status, and formality— make for delays, insensitivity, and large amounts of paperwork and routine. Nevertheless, Korean decision-making has improved considerably in recent years in speed, flexibility, and responsiveness to requirements, particularly in the area of economic planning and control.

Carrying Out Decisions

Once made, political decisions are authenticated (and occasionally side-tracked) by laws enacted in the National Assembly, and by executive orders of the President or cabinet members on the basis of State Council action, in accordance with the laws (except for emergency decrees, of which there were none as of 1987). Laws and orders are executed by the central and local bureaucracy, related governmental and quasi-governmental agencies, and to some degree by non-governmental organizations such as banks, operating according to government instructions. Individual members of the National Assembly may introduce legislative bills, but few are passed, and those mostly on minor matters.

The government hierarchy includes eighteen executive ministries, each with a vice minister and assistant ministers, under whom are bureaus, divisions, and smaller units similar to those of all modern governments. Figure 4.2 is a chart of government organization. There are also offices at a level between ministries and bureaus—some of them under the President or Prime Minister, some attached to ministries. As governmental responsibility has grown more complex, delegation of authority down the line has increased; its high degree of centralization is often frustrating, but, even so, the effectiveness of the bureaucracy has greatly increased in the past twenty years.

Geographically, the Republic is divided into nine provinces, four special cities with provincial status (Pusan, Taegu, Inch'on, and Kwangju), and the Special City of Seoul. Each is headed by a presidentially appointed chief executive (provincial governor or city mayor) who has about six executive departments under him. One of these, the police bureau, reports directly to the National Police Director in all matters except those peculiar to the individual province or city. Other bureaus, also, have close relations with their national counterparts, in addition to regional offices of national ministries. The Mayor of Seoul reports directly to the President; the other governors and mayors report through the Minister of Home Affairs.

Provinces (to) are subdivided into counties (kun) and cities (si). Within the kun are towns (up) and townships (myon), according to population and urban character; these in turn are subdivided into precincts (tong) or villages (ri). Cities are subdivided into tong; special cities (chikhwal si) are divided into wards (ku), and those into districts (tong). In 1984 (before Kwangju became a special city), there were 37 special city wards, 139 counties, and 45 cities. Including the township level, there was a total of about 6,000 incorporated government units.[7] At the village and town level, the head is appointed from among local residents; at higher levels, incumbents are career civil servants, and as of old, tend not to be natives of the area where they are stationed. Since 1985 there has been discussion of electing local councils, provided for inboth the 1980 Constitution and the 1987 amendment. The councils, abolished in 1961, may be reconstituted in 1988. The police have an organization paralleling local administration down to the larger villages; there are also paramilitary combat police units for riot control in the larger centers.

To a limited extent, the execution of laws and regulations is subject to judicial review. Although the courts have not been really independent of the executive branch—both because the Continental legal system is used, and

128

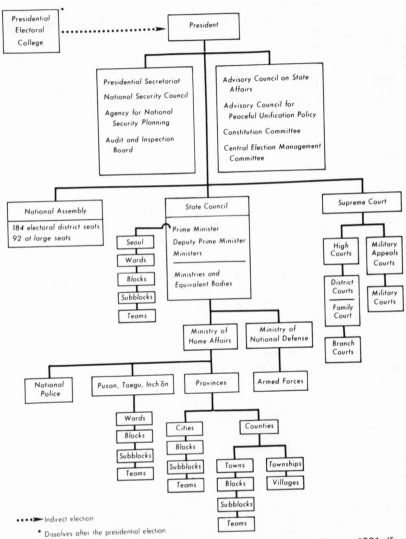

FIGURE 4.2 Chart of government organization, Republic of Korea, 1981 (from Frederica Bunge, ed., *South Korea: A Country Study*, 3d ed. [Washington, D.C.: U.S. Government Printing Office, 1982], p. 168)

because of the Korean tradition of centralized control—they have more than nominal freedom to reach objective decisions on the law. In the last decade, the courts have begun to levy damages against government agencies for injustices done to private citizens and groups. However, in political cases, the prosecution's view has usually prevailed. In late 1987, Amnesty International was endeavoring to secure the release of twenty-one "prisoners of conscience" whose sentences it considered unjustified.

The Supreme Court, which in 1987 had fifteen justices, is the final court of appeal. There are three superior (appeal) courts, in Seoul, Taegu, and Kwangju, and twelve district courts, with both criminal and civil jurisdiction. There are also magistrate courts for minor offenses, family courts, and other specialized courts. Judges are appointed by the President for constitutionally prescribed terms of office, except that his appointment of the Chief Justice of the Supreme Court is subject to confirmation by the National Assembly. The military services have a separate court-martial system, which is subject to Supreme Court review.

Under Korea's version of the Continental legal system (originally drawn from Germany and France through Japan), the role of the prosecutors (sometimes termed procurators) is very important. These officials, organized in a fashion parallel to the courts, are under a quasi-independent office of the Ministry of Justice, headed by a prosecutor-general. They investigate all cases prior to trial; once they determine that a trial is merited, their recommendations are commonly upheld by the courts, although the courts frequently modify the recommended penalties. There are no citizen juries, but panels of three or five judges sit on serious cases, deciding by majority vote. Although defendants are entitled to counsel, the theory of equality between the state and the defendant is not recognized. The Korean Constitution provides for the writ of habeas corpus (under which the government may be required to show cause for arrest and detention), and court warrants are required for police or prosecutor arrests and searches in most circumstances. The courts, however, have not usually been assertive toward executive branch authorities, especially in politically sensitive cases; and defense lawyers do not enjoy the social or procedural status taken for granted in the United States.

Civil suits are a small but growing part of court business—particularly in business matters. Continuing in the old tradition, individuals are reluctant to take their private or family affairs to the authorities. (Family law is still based on native Korean tradition, although changes were under discussion in 1987 to meet new social circumstances, such as increased women's rights.) Private lawyers have not traditionally enjoyed great social respect as such, although they have status as college graduates and as passers of the national examinations. This situation, however, is changing as large businesses find it necessary to seek court remedies for their problems.

Politically Important Groups

Components of south Korean society with politically relevant power or influence, or access to decision-makers, or both—in addition to the President and his entourage—determine the performance of the political system. At present, the armed forces, the bureaucracy, business people, internal security forces, politicians and political parties, mass media, intellectuals, church groups, students, labor, and farmers/fishermen are the most important.

The listed groups vary in organization and coherence. Several of them, in various ways, reflect the growing Korean middle class.[8] They act upon, through, and around the constitutionally or traditionally mandated governmental institutions. Each of them is discussed briefly below.

Armed Forces

The Republic's three armed services are described in Chapter 7. Among them, the Army of about 525,000 persons is politically most significant because of its numbers, coercive power on the ground, managerial ability, and capacity to provide channels of upward mobility for the common citizen.

Prior to 1960, the Army's political role was chiefly a latent one. Its Counterintelligence Corps for a time was an information channel for President Rhee, and Rhee organized a nominally military Joint Provost Marshal General Command under a trusted lieutenant to enforce his political will. The organization of the National Defense College in 1956 may have encouraged the development of political consciousness among senior Army officers. However, the U.S. training of most senior Army officers in the early years of the Republic reinforced a Korean tradition of civilian supremacy. Moreover, in the early years the various factions (grouped by individual allegiance, provincial origin, or previous training and experience) tended to neutralize one another.

During most of his twelve years in the Presidency, Rhee carefully played off factional military leaders against one another and distributed rewards and recognition so as to minimize discontent. The Army was permitted to run a miniature economic empire of its own to supplement the miserable pay of officers and men. After the 1960 upheaval, Prime Minister Chang Myon sought to reduce the size of the Army, in part because of U.S. pressure, to reduce the economic load. Chang lacked Rhee's skill in coping with ambitious military leaders. Most of them were young, even at the highest levels; they were in severe competition for the relatively few top posts not only with one another, but with slightly younger field-grade graduates of the new Korea Military Academy, whose loyalties were by class rather than faction. The resulting internal frustrations were in large part responsible for the military coup d'état of 1961, although social unrest, acting upon a conscript Army, was also a factor.

The declared purpose of the coup leaders was to reform the corrupt and economically stagnant Korean polity and strengthen it against north Korean subversion. Their six-point program of May 1961 set forth these themes and promised restoration of civilian government—a promise eventually kept, under strong U.S. pressure, two years later.

After 1961, however, it was obvious to all civilian leaders that they could not hold political power without military consent and implicit support; and that Army people's ambitions and perceptions of the national interest would have to be taken into account by utilizing their managerial talents in appropriate governmental or industrial positions. General Park Chung Hee and some of his associates resigned their Army affiliation to hold governmental office. Over time their viewpoints approached those of Korean leaders generally, although their own careers made them acutely mindful of the need for military support, and receptive to military viewpoints. Since reestablishment of civilian government in 1963, military personnel have resigned or retired before entering civilian positions.

The second exercise of military power by Army officers, in 1980, was again due in part to internal military problems. It was also due in part to the personal loyalty of certain senior Army officers to the assassinated President. But, as in 1961, the Army officers' actions reflected sincere concern at the apparent weakness of civilian political direction and control in the face of the north Korean threat and the struggles of civilian politicians for power. The return to normal civilian government and competent civilian leadership was swift.

At present, as in most years since 1961, retired military officers are found at middle and senior levels in all areas of civilian government and in major business enterprises. Their numbers are not dominant, however, nor are their viewpoints necessarily those of the military establishment. The 1986 cabinet included two former professional soldiers out of a total membership of twenty-five (the President included).[9] The political role of the military has not been one of day-to-day intervention in civilian affairs (except as any group in society pursues its own interest). Rather, its role is one of watchful surveillance, based on the power of well-organized and heavily armed soldiers backing an educated, talented, and ambitious career officer corps of around forty thousand (with a few thousand Korea Military Academy graduates at their core), which no politician can ignore. No person could likely enter or long remain in the office of President without the acquiescence of the armed forces. Yet the President's governmental policies and administration have not recently been under military control in any direct sense.

The military do, however, play some direct role in internal security through the Defense Security Command, a military intelligence organization that has its own agents in civilian as well as military areas. President Chun headed this agency at the time that he moved to political power, and its present direction presumably has direct access to him as an additional channel of information on the domestic situation. Under President Park, some of the staff of the Korean Central Intelligence Agency came from the military forces. This is true to some extent of the successor Agency for National Security Planning; but the new agency's domestic role is much more limited. Moreover, thousands of ex-Army officers are scattered through the civilian bureaucracy, where they can reflect the views of their military class networks in influencing government behavior.

The Bureaucracy

The Republic's executive branch in 1986 was staffed by somewhat over 650,000 civil servants, or about 1.5 percent of the population. One-quarter of them were in local governments. The remaining three-quarters comprised a special category of top-ranking officials (equivalent to vice-minister and above); a general civil service category of nine grades, the top five of which have presidential appointments; a separate category for administration and faculty of the public schools at all levels; and a career Foreign Service. Police personnel (64,100, not counting 60,000 or more paramilitary riot police) and those of the Agency for National Security Planning were also included; but not employees of public corporations.[10] Entry was by competitive examination. Graduates of Seoul National University had a disproportionate share of higher positions. The Ministry of Government Administration managed recruitment, training, and promotion.

Basic legislation purports to insulate civil servants from political activity or pressure, and provides that they may not be discharged without cause. The Constitution denies civil servants the right of collective bargaining. Nonetheless, the bureaucracy as a whole is a potent political force, both for its own interests and because of its key role in carrying on the business of government. Its members are proud of their status, and still enjoy something of the public awe of officialdom which characterized the Choson Dynasty. Despite constitutional and legal provisions, the civil service acts in accordance with long tradition to support the ruler and regime in power, in subtle and sometimes in blatant ways.

In late 1987 it was uncertain what policies the next south Korean administration would follow toward the bureaucracy and what impact its policies would have on bureaucratic attitudes and effectiveness. In 1960, the new administration launched a wide purge of governnment officials, with adverse results. The main opposition presidential candidates in 1987 pledged not to launch a purge, but any leader upon taking office is under great pressure to settle old scores and reward his followers.

Politicians and Political Parties

In south Korea, the idea of using private organizations as interest groups to put pressure on the government is still very new, and the taint of factionalism still clouds the public perception of political parties and politicians. The role of parties in the political process is therefore imperfectly understood, even by party leaders, and leaders and parties alike tend to be viewed by both the elite and the citizenry as extraneous, untrustworthy, or both.

Nevertheless, the Constitution recognizes the role of political parties in elections and legislative activity, and the party role in the proceedings of the National Assembly has been well established since the early 1950s. Election to the Assembly legitimizes politicians to some extent as part of government. They can be viewed, in traditional terms, as a latter-day equivalent of the Choson Dynasty Censorate, criticizing and investigating government performance and sanctioning executive proposals by enacting them into law. Moreover, opposition parties have given voice to popular dissatisfaction, although their voice has often gone unheeded.

Aside from a few short periods in post-liberation history, the legislative branch of government has not been very influential. It has generally been a forum for the expression of members' opinions, which may or may not reflect those of their constituents, although Assembly members do play to their districts for re-election in ways similar to their counterparts elsewhere. The Assembly also provides rewards for politicians, even those of the opposition, through salaries and privileges. Thus the Assembly has been a significant stimulus to the creation and functioning of political parties as a supplementary means of expressing and aggregating public demands. Yet twice in the Republic's history, in 1961 and in 1980, all political parties were dissolved and their leading figures arrested or proscribed from political activity without greatly disturbing the political process. Party activity resumed in early 1981, and the most recent proscriptions were lifted gradually thereafter (the remainder in early 1985).[11]

The first south Korean political parties formed under the U.S. occupation, with American encouragement (the conservative Han'guk Democratic party was organized even before the U.S. troops arrived in August 1945). There were from 40 to over 200 of them, depending on definition, by mid-1947. By the mid-1950s, two major conservative parties were vying for power, while half a dozen smaller parties led a precarious existence—the more liberal or "progressive" among them often hounded by police. Since that time, each administration has sought to build a mass party in its support, and at the same time to encourage factionalism and division among opposition ranks.[12]

The National Assembly Law, and laws regulating political parties, have been written since 1963 in such a way as to discourage small parties and independent representatives in the Assembly. There have usually been one or two principal opposition parties and several smaller ones, the latter typically motivated by support of a single leader or faction. The long-range trend is toward fewer, stronger, and better organized parties. In accordance with law, even the opposition gets a modicum of public financial support, and all parties look to donations from members and from businesses, especially at election time.

As a result of the parliamentary elections of February 1985 and subsequent adjustments, the government's Democratic Justice party (DJP)—headed by the President of the Republic—held 147 of 276 seats in the Assembly in mid-1987 (although it had only a little more than a third of the 1985 popular vote). The DJP was in the process of organizing a mass base, with government support. President Chun was concurrently president of the DJP until May 1987. At that time Roh Tae Woo, a close associate of the President who had been chairman of the party since its leadership reorganization of 1986, succeeded Chun as party president. As already noted, the DJP held a national convention in June, at which Roh was named its presidential candidate in circumstances making it clear that he was President Chun's choice.

The opposition New Korea Democratic party (NKDP) emerged from the previous opposition when its principal figures, Kim Dae Jung (just returned from two years of exile in the United States) and Kim Young Sam, split off from the party only weeks before the Assembly election in 1985. The NKDP captured over a quarter of the popular vote and for a time had 101 legislative seats; but it had five publicly identified factions within it, of which two—those of Kim Dae Jung (then under suspended sentence for sedition, therefore not a party member) and Kim Young Sam were the "mainstream," and the others "non-mainstream." (The two Kims were also co-chairmen of a Council for the Promotion of Democracy, organized in 1984 as a device to give the two leaders a credible forum for their "democratization" campaign.) The party was reduced to minor status in April, 1987, when most of its Assembly adherents—led by the two Kims—bolted to form the Reunification Democratic party, with 68 seats to the NKDP's 20.[13] The new grouping split again when the two Kims could not agree on which of them would be the presidential candidate. By November 1987, each of the two Kims, now declared registered candidates, headed his own opposition party: the Peace and Democracy party of Kim Dae Jung and the remainder of the Reunification Democratic party, headed by Kim Young Sam.

Among minor parties, a Korea Nationalist party (KNP) included members of the former government party of the Park administration; it held 21 seats until the fall of 1987, when it became the base for a wider grouping to support the presidential candidacy of Kim Jong Pil, a principal figure of the former Park administration, under the name New Democratic Republican party. Former major opposition parties were reduced to insignificant minor status, along with a handful of other minor parties.

The frequent shifting of opposition groups since 1985 is not a new thing. Korean political parties, including pro-government parties, have all been plagued by internal factionalism throughout their existence—a function of their hazy role and the contending individual ambitions of leaders. Factionalism complicates the formulation of party positions and the choice of official candidates in elections.

Internal Security Agencies

The national police, the Agency for National Security Planning (ANSP), and the Defense Security Command (DSC) are the principal internal security agencies of the Republic. Under the administration of President Chun, the national police appear to be the lead agency in internal security. The ANSP was formerly called the Korean Central Intelligence Agency (KCIA); its pervasive presence and harsh methods during the Park administration gained it such opprobrium that it was renamed and its activities oriented principally toward the external threat. The DSC is responsible principally for security within the armed services, but since all south Korea is the military forces' rear area, DSC concerns include civilian subversive activities as well.

Internal security responsibilities include maintenance of public order (ranging from dealing with riots to traffic control) and protection against internal or external subversion. Many investigations in pursuit of these objectives have been criticized as intrusive, oppressive, and coercive. Repeated allegations of arrests without warrant, search and seizure, prolonged detention without trial, and torture have been voiced by both domestic and foreign observers. Government officials have repeatedly asserted that such acts are illegal and unauthorized; a few police officers have been disciplined, tried, and sentenced for them. There may have been a diminution in their frequency over the years, but their continued existence is well documented.[14] It must be recognized, of course, that south Korea is still in a state of suspended hostilities with north Korea, and that the north has constantly sought to subvert the Republic by any means, including sabotage and assassination. Internal security is therefore a vital function of government, although its means are sometimes open to question.

The security agencies also serve as a source of information about public attitudes that—despite obvious shortcomings—has been utilized by every Korean administration, or ignored at its peril. This role as informal articulator of public demands is particularly important because the mass media, speech, and assembly are controlled in varying degree despite constitutional guarantees, and because among a volatile people unaccustomed to democratic process, those who shout the loudest may not be representative, or may be creating the very opinion they claim to represent. Even in Japanese times, the reports of the military police (*kempeitai*) seem to have provided some frank and objective information about public opinion. More recently, in late 1979, President Park was being counseled by his hard-line advisers to apply force against mounting labor and student demonstrations. The Korean CIA Director, Kim Chae-kyu—a trusted associate of the President—was convinced, on the basis of his information, that applying further coercive measures to control dissent would not work. Unable to persuade the President, and thus caught in a no-win situation, the frustrated Director shot the President at the dinner table.

Business Groups

The business community as a political force is very new, reflecting the economic development of Korea and the emergence of the business sector as an important and prestigious aspect of national life. The greatest political clout is in the hands of chief executives of a dozen or so large general trading companies known as *chaebol*. Except that they do not control their own banks, the *chaebol* are comparable to the *zaibatsu* of pre–World War II Japan (the same Chinese characters represent both terms), with vertically and horizontally integrated operations. Most of them are still controlled by the founders or their sons or relatives, although they have been under government pressure to "go public" through the sale of stock. The heads of the firms are thus men of great wealth and economic power. A list of the larger firms appears in Chapter 6 (Table 6.3).

In addition to the large individual firms, the business sector speaks to government (and vice versa) through such organizations as the Korea Chamber of Commerce and Industry, the Federation of Korean Industries, the Korea Federation of Small Business, the Korea Traders' Association, and over a hundred associations of firms in various manufacturing and trading lines. There are also informal lines of communication based on shared college, military, regional, or other ties.

Intellectuals

The high status of educated persons in Korea derives from the Confucian tradition of the scholar-official. The prestige of the doctorate, particularly in the humanities, is very high, especially if it comes from a prestigious university in Korea or abroad. College and university faculty and, to a much lesser degree, teachers below college level enjoy high status, as do authors and journalists. There is some interchange of talent between government and the academic world. The poet and social critic, Kim Chi-ha, evoked such a public reaction with his caustic Aesopian writings about the government that he was imprisoned for several years.

FIGURE 4.3 Antigovernment demonstrators in Inch'on, May 1986, charging into a police cordon with a truck they seized from police and set on fire (photo used by permission of AP/Wide World Photos)

To some degree, persons in these categories, and even college graduates generally, form a vaguely identified class of intellectuals whose views carry special weight with the public—particularly in the relatively few cases where there is an intellectual consensus, as there was in 1960. The intellectuals can, to a certain extent, articulate popular demands and grievances to the political system because of their prestige. They can also create or amplify popular demands, which is the basis for governmental concern about them.

There are some intellectual organizations, as already noted, including an association for the defense of human rights. However, there is no specific intellectual consensus or plan of action, unless it be a general desire for more freedom of speech and behavior, more opportunities for political leadership and economic benefit, more democracy in the national political process, and more attention to human rights. Some intellectuals, particularly the younger generation, have been attracted by socialism, Marxism, and Latin American dependency theory. They favor more public ownership, worker participation, and equitable distribution of wealth. A few of them may be responsive to north Korean propaganda.

Intellectuals, together with students and church groups, were in the vanguard of growing discontent at the repressive policies of the Chun administration and the slow pace of political liberalization (Fig. 4.3). The events of early 1987 led to the emergence of an umbrella organization, the National Coalition for a Democratic Constitution, which gave voice and structure to popular opposition outside the established opposition parties.

Press and Mass Media

Notwithstanding government control over editorial policy and content, the print media are politically important. Respect for the written word and a high literacy rate make Koreans enthusiastic readers of newspapers, magazines, and books. There are 23 daily newspapers, published in Seoul and provincial cities. The independent *Chosun Ilbo* and conservative opposition *Dong A Ilbo*, both published in Seoul, are the most influential; they have a national circulation of millions. *Seoul Shinmoon* speaks for the government, as do several other smaller papers.

Newspapers and other publications are the major vehicle for expression of intellectual views, as well as for news reporting. Traditionally, the Korean press has been as critical of government as it dared to be, beginning with *The Independent*, started by Philip Jaisohn and other young reformist leaders of the Independence Club in 1897 (see Chapter 2). However, censorship and government control are equally traditional. The degree of freedom permitted the print media has varied from the tight controls of the Japanese colonial regime to virtually complete liberty under the short-lived Second Republic in 1960–1961. During some years of Park Chung Hee's presidency, newspapers had to submit to pre-publication censorship, sometimes by officials placed in editorial offices for the purpose. Beginning in the Japanese period, editors have developed a talent for conveying messages between their lines and testing the limits of government tolerance.

Since 1980, under the Fifth Republic, there has been gradual but considerable relaxation of control over the press; but full press freedom, which has become a major public demand, has not been realized. By 1986, the activities and statements of opposition leaders were being quite fully reported, in a way that would have been unthinkable in the late 1970s. Yet in mid-1986 the security authorities started cracking down on publications and statements that appeared supportive of north Korean positions or critical of "liberal democracy." In the second half of 1987, controls were again relaxed, and the Press Law was liberalized by amendment.

Radio, and in recent years television, reach virtually every citizen in Korea. With few exceptions, however, they are government owned or closely controlled. Their emphasis, in news and commentary, on the doings of the President and senior officials and the official propaganda line have led to public distrust. In late 1985, church and student groups launched a campaign for a public boycott of "listening fees" (a tax on use of television sets) for the Korea Broadcasting Corporation's television programs. The campaign was picked up by the opposition New Korea Democratic party. To the government's credit, it reacted to the campaign by appointing a commission to study the problem, rather than by launching a crackdown, and promised to reduce advertising volume (a major focus of complaint) after the 1988 Olympics. The 1987 presidential election campaign was the first in south Korea in which television played a major role; but opposition candidates accused the government-owned broadcasting companies of slanting coverage to favor the pro-government candidate—a charge with which Western journalists' observations agreed.

Students

Students have already been discussed in connection with education, in Chapter 3. As a political factor, students in Korea are important in five ways: They have the social status of apprentice intellectuals, and the communication skills derived from their education; they have a tradition as a leading force in nationalist movements since 1919; they have the simplistic dedication and exuberance (particularly in the springtime) of youth and a sense of generation gap magnified by the rapidity of social change; they have organization and esprit de corps; and there are a lot of them. They are a key factor in the nation's future, and they know it—which adds to their frustration when they cannot find jobs in times of recession.

Students by themselves are generally a manageable political problem, so long as actions to control them do not escalate into violence and create martyrs. Their causes do not always represent broad public issues (for example, their excitement over campus problems); hence they do not necessarily enjoy public sympathy or support. If, however, they articulate genuine grievances and combine with other political groups, sharing leadership abilities and organization and communication skills, their impact can be politically destabilizing. Their importance in 1960 was that they gave voice to broad popular discontent. At times, opposition political leaders have used students for their own cause, as occurred in the anti-Japanese treaty riots of 1964 and 1965.[15]

In recent years, when labor demands for better wages have been curtailed because of the need for competitiveness in world markets, there has been apprehension over student participation or leadership in labor demonstrations. The extremist and extra-legal *minmint'u* student group, which according to government sources had 46,000 members on twenty-six university campuses in May 1986, was apparently seeking linkages with labor and other groups in its campaign for "mass democracy" and anti-imperialism, but without great success—owing in part to arrests of its leaders and suppression of its activity.

Churches

Of the three largest groups of religious adherents in south Korea—
Buddhist, Christian, and Confucian[16]—only the Christians have the high
degree of organization among the laity that gives them significant capability
for political influence. Moreover, because of the leading Christian role in the
modernization of Korea, the role of the churches as the major channel of
expression and upward mobility during the Japanese regime, the association
of Christianity with the nationalist movement, and the international support
traditionally given to the Christians, the incentive for political activism among
church members is greater than for their fellow-communicants in the United
States or Europe.

Accordingly, a Christian minority, including a few foreign missionaries,
has been in the forefront of movements for improving labor conditions,
alleviating poverty and injustice, and promoting human rights. In so doing,
some activists have gotten themselves in serious trouble with the authorities.
The extreme was probably reached in 1981, when a Catholic priest sheltered
a young man who torched the American Cultural Center in Pusan, the
Republic's second city. The young man did so in protest against what he
perceived as the failure of the United States to support democracy and
human rights in Korea against government oppression. However, it would
appear that only a small minority of the nine million Christians support
political action, and a far smaller minority condone arson or violence.
Moreover, Christians fill a proportion of government and business leadership
positions that is more than commensurate with their share of the population
as a whole. Many of the Christian clergy, as intellectuals, have prestige
beyond their own communion. Stephen Cardinal Kim, head of the Korean
Catholic church, is a leading example.

Labor

The Korean labor force of 15 million is far from completely organized.
It is officially represented by the national Korean Federation of Trade Unions
(KFTU), with a nominal membership of about two million in 1985. The
KFTU had been closely controlled by the government until the mid-1987
change in the political climate; it has not been in the vanguard of the effort
for improved benefits.In recent years the government has sought to decen-
tralize to the plant level such collective bargaining as law and regulation
permit. Nationwide industrial unions exist in name, but they cannot organize
collective action.Unions in individual plants are legally able to act on behalf
of workers, including collective action, but their activities were closely
restricted in practice until mid-1987.

Strikes were, for practical purposes, illegal until late 1987. There were
nevertheless some significant work stoppages and sit-ins, even before the

outburst of strikes in August 1987, including two in 1985 against one of Korea's largest conglomerates. Criminal action was taken against the ringleaders of both strikes. By the standards of Western industrialized nations, labor's rights and benefits have been narrowly circumscribed, and wages and working conditions are poor, especially in smaller enterprises. Labor discontent is a constant worrisome contingency, especially in times of economic adversity.

On the whole, Korean workers have acquiesced in the government's policy to hold wage and benefit increases within productivity limits. The ability to compete in world markets is the key to continued economic growth and therefore to job availability. Economic growth of at least 6 percent a year is required to absorb new members of the labor force. Toward the end of the Park regime, however, rapid inflation necessitated large wage increases to avoid labor unrest. This and other factors contributed to the recession of 1979-80, and the concurrent political instability—in which labor unrest was a significant factor.

Following the changes of government policy in mid-1987, pent-up grievances of labor regarding wages and working conditions exploded into over 3,000 work stoppages and sit-ins, accompanied by violence and police counteraction in some cases, and government mediation and peaceful settlement in others. The largest involved the giant Hyundai shipbuilding plant in southeastern south Korea, where 20,000 workers went on strike. The government allowed more latitude to peaceful union activity, and changes in the restrictive labor laws were made in late 1987. (See also the discussion of labor in Chapter 6.)

Farmers and Fishers

Industrialization in Korea has proceeded so fast that the farm to non-farm population ratio has reversed since 1950; now less than a third of the south Korean people are primarily agricultural, and less than 10 percent of that number are engaged in fishing. Although recent surveys have demonstrated that farmers, as much as their urban counterparts, have acquired modern social attitudes, their political behavior continues to be more traditional than that of people in the cities. Voting turnout is greater in rural than in urban areas. Rural voters appear more responsive to government pressure and simple electoral appeals, including entertainment and gifts. They also tend to support the administration in power.

During the Rhee administration, rural support was taken for granted; but in more recent years there have been signs of erosion. Subsequent Korean governments have therefore sought to preserve good relations with the rural voters. The New Community Movement, launched in 1971 (when there seemed to be some erosion of rural support), and other steps to improve rural life and income—especially high agricultural price support levels—are prime examples. In recent years, budgetary pressures have lessened price supports, and agricultural household debt has risen to a level approaching a year's income, raising questions about future rural attitudes.

National farmers' associations have never been effective in Korea, although the government or ruling political party has sought to organize them. The National Agricultural Cooperative Federation is the principal farm organization, apart from the New Community Movement. It is a quasi-governmental association that provides farm credit, supply, and marketing facilities and speaks more for the administration than for the farmers themselves. At the local level, various types of cooperatives and New Community Movement units, as well as the local governments, respond to the farmers' interests, while at the same time keeping these interests under control. In recent years, both Catholic and Protestant activists have organized regional farmers' associations, which have called for—and demonstrated in support of—better treatment for the rural sector.

Constitution and Formal Government Structure

The original Constitution of the Republic of Korea was adopted by a constituent assembly elected under UN observation in 1948. It has been amended nine times: in 1952, 1954, 1960 (twice), 1963, 1969, 1972, 1980, and 1987. Four of the amendments—1960, 1963, 1972, and 1980—constituted essentially new constitutions; the corresponding governments are often referred to as the First, Second, Third, Fourth, and Fifth (present) Republics. The principal changes made by the 1987 amendment are to restore popular election of the President and to strengthen guarantees of individual rights; in other respects, the basic structure of government remains essentially the same. It remains to be seen whether the new amendment of the Constitution will result in major reforms in the political system.

The 1987 amendment was overwhelmingly approved by popular referendum in October 1987, on the basis of a draft developed by a bipartisan legislative committee and approved by the National Assembly. As amended, the Constitution now consists of a preamble, ten chapters with 130 articles, and six supplementary articles covering the transition from the previous regime. The Constitution defines the formal, outward structure of government—within and around which the actual political process goes on. Political power realities and interrelationships do not always correspond to those specified in the Constitution. Nevertheless, the requirements of the Constitution have usually been carefully met. The main exceptions, aside from disregard of human rights provisions, were the failure to implement constitutional requirements for an upper legislative house, from 1952 to 1960, and failure from 1959 to 1960 and after 1980 to provide for meaningful autonomy of local government. The amended Constitution is briefly summarized below.[17]

Rights and Duties of Citizens

Chapter II of the Constitution guarantees basic rights and freedoms: equality; non-discrimination; due process of law (including the right to court review of arrest or detention); freedom of movement, residence, and occupation; privacy of person, correspondence, and domicile; freedom of religion, speech, press, and petition; the rights to property ownership, education, employment, voting, and holding public office; the right to work; and the right of labor association and collective action (unqualified except for employees of government and defense industries, in constrast to the 1980 version). Most of these rights and freedoms are unconditional; they are, however, qualified by Article 37(2), which states that they "may be restricted by law only when necessary for national security, the maintenance of law and order or for public welfare. Even when such restriction is imposed, no essential aspect of the freedom or right shall be violated." (The 1987 language of this article is identical with that of 1980.)

Some of the guarantees of rights are further-reaching than those of the U.S. Constitution—such as free compulsory education, entitlement to "a healthy and pleasant environment" and "a life worthy of human beings," protection of women and the young and old, and state protection of the health of all citizens. In addition to rights, Chapter II also specifies the duty of citizens to work, pay taxes, and support national defense.

President and Executive Branch

An interesting symbolic change in the 1987 constitutional amendment was to place the chapter on the legislature (Chapter III) before that on the Executive (Chapter IV), a reversal in the order of all previous versions, and a reflection of the order in the U.S. Constitution. On the hypothesis that the executive will remain the preeminent branch, I deal with it first.

Chapter IV provides that the President is head of state, head of the executive branch, and commander-in-chief of the armed forces. The President chairs the State Council; appoints the Prime Minister, subject to National Assembly confirmation; appoints State Council members (in practice, mostly heads of executive agencies) on the Prime Minister's recommendation; and appoints other public officials. The President issues decrees to implement the laws; may refer important matters to national referendum; may grant amnesty, commutation of sentences, and restoration of rights; and may award decorations and other honors.

In time of crisis, and subject to National Assembly concurrence, the President may "take . . . the minimum necessary financial and economic actions or issue orders having the effect of law, only when it is required to take urgent measures for the maintenance of national security or public peace and order, and there is no time to await the convocation of the National Assembly" (Article 76[1]). A similar provision deals with "major hostilities affecting national security" (Article 76[2]). In time of "war, armed conflict or similar national emergency" the President may declare martial law of two types, one more sweeping than the other, but must lift it if a majority of the Assembly so requests. The President may attend or address the National Assembly. Presidential power to dissolve the Assembly was deleted by the 1987 amendment.

The President is to be elected for a single five-year term by "universal, equal, direct and secret ballot by the people" (Article 67[1]) and must receive no less than one-third of the votes. To be elected President, a person must have reached the age of forty years and be eligible for election to the National Assembly. The previous requirement of residence within the country for five years was deleted. If the office becomes vacant, a successor must be elected within sixty days; in the interim, the Prime Minister (or other member of the State Council, as provided by law) acts as President. A President may not be re-elected; but "matters pertaining to the status and courteous treatment of former Presidents shall be determined by law."

The 1972 and 1980 constitutions provided for election of the President by an electoral college; this provision was the principal focus of opposition criticism. Although there are valid objective arguments for it, the Korean public viewed it as a device to influence voting to favor the government, since there were a relatively small number of electors (2,500 under the 1972 Constitution; more than 5,000 under the 1980 Constitution) and they cast their votes in public view. Electors were chosen by direct popular vote in districts roughly corresponding to townships (*up* and *myon*). Although electors after 1980 could be political party members and publicly state their preferred candidate, local officials and notables had a major say in choosing them.

The Prime Minister, who must be a civilian, "shall assist the President and shall direct the Executive Ministries under order of the President." The Prime Minister is vice president of the State Council, a body consisting of from fifteen to thirty members that "shall deliberate on important policies that fall within the power of the Executive." (Article 89 lists sixteen specific categories that must be referred to the State Council.) Members of the Council "assist the President in the conduct of State affairs," and the heads of Executive Ministries are appointed from among State Council members. Ministries are established by law, and not listed in the Constitution.

The other appointive Executive Branch agencies specified in the Constitution are as follows:

- an Advisory Council of Elder Statesmen, whose chairperson is the immediate past President, to "advise the President on important affairs of State";
- a National Security Council, similar to the U.S. body of the same name, to advise the President on national security policies "prior to their deliberation by the State Council";
- an Advisory Council on Democratic and Peaceful Unification, to support the President in his constitutional mandate to "pursue sincerely the peaceful unification of the homeland";
- a National Economic and Advisory Council "to advise the President on the formulation of important policies for developing the national economy";
- a Board of Audit and Inspection, composed of five to eleven members, the chairman of which must have National Assembly concurrence for his appointment and serves no more than two four-year terms. The Board's functions are roughly comparable to those of the U.S. General Accounting Office, although it is an executive, not legislative, agency.

Legislative Branch

Chapter III of the Constitution establishes a one-chamber National Assembly that must have more than 200 members (in 1987, under the same provision of the 1980 Constitution, there were 276). Members are elected for four-year terms by "universal, direct and secret ballot by the citizens." "Constituencies of members, proportional representation and other matters" are to be prescribed by law.

This provision leaves major questions unsolved, such as the size of constituencies, the number of members representing each (there have been two per district since 1973), the number of votes to be cast by each voter, and the basis for determining winners (simple plurality or proportional representation). Whether some proportion of Assembly members should continue to be drawn from national party slates, as at present, must also be determined. Since Article 3 of the Supplementary Provisions requires election of the Assembly within sixty days after entry into force of the new Constitution in February 1988 it seemed probable in late 1987 that difficult debate was in prospect before a new Assembly election law could be passed and enforced.

The Assembly convenes once a year in regular session for not over one hundred days but may be convened by the President or by one-fourth of its members for special sessions of not over thirty days each. Bills may be introduced either by the Executive or by Assembly members. A majority of the membership constitutes a quorum, and majority vote of members

6 ECONOMICS

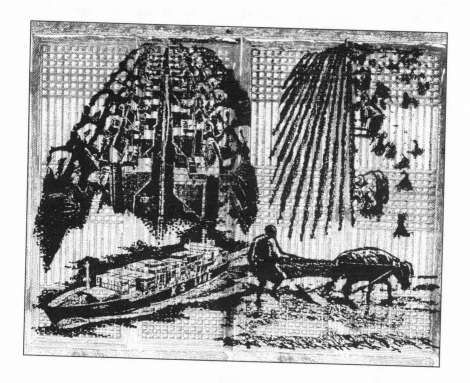

Introduction

"Miracle on the Han" is an apt, if overworked, description of south Korea's amazingly rapid and successful transition from a traditional agrarian subsistence economy to a primarily industrialized one. This transition has involved social and political as well as purely economic change. In the old Confucian tradition, both industry and commerce were looked down upon, whereas agriculture (next to learning and government) was viewed as the most worthy human pursuit. It is only in the last twenty years or so that business has begun to rank with other callings as a respectable life work.

Another significant shift in attitude concerns belief in the possibility of future security and betterment. It has already been mentioned that the Korean cultural tradition assumes an essentially static human condition, in which there may be good times and bad times, but a marginal existence is the lot of most people. More than a century of economic adversity,

Local Government

Under Chapter VIII, local governments "shall deal with . . . welfare of local residents, manage properties and may enact provisions relating to local autonomy, within the limits of laws and regulations." The Constitution specifies that local governments shall have councils, organized and elected according to law, and provides for election of heads of local government bodies. Local councils were also provided for in the 1980 Constitution, but a supplementary provision (deleted in 1987) stated that they were to be "established on a phased basis taking into account the degree of financial self-reliance attained by local governments." Legislation to establish local councils has been under discussion since 1982, but no specific action has been taken on it. Both government and opposition are pledged to establish local autonomy in 1988.

Economic Provisions

Chapter IX provides a mixture of provisions accepting respect for "freedom and creative ideas of the individual in economic affairs," coupled with State regulation "in order to maintain the balanced growth and stability of the national economy to insure proper distribution of income, to prevent the domination of the market and the abuse of economic power and to democratize the economy through harmony among the economic agents." The clauses concerning state regulation have been somewhat changed from the 1980 version, clearly reflecting the populist themes of Kim Dae Jung.

Article 127 states, "Private enterprise shall not be nationalized or transferred to ownership by a local government, nor shall their management be controlled or administered by the State, except in cases determined by law to meet urgent necessities of national defense or the national economy." Natural resources may be licensed for exploitation "for a period of time"—implying State ownership of them. "Land and natural resources shall be protected by the State." The State is required to plan for appropriate utilization of natural resources.

According to Articles 121 to 127, the state is required to protect and foster agriculture, fisheries, and small and medium enterprises; "guarantee the consumer protection movement"; foster regional economies "to ensure the balanced development of all regions"; foster foreign trade, with the power to regulate and coordinate it; and "strive to develop the national economy by developing science and technology, information and human resources and encouraging innovation." Tenant farming is prohibited, and "the State shall endeavor to realize the land-to-the-tiller principle," but leasing and management are recognized for efficient utilization of farmland.

Amendment

According to Chapter X, amendments to the Constitution may be proposed either by the President or by a majority of members of the National Assembly. They must be put before the public for at least twenty days, adopted by two-thirds or more of the total Assembly membership within sixty days, and approved in a national referendum not later than thirty days after Assembly action by majority vote of more than half the eligible voters. No amendment may change the term or eligibility for re-election of the President who is in office when it is proposed.

Basic Laws

Several basic laws were enacted by an appointive interim legislature in late 1980 to shape the government of the Fifth Republic. Principal among them were laws on the election of the National Assembly and President, the organization of the executive and judicial branches, labor organization and policies, and regulation of the media. Opposition members of the National Assembly focused critical attention on these laws, particularly regarding elections, labor, and the press. Up to mid-1987 only minor changes had been made, but in the new political climate the Assembly thereafter liberalized the labor and press laws and passed a new presidential election law, among other changes. As already noted, major matters remained to be acted upon, including the Assembly election law and the implementation of elective local government organizations.

Performance of the Political System

Since 1945, the South Korean political system has virtually completed the destruction of the old concentration of wealth and power in the hands of the *yangban* aristocracy—a process that had begun under the Japanese. The Korean War accelerated the process through massive population movement, physical destruction, and inflation. Effective land reform, begun by the U.S. military government and completed by 1952, virtually eliminated landlordism. Growing emphasis on merit and competence in government and industry has greatly reduced family influence and favoritism in filling government positions, and increased access to education has improved career opportunity for the average citizen.

Studies show, however, that elite families (now including a new plutocracy) still have an advantage in access to higher levels of Korean society, in and out of government, because of their education and connections.[18] In business enterprises and other social institutions, members of the founders' families often hold senior positions.

smuggling) included a trading station that the Japanese were permitted to maintain near the southeast port city of Pusan and some private trade with China. There were wealthy merchants and artisans, but they did not develop a financial or cultural network such as existed among their counterparts in Japan or China; rather, they tended to enter the aristocracy—often by purchasing rank.

In accordance with Confucian teachings, the *yangban* disdained commercial activity ; but they nonetheless amassed wealth from the perquisites of office and the product of their estates. From the middle of the dynasty, despite efforts at reform, the gap between wealth and poverty widened, and state revenues shrank. Wealthy landlords and officials, however, did not often invest in manufacture or commerce, as did their Japanese counterparts. Although one north Korean scholar has maintained that Korean private investment in enterprise such as mining and iron manufacturing activity began as early as the eighteenth century,[1] it did not appear on a significant scale until after the Western penetration had begun, toward the end of the nineteenth century, and did not reach major proportions until the period of Japanese control, beginning in 1905.

The Economy Under the Japanese

It was chiefly the Japanese who brought capitalist economic patterns of industrialization and trade to Korea. They treated Korea as an extension of the Japanese economy, principally to serve Japanese interests. A major example was the Japanese export of the Korean rice crop to Japan to fill the shortfall in Japanese rice production. Cheaper grains were imported to meet Korean food requirements. Industries were established in accordance with imperial, not Korean, needs.

The result of these Japanese policies was a typical colonial dual economy, in which over a half million Japanese residents managed the modern industrial sector and enjoyed its fruits, while most Koreans—except the urban labor force—remained in the traditional agrarian economy. In this situation, it was easy for Korean nationalists, economically naive as they were, to castigate capitalism along with the Japanese occupation itself. Marxist ideas spread. It was largely the minority of Koreans who kept their property and wealth under the Japanese that opposed socialist principles of public ownership and land redistribution.

The forty-year Japanese occupation brought some benefits to Korea. The Japanese built a substantial economic infrastructure of roads, railroads, and public works; they expanded the education of the Korean people at elementary-school level (from an enrollment of 20,000 in 1919 to 900,000 in 1937); they introduced factory discipline to an industrial labor force totalling nearly 200,000 by 1938 and more during the war years (chiefly in north Korea), not counting those among the 2 million Koreans in Japan who worked in industrial plants.[2]

Despite these seeming signs of progress, however, the welfare of the general public was not improved. Grain consumption per capita by Koreans, according to Japanese statistics, diminished from 2.032 *koku* in 1915–19 to 1.668 *koku* in 1930–33 (1 *koku*, called *sok* in Korean, is equal to about 35 liters or 5 U.S. bushels).[3] Rural starvation in the spring grew worse. Gross value of production in Korea for 1938 was 126 yen per capita, compared with 358 for Japan (the yen was then worth about 50 U.S. cents.)

Although net commodity product in Korea grew at a rate of 2 percent per capita over the three decades before World War II,[4] this growth probably did not do most Koreans much good—no more than they would have gained from even an inefficient native rule. Notwithstanding Japanese efforts at educating the Koreans, 87 percent of the Korean population had less than six years of education in 1945. Perhaps the greatest contribution of the Japanese was to engender a Korean determination to equal or outdo them.

During the World War II years, the Japanese drew heavily on Korean resources (as, of course, they did on their own). Factories were diverted to military production; forested hillsides were stripped for timber and fuel; industrial plant depreciated; metals, including family heirlooms of brass, were ruthlessly collected and melted down to make ammunition. In their final weeks, when surrender appeared certain, the Japanese gave their workers a year's salary in advance and paid savings deposits and insurance policies in full, flooding the currency market and creating galloping inflation. The departure of all the hated Japanese expatriates at the end of the war, including the managerial elite, was politically necessary. But the Koreans were left without managers, markets, or (in south Korea) raw materials for a rundown industrial plant that was not designed to serve Korean needs.

The Korean Economy, 1945–1960

Division of Korea between U.S. and Soviet occupying forces in 1945 added still further to Korean economic problems. Most of the natural resources, heavy industry (including fertilizer production), and electric power generation were concentrated in the north; the country's food-basket and center of textile and other light industry were in the south. Although trade between the two zones was not totally suspended until the Korean War, it was severely impeded. North Korea cut the supply of electricity in May 1948, depriving the south of over half of its already inadequate power. In south Korea, initial U.S. policies made the situation even worse. The U.S. occupiers, prepared only with complete faith in free private enterprise and sublime ignorance, removed wartime economic controls. Hoarding, speculation, food shortages, and galloping inflation resulted.[5]

the shame and humiliation of the Japanese period. This effort is in contrast to attempts during the Rhee regime to motivate the people through the negative appeal of anti-Japanism and anti-communism (although anti-communism continues as a major theme). The new spirit, coupled with the evident economic success of the nation, has resulted in a material change in public attitude. The Korean armed forces and their impressive displays are a source of national pride, as well as concern. Such policies as sponsorship of the 1988 Summer Olympic Games, aside from their economic and diplomatic payoff, are also important as symbols for the Korean people of their heightened status in the international community.

One of the primary bases for Korea's rapid economic development since the mid-1960s has been greatly improved tax collection and saving, permitting increased capital investment. Similarly, the military draft has been effectively implemented since the early 1960s. The New Community Movement, while primarily an instrument to mobilize and motivate the people, increased the popular contribution to the general welfare, although there are indications that it has passed the peak of its accomplishment. Perhaps the most evident accomplishment, aside from the general economic progress, is reforestation. Twenty-five years ago the countryside was so completely brown, denuded, and eroded from overcropping that many people feared it could never be restored. Today it is green and attractive.

A major unsatisfied demand of all Korean people in both north and south is the reunification of the country. Reunification emerged as a major issue in the south Korean presidential election campaign of 1987. This problem remains a hostage of ideological conflict and great-power rivalry; efforts to solve it have been mostly posturing. Thus far, however, most Koreans themselves recognize the difficulty of the problem and are content to wait as long as their rulers display a reasonable amount of intelligent attention to it.

The ultimate test of political performance is the maintenance of political equilibrium. Thus far, the south Korean political system has been very effective in maintaining a relatively stable political process. Even the major political crises of 1952, 1960-1961, and 1979-80, involved violence on a scale that was minor indeed in comparison with the general experience of Third World countries. In the face of constant attempts from north Korea to weaken and subvert the system, south Korea has managed the demands upon it either by responding to them (albeit often partially or belatedly) or by controlling or suppressing them through various combinations of persuasion and coercion, with remarkably little large-scale internal violence or rebellion. Government operation, ever since 1945, has had much more continuity and evolutionary improvement than upheaval. This record provides a basis for hope that equilibrium will also be maintained in the years ahead.

The legitimacy of the UN-sponsored Republic and its respected nationalist leader, Syngman Rhee, were the primary basis of south Korea's stability in the first fifteen years after liberation. Strong U.S. security and economic support was also an important factor. Since 1961, no south Korean government has had the same degree of legitimacy. Economic progress and firm control have been the main forces for stability, with U.S. support a continuing but diminishing factor. For the future, the prospects for stability—that is, effective government performance that will avoid violence, bloodshed, repression, and revolt—are somewhat less certain, but still quite good.

An increasingly sophisticated Korean public will be less likely in coming years to accept government orders and preaching instead of performance in meeting popular demands. The demands are becoming more political and social, and less centered on basic livelihood items. Economic progress cannot be maintained indefinitely at the high rate of the 1970s; threfore, there is less to trickle down, with consequent increase in demands for equity. Thus government efficacy cannot so easily substitute for government legitimacy. Other bases must be found for popular support of government. Yet for greater political freedom and government responsiveness, a new national consensus will have to develop, and it may not develop so fast as the demands increase.

However, there is good reason to believe that the leadership groups of the Republic recognize these facts and the dangers of failure to take account of them. Korean elites have shown themselves to have flexibility and awareness along with their stubbornness and traditional political values. Korean political process has changed considerably since 1945 and will continue to change. If a peaceful transfer of power is realized in 1988 in a way that is accepted by the people, it will be an important milestone in Korean political development.

There is no reason why south Korea cannot achieve the same dramatic successes in the political arena—although at a slower rate—that it has already demonstrated in the military and economic areas. Given a reasonably stable international and regional environment, the prospects for continued political stability and orderly evolution seem good.

Notes

1. This story was related to me by a reliable and knowledgeable Korean political observer, who was personally acquainted with the people involved.

2. "Gist of President Chun Doo Hwan's Special Statement on Constitutional Reform" Korea News/Views No. 87-08, Korean Information Office, Washington, D.C., Apr. 13, 1987. 3 pp., mimeographed.

3. Although this poll is common knowledge among Korean analysts, I have been unable to locate the published record of it.

of an additional $7 billion in military assistance.[10] Exact comparable figures for north Korea are not available, but it is estimated that grant economic aid to the DPRK from the Soviet Union, Eastern European countries, and China totalled about $1.4 billion from 1946 to 1960, after which it dropped sharply.[11]

The patterns of economic development in the two halves of Korea, which were already divergent before the war, moved rapidly in the direction of capitalism in the south and communism in the north. In the south, what was left of the industrial plant was mostly turned over to private owners— some of whom, however, were chosen as much for political loyalty as for economic acumen. Although there was some investment in import-substitution industries and textiles, primary emphasis was on food and other consumer goods to meet minimal living requirements. With revenues from foreign aid supporting over half the Republic's government budget (including defense costs) and constrained by foreign advisers to exercise financial discipline, the south Korean economy had fairly well stabilized by 1957, and living standards had recovered to pre–World War II levels.[12] Yet the diet of most south Koreans in the late 1950s was no more than the minimum requirement, and below that for many.

President Rhee and his supporters had scant understanding of economics. Their strategy was to maximize foreign aid, overvalue their currency, meet the government deficit by printing money and bonds, keep interest rates artificially low, and focus on import substitution for economic growth. Business loans and titles to former Japanese enterprises often were granted for political rather than economic reasons. The future economic outlook was pessimistic. The result was inflation, speculation in land and goods, and discouragement of saving and investment. Although U.S. advice mitigated some of the economic naivete and misdirection, much of it was resisted by the Koreans—as it had been since 1948—for reasons of both principle and political expediency. Moreover, not all U.S. advice was sound, from the Korean point of view. For example, U.S. agricultural representatives pushed wheat sales to the detriment of Korean rice farmers.

Korean reconstruction was also hampered by the U.S. prejudice against national economic planning and by policy disputes among U.S. agencies and between officials of the United States and those of the United Nations Korea Reconstruction Agency (UNKRA). Moreover, it was not until late in the 1950s that U.S. officials and scholars began to understand the problems of the developing world. From 1958 to 1960, the approaching south Korean political crisis inhibited and distorted the economy, at the same time that foreign aid was being reduced in response to domestic U.S. pressures. The situation was worsened by poor crops. Resultant popular frustration at the lack of economic progress was a contributing factor in the political upheaval of 1960. The brief ensuing experiment in free parliamentary democracy in

1960–61 further unsettled the economy, although it did bring the beginning of Korean multi-year development planning.

Under these conditions, the south Korean economy showed approximately a 4 percent average annual real economic growth rate for the period 1953–1962. (In comparison, the Philippine economy grew by 5.4 percent and Taiwan 7.0 percent during the same period.)[13] Population growth of nearly 3 percent a year absorbed most of the economic growth. The remaining per capita increase of around 1 percent—probably dropping to zero or less in the last Rhee years—was not enough to meet popular expectations. In these years, U.S. grant aid was becoming counterproductive by fostering dependence and by discouraging Korean agricultural and industrial growth.

[President] Rhee used this massive grant assistance as a protection against the necessity of policy changes that would have made the economy more productive and self-supporting and against normalization of relations with Japan. . . . As in so many recorded instances in USAID [U.S. Agency for International Development] relationships, it was the weaker power that held the whip hand.[14]

South Korean Economic Development, 1961–1985

Following their seizure of political power in 1961, General Park Chung Hee and his military associates clearly recognized the importance of rapid economic progress and committed themselves to bring it about. At first, however, they embarked on a series of rash and ill-advised economic policies—born of naive populism and a desire to raise political funds—including deliberate rigging of the stock market, a purge of leading businessmen, manipulation of the banks, and an abortive capital levy in conjunction with currency reform, which brought about further confusion and confrontation with U.S. aid officials.

Nevertheless, the military government learned quickly from its mistakes. Taking the plans of the short-lived Chang Myon administration as a base, it developed a five-year plan for rapid export-led development, with the assistance of the United States (the Kennedy administration accepted new ideas on economic development). The military leaders stabilized the economy and under U.S. pressure brought their budget under control. They managed the economy with far more energy and effectiveness than any previous south Korean administration, utilizing the expertise of U.S.-trained civilian economists.

Domestic savings increased as a result of increased interest rates and stability. Production for export was spurred by an improved foreign exchange regime: The south Korean won (the new unit of currency introduced by the

5 POLITICS AND GOVERNMENT OF NORTH KOREA (DEMOCRATIC PEOPLE'S REPUBLIC OF KOREA)

Introduction

Korea is one of three places in the world where both Communist and non-Communist political and social systems operate in one divided nation.[1] Given the long tradition of Korea as a single, integrated country, the contrast of the two political systems is all the more dramatic. Unfortunately, however, the Democratic People's Republic of Korea is one of the most closed societies in the world. The picture of north Korea has to be inferred from what was known of the Korean people prior to 1950, oral and written statements from north Korean sources, the principles of Marxism-Leninism as it was received by north Korea from the Soviet Union, and the limited information provided by foreign observers.

South Korea's Current Economic Situation

Overview

The gross national product of the Republic of Korea in 1985 was the equivalent of U.S. $83.1 billion at the year-end exchange rate of 890 won to $1, or $1,976 per capita—a 5.1 percent real increase over the previous year.South Korea ranked twenty-first among the world's nations in gross national product and fortieth in per capita GNP.[22] (A tabulation of south Korean major economic indices is presented in Table 6.2.)

The largest component of the total national product (based on 1984 figures) was services, at 56.6 percent, followed by manufacturing and mining, 29.9 percent, and agriculture and fisheries, 13.5 percent. Merchandise exports and imports in 1985 each were slightly over a third of GNP (exports, $30.3 billion; imports, $31.1 billion). Invisible trade receipts totalled $6.6 billion (of which overseas construction was a large component) and payments, $8.4 billion (including $4 billion in debt service).

The international current account ("balance of payments"), including invisible exports and imports, was a negative $882 million; but this amount compared with $1.4 billion deficit in 1984, $1.6 billion in 1983, and $5.32 billion in the peak year of 1980. Cumulative gross foreign debt amounted to $46.7 billion at the end of 1985, of which $10.7 billion (23 percent) represented short-term commercial loans; the Republic's own foreign assets totalled an offsetting $10.2 billion.[23] Although the gross debt magnitude put Korea fourth among the world's debtor nations, the debt-service ratio (principal and interest to exports) was about 21 percent, which is generally considered a manageable amount.[24]

In 1986, the Republic's national product grew 12.2 percent, to approximately $94 billion (over $2,300 per capita), and south Korea for the first time since the Korean War achieved a significant surplus of over $4 billion in its international trade, enabling a reduction in foreign debt to $45 billion.[25] Commensurate growth and a continued trade surplus were anticipated for 1987.

South Korea's economic system, still in evolution, is intermediate between state capitalism and free enterprise. Government economic powers—both formal and informal—are pervasive and are facilitated by a long tradition of political supremacy over economics. Public ownership (chiefly utilities, fertilizer, iron and steel, chemicals, and other heavy industry) is as high a percentage of Korea's industrial plant as in India, which calls itself a socialist state but has a large private sector.[26] The government sets overall goals, both in successive five-year plans (the Sixth Five-Year Plan began in 1987— see below) and in yearly programs, and guides industry by means of export and production targets, the control of credit (probably its most powerful

TABLE 6.2   South Korean Economic Indicators

	(US $ million unless otherwise stated) [h]			
	1983	1984	1985	1986 [h]
Socio-Economic Indicators				
Population (millions)	40.0	40.6	41.2	41.6
Population growth (%)	1.6	1.6	1.6	1.3
Economic Indicators				
GNP [a], current dollars	75,318	81,118	81,435	95,100
Real GNP growth rate (%)	9.5	7.6	5.0	12.5
Inflation rate (%)	3.4	2.3	3.2	2.3
Per capita GNP ($)	1,885	1,999	1.976	2,395
Per capita real GNP growth (%)	7.9	6.0	3.4	11.2
Unemployment rate (%) [b]	4.1	3.8	4.0	3.8
Investment/GNP ratio (%)	31.5	31.9	31.2	30.8
Govt. expenditure ratio (%)	21.5	21.4	21.4	18.9
Govt. budget balance/GNP ratio (%)	-1.6	-1.4	-1.5	+1.0
Balance of Payments				
US exports to ROK [c]	5,710	5,839	5,720	5,909
US imports from ROK [d]	7,657	10,027	10,711	13,497
US/ROK trade balance [e]	1,947	4,188	4,991	7,400
Total ROK exports	23,204	26,335	26,400	33,000
Total ROK imports	27,464	30,108	29,800	30,000
Trade balance with world	-4,260	-3,773	-3,400	-3,000
Current account balance	-1,606	-1,373	-882	+4,600
Current Finance				
Foreign exchange reserves	6,889	7,629	7,729	7,900
Avg. exchange rate (won/$)	776	806	870	880
Gross external debt [f]	28,400	31,700	36,000	35,200
Annual debt service	6,173	6,757	7,140	9,280
Debt service/export ratio (%)	18.8	20.1	21.7	22.2
Official Foreign Aid				
US economic assistance	0.0	0.0	0.0	0.0
US military assistance [g]	186.7	231.8	231.9	164.5
Total foreign dev. assistance	8.8	n/a	n/a	n/a

[a] GNP = Gross national product
[b] Official rate, by ILO standards
[c] Value free alongside ship (FAS)
[d] Value includes cost, insurance, freight (CIF)

[e] ROK surplus is positive
[f] Medium and long term only
[g] Includes grants and credits
[h] Preliminary

Source: Economic Fact Sheets, US Department of State, Jan. 4, 1987, and June 2, 1987, from statistics of Asian Development Bank, International Monetary Fund, Data Resources Asia Review, and US Embassy reports.

of Russia in the Bolshevik Revolution of 1917, communism developed a conspiratorial flavor and a reputation for an emphasis on revolution, violence, guile and deceit that still continue, even though the leaders in most Communist countries are conservative in maintaining the basic structure of their domestic regimes.

Central to the Communist polity is the Communist Party (in north Korea, the Korean Workers' party), which directs the policies and activities of the government in the interests of the proletariat it represents. Token parties may be permitted under other names, but they have no real political significance.

A basic element in Communist political culture is democratic centralism, the doctrine that everyone should have a chance to voice his or her views and preferences, but once these views have been taken into account in Party decisions, it is everyone's duty to carry those decisions out loyally and completely, as directed by the Party leaders. Related to this is the "mass line," which makes the Party responsible both for hearing the views of the people and for educating them in Party policies, through both propaganda and personal contact. Kim Il Sung, particularly, has emphasized the need for leaders and officials to get out among the people and has set an example with his numerous famous "on-the-spot guidance" visits.

In recent years, north Korea has developed an ideology of its own, called *juche*—self-reliance. Juche has been elevated to the status of national doctrine as a new and higher stage of Marxism-Leninism, responding to north Korea's own conditions and those of other developing countries. The following excerpts from a 1974 speech by Kim Jong Il, Kim Il Sung's son and designated successor, illustrate the nature of the ideology. The speech is quoted at length because it offers some flavor of north Korean ideological writings.

The *juche* philosophy is a new philosophy focusing on the leader [Kim Il Sung] . . . elaborated and systematized, focusing on man.

*   *   *

The *juche* philosophy made it clear for the first time that *chajusong* [concept of standing for oneself], creativity, and consciousness are the essential features of man, the social being. Thus it gave a perfect conception of man and a correct philosophical answer to his position and role as master who dominates and transforms nature and society.

*   *   *

The *juche* philosophy and human[ist bourgeois] philosophy have fundamentally different viewpoints of man. The former regards man as an independent, creative and conscious social being [who is master of everything and decides everything], whereas advocates of the latter deny man's social character and consider him to be a being dominated by his instinct, a powerless being isolated from the world. The bourgeois human[ist] philosophy which negates a scientific understanding of the world and revolutionary changes, inspires sorrow, pessimism and ultra-egotism.

*   *   *

The world is, in essence, a material entity . . . and . . . moves, changes, and develops in accordance with its inherent laws. The *juche* philosophy . . . elucidated a new idea of the world that nature and society are dominated and transformed by man, and thus fulfilled brilliantly the philosophical task of our time when the popular masses are masters of their own destiny and history.

*   *   *

Man's *chajusong* is different in quality from the simple instinct of other living matter to maintain their physical existence. It is an attribute to live and develop as a social being. . . . *Chajusong* is the main attribute of man, but . . . along with [it], creativity and consciousness constitute his social attributes. . . . *Chajusong* is an attribute of man who is desirous of living independently as master of the world and his own destiny; creativity is an attribute of man who transforms the world and shapes his own destiny purposefully; and consciousness is an attribute of man who determines all his activities designed to understand and reshape the world and himself. *Chajusong*, creativity and consciousness, though distinguishable from one another, are closely integrated.

*   *   *

The *juche* philosophy newly elucidated the essential features of man and his position and role as dominator and transformer of the world, and thus raised his dignity and value to the highest level possible. This is the great achievement of the *juche* philosophy that no other philosophical thoughts have accomplished.[3]

The emphasis on the supremacy and independence of man seems to echo certain aspects of Christian theology, in contrast to the traditional East Asian emphasis on harmony of man with nature. However, independence in *juche* thought must necessarily refer chiefly to the independence of people as a national whole. The individual's independence lies in loyal obedience to leader and Party. Obedience does not rule out initiative and innovation; as a matter of fact, Kim Il Sung's statements have explicitly encouraged initiative and innovation, within the limits of doctrine and policy, and have decried bureaucratic rigidity.

Political Process

By analogy with the south, it can be assumed that the demands of the north Korean people upon the regime focus upon improvement in the consumer industries (food processing, textiles, electric and electronic goods, footwear), and trading companies (general trading company for import and export, plus domestic consumer outlets and distributing agencies). They do not own banks, although they may hold substantial bank equities and may operate investment services. The larger ones are listed in Table 6.3.

The *chaebol*, like their Japanese counterparts, have high ratios of corporate debt to equity (the money invested by owners and stockholders). They are therefore very vulnerable to economic downturns. This fact was demonstrated by the collapse of the Kukje Group, Korea's seventh-largest conglomerate, in 1985, primarily because of the loss of Middle East markets and over-expansion. In 1985, the ratio of all corporate paid-in capital to total assets was 22.3 percent, slightly down from the previous year and very low by U.S. and European standards. Although the government has been encouraging public sale of stock, most of the firms are wholly or largely owned by the founders and their families.

Although the *chaebol* predominate in production and export, medium and small firms predominate in employment and numbers. Many of these firms supply the *chaebol* with parts or components. There was a total of 41,088 manufacturing and mining firms in south Korea in 1983, employing a total of 2.3 million people; 33,373 of the firms employed fewer than 50 employees each, but collectively accounted for nearly a quarter of these workers. Another quarter of employment was provided by 5,840 firms employing 50 to 199 workers.[29]

Textiles were the principal basis for south Korean export expansion and are still the largest industrial component, with 18.6 percent of total manufacturing value added;[30] products range from very high quality silk and polyester through wool, cotton, and hemp cloth and yarn. Textiles also are a leading export component, representing 9 percent of total exports in 1984. However, the textile industry faces growing competition from other developing countries as its labor cost advantage shrinks. At the same time, it meets with growing protectionist barriers in the United States and Europe. Exports decreased by 1 percent in 1985 from 1984 (including apparel) but were recovering at year's end.[31]

Heavy and chemical industry in south Korea began only in the 1970s, except for modest beginnings in fertilizer and pharmaceuticals. Its growth since then has been extraordinary, comprising iron and steel (14 million metric tons or 15.4 million U.S. short tons of pig-iron and steel ingots in 1984), semi-finished and finished iron and steel products, ships, motor vehicles, machine tools, industrial machinery and equipment, electrical machinery and appliances, cement, fertilizer, petrochemicals, and petroleum products. These industries, particularly shipbuilding, suffered in the mid-1980s from world recession and from the oil glut, which reduced the market for ships and construction materials. Automobile manufacturing, however,

TABLE 6.3 Major South Korean Business Firms
(Sales over US$ 1 billion in 1985)

Name of Company	Ranking 1985 1984		Business Lines	(US $ mil equiv.) 1985 Sales	1985 Income
Samsung Corporation (Samsung Group)	1	3	Trade	4,560	7.3
Dae Woo Corporation (Dae Woo Group)	2	1	Trade	4,530	41.1
Hyundai Corporation (Hyundai Group)	3	5	Trade	3,420	5.3
Yukong Ltd. (Sunkyong Group)	4	2	Chemicals	3,360	38.9
Hyundai Engineering & Construction (Hyundai Group)	5	4	Construction	2,390	39.1
Samsung Electronics (Samsung Group)	6	8	Electronics	2,030	25.9
Sunkyong Ltd. (Sunkyong Group)	7	6	Trade	1,980	9.8
Lucky-Goldstar International (Lucky-Goldstar Group)	8	7	Trade	1,950	2.0
Goldstar Co. (Lucky-Goldstar Group)	9	9	Electronics	1,500	13.0
Korean Air (Hanjin Group)	10	11	Air transport	1,350	5.4
Hyundai Motor (Hyundai Group)	11	15	Automobiles	1,260	34.5
Ssangyong Corp.	12	12	Trade	1,100	0.2

Source: Adapted from Business Korea, May 1986, p. 60. Dollar
equivalents of sales and net income were calculated at the 29
June 1985 exchange rate of $0.0012 per won, and rounded off. Net
income is after taxes.

At the same time, the testimony of defectors suggests that coercion and fear are important in enforcing compliance. The Ministry of Public Security has subordinate units at provincial, county, and local levels, closely monitored by the Party; county units may number 100 or more officers, and agents are assigned to all cooperative farms (which, in the north Korean system, are also the local political units). Citizens are encouraged to inform on each other, even within families, regarding deviant behavior; and there is reportedly an ever-present network of informers.

The north Korean judicial system is patterned after that of the Soviet Union. As in continental European states, it gives primary importance to officials of the State Procurator's Office—an executive agency—and its local counterparts. They are responsible for initiating investigations and presenting cases to the courts, which rule on the validity of the procurators' findings rather than acting as neutral referees between the state and the accused.

More significantly, however, courts and procurators are subject to guidance and control by the Party and are expected to operate in support of Party policies. Thus, the declared purpose of the north Korean penal code is to suppress resistance from the overthrown classes of capitalists and bourgeoisie, counter the "people's enemies," educate the population in the spirit of "socialist patriotism," and reeducate and punish individuals for any relapse into old-style capitalistic thinking or support of the Japanese or other external powers. Political crimes (against the state and the legal order) are handled separately, with investigations conducted in secret by separate state security agencies. Political suspects can be seized, held indefinitely, and tried and sentenced in secret.

Mass media in North Korea are organized with great effectiveness to convey regime policies to the citizens. Newspapers, radio, television, motion pictures, and magazines are all operated by state or Party organs. There are also local loudspeaker networks and mobile broadcast vehicles in rural areas. Mass media are supplemented by Party and other education and indoctrination meetings and by the educational system generally. Radios possessed by the general public can be tuned only to north Korean broadcasts.

The most dramatic distinction in political style between north and south Korea lies in the fact that from the beginning of the Soviet occupation in 1945, there was an unabashed and concerted effort to persuade or, if necessary, force the entire north Korean people into the Communist philosophical and political mold, with no concern for previous tradition or alternative philosophies. Kim Il Sung and his followers (some of whom were purged for dissent) continued after independence where their Soviet mentors had left off. Since the mid-1950s, the principle of *juche* and other tenets of Kim Il Sung's thought have more and more displaced the original Marxism-Leninism, but the intensity of indoctrination (judging from the regime's public pronouncements) has not abated.

FIGURE 5.1 Kim II Sung, President of the Democratic People's Republic of Korea, July 1980 (photo courtesy of Ralph Clough)

Another remarkable feature of north Korean politics is the cult of the Great Leader, Kim II Sung (Fig. 5.1). The adulation accorded him in the official media is extraordinary. His name is invoked on all possible occasions as the source of infinite wisdom, grace, and benevolence. His father, mother, and grandfather also receive praise as nationalist heroes. His birthplace is a national shrine and a mecca for innumerable pilgrims. To some extent, at least, adoration of Kim is a genuine popular attitude. Its expression seems to be universal, whether because of conviction or conformity. It is widely reported in south Korea that when a south Korean religious leader met his north Korean sister in the family exchange visits of September 1985, he nearly twenty years, the government has bought rice at high prices from farmers and sold it at subsidized prices in the cities to encourage production and improve the farmers' living standards; but by 1983 this practice had accumulated a deficit of over $2 billion, so 1984 support was frozen at 1983 level and has only slightly increased since then.

Barley, grown either on upland fields or in paddies between rice crops, is the second most important crop. In recent years, the government has purchased up to 80 percent of it at support prices and distributed it in the cities, where it is often mixed with rice for eating. (To conserve rice supply, the government for some years has required the mixing of 10 percent barley with rice in public restaurants.) The 1984 harvest totalled 804,000 metric tons (885,000 U.S. short tons). Other major crops include potatoes, wheat, maize, cabbage (used for the national dish known as *kimch'i*), and turnips. Korea imports most of its wheat and feed grains and much of its soybean requirements. Production of fruits and vegetables, both for the domestic market and for export, has increased greatly: South Korea produced 1.2 million metric tons (1.3 million U.S. short tons) of fruit in 1984, of which apples made up nearly half (528,000 tons).

Double-cropping can be practiced in the southern part of the country (usually by growing barley in rice paddies during the winter) and is facilitated by the new practice of growing rice seedlings in plastic hothouses. Double-cropping and inter-cropping (one crop sowed between rows of another) gave south Korea a land utilization ratio of 125 percent in 1984.

To increase their incomes, farmers have been encouraged to grow cash crops such as fruit and vegetables. Plastic hothouses for this purpose have become a common feature of the landscape. Animal husbandry—chiefly of pigs and chickens—has also grown. Milk has entered the Korean diet, and the dairy industry, as well as some raising of cattle for beef, has made great strides. Traditional cash crops such as ginseng, tobacco, tea, and silkworm raising remain important. Some cotton and other commercial fibers are grown.

Korean agriculture faced severe problems in the mid-1980s. Despite its tradition as the peninsula's rice basket, south Korea has not been agriculturally self-sufficient for many years. In 1984, imports—mostly wheat and animal feed corn—made up just under half of requirements. A major reason is that population and income growth have outstripped the very respectable increase in agricultural productivity in two ways: by increasing consumption and, through urban growth, by reducing the stock of agricultural land. In recent years, also, high-yield hybrid strains of rice have proved vulnerable to pests and cold weather and have not met the taste standards of Korean consumers. There had been strong government pressure to plant the new varieties; nevertheless, some farmers have returned to the hardier but lower-yielding traditional varieties.

In addition, south Korea must contend with structural problems. Only 20 percent of the land is arable, and rainfall is less than that of Japan and other rice-growing countries. Farmland has been divided over the centuries into tiny plots, so that individual holdings, averaging slightly over one hectare (about 2.5 acres) in 1984, may be divided into several noncontiguous fields. Although the land reform of 1948 to 1953 was a brilliant political and social success, it perpetuated the fractionation of land, making cultivation relatively inefficient and lessening the opportunity for mechanization.

Agricultural labor costs have risen as young people leave for urban jobs; farm work is increasingly done by women and old men. Costs have also been increased by heavier fertilizer and pesticide use, augmented in recent years by the needs of the new high-productivity rice strains. Budgetary pressure on agricultural price supports has reduced farm income. This factor, probably reinforced by increased propensity of farmers to buy machinery and modern durable consumer goods, has led to an increase of farm household debt, which at the end of 1985 averaged two million won (about $2,300) per household, against average annual farm household income of 5,700,000 ($6,500) won.[36]

For some years, the government has been promoting agricultural improvement to offset these problems, working through the agricultural extension service, New Community Movement, and other agencies. In addition to newly developed plant varieties, improvements include irrigation, fertilizer (of which Korea produces a surplus), mechanization, land rationalization (straightening boundaries, combining small fields), and improved cultivation techniques. For years, extension programs have encouraged handicraft industry such as woodcarving and basket-weaving in farm households to supplement income. Efforts are being made to encourage location and relocation of industry in rural areas, so that farmers can augment their income without leaving for the city. In 1985, farmers got 35.3 percent of their income, on the average, from non-farm sources; this proportion is projected to rise by 1991 to 42.3 percent.[37] The government has commissioned extensive land reclamation projects along the west coast both to compensate for land lost to urban sprawl and to utilize construction industry resources returning from the hard-pressed petroleum exporting countries.

Services

The largest category of Korea's service sector in the mid-1980s was retail trade, most of it still in the hands of hundreds of thousands of small merchants in the nation's cities, towns, and villages, each with a modest storefront and stock. Department stores of the Western type were increasingly common, however, many of them operated by the industrial *chaebol*. A total of 26,054 wholesale and 542,548 retail establishments, and 233,834

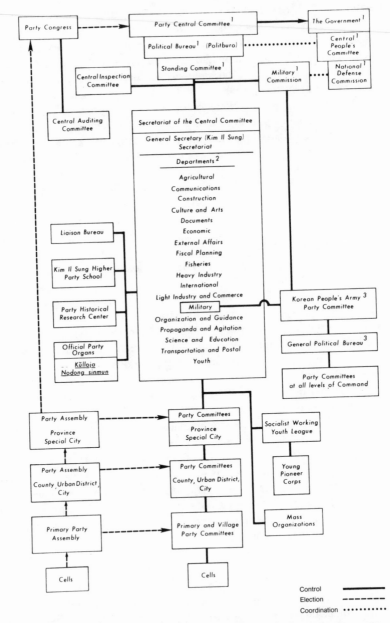

FIGURE 5.2 Chart of organization of the Korean Workers' party, 1981: [1]headed by Kim Il Sung; [2]as of April 1979; [3]headed by some official (from Frederica Bunge, ed., *North Korea: A Country Study,* 3d ed. [Washington, D.C.: U.S. Government Printing Office, 1981], p. 181)

military leaders; the order of their listing is considered to indicate relative prestige and power in the political system.

The Politburo had thirty-three members in 1986, of whom sixteen were alternates. Its Standing Committee—the summit of political power—was comprised of just three men: Kim Il Sung, Kim Jong Il (Kim Il Sung's son), and O Jin U (Defense Minister).[5]

Subordinate to the Politburo is the Party bureaucracy, headed by nine secretaries (including Kim Il Sung as General Secretary), and various central organizations. These include the Central Auditing Committee, fiscal watchdog; Central Inspection Committee, enforcing discipline; Military Commission, which directs the armed forces; and a Liaison Bureau directing clandestine activities against south Korea. The bureaucracy works through the Party organization at provincial, county, and local levels, each of which repeats in miniature the same general organization as at the center. Crucial to the operation of the Party are the doctrines of democratic centralism and mass line. The former permits rank-and-file members to express their views internally, while requiring them to carry out Party decisions without question. The mass line doctrine makes Party members responsible for getting the views of the people, by going out among them, and for ensuring popular knowledge and support of Party decisions.

The Party is reinforced by a number of related organizations that support its work and provide recruits to its ranks. Among them, the most important is the Socialist Working Youth League, for persons of 15 to 26 years of age. (The Socialist Working Youth League and the Korean People's Army are the principal sources of Communist party members.) There is a Young Pioneers' Corps for children 9 to 15. Laborers, agricultural workers, women, scientists, and others have their organizations related to the Party. A Democratic Front for the Reunification of the Fatherland coordinates these and other nominally unrelated groups, such as political and religious organizations (including the People's Revolutionary party, which is claimed to exist in south Korea), to ensure broad support for Party and state policies.

Constitution and Formal Government Organization

General Principles

In contrast to the ROK Constitution, that of the DPRK, as adopted in 1972 (the first and only revision of the original 1948 document), devotes considerable space to explicit definition of the nation's political ideology and to the place of the Korea Workers' party. The state is enjoined to build a "socialist national culture." It is to be guided by the *juche* principle as "a creative application of Marxism-Leninism." Dictatorship of the proletariat and class struggle are recognized, as is the *Chollima* Movement (a north of growing labor impatience with low Korean standards and the growing ability of the educational system to deliver the necessary skills in requisite quantities (the growth of educational enrollments has produced an oversupply of graduates in some categories). There were over three thousand labor actions in the summer of 1987, resulting in an estimated average increase in workers' wages of somewhat over 20 percent.

Although south Korea has had organized labor unions since 1945, they have a tradition of being more politically than economically oriented. At present, however, the officially sanctioned labor organizations concentrate their attention on economic matters. The Communists used unions for political purposes from 1945 to 1948; Syngman Rhee used them for political purposes from 1948 to 1960. Since that time, organized labor activity has been severely circumscribed, both to contain the potential political threat and to prevent wage increases that would hurt Korea's export drive. Until late 1987 Korean labor laws were highly restrictive, although the Constitution guarantees the right of collective organization and action. As noted in Chapter 4, the change in political policy in the summer of 1987 was followed by an upsurge of strikes and other labor actions in support of demands for better wages and working conditions and freedom to organize. The labor laws have already been revised, and a somewhat freer climate for organized labor activity will almost certainly result.

Under the labor laws as they existed in early 1987, a national labor federation (the Federation of Korean Trade Unions) and sixteen national industrial federations existed in south Korea; but they were forbidden to enter into specific negotiations without government permission. Labor unions at individual plants might bargain collectively, and in theory had the right to strike after other remedies were exhausted; but the Ministry of Labor and its constituent divisions and committees played a major role in all labor negotiations. Each plant was required to have a labor-management council, separate from the union, to deal with labor problems, including wages, other benefits, and working conditions. There were strikes and sit-ins even before the upsurge of mid-1987, such as the sit-in by auto workers at a major plant in the port city of Inch'on in early 1985. Nevertheless, the steady, if slow, growth of wages and benefits, together with government controls, was apparently sufficient to avoid massive labor unrest, except at such times as the oil-shock year of 1979 and again in 1987.

In the mid-1980s, although some strikes had involved large plants such as that in Inch'on, the main labor problem areas were small firms. Unsafe and unhealthy working conditions were not uncommon in such establishments and were inadequately controlled by overworked government inspectors. Wages were frequently very low, especially in industries that have traditionally depended upon low-wage labor by young women expecting to get married. Discontent in such sectors has been given voice and support by activist

Christian social groups, particularly the Urban Industrial Mission, which was put under government ban. Increasingly, also, students have disguised their backgrounds, taken blue-collar jobs as "disguised workers," and mobilized the plant work force to improve their wages and working conditions.

The government's response, up to mid-1987, was twofold. On the one hand, it was slowly moving to correct some of the abuses; the draft Sixth Five Year Plan emphasizes social benefits, and a minimum wage was promised for 1988. On the other hand, it moved forcefully to suppress labor disturbances, frequently arresting the leaders, especially when "disguised workers" were involved.

For some years, the Republic of Korea's admission to the International Labour Organisation was opposed by many of its members because of their adverse view of south Korean political and working conditions. Support for south Korea has grown, however; at present the opposition is chiefly by Communist nations, which insist that north Korea also be admitted and which have been able to prevent the necessary two-thirds vote for south Korea. It seems probable that the Republic will be admitted to the ILO within the next few years.

The International Component
in South Korea's Economy

A persisting myth about south Korea is that the country is still receiving large amounts of concessionary assistance from the United States. Such is not the case. The reality is that for nearly two decades, Korea has met its capital investment requirements on a competitive international market and, increasingly, from domestic savings. Commercial banks, the World Bank, and foreign governmental agencies (which are motivated more by their own trade promotion than by Korea's needs) have been the sources of Korean government and private borrowing. Total direct foreign equity investment in south Korea totalled well over $1 billion in the mid-1980s. The government has sought and applied foreign advice, particularly from the World Bank, but it has made its own economic plans and policies. The last resident U.S. aid official left the country in the early 1970s, as remaining U.S.-financed projects were winding up.

South Korea's dependence upon foreign trade means that the nation is highly vulnerable to international market fluctuations, which are largely responsible for Korea's economic cycles. So far, the government's economic management has coped very well with these fluctuations. The large south Korean foreign debt means vulnerability to changes in the availability of foreign money and in international interest rates; here, again, the government's management of its debt has been effective. Both vulnerabilities lead to a south Korean desire to maximize its self-reliance, within the limits set by

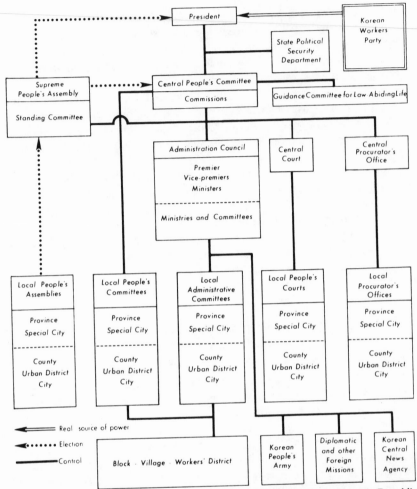

FIGURE 5.3 Chart of government organization of the Democratic People's Republic of Korea, 1981 (from Frederica Bunge, ed., *North Korea: A Country Study*, 3d ed. [Washington, D.C.: U.S. Government Printing Office, 1981], p. 171)

Assembly, and other commissions appointed by the Central People's Committee.

Also under the Central People's Committee is the Administration Council, or cabinet, comprised of a Premier, Vice Premiers, ministers, and other cabinet-level members. The Council prepares the state budget, formulates economic development plans and implementing measures, and may countermand the orders of subordinate bodies. It is responsible for foreign affairs, national defense, public order and safety, and protection of the rights of citizens. As of 1986, there were one first Vice Premier, ten vice-premiers, twenty-five ministries, and about four committees (charged with coordination of functions relating to two or more ministries).[7]

Judiciary

The Constitution establishes a judicial system modelled generally on that of the Soviet Union. It provides that "the court is independent and judicial proceedings are carried out in strict accordance with the law." There are a Central Court, as highest court of appeal; provincial courts as courts of first instance for major civil and criminal cases; and people's courts in cities, counties, and urban districts. Judges and people's assessors are elected by legislative bodies at corresponding levels (those of the Central Court by the Supreme People's Assembly).

There is a parallel hierarchy of officers headed by a Central Procurator's Office, who act as state prosecutors at their respective levels, as well as checking on the activities of all public organs and citizens to ensure "active struggle against class enemies and all lawbreakers." The Chief Procurator is made responsible to the Supreme People's Assembly, the President, and the Central People's Committee. He sits as a statutory member of plenary sessions of the Central Court.

Local Government

Although not spelled out in complete detail in the Constitution, there are three levels of government below the central administration: 13 provinces (including 4 special cities) at the highest level; 17 cities, 152 counties, and 36 urban districts, at intermediate level; and local villages, which are coterminous with agricultural cooperatives, at the lowest level. At all three levels, each governmental entity has a People's Assembly, People's Committee, and Administrative Committee, paralleling the national-level entities. However, the people's committees perform the function of standing committee for the assemblies between sessions.

North Korean System Performance

To all outward appearances, the north Korean political system has been successful in terms of stability and order. The leadership has had substantial success in implanting its version of Communist political culture in the people—by persuasion, coercion, and denial of information about competing ideologies. In a sense, Kim Il Sung's inculcation of communism is reminiscent of King T'aejo's inculcation of Confucianism at the beginning of the Choson Dynasty, although Kim Il Sung seems to have injected more of his own thinking than T'aejo did and to have proceeded with more speed. In both milestone of progress was south Korea's agreement with the United States in mid-1986 to open its insurance industry, remove the ban on foreign cigarettes, and move toward stiffer copyright protection.

For the first twenty years of its existence, south Korea depended heavily on the United States for economic and technical aid. As its economy grew, the Republic looked to the United States for an export market and for investment and technology. Since 1965, Japan has also been a major market and investment source, overtaking the United States in some years as principal trading partner. In 1985, the United States provided a market for 35.5 percent of Korea's exports and Japan, 15.0 percent; the two nations' shares of total Korean imports were 20.8 and 24.3 percent, respectively.

In recent years, the Republic has vigorously sought to diversify its trade, both to reduce its dependence and to combat growing protectionism. The President, Prime Minister, other senior officials, and business leaders have travelled extensively to promote trade. Although the United States and Japan still dominate foreign trade, the diversification policy has had significant results. In 1985, Hong Kong (surrogate for Mainland China) took 5.2 percent of south Korean exports; Canada, 4.1 percent; West Germany, 3.2 percent; Saudi Arabia, 3.2 percent; United Kingdom, 3.0 percent. The remaining 31 percent of exports (after the 50.3 percent to the United States and Japan) was widely distributed among European, Middle Eastern, African, Asian, and Latin American countries, with European countries and Australia predominating.

On the import side (apart from Japan and the United States), 4.0 percent came from Malaysia, 3.6 percent from Australia, and 3.1 percent from West Germany. As would be expected, oil-exporting states were significant import sources: Indonesia (2.1 percent), Saudi Arabia (2.1 percent), and Kuwait (1.7 percent). Hong Kong provided only 1.6 percent of imports. The remaining import shares were widely distributed.

South Korean Economic Prospects:
The Sixth Five-Year Plan

Three forces are inducing a reorientation of Korea's basic development policy: first, increasing resistance in the industrialized countries—south Korea's primary markets; second, competition from other developing nations with cheaper labor; third, growing popular pressure at home for improvement in the quality of life and social welfare. The latter factor, in its economic dimension of upward pressure on wage levels, is also reducing Korea's competitiveness in the international market as newly emerging suppliers (such as China, India, Indonesia, Thailand, and Malaysia) enter the market for traditional labor-intensive commodities.

The response of Korea's planners has been to lower the expected level of future annual GNP growth to a range of 7 to 7.5 percent, in contrast to levels of 9 to 10 percent in earlier years (although growth was 12.2 percent in 1986 and probably over 10 percent in 1987, because of the boost to the Korean economy given by the "three lows"—lower oil prices, lower interest rates, and lower value of the dollar, hence the won, against the Japanese yen). Future planning includes diversification of export markets, including joint ventures with industrialized countries to meet the needs of developing nations; more emphasis on meeting domestic needs for goods and services; emphasis on growth of capital-intensive, high-technology industrial sectors; and reduction of foreign indebtedness.

Such growth, in turn, means more foreign participation, since although Korea has produced its own technological breakthroughs, the primary sources remain foreign. Moreover, the two-decade-long outward orientation of south Korea's economy, even if somewhat modified, will undoubtedly continue. Korea's domestic market, "while growing rapidly, remains too small to support 7 to 7.5 percent growth. Within that export-oriented model, however, major adjustments are necessary. . . . Korean economic policy-makers must try to reduce trade frictions by diversifying their export goods and the markets for those goods."[41]

For the next several years, Korea's past baby boom will require at least a 7.5 percent annual increase in national product to absorb new entrants into the job market and perhaps more, even assuming continuation of current capital-labor ratios. (One recent study, by the Bank of Korea, suggests that 10 percent annual growth would be needed to produce enough jobs.) Movement toward capital-intensive industry and increasing demands for employment by women not now listed as economically active (such as housewives) would aggravate the problem. More education may alleviate the problem but cannot solve it. However, by the mid-1990s the number of young entrants into the job market will fall off. The new problem (like that of Japan and the United States) will be how to maintain or improve social welfare levels for an increasing aged population out of contributions by a diminishing active population.

South Korea's inflation and recession of the late 1970s was brought on partly by adverse international economic circumstances, especially the "second oil shock," and partly by a forced-draft drive for increased self-sufficiency in defense-related industry in response to perceived weakening of the U.S. presence and commitment in East Asia. The economy made a successful recovery; and as of 1986, the international climate for continued growth seemed at its most favorable in some years.

Credible reassurance of the U.S. security commitment since 1980 reduced the south Korean preoccupation with self-sufficiency. Nevertheless, Korea's national interest continued to dictate some reasonable degree of economic name only since 1980 (prior to that time, he was referred to in north Korea as "the Party center"). Some analyses suggest that he has been building a base of support in the principal Party and state organs. He has the aura of his father's preeminent, almost superhuman, status to bolster his own prestige. But his real test is yet to come; and he faces challenges that may be even greater than his father's, although of a different order.

In meeting popular demands, the north Korean regime faces a difficult dilemma. On the one hand, internal technical and organizational difficulties seem to be leading north Korea to look for foreign technical assistance: A mission of the United Nations Development Program has been stationed in the country for several years, and in 1985 the regime went so far as to enact a joint venture law to encourage foreign economic participation in the north Korean economy. On the other hand, opening the country to foreign assistance will inevitably heighten expectations as the general public learns more of what other countries have achieved. Similarly, the demand for reunification obliges the regime to enter into at least cosmetic negotiations with south Korea; but as these negotiations result in concrete exchanges, such as the exchange of separated family members in 1985, north Korea's lag behind the south—both economic and political—will become more apparent.

It thus appears that Kim Il Sung, Kim Jong Il, and their supporters will face a steadily mounting gap between the expectations of the north Korean people and the capacity of the system to meet them. Moreover, it will be less and less practical for the north Korean leaders to insulate their people from the rest of the world or to control the level of popular demands, as in the past. Either the political system will have to adapt itself to the new challenge, as has been happening in China, or it will have to resort to increased repression to maintain order. The former will cause confusion; the latter, eventually, anger and rebellion. Either contingency exposes north Korea to increased outside influence. The direction of north Korea's political evolution will thus influence the future of all Korea.

Notes

1. The other two places are China and Germany. The countries that in the United States are referred to as "Communist" (the Soviet Union, Eastern Bloc countries, China, north Korea, Vietnam, Cuba) describe their own political systems as socialist, not communist, because in Marxist theory they have not yet reached the communist stage of social development. However, to avoid confusion for Western readers, the term "Communist" will be used in this discussion to describe nations that have the goal of communism as state policy, and that—unlike socialist states and parties of Western Europe—have eliminated or severely limited private ownership of property.

2. U.S. Information Service, Seoul, "Human Rights Report for Democratic People's Republic of Korea," *Backgrounder,* February 21, 1986, p. 1.

3. Federal Broadcast Information Service, Asia-Pacific Daily Summary, April 10, 1984, vol. 4, pp. D16–19, citing *Kulloja,* No. 4, 1984, reporting Kim Jong Il's speech to Korea Workers' party propagandists on its tenth anniversary.

4. See Ch'oe, Yong-ho, "Christian Background in the Early Life of Kim Il-song." *Asian Survey* 26 (No. 10, October 1986):1082–91.

5. O Jin U, one of Kim Il Sung's original comrades-in-arms, disappeared from public view in 1986, but reappeared in 1987. He was reported to have been badly injured in an automobile accident. Nevertheless, his name continued to appear on official documents, and he was listed as third-ranking among north Korean leaders, after Kim Il Sung and Kim Jong Il.

6. Federal Broadcast Information Service, *Daily Report—Asia-Pacific,* December 31, 1986, pp. D1–D20.

7. U.S. Central Intelligence Agency. *Directory of Officials of the Democratic People's Republic of Korea* (Washington, D.C., April 1985). The number of ministries is determined by counting entries. The number of committees is not specified but is inferred from the titles of vice premiers. See also *North Korea: A Country Study* (Washington: Foreign Area Studies, The American University, 1981), p. 173.

8. Observations of north Korea by a group of U.S. scholars of ethnic Korean descent in 1979 are recorded in C.I. Eugene Kim, ed., *Journey to North Korea: Personal Perceptions* (Berkeley: Institute of East Asian Studies, University of California, 1983).

6 ECONOMICS

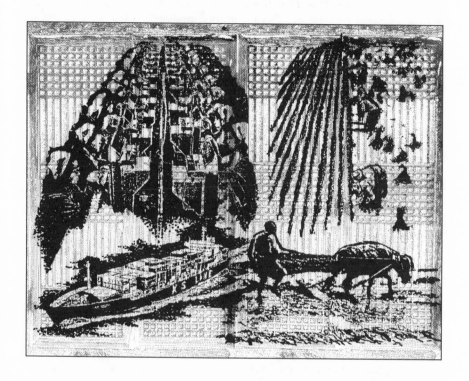

Introduction

"Miracle on the Han" is an apt, if overworked, description of south Korea's amazingly rapid and successful transition from a traditional agrarian subsistence economy to a primarily industrialized one. This transition has involved social and political as well as purely economic change. In the old Confucian tradition, both industry and commerce were looked down upon, whereas agriculture (next to learning and government) was viewed as the most worthy human pursuit. It is only in the last twenty years or so that business has begun to rank with other callings as a respectable life work.

Another significant shift in attitude concerns belief in the possibility of future security and betterment. It has already been mentioned that the Korean cultural tradition assumes an essentially static human condition, in which there may be good times and bad times, but a marginal existence is the lot of most people. More than a century of economic adversity, imperialist domination, and war reinforced this attitude. Until the 1960s, there was no incentive for either leaders or people to make plans for a better future, or to lay aside resources for it, since faith in the future was essentially lacking.

A friend of mine illustrated the profound shift in south Korean attitudes with a personal experience. During a trip through a rural area of North Kyongsang Province to observe the effects of U.S. aid programs, he came upon an old farmer planting fruit tree seedlings. "Why are you planting those trees?" my friend asked the farmer. "They won't bear fruit for many years, and they're taking up space you could use for crops." "I know," said the farmer; "I'm planting them for my son. He'll be able to harvest them and profit from them." The farmer's act demonstrated the new trend: One could invest in the future with confidence.

In this chapter, we shall see how this new confidence, in combination with entrepreneurial spirit, a capable work force, able and energetic government management, foreign assistance, and a favorable world economic environment, contributed to Korea's rise from abject poverty to top rank among the world's developing nations in hardly more than a generation. (A statistical summary of this growth is shown in Table 6.1.)

The Traditional Korean Economy

For centuries, most Koreans were subsistence farmers of rice and other grains, supplying most of their basic needs through their own labor or through barter. Markets at five-day intervals in larger towns and itinerant peddlers supplied needs the villages could not meet. Officials were compensated in grain; until late in the Choson Dynasty, the grain came from lands assigned to them for that purpose. In principle, other land was allotted to all the people in accordance with their needs and taxed for support of government activity. In practice, land gravitated into the hands of the aristocratic *yangban* class, whose members exempted themselves from taxation. Taxes grew on the decreasing base of non-exempt land, forcing many into tenancy or day labor. From the mid-seventeenth century on, money increasingly took the place of grain for taxes and purchases of goods by the court and aristocracy, although the value of the money depreciated because of deficit financing.

The simple manufactures of the period—principally cloth, furniture, cooking and eating utensils, articles of personal adornment, and paper— were largely produced by artisans of low social status in a few population centers. Many of the artisans were in the service of, or commissioned by, the court and aristocracy. Such items as hemp cloth and paper were produced for export to China on the periodic tribute missions, which also served as a principal channel of foreign trade. Other channels (apart from

TABLE 6.1   Growth of the South Korean Economy after World War II

Year	Midyear Popu- lation, millions	Growth rate, %	GNP at cur- rent prices, billion US $	GNP per capita, US $	Real GNP growth %	Exports, billion US $
1949	20.2	1.4	1.8	89	-	.01
1953	21.5	1.6	1.4	65	6.0	.35
1957	22.3	3.1	1.7	80	8.8	.43
1962	26.5	2.9	2.3	87	2.2	.05
1963	27.3	2.8	2.7	99	9.1	.09
1964	29.0	2.6	2.9	104	9.6	.12
1965	28.7	2.5	3.1	108	5.8	.18
1966	29.4	2.6	3.7	126	12.7	.25
1967	30.1	2.4	4.3	143	6.6	.32
1968	30.8	2.4	5.2	169	11.3	.46
1969	31.5	2.3	6.6	209	13.8	.62
1970	32.2	2.2	8.0	248	7.6	.84
1971	32.9	2.0	9.4	286	8.8	1.07
1972	33.5	1.9	10.6	316	5.7	1.62
1973	34.1	1.8	13.5	396	14.1	3.23
1974	34.7	1.7	18.5	533	7.7	4.46
1975	35.3	1.7	20.9	592	6.9	5.08
1976	35.8	1.6	28.7	801	14.1	7.72
1977	36.4	1.6	37.4	1027	12.7	10.05
1978	37.0	1.5	52.0	1407	9.7	12.71
1979	37.5	1.5	62.4	1662	6.5	15.06
1980	38.1	1.6	60.3	1582	-5.2	17.50
1981	38.7	1.6	66.2	1710	6.6	21.25
1982	39.3	1.5	69.3	1762	5.4	21.85
1983	39.9	1.5	76.0	1903	11.9	24.45
1984	40.5	1.3	82.4	2034	8.4	29.24
1985	41.1	1.3	83.1	2024	5.1	30.28
1986	41.6	1.2	94.3	2274	12.5	34.72

Sources: Republic of Korea Economic Planning Board, Major Statistics of Korean Economy (Seoul, 1982 and 1986); Korean Economic
Institute, Korea's Economy 3 (No. 3, Aug. 1987); Robert W. Cole
and Princeton N. Lyman, Korean Development: The Interplay of
Politics and Economics (Cambridge, Mass.: Harvard University
Press, 1971); Paul W. Kuznets, Economic Growth and Structure in
the Republic of Korea (New Haven, Conn.: Yale University Press,
1977); United Nations Statistical Yearbook, 1951 and 1958. Population growth figures for 1949 and 1953 are multi-year averages;
1953 population is as of Dec. 31.

smuggling) included a trading station that the Japanese were permitted to maintain near the southeast port city of Pusan and some private trade with China. There were wealthy merchants and artisans, but they did not develop a financial or cultural network such as existed among their counterparts in Japan or China; rather, they tended to enter the aristocracy—often by purchasing rank.

In accordance with Confucian teachings, the *yangban* disdained commercial activity ; but they nonetheless amassed wealth from the perquisites of office and the product of their estates. From the middle of the dynasty, despite efforts at reform, the gap between wealth and poverty widened, and state revenues shrank. Wealthy landlords and officials, however, did not often invest in manufacture or commerce, as did their Japanese counterparts. Although one north Korean scholar has maintained that Korean private investment in enterprise such as mining and iron manufacturing activity began as early as the eighteenth century,[1] it did not appear on a significant scale until after the Western penetration had begun, toward the end of the nineteenth century, and did not reach major proportions until the period of Japanese control, beginning in 1905.

The Economy Under the Japanese

It was chiefly the Japanese who brought capitalist economic patterns of industrialization and trade to Korea. They treated Korea as an extension of the Japanese economy, principally to serve Japanese interests. A major example was the Japanese export of the Korean rice crop to Japan to fill the shortfall in Japanese rice production. Cheaper grains were imported to meet Korean food requirements. Industries were established in accordance with imperial, not Korean, needs.

The result of these Japanese policies was a typical colonial dual economy, in which over a half million Japanese residents managed the modern industrial sector and enjoyed its fruits, while most Koreans—except the urban labor force—remained in the traditional agrarian economy. In this situation, it was easy for Korean nationalists, economically naive as they were, to castigate capitalism along with the Japanese occupation itself. Marxist ideas spread. It was largely the minority of Koreans who kept their property and wealth under the Japanese that opposed socialist principles of public ownership and land redistribution.

The forty-year Japanese occupation brought some benefits to Korea. The Japanese built a substantial economic infrastructure of roads, railroads, and public works; they expanded the education of the Korean people at elementary-school level (from an enrollment of 20,000 in 1919 to 900,000 in 1937); they introduced factory discipline to an industrial labor force totalling nearly 200,000 by 1938 and more during the war years (chiefly in north Korea), not counting those among the 2 million Koreans in Japan who worked in industrial plants.[2]

Despite these seeming signs of progress, however, the welfare of the general public was not improved. Grain consumption per capita by Koreans, according to Japanese statistics, diminished from 2.032 *koku* in 1915–19 to 1.668 *koku* in 1930–33 (1 *koku*, called *sok* in Korean, is equal to about 35 liters or 5 U.S. bushels).[3] Rural starvation in the spring grew worse. Gross value of production in Korea for 1938 was 126 yen per capita, compared with 358 for Japan (the yen was then worth about 50 U.S. cents.)

Although net commodity product in Korea grew at a rate of 2 percent per capita over the three decades before World War II,[4] this growth probably did not do most Koreans much good—no more than they would have gained from even an inefficient native rule. Notwithstanding Japanese efforts at educating the Koreans, 87 percent of the Korean population had less than six years of education in 1945. Perhaps the greatest contribution of the Japanese was to engender a Korean determination to equal or outdo them.

During the World War II years, the Japanese drew heavily on Korean resources (as, of course, they did on their own). Factories were diverted to military production; forested hillsides were stripped for timber and fuel; industrial plant depreciated; metals, including family heirlooms of brass, were ruthlessly collected and melted down to make ammunition. In their final weeks, when surrender appeared certain, the Japanese gave their workers a year's salary in advance and paid savings deposits and insurance policies in full, flooding the currency market and creating galloping inflation. The departure of all the hated Japanese expatriates at the end of the war, including the managerial elite, was politically necessary. But the Koreans were left without managers, markets, or (in south Korea) raw materials for a rundown industrial plant that was not designed to serve Korean needs.

The Korean Economy, 1945–1960

Division of Korea between U.S. and Soviet occupying forces in 1945 added still further to Korean economic problems. Most of the natural resources, heavy industry (including fertilizer production), and electric power generation were concentrated in the north; the country's food-basket and center of textile and other light industry were in the south. Although trade between the two zones was not totally suspended until the Korean War, it was severely impeded. North Korea cut the supply of electricity in May 1948, depriving the south of over half of its already inadequate power. In south Korea, initial U.S. policies made the situation even worse. The U.S. occupiers, prepared only with complete faith in free private enterprise and sublime ignorance, removed wartime economic controls. Hoarding, speculation, food shortages, and galloping inflation resulted.[5]

The desperate south Koreans sought fuel and saleables where they could, further denuding the already bare hillsides and actually ripping up Japanese-owned houses and factories for firewood. An influx of Korean repatriates from Japan and elsewhere and a flood of refugees from the Communist regime in the north—perhaps four million or more in both categories by 1951—increased the population by 20 percent. Food production was hindered by fertilizer shortage. South Korean daily caloric intake fell to less than 1,500 per person in 1946–47.

Mass starvation was averted only by U.S. emergency relief under the GARIOA (Government Aid and Relief in Occupied Areas) program, intended to avert disease and unrest that might threaten U.S. forces. From 1945 to 1948, $400 million in aid was given to south Korea, 90 percent of it in food, clothing, fuel, other consumer commodities, and fertilizer. The U.S. military government soon reversed its free-market policies, and rationalized grain collection. Some industry revived with whatever encouragement the U.S. authorities could provide.

In the final months of the occupation, the U.S. authorities made their greatest non-military contribution to Korea's future: the distribution of all Japanese-owned farmland (about 25 percent of the total) to the tillers, to be paid for at the rate of 1.5 times the annual crop, spread over a fifteen-year term. This program constituted the model for eventual redistribution of Korean-owned farmland, largely completed by the south Korean government (under pressure from the United States) during the latter two years of the Korean War.

Because of the U.S. priority for negotiation of reunification with the Soviets and because of U.S. prejudice against centralized state economic planning, there was little overall thought for economic development until 1948; even had there been, no resources were available (GARIOA money could not be used for such purposes). Nevertheless, U.S. and Korean pragmatism and ingenuity managed to keep minimum services operating and even to improve them. For example, the occupation authorities managed to import 101 U.S. locomotives in 1947, thus increasing the locomotive inventory by about two-thirds. When the north Koreans cut off the supply of electricity, the military government brought in power barges. To obtain needed trucks and other items, the military government, acting as the sovereign government of Korea, negotiated a $25 million loan to buy surplus military property (a loan that the new Republic of Korea was forced to assume in 1948, becoming a bone of contention between the two governments for many years thereafter). For their part, the Koreans showed surprising capacity for improvising shoestring repairs to obsolescent equipment and maintaining family and communal existence by hook or crook. When the Republic was declared in 1948, the departing U.S. rulers turned over to it a balanced budget and a reserve in the treasury.

The economic policies of the new Republic of Korea at first were naive, populist, undisciplined, and inflationary. Neither President Rhee nor his new senior appointees understood economics, and for nationalist reasons they were disinclined to take U.S. advice. Besides, they were preoccupied with a large-scale guerrilla challenge to their political control. It took eighteen months of sad experience and a stern U.S. diplomatic demarche (based on the leverage of economic aid, long-delayed but finally enacted) to turn things around.[6] Nevertheless, there were good harvests in 1948 and 1949. A U.S.-financed consultant firm produced a rudimentary economic development plan, stressing coal, electric power, and fertilizer production. Industrial production rose by 50 percent in 1949-1950; coal, by 40 percent; electric power, 33 percent. "For south Koreans as a whole, 1949-1950 was probably the best year they had had in a decade." Despite formidable obstacles, the south Korean economic outlook in the spring of 1950, in the eyes of U.S. observers, was reasonably optimistic.[7]

Meanwhile, north Korea was following a very different economic path. The Soviets, acting through the Korean administration they had established, expropriated all land from former owners—Japanese and Korean—in 1946 and distributed it free of charge to the tillers. All large industry (most of it Japanese-owned) was nationalized,[8] but smaller businesses were not initially seized. These moves were popular with the majority of the population, and the apparent progress and reform were attractive to many people in south Korea as well (notwithstanding the exodus of many north Korean property-owners and professionals to the south). Preparations were made for movement toward collectivization of agriculture and for Soviet-style centralized economic management.

The Korean War shattered the economy of both south and north Korea. In addition to the millions of people killed and injured, physical loss in the south alone was estimated at 400 billion hwan (the unit of currency at the time, officially worth about two US cents) at 1953 prices, nearly the equivalent of the Republic's gross national product for that year.[9] Because of U.S. saturation bombing, the north Korean economic plant was almost totally destroyed, and human casualties were enormous. In addition, north Korea lost many of its most qualified people as refugees to the south, both before and during the war.

Reconstruction began in both halves of Korea after the 1953 Armistice—hindered, on both sides, by the burden of maintaining huge armed forces (over 700,000 in south Korea, and about the same in the north, in the early post-Armistice years). The United States committed $1 billion in grant aid over three years for south Korea, in addition to about $600 million through the United Nations Korea Reconstruction Agency. Total external economic aid to south Korea from 1953 to the mid-1970s, when concessionary U.S. aid ceased, amounted to about $6 billion, not counting the economic impact of an additional $7 billion in military assistance.[10] Exact comparable figures for north Korea are not available, but it is estimated that grant economic aid to the DPRK from the Soviet Union, Eastern European countries, and China totalled about $1.4 billion from 1946 to 1960, after which it dropped sharply.[11]

The patterns of economic development in the two halves of Korea, which were already divergent before the war, moved rapidly in the direction of capitalism in the south and communism in the north. In the south, what was left of the industrial plant was mostly turned over to private owners—some of whom, however, were chosen as much for political loyalty as for economic acumen. Although there was some investment in import-substitution industries and textiles, primary emphasis was on food and other consumer goods to meet minimal living requirements. With revenues from foreign aid supporting over half the Republic's government budget (including defense costs) and constrained by foreign advisers to exercise financial discipline, the south Korean economy had fairly well stabilized by 1957, and living standards had recovered to pre–World War II levels.[12] Yet the diet of most south Koreans in the late 1950s was no more than the minimum requirement, and below that for many.

President Rhee and his supporters had scant understanding of economics. Their strategy was to maximize foreign aid, overvalue their currency, meet the government deficit by printing money and bonds, keep interest rates artificially low, and focus on import substitution for economic growth. Business loans and titles to former Japanese enterprises often were granted for political rather than economic reasons. The future economic outlook was pessimistic. The result was inflation, speculation in land and goods, and discouragement of saving and investment. Although U.S. advice mitigated some of the economic naivete and misdirection, much of it was resisted by the Koreans—as it had been since 1948—for reasons of both principle and political expediency. Moreover, not all U.S. advice was sound, from the Korean point of view. For example, U.S. agricultural representatives pushed wheat sales to the detriment of Korean rice farmers.

Korean reconstruction was also hampered by the U.S. prejudice against national economic planning and by policy disputes among U.S. agencies and between officials of the United States and those of the United Nations Korea Reconstruction Agency (UNKRA). Moreover, it was not until late in the 1950s that U.S. officials and scholars began to understand the problems of the developing world. From 1958 to 1960, the approaching south Korean political crisis inhibited and distorted the economy, at the same time that foreign aid was being reduced in response to domestic U.S. pressures. The situation was worsened by poor crops. Resultant popular frustration at the lack of economic progress was a contributing factor in the political upheaval of 1960. The brief ensuing experiment in free parliamentary democracy in

1960–61 further unsettled the economy, although it did bring the beginning of Korean multi-year development planning.

Under these conditions, the south Korean economy showed approximately a 4 percent average annual real economic growth rate for the period 1953–1962. (In comparison, the Philippine economy grew by 5.4 percent and Taiwan 7.0 percent during the same period.)[13] Population growth of nearly 3 percent a year absorbed most of the economic growth. The remaining per capita increase of around 1 percent—probably dropping to zero or less in the last Rhee years—was not enough to meet popular expectations. In these years, U.S. grant aid was becoming counterproductive by fostering dependence and by discouraging Korean agricultural and industrial growth.

> [President] Rhee used this massive grant assistance as a protection against the necessity of policy changes that would have made the economy more productive and self-supporting and against normalization of relations with Japan. . . . As in so many recorded instances in USAID [U.S. Agency for International Development] relationships, it was the weaker power that held the whip hand.[14]

South Korean Economic Development, 1961–1985

Following their seizure of political power in 1961, General Park Chung Hee and his military associates clearly recognized the importance of rapid economic progress and committed themselves to bring it about. At first, however, they embarked on a series of rash and ill-advised economic policies—born of naive populism and a desire to raise political funds—including deliberate rigging of the stock market, a purge of leading businessmen, manipulation of the banks, and an abortive capital levy in conjunction with currency reform, which brought about further confusion and confrontation with U.S. aid officials.

Nevertheless, the military government learned quickly from its mistakes. Taking the plans of the short-lived Chang Myon administration as a base, it developed a five-year plan for rapid export-led development, with the assistance of the United States (the Kennedy administration accepted new ideas on economic development). The military leaders stabilized the economy and under U.S. pressure brought their budget under control.They managed the economy with far more energy and effectiveness than any previous south Korean administration, utilizing the expertise of U.S.-trained civilian economists.

Domestic savings increased as a result of increased interest rates and stability. Production for export was spurred by an improved foreign exchange regime: The south Korean won (the new unit of currency introduced by the

Park regime), which had had various exchange rates for different purposes, averaging around 130 to the dollar, was devalued to 260 and a single exchange rate established; and export regulations were simplified. Preferential credit was extended to firms with good export performance. Family planning programs, begun in the 1950s, were energetically and effectively pushed. In 1965, encouraged behind the scenes by the United States, the south Koreans normalized relations with Japan, bringing an assistance package of $800 million in various forms of grants and credits. These measures permitted full advantage to be taken of elements of strength that had been accumulating, almost unnoticed, since 1945. They also made the economy credit-worthy, permitting the induction of foreign investment capital for expansion.

By 1965, south Korea was well launched on a course of rapid sustained economic growth, in accordance with its successive five-year plans. As yearly population growth fell to about 1.5 percent, the per capita share of economic growth increased. Real GNP growth averaged 10 percent per year until the second oil shock of 1979; growth was negative in 1980, but resumed in 1981, and averaged 6.8 percent from 1981 through 1985.[15] (Between 1964 and 1985, there were three cycles of high growth followed by recession.)[16] Exports grew from $30 million in 1960 to $30 billion in 1985—a thousand-fold increase at current prices, despite oil shocks and world recession. From 1962 to 1985, real GNP per capita tripled, reaching $2,032. This performance is a principal factor in the restoration of Korean political stability and of Korean pride and self-confidence as a nation.

As the south Korean economy has grown, it has drastically altered in nature from a basically agrarian to an industrialized one. Agriculture made up 50 percent of domestic product in 1953-1955, but dropped to 30 percent by 1970-1972, while the industrial sector's share rose from 11 to 35 percent. Since then, agriculture's share has continued to decline, but in later phases it is the service sector that has expanded most. It is noteworthy that although a similar shift occurred in such countries as Japan or Sweden, it took 40 to 45 years, compared with 20 for Korea.[17]

Income distribution, as well as per capita averages, is an important indication of economic performance. In this respect, south Korea has done much better than most developing countries. A World Bank study published in 1975 showed an inequality between the top and bottom 20 percent of the population roughly comparable to that of the United States, although at a much lower level.[18] Inequality increased during the latter 1970s because of emphasis on heavy industry, inflation, land speculation, and the unequal impact of rural support programs. Since 1980, the situation has somewhat improved. (The Republic's statistics show continuing approximate parity between urban and rural working households, but substantial inequalities continue within both sectors.) In general, south Korea's record continues better than most other comparable countries.[19]

Until 1982, a high rate of inflation (from 15 to over 30 percent per year, averaging an annual 20 percent) had characterized the south Korean economy in most years since 1945. After 1963, inflation was both a means and a cost of rapid growth. In part, it reflected the world situation and internal social pressures (for higher wages and more social services); in part, it was due to inflationary expectations; and in the late 1970s, it was aggravated by overemphasis on investment in heavy industry for greater economic and military independence and export growth. However, new government policies restricting credit and the money supply brought inflation down to single digits in 1982 for the first time since Liberation. Consumer price increases were 3.0 percent in 1985.[20]

A comprehensive Harvard University study of Korea's economic development sought to determine the reasons for south Korea's extraordinary economic performance. It listed the following factors:

- A work ethic, probably derived from the Confucian tradition, comparable to the Protestant ethic of Western Europe;
- The residue left by Japan, including access to techology and management;
- Social mobility and destruction of the traditional structure by liberation, division, social confusion, war, and the return of overseas residents;
- Cultural homogeneity;
- Foreign financial and technical assistance;
- A rapidly expanding educational system.

These factors, according to the Harvard study, produced a disciplined and well-educated work force; an influx of added workers as agricultural productivity increased; access to investable funds from abroad; increased domestic savings; an expanding stock of entrepreneurs; access to foreign technologies. Additional factors were basic political stability and the shift in government policies from inward-looking import substitution to outward-looking export orientation.[21]

In my opinion, the following additional factors can be listed:

- The assurance of national security by the presence of an American shield;
- Korea's earnings from contribution of men and supplies to the United States in Vietnam;
- Improved nutrition levels;
- The precipitous drop in chronic intestinal and other infections that had for centuries drained the Korean people's energy;
- Improvement in the quality of government administration.

South Korea's Current Economic Situation

Overview

The gross national product of the Republic of Korea in 1985 was the equivalent of U.S. $83.1 billion at the year-end exchange rate of 890 won to $1, or $1,976 per capita—a 5.1 percent real increase over the previous year.South Korea ranked twenty-first among the world's nations in gross national product and fortieth in per capita GNP.[22] (A tabulation of south Korean major economic indices is presented in Table 6.2.)

The largest component of the total national product (based on 1984 figures) was services, at 56.6 percent, followed by manufacturing and mining, 29.9 percent, and agriculture and fisheries, 13.5 percent. Merchandise exports and imports in 1985 each were slightly over a third of GNP (exports, $30.3 billion; imports, $31.1 billion). Invisible trade receipts totalled $6.6 billion (of which overseas construction was a large component) and payments, $8.4 billion (including $4 billion in debt service).

The international current account ("balance of payments"), including invisible exports and imports, was a negative $882 million; but this amount compared with $1.4 billion deficit in 1984, $1.6 billion in 1983, and $5.32 billion in the peak year of 1980. Cumulative gross foreign debt amounted to $46.7 billion at the end of 1985, of which $10.7 billion (23 percent) represented short-term commercial loans; the Republic's own foreign assets totalled an offsetting $10.2 billion.[23] Although the gross debt magnitude put Korea fourth among the world's debtor nations, the debt-service ratio (principal and interest to exports) was about 21 percent, which is generally considered a manageable amount.[24]

In 1986, the Republic's national product grew 12.2 percent, to approximately $94 billion (over $2,300 per capita), and south Korea for the first time since the Korean War achieved a significant surplus of over $4 billion in its international trade, enabling a reduction in foreign debt to $45 billion.[25] Commensurate growth and a continued trade surplus were anticipated for 1987.

South Korea's economic system, still in evolution, is intermediate between state capitalism and free enterprise. Government economic powers—both formal and informal—are pervasive and are facilitated by a long tradition of political supremacy over economics. Public ownership (chiefly utilities, fertilizer, iron and steel, chemicals, and other heavy industry) is as high a percentage of Korea's industrial plant as in India, which calls itself a socialist state but has a large private sector.[26] The government sets overall goals, both in successive five-year plans (the Sixth Five-Year Plan began in 1987— see below) and in yearly programs, and guides industry by means of export and production targets, the control of credit (probably its most powerful

TABLE 6.2   South Korean Economic Indicators

| | (US $ million unless otherwise stated) | | | |
	1983	1984	1985	1986[h]
Socio-Economic Indicators				
Population (millions)	40.0	40.6	41.2	41.6
Population growth (%)	1.6	1.6	1.6	1.3
Economic Indicators				
GNP[a], current dollars	75,318	81,118	81,435	95,100
Real GNP growth rate (%)	9.5	7.6	5.0	12.5
Inflation rate (%)	3.4	2.3	3.2	2.3
Per capita GNP ($)	1,885	1,999	1.976	2,395
Per capita real GNP growth (%)	7.9	6.0	3.4	11.2
Unemployment rate (%)[b]	4.1	3.8	4.0	3.8
Investment/GNP ratio (%)	31.5	31.9	31.2	30.8
Govt. expenditure ratio (%)	21.5	21.4	21.4	18.9
Govt. budget balance/GNP ratio (%)	-1.6	-1.4	-1.5	+1.0
Balance of Payments				
US exports to ROK[c]	5,710	5,839	5,720	5,909
US imports from ROK[d]	7,657	10,027	10,711	13,497
US/ROK trade balance[e]	1,947	4,188	4,991	7,400
Total ROK exports	23,204	26,335	26,400	33,000
Total ROK imports	27,464	30,108	29,800	30,000
Trade balance with world	-4,260	-3,773	-3,400	-3,000
Current account balance	-1,606	-1,373	-882	+4,600
Current Finance				
Foreign exchange reserves	6,889	7,629	7,729	7,900
Avg. exchange rate (won/$)	776	806	870	880
Gross external debt[f]	28,400	31,700	36,000	35,200
Annual debt service	6,173	6,757	7,140	9,280
Debt service/export ratio (%)	18.8	20.1	21.7	22.2
Official Foreign Aid				
US economic assistance	0.0	0.0	0.0	0.0
US military assistance[g]	186.7	231.8	231.9	164.5
Total foreign dev. assistance	8.8	n/a	n/a	n/a

[a]GNP = Gross national product   [e]ROK surplus is positive
[b]Official rate, by ILO standards   [f]Medium and long term only
[c]Value free alongside ship (FAS)   [g]Includes grants and credits
[d]Value includes cost, insurance,   [h]Preliminary
   freight (CIF)

Source: Economic Fact Sheets, US Department of State, Jan. 4, 1987, and June 2, 1987, from statistics of Asian Development Bank, International Monetary Fund, Data Resources Asia Review, and US Embassy reports.

lever), and various informal means of pressure and persuasion, as well as the usual fiscal and monetary controls of the economy as a whole.[27] Thus, as of the mid-1980's, the Korean government was still playing a major role in the national economic enterprise and remained its senior partner.

Nevertheless, south Korea has basically a market economy, and its government planners are committed to liberalization. They recognize that Korea already has such a highly developed and complex economy that market forces, rather than government fiat, must be the primary regulator. Private industry has growing latitude to develop products, processes, and markets. The expanding economic power of the leading industrialists gives them increasing independence of action and capacity to influence government policies—several of the Korean conglomerates are listed among *Fortune* magazine's top 500 firms of the world.[28] Business has become socially respectable in recent years and now attracts the best talent. Commercial banks have been returned to private ownership (although they are still closely controlled through the Monetary Board and Ministry of Finance). Restrictions on foreign trade and investment are being relaxed, both to improve domestic industry by foreign competition and to meet complaints from the United States and other trading partners.

The main locus of government economic planning and direction is the Economic Planning Board (EPB), headed by a Deputy Prime Minister. This organization has a sustained reputation for high intellectual ability and competence. It is supported by the Korea Development Institute, a research organization funded by the government but with considerable independence in operation. Other major governmental actors are the Office of the President (which has a senior secretary for economic affairs), the ministries of Finance, Trade and Industry, and Labor, and the central bank (Bank of Korea)—which, however, is controlled by the Ministry of Finance. In 1982, some economic responsibilities, particularly those relating to foreign investment, were transferred from the Economic Planning Board to the functional ministries; but the result was to inhibit rather than facilitate decisions because each of the ministries had its particular interests and its turf to defend. An office has since been installed in the EPB specifically to ensure prompt inter-ministerial coordination and decision when difficulties are encountered, particularly by foreign investors.

Until the 1980s, government policy favored the large combines because large enterprises had lower production costs and could be controlled more easily by the government to assure compliance with its policy of maintaining high export growth. In recent years, however, the government has become concerned at the degree of industrial concentration. It has also recognized the contribution of medium and small enterprises to employment and to innovation, despite their high failure rate—nearly half the small firms organized each year fail. Accordingly, more attention is being given to credit facilities

FIGURE 6.1 A modern south Korean factory (photo courtesy of Korea Overseas Information Service)

through the Medium and Small Industry Bank, quotas of loans from other banks, and other means of encouragement, such as facilitation of exports.

Industry

South Korean industry began in such lines as textile manufacturing, food processing, and light machinery. It was concentrated in Seoul and a half-dozen other major cities. Since the mid-1960s, the government has promoted the development of industrial complexes, such as Ulsan and Pohang on the southeast coast, to reduce the concentration of industry close to the military truce line, mitigate rapid urban growth, and spread employment opportunities more widely. However, in the mid-1980s Seoul and the surrounding areas encompassed almost half the total economic activity (Fig. 6.1).

South Korea's industrial sector is dominated by the huge conglomerates, or *chaebol*. These large firms are both vertically and horizontally integrated (that is, some of the units within a conglomerate produce components for other units' products, while several different units may be engaged in different industries or services, more or less independent of one another). The thirty largest firms represented 16 percent of the Republic's gross national product in 1983, according to a newspaper report (compared with the 20 percent taken by the government's budget). These firms typically include various heavy industries (such as shipbuilding, motor vehicles, machinery, chemicals), consumer industries (food processing, textiles, electric and electronic goods, footwear), and trading companies (general trading company for import and export, plus domestic consumer outlets and distributing agencies). They do not own banks, although they may hold substantial bank equities and may operate investment services. The larger ones are listed in Table 6.3.

The chaebol, like their Japanese counterparts, have high ratios of corporate debt to equity (the money invested by owners and stockholders). They are therefore very vulnerable to economic downturns. This fact was demonstrated by the collapse of the Kukje Group, Korea's seventh-largest conglomerate, in 1985, primarily because of the loss of Middle East markets and over-expansion. In 1985, the ratio of all corporate paid-in capital to total assets was 22.3 percent, slightly down from the previous year and very low by U.S. and European standards. Although the government has been encouraging public sale of stock, most of the firms are wholly or largely owned by the founders and their families.

Although the chaebol predominate in production and export, medium and small firms predominate in employment and numbers. Many of these firms supply the chaebol with parts or components. There was a total of 41,088 manufacturing and mining firms in south Korea in 1983, employing a total of 2.3 million people; 33,373 of the firms employed fewer than 50 employees each, but collectively accounted for nearly a quarter of these workers. Another quarter of employment was provided by 5,840 firms employing 50 to 199 workers.[29]

Textiles were the principal basis for south Korean export expansion and are still the largest industrial component, with 18.6 percent of total manufacturing value added;[30] products range from very high quality silk and polyester through wool, cotton, and hemp cloth and yarn. Textiles also are a leading export component, representing 9 percent of total exports in 1984. However, the textile industry faces growing competition from other developing countries as its labor cost advantage shrinks. At the same time, it meets with growing protectionist barriers in the United States and Europe. Exports decreased by 1 percent in 1985 from 1984 (including apparel) but were recovering at year's end.[31]

Heavy and chemical industry in south Korea began only in the 1970s, except for modest beginnings in fertilizer and pharmaceuticals. Its growth since then has been extraordinary, comprising iron and steel (14 million metric tons or 15.4 million U.S. short tons of pig-iron and steel ingots in 1984), semi-finished and finished iron and steel products, ships, motor vehicles, machine tools, industrial machinery and equipment, electrical machinery and appliances, cement, fertilizer, petrochemicals, and petroleum products. These industries, particularly shipbuilding, suffered in the mid-1980s from world recession and from the oil glut, which reduced the market for ships and construction materials. Automobile manufacturing, however,

TABLE 6.3 Major South Korean Business Firms
(Sales over US$ 1 billion in 1985)

Name of Company	Ranking 1985 1984		Business Lines	(US $ mil equiv.) 1985 Sales	1985 Income
Samsung Corporation (Samsung Group)	1	3	Trade	4,560	7.3
Dae Woo Corporation (Dae Woo Group)	2	1	Trade	4,530	41.1
Hyundai Corporation (Hyundai Group)	3	5	Trade	3,420	5.3
Yukong Ltd. (Sunkyong Group)	4	2	Chemicals	3,360	38.9
Hyundai Engineering & Construction (Hyundai Group)	5	4	Construction	2,390	39.1
Samsung Electronics (Samsung Group)	6	8	Electronics	2,030	25.9
Sunkyong Ltd. (Sunkyong Group)	7	6	Trade	1,980	9.8
Lucky-Goldstar International (Lucky-Goldstar Group)	8	7	Trade	1,950	2.0
Goldstar Co. (Lucky-Goldstar Group)	9	9	Electronics	1,500	13.0
Korean Air (Hanjin Group)	10	11	Air transport	1,350	5.4
Hyundai Motor (Hyundai Group)	11	15	Automobiles	1,260	34.5
Ssangyong Corp.	12	12	Trade	1,100	0.2

Source: Adapted from Business Korea, May 1986, p. 60. Dollar equivalents of sales and net income were calculated at the 29 June 1985 exchange rate of $0.0012 per won, and rounded off. Net income is after taxes.

was on the upswing.The Korean Hyundai Excel sub-compact sold well in Canada in 1985 and entered the U.S. market in 1986, selling a phenomenal 160,000 units in its first year. Machine tool production was increasing for both export and domestic markets—the latter in response to government-encouraged plant expansion.

South Korea's construction industry made enormous inroads into the Middle East during the 1970s, when the oil exporting countries used their high revenues for investment in local industry and social overhead. Korean construction firms, which had developed their skills as contractors for the U.S. military program in Vietnam, successfully transferred and improved these skills, mobilizing several hundred thousand Korean workers to build roads, industrial facilities, public buildings, and housing in several Middle Eastern states.

The decline in the world oil market—and producer revenues—at the end of the decade brought 150,000 Korean construction workers home and sharply reduced this source of foreign earnings. Some companies failed; others reduced their size and scope. Their skills were turned to domestic projects such as land reclamation, government and commercial office buildings, and preparations for the Asian Games in 1986 and the Olympic Games in 1988. Attention was being given to joint ventures with the United States and other countries in the Pacific Basin and elsewhere, especially the member countries of the Association of Southeast Asian Nations (ASEAN),[32] India, and Pakistan.

A period of rapid growth in electrical appliance manufacture and export (radios, watches, television sets, microwave ovens) led to protectionist obstacles, which Korean firms answered through the establishment of manufacturing subsidiaries in the United States. The firms also moved into more sophisticated electronics, some in joint ventures with foreign concerns as a source of advanced technology. Four large Korean firms were manufacturing semiconductors in the mid-1980s; one of them was going into production of advanced (256-kilobyte) random access memory (RAM) chips. Because Korea got a relatively early start in this high-technology field and had a cost advantage over the United States and Japan, it was doing well, although continued growth would depend upon technological advance and high-quality production.

Other major manufacturing activity includes plywood (1 million cubic meters or 1.3 million cubic yards in 1984, down from over 2.5 million cubic meters or 3.3 million cubic yards in the late 1970s because of world market conditions), flour, sugar refining, food canning and processing, paper, and rubber goods (footwear, tires and tubes, industrial rubber), pottery and porcelain.

Energy

Government enterprises dominate the energy field, although there are privately operated coal mines, and oil refineries are mostly in private hands. Korea has as yet no proven oil reserves, although offshore areas on the continental shelf are being explored. The Republic's coal is insufficient and of low quality. Hydroelectric resources are limited and are subject to great seasonal variations because of the concentration of rainfall in the summer. The government has therefore put heavy emphasis on nuclear power generation. Nine plants were in operation or under construction in 1985, with two more in the planning stage; the fifth and sixth units were dedicated in June 1986, bringing nuclear power capacity to 3.8 million kilowatts, or 22.3 percent of total capacity.[33] Of the total of 54 million megawatt-hours of electricity generated in 1985, 22 percent came from the nuclear plants then in operation, 74 percent from thermal plants (oil and coal), and 4 percent from hydroelectric sites.

Armaments

In response to the post-Vietnam shift in U.S. policy, President Park stressed self-reliance in armaments, and the country built up its own weapons manufacturing capacity as well as the heavy industry to support it. In this venture, Korea had the support of the United States, which transferred large quantities of technical data. Although details are secret, south Korea has become almost self-sufficient in conventional weapons—including M-16 rifles, artillery, ammunition, tanks, other military vehicles, and ships. Aircraft are assembled under co-production arrangements with U.S. firms. In the absence of actual combat, armaments production is approximately half of capacity; hence the nation seeks exports. The Koreans complain that the United States, for reasons of both foreign policy and domestic commercial interest, has refused some south Korean requests for export of items manufactured under U.S. license. (Sources in the U.S. Embassy in Seoul stated that the United States turns down no more than about 15 percent of south Korean requests for third-country sales.) Korean arms exports have grown, amounting to $370 million (1.5 percent of total exports) in 1983, but they have grown only half as fast as those of other developing countries.[34]

Agriculture

Rice is Korea's basic crop; and south Korea's yields are impressive, although rising wage levels and land values have made it costly (the retail price of rice is about twice what imported rice would cost). Korea's 1984 rice crop of 5.68 million metric tons (6.2 million U.S. short tons) represented a yield of 4.62 metric tons per hectare (2.06 U.S. tons per acre).[35] For nearly twenty years, the government has bought rice at high prices from farmers and sold it at subsidized prices in the cities to encourage production and improve the farmers' living standards; but by 1983 this practice had accumulated a deficit of over $2 billion, so 1984 support was frozen at 1983 level and has only slightly increased since then.

Barley, grown either on upland fields or in paddies between rice crops, is the second most important crop. In recent years, the government has purchased up to 80 percent of it at support prices and distributed it in the cities, where it is often mixed with rice for eating. (To conserve rice supply, the government for some years has required the mixing of 10 percent barley with rice in public restaurants.) The 1984 harvest totalled 804,000 metric tons (885,000 U.S. short tons). Other major crops include potatoes, wheat, maize, cabbage (used for the national dish known as *kimch'i*), and turnips. Korea imports most of its wheat and feed grains and much of its soybean requirements. Production of fruits and vegetables, both for the domestic market and for export, has increased greatly: South Korea produced 1.2 million metric tons (1.3 million U.S. short tons) of fruit in 1984, of which apples made up nearly half (528,000 tons).

Double-cropping can be practiced in the southern part of the country (usually by growing barley in rice paddies during the winter) and is facilitated by the new practice of growing rice seedlings in plastic hothouses. Double-cropping and inter-cropping (one crop sowed between rows of another) gave south Korea a land utilization ratio of 125 percent in 1984.

To increase their incomes, farmers have been encouraged to grow cash crops such as fruit and vegetables. Plastic hothouses for this purpose have become a common feature of the landscape. Animal husbandry—chiefly of pigs and chickens—has also grown. Milk has entered the Korean diet, and the dairy industry, as well as some raising of cattle for beef, has made great strides. Traditional cash crops such as ginseng, tobacco, tea, and silkworm raising remain important. Some cotton and other commercial fibers are grown.

Korean agriculture faced severe problems in the mid-1980s. Despite its tradition as the peninsula's rice basket, south Korea has not been agriculturally self-sufficient for many years. In 1984, imports—mostly wheat and animal feed corn—made up just under half of requirements. A major reason is that population and income growth have outstripped the very respectable increase in agricultural productivity in two ways: by increasing consumption and, through urban growth, by reducing the stock of agricultural land. In recent years, also, high-yield hybrid strains of rice have proved vulnerable to pests and cold weather and have not met the taste standards of Korean consumers. There had been strong government pressure to plant the new varieties; nevertheless, some farmers have returned to the hardier but lower-yielding traditional varieties.

In addition, south Korea must contend with structural problems. Only 20 percent of the land is arable, and rainfall is less than that of Japan and other rice-growing countries. Farmland has been divided over the centuries into tiny plots, so that individual holdings, averaging slightly over one hectare (about 2.5 acres) in 1984, may be divided into several noncontiguous fields. Although the land reform of 1948 to 1953 was a brilliant political and social success, it perpetuated the fractionation of land, making cultivation relatively inefficient and lessening the opportunity for mechanization.

Agricultural labor costs have risen as young people leave for urban jobs; farm work is increasingly done by women and old men. Costs have also been increased by heavier fertilizer and pesticide use, augmented in recent years by the needs of the new high-productivity rice strains. Budgetary pressure on agricultural price supports has reduced farm income. This factor, probably reinforced by increased propensity of farmers to buy machinery and modern durable consumer goods, has led to an increase of farm household debt, which at the end of 1985 averaged two million won (about $2,300) per household, against average annual farm household income of 5,700,000 ($6,500) won.[36]

For some years, the government has been promoting agricultural improvement to offset these problems, working through the agricultural extension service, New Community Movement, and other agencies. In addition to newly developed plant varieties, improvements include irrigation, fertilizer (of which Korea produces a surplus), mechanization, land rationalization (straightening boundaries, combining small fields), and improved cultivation techniques. For years, extension programs have encouraged handicraft industry such as woodcarving and basket-weaving in farm households to supplement income. Efforts are being made to encourage location and relocation of industry in rural areas, so that farmers can augment their income without leaving for the city. In 1985, farmers got 35.3 percent of their income, on the average, from non-farm sources; this proportion is projected to rise by 1991 to 42.3 percent.[37] The government has commissioned extensive land reclamation projects along the west coast both to compensate for land lost to urban sprawl and to utilize construction industry resources returning from the hard-pressed petroleum exporting countries.

Services

The largest category of Korea's service sector in the mid-1980s was retail trade, most of it still in the hands of hundreds of thousands of small merchants in the nation's cities, towns, and villages, each with a modest storefront and stock. Department stores of the Western type were increasingly common, however, many of them operated by the industrial *chaebol*. A total of 26,054 wholesale and 542,548 retail establishments, and 233,834 hotels and restaurants, employed a total of 1.7 million people (probably not counting family members in small stores).

Communications and rail transportation were in the hands of government ministries or government corporations, but Korean Air Lines, sold by the government to private interests in the 1970s, and all intercity and municipal bus transport were in private hands. Tourism was a rapidly growing industry; the Koreans themselves are enthusiastic travelers, and well over a million foreigners came to south Korea in 1985.

Finance

Although the Government disposed of most of its equity in the five major commercial banks, it retained close control over their policies and operation through the Monetary Board and central Bank of Korea, which are responsible to the Ministry of Finance, and through other regulatory procedures of the Ministry. (A number of smaller banks throughout the country remained in private hands, but their operations were limited.) The principal government lever has been credit policy: Export growth has been promoted by favorable allocation of credit to firms with a good track record.

Korea's domestic savings, particularly public and corporate savings, are growing. In 1984, private savings were 13.8 percent of income, while total domestic savings were over 20 percent. In recent years, such savings have accounted for two-thirds or more of total investment. In the earlier development phases, funds for investment came almost wholly from foreign borrowing. The money came from bilateral government loans (chiefly from the United States and Japan), international lending institutions, and commercial banks. Public ownership of business (in the sense of equities owned by individuals and freely bought and sold) is still in its beginning stages in Korea. There is a stock exchange, with a number of listed securities and daily published listings of transactions; but the majority of enterprise is still family owned. Business financing is primarily through bank loans or borrowing on the informal (and high-interest) "curb market" of private lenders; the result is that Korean corporations have very high ratios of debt to equity and are very vulnerable to changes in credit cost and availability. Among private sources of money are *kye*, informal groups of people who contribute to a pool of money that is loaned out at high interest by each member of the group in turn for an agreed period. Altogether, the scale of curb market operations is quite large because money is not readily available from banks, particularly for small-scale or venturesome operations.

The banks, also, have been in a difficult position because some of their loans have been made according to government policies rather than profitability or even credit-worthiness. They thus face non-repayment of loans and falling profits in times of economic contraction. The ability of the central bank to control the money supply through traditional means such as the rediscount rate and reserve requirements is therefore limited, making further resort to political controls rather than traditional monetary levers necessary.

Labor

In 1985, according to government statistics, south Korea had an economically active population of 15.5 million people. This figure does not include approximately 2 million high school and college students, nor many family members participating in small businesses. It also omits women not working or not actively seeking work; many of these are sure to enter the job market, in view of the growing movement for women's rights. Statistically, 300,000 young people are expected to enter the labor force each year for some years to come, until the surge from the postwar baby boom abates by the mid-1990s.

The average worker's wage was 269,000 won (about $300) per month in 1985. The International Labour Organisation (ILO) reported the average south Korean workweek that year as 53 hours. Although the Ministry of Labor stated that workers received an average of 19 days off per year, the prevailing impression is that few get so many days. Construction workers earned 528,000 won. However, at the end of 1985, 8.9 percent of manufacturing workers received less than 100,000 won (about $110) per month, which was the anticipated level of a minimum wage projected for adoption in 1988. Of these low-wage workers, 29.7 percent were in the textile industries, which have traditionally employed young women—many of them housed in dormitories—who augment their families' incomes and save up for marriage. In other industries, as well, most of the low-wage workers were unmarried women. Altogether, the wages of three to five hundred thousand workers were at or below 100,000 won per month.[38]

Officially registered unemployment in Korea has been low for many years. In 1985, the rate was 4.0 percent (computed according to ILO standards, which classify as employed a person who works one hour or more per week). This figure is not fully comparable with American unemployment statistics—which are based on a broader definition—and probably conceals a great deal of underemployment in agriculture and small business. Nevertheless, it reflects the success of the south Korean economy, since the mid-1960s "take-off," in harnessing its abundant human resources.

Wage levels have risen, in both real and nominal terms, over most of the period since the early 1960s. In the late 1970s, because of high inflation, they rose faster than productivity, thus threatening Korea's competitiveness on world markets. The downward trend in productivity continued until 1984, when it again began to rise.[39] Wages for blue-collar workers, in most recent years, have risen faster than those for white-collar workers as a consequence of growing labor impatience with low Korean standards and the growing ability of the educational system to deliver the necessary skills in requisite quantities (the growth of educational enrollments has produced an oversupply of graduates in some categories). There were over three thousand labor actions in the summer of 1987, resulting in an estimated average increase in workers' wages of somewhat over 20 percent.

Although south Korea has had organized labor unions since 1945, they have a tradition of being more politically than economically oriented. At present, however, the officially sanctioned labor organizations concentrate their attention on economic matters. The Communists used unions for political purposes from 1945 to 1948; Syngman Rhee used them for political purposes from 1948 to 1960. Since that time, organized labor activity has been severely circumscribed, both to contain the potential political threat and to prevent wage increases that would hurt Korea's export drive. Until late 1987 Korean labor laws were highly restrictive, although the Constitution guarantees the right of collective organization and action. As noted in Chapter 4, the change in political policy in the summer of 1987 was followed by an upsurge of strikes and other labor actions in support of demands for better wages and working conditions and freedom to organize. The labor laws have already been revised, and a somewhat freer climate for organized labor activity will almost certainly result.

Under the labor laws as they existed in early 1987, a national labor federation (the Federation of Korean Trade Unions) and sixteen national industrial federations existed in south Korea; but they were forbidden to enter into specific negotiations without government permission. Labor unions at individual plants might bargain collectively, and in theory had the right to strike after other remedies were exhausted; but the Ministry of Labor and its constituent divisions and committees played a major role in all labor negotiations. Each plant was required to have a labor-management council, separate from the union, to deal with labor problems, including wages, other benefits, and working conditions. There were strikes and sit-ins even before the upsurge of mid-1987, such as the sit-in by auto workers at a major plant in the port city of Inch'on in early 1985. Nevertheless, the steady, if slow, growth of wages and benefits, together with government controls, was apparently sufficient to avoid massive labor unrest, except at such times as the oil-shock year of 1979 and again in 1987.

In the mid-1980s, although some strikes had involved large plants such as that in Inch'on, the main labor problem areas were small firms. Unsafe and unhealthy working conditions were not uncommon in such establishments and were inadequately controlled by overworked government inspectors. Wages were frequently very low, especially in industries that have traditionally depended upon low-wage labor by young women expecting to get married. Discontent in such sectors has been given voice and support by activist

Christian social groups, particularly the Urban Industrial Mission, which was put under government ban. Increasingly, also, students have disguised their backgrounds, taken blue-collar jobs as "disguised workers," and mobilized the plant work force to improve their wages and working conditions.

The government's response, up to mid-1987, was twofold. On the one hand, it was slowly moving to correct some of the abuses; the draft Sixth Five Year Plan emphasizes social benefits, and a minimum wage was promised for 1988. On the other hand, it moved forcefully to suppress labor disturbances, frequently arresting the leaders, especially when "disguised workers" were involved.

For some years, the Republic of Korea's admission to the International Labour Organisation was opposed by many of its members because of their adverse view of south Korean political and working conditions. Support for south Korea has grown, however; at present the opposition is chiefly by Communist nations, which insist that north Korea also be admitted and which have been able to prevent the necessary two-thirds vote for south Korea. It seems probable that the Republic will be admitted to the ILO within the next few years.

The International Component
in South Korea's Economy

A persisting myth about south Korea is that the country is still receiving large amounts of concessionary assistance from the United States. Such is not the case. The reality is that for nearly two decades, Korea has met its capital investment requirements on a competitive international market and, increasingly, from domestic savings. Commercial banks, the World Bank, and foreign governmental agencies (which are motivated more by their own trade promotion than by Korea's needs) have been the sources of Korean government and private borrowing. Total direct foreign equity investment in south Korea totalled well over $1 billion in the mid-1980s. The government has sought and applied foreign advice, particularly from the World Bank, but it has made its own economic plans and policies. The last resident U.S. aid official left the country in the early 1970s, as remaining U.S.-financed projects were winding up.

South Korea's dependence upon foreign trade means that the nation is highly vulnerable to international market fluctuations, which are largely responsible for Korea's economic cycles. So far, the government's economic management has coped very well with these fluctuations. The large south Korean foreign debt means vulnerability to changes in the availability of foreign money and in international interest rates; here, again, the government's management of its debt has been effective. Both vulnerabilities lead to a south Korean desire to maximize its self-reliance, within the limits set by the character of its economy. Not only is it in the national interest to do so, but there is also a feeling among Koreans, voiced largely by intellectuals and students, but more generally shared, that too much foreign penetration puts the nation's own personality and identity at risk. There are fears, also, of social dislocation resulting from the impact of foreign competition on Korean industry and agriculture.

South Korea's growing economic power and importance have attracted foreign businesspeople in increasing numbers. Most visible are the foreign banks (including several U.S. banks), which are gradually becoming competitive with domestic banks as restrictions on them are eased (but like all south Korean banks, they are subject to close regulation). In 1985, fifty-two foreign banks collectively made an estimated profit of over $100 million on their Korean business. Larger equities, however, are held by a long list of U.S., Japanese, and other firms doing business in south Korea either as joint ventures or as wholly owned subsidiaries, including such giants as General Motors, Ford, Du Pont, and International Business Machines (IBM). (South Korean investment in the United States is also significant: Korean firms own coal mines in Alaska and Pennsylvania and manufacturing plants in Alabama and New Jersey.)

Since the late 1970s, south Korean economic planners have favored liberalization of their government's restrictions on international trade and on foreign participation in Korean business. In part, this policy responds to demands from the United States and other countries for free access to Korean markets; in part, it reflects a conviction that south Korea will benefit from foreign competition in terms of its own production quality and efficiency, as well as from availability of certain foreign goods. Above all, it is recognized that the Republic must compete internationally on a level of constantly advancing technology, the source of which is largely the industrialized countries.

In July 1985, the south Korean government officially changed its control policy on foreign investment from a "positive list" to a "negative list" basis—that is, any activity not specifically restricted or prohibited was open to investment. Full foreign ownership of a business was possible in many of the areas not on the negative list. In the area of commodity trade, as well, import restrictions have been significantly eased. By the end of 1985, the south Korean government claimed that 78 percent of imports had been freed of prohibitions or restrictions (although not necessarily from import tariff) and that tariff rates had been reduced to an average level of 33 percent.[40] President Chun Doo Hwan, in his visit to European capitals in the Spring of 1986, stressed south Korea's support for a free international trading system.

Despite the evident sincerity of this liberalization policy on the part of the economic planners, the actual situation was much more complicated from the foreign businessperson's point of view. One reason was that the government was still seeking to control imports in order to reduce its balance of payments deficit. Also, strong vested interests both within the bureaucracy and in business circles resisted liberalization, both on the basis of principle—avoidance of foreign economic influence—and of self-interest—maintenance of traditional protection from competition from abroad. In addition, the dismantling of long-established bureaucratic controls and prerogatives is a complex and painful process. Moreover, many Koreans still believed that the United States, as a rich and powerful nation with special responsibilities toward Korea, should continue the preferential treatment of the past and were resisting U.S. moves to reduce Korean benefits under the Generalized System of Preferences (giving special consideration to imports from developing countries).

Basic differences in philosophy and practice between Korean and Western ways of doing business greatly complicate the operation of foreign business in Korea. In addition, there is a combination of die-hard nationalism, self-interest, and inertia among some influential Korean circles (including intellectual opposition to the specter of imperialist domination and opposition politicians' exploitation of the foreign trade issue to make any Korean concessions seem like toadyism). Foreign businesspeople react with indignation and frustration and call for support of their own governments to get treatment more like what they would expect at home. U.S. trade with south Korea showed a negative balance of $3.5 billion in 1985—the third year of deficit after twenty years of surplus (and may rise to $10 billion in 1987). Although the amount was small in comparison with the total U.S. trade deficit, or even the deficit of $35 billion with Japan, it added urgency to U.S. demands for better access to the Korean market.

In the mid-1980s, such demands centered on the service industries, where U.S. and other foreign competitive advantage tended to be high—financial services, insurance, and professional services such as law and accounting. Also at the center of controversy was Korea's traditional lack of concern for intellectual and other non-tangible property rights, such as copyrights and trademarks. The pirating of foreign-language books by Korean publishers was essentially uncontrolled. More serious, the pirating of sophisticated computer software challenged the whole concept of protection that had evolved with the computer industry in the United States.

The south Korean government at that time was moving slowly toward opening the service sector and toward enforcement of intellectual property rights. It was nevertheless encountering stiff resistance from Korean entrepreneurs and professionals. Such people claimed, not without reason, that the Korean service industry was still in its infancy, especially in the leading sectors where foreign entry was being sought, and that foreigners would soon dominate the whole area if protection were denied. An important milestone of progress was south Korea's agreement with the United States in mid-1986 to open its insurance industry, remove the ban on foreign cigarettes, and move toward stiffer copyright protection.

For the first twenty years of its existence, south Korea depended heavily on the United States for economic and technical aid. As its economy grew, the Republic looked to the United States for an export market and for investment and technology. Since 1965, Japan has also been a major market and investment source, overtaking the United States in some years as principal trading partner. In 1985, the United States provided a market for 35.5 percent of Korea's exports and Japan, 15.0 percent; the two nations' shares of total Korean imports were 20.8 and 24.3 percent, respectively.

In recent years, the Republic has vigorously sought to diversify its trade, both to reduce its dependence and to combat growing protectionism. The President, Prime Minister, other senior officials, and business leaders have travelled extensively to promote trade. Although the United States and Japan still dominate foreign trade, the diversification policy has had significant results. In 1985, Hong Kong (surrogate for Mainland China) took 5.2 percent of south Korean exports; Canada, 4.1 percent; West Germany, 3.2 percent; Saudi Arabia, 3.2 percent; United Kingdom, 3.0 percent. The remaining 31 percent of exports (after the 50.3 percent to the United States and Japan) was widely distributed among European, Middle Eastern, African, Asian, and Latin American countries, with European countries and Australia predominating.

On the import side (apart from Japan and the United States), 4.0 percent came from Malaysia, 3.6 percent from Australia, and 3.1 percent from West Germany. As would be expected, oil-exporting states were significant import sources: Indonesia (2.1 percent), Saudi Arabia (2.1 percent), and Kuwait (1.7 percent). Hong Kong provided only 1.6 percent of imports. The remaining import shares were widely distributed.

South Korean Economic Prospects:
The Sixth Five-Year Plan

Three forces are inducing a reorientation of Korea's basic development policy: first, increasing resistance in the industrialized countries—south Korea's primary markets; second, competition from other developing nations with cheaper labor; third, growing popular pressure at home for improvement in the quality of life and social welfare. The latter factor, in its economic dimension of upward pressure on wage levels, is also reducing Korea's competitiveness in the international market as newly emerging suppliers (such as China, India, Indonesia, Thailand, and Malaysia) enter the market for traditional labor-intensive commodities.

The response of Korea's planners has been to lower the expected level of future annual GNP growth to a range of 7 to 7.5 percent, in contrast to levels of 9 to 10 percent in earlier years (although growth was 12.2 percent in 1986 and probably over 10 percent in 1987, because of the boost to the Korean economy given by the "three lows"—lower oil prices, lower interest rates, and lower value of the dollar, hence the won, against the Japanese yen). Future planning includes diversification of export markets, including joint ventures with industrialized countries to meet the needs of developing nations; more emphasis on meeting domestic needs for goods and services; emphasis on growth of capital-intensive, high-technology industrial sectors; and reduction of foreign indebtedness.

Such growth, in turn, means more foreign participation, since although Korea has produced its own technological breakthroughs, the primary sources remain foreign. Moreover, the two-decade-long outward orientation of south Korea's economy, even if somewhat modified, will undoubtedly continue. Korea's domestic market, "while growing rapidly, remains too small to support 7 to 7.5 percent growth. Within that export-oriented model, however, major adjustments are necessary. . . . Korean economic policy-makers must try to reduce trade frictions by diversifying their export goods and the markets for those goods."[41]

For the next several years, Korea's past baby boom will require at least a 7.5 percent annual increase in national product to absorb new entrants into the job market and perhaps more, even assuming continuation of current capital-labor ratios. (One recent study, by the Bank of Korea, suggests that 10 percent annual growth would be needed to produce enough jobs.) Movement toward capital-intensive industry and increasing demands for employment by women not now listed as economically active (such as housewives) would aggravate the problem. More education may alleviate the problem but cannot solve it. However, by the mid-1990s the number of young entrants into the job market will fall off. The new problem (like that of Japan and the United States) will be how to maintain or improve social welfare levels for an increasing aged population out of contributions by a diminishing active population.

South Korea's inflation and recession of the late 1970s was brought on partly by adverse international economic circumstances, especially the "second oil shock," and partly by a forced-draft drive for increased self-sufficiency in defense-related industry in response to perceived weakening of the U.S. presence and commitment in East Asia. The economy made a successful recovery; and as of 1986, the international climate for continued growth seemed at its most favorable in some years.

Credible reassurance of the U.S. security commitment since 1980 reduced the south Korean preoccupation with self-sufficiency. Nevertheless, Korea's national interest continued to dictate some reasonable degree of economic independence, to insulate the country from further unforeseen shocks. One obvious response to this problem (as well as to increased foreign protectionism) is increased import substitution—a strategy not followed in south Korea since the early 1960s. The potentialities are limited, however, because of south Korea's dearth of raw materials.

The Korea Development Institute, in a study of south Korea's development to the year 2000, foresaw a population of 49.4 million, increasing 1.1 percent a year (compared with the present 1.5 percent). The EPB also projected per capita income of slightly over $5,000 in 1984 prices; price stability at 3 to 4 percent inflation throughout the period; agriculture diminishing from 13.7 percent of GNP (1984) to 8.3 percent; mining and manufacturing increasing proportionately (from 29.7 to 33.2 percent), while services, including social overhead capital, would remain about constant. Heavy industry's share of manufacturing (in terms of value added) is projected to double, reaching about 50 percent; automobile manufacturing will play a leading role, with exports increasing 30 percent a year at first, 22 percent later.[42]

These projections (assuming other countries continue growth at their present rates) would move south Korea from a "medium" to a "large" economic power—perhaps the ninth-largest international trader. Yet south Korea's income levels would still be below those of the leading industrialized countries. Thus, Korea's continuing competitive advantage would be offset by protectionist reaction to the greater challenge posed by her larger economy.[43]

In early 1987, after two years or more of study and discussion, the Republic of Korea published its Sixth Five-Year Plan for the years 1987–1991, moving toward the goals for the year 2000 already described.[44] The broad overall economic targets of the plan are summarized in Table 6.4. They include a gross national product of $175 billion ($4,000 per capita) in 1991; exports reaching $55.8 billion; a current account surplus of $5 billion; and a total foreign debt of $32.9 billion, representing a reduction of nearly $12 billion, or over a quarter of the total at the end of 1986.

However, the Sixth Five-Year Plan emphasizes balance and adjustment, as well as growth. Externally, emphasis is to be given to expansion into new markets in Europe and the Third World, making use of joint ventures with industrialized countries and locating manufacturing subsidiaries abroad. Traditional export industries such as textiles, overseas construction, and shipping will give place to more competitive sectors, and painful domestic adjustments will probably ensue.

Internally, more attention is to be given to small and medium industry in an effort to reduce the economic domination of the *chaebol* and increase employment and innovation. More important from the standpoint of domestic popular demands will be balanced growth among economic sectors and

TABLE 6.4   Targets of the Sixth Five-Year Plan, Republic of Korea

Item	Amount, 1987	Amount, 1991	% change[a]
Gross National Product (billion US $)	108.9	175	+61
GNP per capita (US $)	2,600	4,000	+54
Commodity exports (billion US $)	39	55.8	+43
Commodity imports (billion US $)	35.3	52.5	+49
Current account surplus (billion US $)	5	5	0
Total foreign debt (billion US $)	41.8	32.9	-21
Total investment ratio (%)	29.7	31.3	+ 5
Domestic savings (%)	32.8	33.5	+ 2
Tax burden (%)	18.4	20.0	+ 9
Unemployment (%)	3.6	3.7	+ 3

[a]Percentages calculated by the author to show the scale of increases (+) or decreases (-) between the first and final years of the Sixth Five-Year Plan. These are crude figures, since they are not adjusted for inflation or exchange-rate changes.

Source: Korea's Economy 3 (No. 2, 1987), p. 2, citing the American Chamber of Commerce in Korea.

geographic regions, and among people of various income levels. Some steps in this direction will be the development of industry outside the great urban centers; more autonomy for local governments in budgeting and expenditure; establishment of a national pension program in 1989, and extension of medical insurance to the entire population by that year. Establishment of a minimum wage is expected in 1988, as is the extension of elementary education to include nine grades, instead of the present six.

A further goal of the Sixth Five-Year Plan is the "internationalization" of Korea, both through economic measures such as import and exchange rate liberalization and through increasing the people's awareness of the outside world by programs such as augmented foreign language instruction.

In moving toward its five-year goals, the south Korean government faces the inevitable trade-off between economic and managerial efficiency, on the one hand, and the greater freedom associated with political development, on the other. "The advantages of political decentralization in opening up the political process are indisputable; the obvious corollary, however, is a diminution in the national government's ability to rapidly carry out new initiatives."[45] Nevertheless, south Korea has done very well in fulfilling or exceeding its previous five-year program goals. Given a reasonably stable international environment, the odds seem fairly good that the 1991 targets will be fulfilled along with the inevitable political changes.

Evolution of the North Korean Economy

The Democratic People's Republic of Korea, since its establishment in 1948, has sought to maximize the individual and collective welfare of its citizens by doing away with what it considers the evils of capitalism and enforcing the doctrines of Karl Marx, as interpreted by Lenin and Stalin in the Soviet Union. Unlike China and most Communist states of Eastern Europe, which also became Communist during Stalin's time, north Korea has adhered to the rigid authoritarianism and state planning of the Stalinist model more closely than the Soviet Union itself. However, north Korea, under the leadership of Kim Il Sung, has made its own modifications in both ideology and practice to meet its own conditions. The desire for an independent national personality, and probably the impact of reductions in levels of support from the Soviet Union and China in the early 1960s, gave birth to the doctrine of *juche* (self-reliance).

Economic Theory and Organization

In accordance with Marxist doctrine, private ownership in north Korea is limited to personal and household possessions. All means of production are owned either by groups of citizens organized as cooperatives or by various organs of the state at national or local level. Neither north Korea nor any other Communist state has reached the stage of communism as envisaged by Marx because the state (which is to wither away when true communism is practiced) still exists and because ownership of most agricultural land is still in the hands of individual collectives, rather than of the people as a whole. Kim Il Sung himself has stated that the communist stage is still far in the future because reactionary capitalism is still obstructing development and class enemies still exist even within the country. However, the "socialism" of north Korea and other Communist states is very different from the democratic socialism of such countries as Sweden, in which the economy responds to the laws of the market rather than to central government plans.[46]

The economic and political structures of north Korea, for practical purposes, are one and the same. By far the largest proportion of government agencies and personnel are devoted to the management of manufacturing, agriculture, finance, trade, and related services and activities; only such ministries as Foreign Affairs, Security, and Justice, out of the thirty-odd agencies represented on the State Administrative Council, are political in nature. The ministries—in coordination with inter-ministerial committees—control the largest plants and state farms directly; smaller enterprises are administered by provincial and local agencies. Agricultural collectives are controlled by county officials.[47]

Key economic decisions are centered in the State Planning Commission, a cabinet-level agency that sets production and activity levels for all economic entities. In the absence of a competitive market, the requirements and outputs of all economic units must be matched against one another and against estimates of over-all needs. Quotas are assigned to each mine, factory, and farm for the complex process in which mines produce for factories, factories produce for other factories and farms, and the whole structure then produces consumer goods for the people, the government, and the armed forces. Actual performance is monitored and necessary adjustments of quotas are made as necessary. Prices at all levels are set on the basis of costs of production, and wages are set on the basis of the cost of living, with some recognition for superior skills and service.

In carrying out its task, the State Planning Commission draws upon the recommendations of the individual plants and farms, the national ministries, the provincial and local government agencies (which themselves handle some of the planning process at their levels), the experience of previous years, and the goals of the overall multi-year plans. Once the quotas are assigned, they are enforced by the various operating ministries and local government agencies. Broad overall policies and goals are determined (on behalf of all the people) by the senior officials of the Korean Workers' Party, which monitors the work of the Commission and other government agencies through its members' presence in them (the Party has its own bureaucracy, paralleling that of the government), and through the agencies' reports.

This, in the view of Communist thinkers, is a better way of operation than capitalism because no unit makes a profit (surpluses revert to the state, a system that made it possible for north Korea to abolish taxes); nobody pays interest to parasitic moneylenders; and all benefits generated from the national economy accrue to the people as a whole, since the people own everything. Moreover, the workers and peasants, since they are all working for themselves and for their fellow comrades, are expected to do their best for the common good, without the motive of selfish personal gain which leads to inequality and injustice under capitalism. (Exhortations to workers and peasants for redoubled unselfish devotion to work are daily fare in north Korean leaders' statements and in mass media, and many hours are devoted to public education along these lines.) In a capitalist system, benefits would accrue to a small handful of monopolistic entrepreneurs and moneylenders, manipulating the entire system for their own selfish profit. In the Marxist-Leninist-Kim Il Sungist system, benefits are supposed to be distributed equally among all the people. This supposition is, of course, based on the assumption that the leaders use their power only to make the system work and not to benefit themselves (an assumption similar to that concerning scholar-officials in the traditional Confucian state).

Historical Experience

In earlier years, the theory—supported by strong central planning and centralized, vigorous authoritarian administration—seems to have worked well. Starting from a completely shattered economy in 1951, with the benefit of foreign aid for the first few years, north Korea scored very impressive gains that far outdistanced the then stagnant south Korean economy. Yearly growth in national product reached as high as 20 percent.[48]

These gains did not necessarily produce a proportionate improvement in general living standards, because Communist economic doctrine gives priority to heavy industry, deferring consumer benefits until the basic industrial structure is in place (whereas in south Korea the emphasis was on meeting basic individual needs first). However, the north Korean people, comparing their lot to their experience under Japanese domination and virtually cut off from the rest of the world by a totalitarian regime, seem generally to have accepted what they got, although there may have been a leadership dispute over the priority given heavy industry at the expense of consumer goods. A Five-Year Plan for economic growth was apparently completed a year ahead of schedule, in 1960 rather than 1961, although it took a forced-draft Chollima (Flying Horse) Movement, similar to China's Great Leap Forward, to do so.

Subsequently, however, the north Korean economy seems to have run into trouble. The government stopped publishing quantitative production statistics in the mid-1960s and has never resumed doing so except for individual products at various times—announcing results only in terms of percentage increases. The First Seven-Year Plan (1961–1967) had to be extended three additional years, to 1970. There have been two subsequent multi-year plans—the Six-Year Plan (1971–1976) and the Second Seven-Year Plan (1978–1984); but during this period there have been internal readjustments in organization and method and constant exhortations for redoubled effort by workers, particularly in apparent bottleneck areas such as mining and transportation, coupled with criticisms of bureaucratism. A U.S. government study in 1977 concluded that the falling north Korean economic growth rate intersected with the rising south Korean growth rate around 1975.[49] South Korean scholars maintain that the south's GNP is over five times the north's, or nearly two and one-half times as large on a per capita basis.[50]

Given the lack of reliable information on north Korea's economy, the reasons for the economic slowdown cannot be precisely stated. The north Koreans themselves attributed it to the burden of a defense buildup; they put their military expenditures at around 15 percent of their national budget (which constitutes about 80 percent of the national economy). Other estimates of military expenditure run as high as 25 percent of national product.

In addition, it is known that external aid declined steeply—first from the Soviet Union under Khrushchev, in the late 1950s, and then from China during the Great Cultural Revolution. Furthermore, north Korea has suffered from labor shortage, both from wartime losses by death and defection and from the high proportion of men under arms (over 800,000 in 1985, out of a population of about 20 million). It was presumably for this reason that north Korea persuaded 100,000 Korean residents of Japan to immigrate[51] in the late 1950s and has encouraged a very high birthrate (population increase was estimated at 2.8 percent annually in earlier years and 2.6 percent per year from 1973 to 1984, almost 50 percent above the rate of the south).[52]

The tone of north Korean internal propaganda, together with some apparent decentralization of controls to lower governmental levels—including an accounting system that makes individual plants responsible for balancing their costs and revenues—suggests that the highly centralized economic control system is working less well as the economy grows more complex. It presumably suffers from the usual problems of inertia, time-serving, and assertion of status that are common to large established bureaucracies and has had trouble in controlling the many variables of the economic system without the discipline of impersonal market forces.

Moreover, the north Koreans have increasingly resorted to financial incentive devices, as well as non-material awards, to promote worker and management productivity, suggesting that notwithstanding Marxist theory, communist principles have not yet found altruism to be a driving force equal to old-fashioned monetary benefits in practice. Farmers are allowed, for example, to cultivate "private plots" of up to about 100 square meters (1,076 square feet), the crops from which can be sold at periodic peasant markets at uncontrolled prices. Both industrial and agricultural enterprises can distribute some earnings above quota, and work teams can earn extra financial benefits if their quotas are exceeded.

A major administrative reform was inaugurated in 1960. Kim Il Sung, in the course of one of his many "on-the-spot guidance" visits around the country, called for a new form of agricultural collective organization in which a local Party committee worked with the administrative manager to set policies and itself had responsibility for ideological work. This dual directorate, called the Chongsan-ni Method after the place it was announced, was extended the following year to industry in a similar visit by Kim Il Sung to a factory at T'aean.

In the early 1970s, notwithstanding their heavy emphasis on self-reliance, the north Koreans sought to import Western plants and techniques to upgrade their own obsolescent industry. This move backfired partly because of the 1973 oil crisis; the government was unable to discharge its debt obligations, totalling over $2 billion, and has been more or less in default ever since to Japan and several other countries, including Sweden, Finland, Austria, and Indonesia. Foreign-exchange problems were apparently so severe that north Korean diplomatic missions abroad were required to support themselves. Some embassies resorted to smuggling through their diplomatic pouches.

Another means of attacking north Korean problems was the campaign of Three Revolutions—technological, ideological, and cultural—launched in the early 1970s, apparently under the leadership of Kim Il Sung's son and heir-apparent, Kim Jong Il. This campaign sought to encourage innovation and to eliminate the barriers of negative bureaucratic attitudes. It included the organization of Three Revolutions teams composed of qualified party and government officials who visited industrial sites to upgrade management and productivity.

Most recently, the Supreme People's Assembly approved a policy, promulgated as law in September 1984, for organizing joint ventures with foreign governments or concerns to promote the north Korean economy. This innovation may have reflected a similar and earlier Chinese move. The first two such ventures were a Japanese department-store chain and a French tourist hotel. In 1987, north Korea signed a joint-venture agreement with the Soviet Union, and ground was broken for the rehabilitation of a gold mine by a joint venture between Korean residents of Japan and a north Korean agency. There may be as many as fifty joint ventures as of late 1987.

Present State of the North Korean Economy

The gross national product of the Democratic People's Republic of Korea for 1984 was estimated by the south Korean government's National Unification Board at U.S. $14.7 billion or $762 per capita. This figure is somewhat speculative both because of the absence of reliable data on north Korea and because there is no real basis on which to establish an exchange rate

TABLE 6.5   North Korean Economic Indicators

	Year	Amount
Population	1987	21.4 million
Population growth rate	1987	2.5 percent
Gross national product	1985	$24-30 billion[a]
GNP growth rate	1984	2.7 percent
Per capita GNP	1985	$900-1500[b]
Government budget		
Revenues	1987	$15.2 billion[c]
Expenditures	1987	$15.2 billion[c]
Exports	1985	$1.38 billion
Imports	1985	$1.72 billion
External debt	1985	$2-3 billion

[a]Approximate range of estimates; firm statistics are unavailable, and the exchange rate is arbitrary.

[b]Range of estimates.

[c]Calculated on the arbitrary exchange rate of 2 north Korean won to one U.S. dollar.

Sources: The Economist Intelligence Unit, Country Profile: China, NorthKorea 1987-88 (London, 1987); U.S. Central Intelligence Agency, Handbook of Economic Statistics 1986: A Reference Guide (Washington, D.C., 1986); U.S. Central Intelligence Agency, The World Factbook, 1987 (Washington, D.C., 1987); U.S. Department of State, [North] Korea: Background Notes (Washington, D.C., May 1986)

between the north Korean won and the dollar (or south Korean won).[53] Given the source of the estimate, it is probably quite conservative. The *World Development Report* puts north Korean per capita GNP in the "lower middle income economies" (the category next below south Korea's), with a per capita GNP between $700 and $1,600 for 1984. The south Korean figure for 1984 was $1,999.[54] A south Korean compilation of major north Korean economic indices is presented in Table 6.5.

Official north Korean statements have promised increased attention to consumer goods production, in terms of both quantity and quality—responding, presumably, to long pent-up demand. There is no firm statistical evidence to indicate whether such promises have been translated into action. Foreign visitors to north Korea agree that amenities are far behind those readily available in the south; however, there seems to be no evidence of severe deprivation. The north Koreans have succeeded fairly well in enforcing equal distribution of poverty. Upper-level government and party officials apparently have access to special stores and other benefits, as in the Soviet Union.

The Second Seven Year Plan was scheduled for completion in 1984. The relative lack of specific data in official north Korean statements at the time raised a question as to whether its targets had been fulfilled. One of the few quantitative announcements was the report to the Supreme People's Assembly in early 1985 that 10 million metric tons (11 million U.S. short tons) of grain had been produced the previous year, or two-thirds of the 1990 target, which may have brought the country to agricultural self-sufficiency.[55]

In April 1987, in announcing the Third Seven Year Plan, Prime Minister Li Kun Mo explained that 1985 and 1986 had been years of adjustment, but that the previous plan had been "successfully fulfilled on schedule." He then announced the results, including increase of industrial output of 2.2 times, attainment of the annual production targets of 70 million metric tons (77 million U.S. tons) of coal, 5 million metric tons (5.5 million U.S. tons) of chemical fertilizer, and 12 million tons (13 million U.S. tons) of cement. Over 800 million meters (872 million yards) of annual textile production and 3.6 million tons (4 million U.S. tons) of marine products were produced annually. Application of chemical fertilizer per hectare exceeded 2 metric tons (2.2 U.S. tons); 1,500 kilometers (930 miles) of railroad had been electrified, bringing electrically hauled freight to 88.3 percent. A total of 17,785 new modern factories and workshops were built. National income had been increased 80 percent.[56]

Because of north Korea's endowments of natural resources, it is far less dependent upon foreign trade than the south. However, it is also far less competent, because of its economic reclusiveness, to compete on the world market. Its principal trading partners are the Soviet Union, China, and Japan, in that order. In 1979, according to a south Korean tabulation, 51.5 percent of north Korean international trade was with Communist countries, 24 percent with industrialized Western countries, and 24.4 percent with developing nations, totalling U.S. $2,889,764,000.[57]

North Korea's imports consist primarily of petroleum (from the Soviet Union and China—like the south, north Korea has no petroleum resources), machinery, cotton, and foodstuffs (primarily wheat). Exports are mainly minerals, processed metals, textiles, agricultural products, precious metals, and (to developing countries) military arms. Beginning in 1985, after a virtual boycott for many years, the Soviet Union again began furnishing advanced weaponry to north Korea.

In most of the years since the Korean War, the north Korean foreign trade balance has been positive, as a means of paying off foreign aid obligations. However, from 1967 to 1977, the balance was negative, reflecting the ill-fated industrial modernization drive and the oil crisis. The foreign trade objective for the decade, announced in 1980, was to increase exports from the then approximately $500 million per year to over $2 billion— which presumably would ensure a balance or a surplus on the international account.

Prospects

At the Sixth Congress of the Korean Workers' Party in 1980, Kim Il Sung announced "ten major targets" for the 1980s: 100 billion kilowatts of power, 120 million metric tons (132 million U.S. tons) of coal, 15 million metric tons (16.5 million U.S. tons) of steel, 1.5 million metric tons (1.65 U.S. tons) of nonferrous metals, 20 million metric tons (22 million U.S. tons) of cement, 7 million metric tons (7.7 million U.S. tons) of agricultural fertilizer, 5 million metric tons (5.5 million U.S. tons) of aquatic products, 15 million metric tons (16.5 million U.S. tons) of grain, 1.5 billion meters (1.6 billion yards) of fabrics, and the reclamation of 300,000 *chongbo* (about 330,000 hectares or 810,000 acres) of tidelands.[58]

President Kim Il Sung's policy speech of December 1986 and Prime Minister Li Kun Mo's summary of the Third Seven Year Plan (1987–1993) gave the north Korean regime's targets for the future. The ten long-range goals set forth in 1980 were reaffirmed, except that the steel target was reduced from 15 to 10 million metric tons (11 million U.S. tons) per year. During the Third Seven Year Plan, industrial output is to increase 10 percent annually; national income is to increase 1.7 times. The long-range targets are to be reached. Attention is to be placed on finding new ore deposits. Development of electronic industry is to emphasize minicomputers and automation. Foreign trade is to be increased 3.2 times, to develop science and technology; economic collaboration and joint ventures with socialist and other countries are to be brisk. The number of technical specialists is to reach 2 million (from the present 1.25 million); the number of doctors is to reach 43 per 10,000 population. Consumer industry is to grow at approximately the same rate as heavy industry. Yet, unlike China and the Soviet Union, north Korea is to move toward universal state ownership of the means of production, in place of the existing agricultural cooperatives, as a necessary step toward building a classless society.[59]

As the foregoing summary suggests, north Korea's economic problems in recent years have apparently led to recognition of the need for opening

up to the world as a means of accelerating economic growth and modernization. The growing economic gap between north and south Korea must
be of great concern to north Korean leaders. The joint venture law is a
small step in this direction—the first one since the unsuccessful attempt
of the early 1970's. Kim Il Sung has already made clear that cooperation
with other countries for mutual benefit is consistent with the ideals of *juche*.
If this policy trend continues, it seems almost inevitable that the north must
follow the lead of China's economic reforms as another means of accelerating
economic growth. Yet the country's tradition of quasi-autarchy and Stalinist
controls act as a brake on this process. Once the leadership succession
has been accomplished, north Korea may well move ahead, somewhat as
China is doing. In the meantime, however, it will continue on its present
level of low to moderate growth. Continued priority assigned to heavy
industry, a large defense expenditure, and high population growth will limit
improvements in living standards, unless popular discontent reaches levels
that force modification of current policies.

Notes

1. Ch'oe Chin Hyok, "Choson Minjujuui Inmin Konghwagukeso ui Rijo Sigi ui
Ryoksawa Munhwa Yon'gue Taehayo" (Regarding Research on the History of the Yi
Dynasty in the Democratic People's Republic of Korea), paper delivered to the annual
conference of the Mid-Atlantic Region, Association for Asian Studies, Washington,
November 1985.
2. Andrew Grajdanzev, *Modern Korea* (New York: distributed by John Day Co.
for the International Secretariat of the Institute of Pacific Relations, 1945); *Korea
Under Japanese Colonial Rule*, Andrew H. Nahm, editor (Kalamazoo, Mich.: Institute
for Korean Studies, Western Michigan University, 1973); George M. McCune, *Korea
Today* (Cambridge, Mass: Harvard University Press, 1950), pp. 29–34.
3. Grajdanzev, *Modern Korea*, p. 119.
4. Paul Kuznets, *Economic Growth and Structure in the Republic of Korea* (New
Haven, CT: Yale University Press, 1977), p. 22.
5. Kuznets, *Economic Growth and Structure*, p. 30.
6. A Korean aid bill failed in the U.S. House of Representatives by one vote in
January 1949 (*New York Times*, July 2, 1949). Later, an appropriation of $350
million for economic assistance was made, but little of it had arrived when the
Korean War started; the U.S. aid program was still running largely on the remaining
GARIOA funds.
7. Kuznets, *Economic Growth and Structure*, p. 32; David C. Cole and Princeton
N. Lyman, *Korean Development: The Interplay of Politics and Economics* (Cambridge,
Mass.: Harvard University Press, 1971), p. 21.
8. Some plants were reportedly taken by the Soviets as war reparations; exactly
how many is not known.
9. Cf. United Nations Command, Office of the Economic Coordinator, *Stabilization
and Program Progress; Fiscal Year 1958* (Seoul, 1958), p. 11. The Korean currency

was called *hwan* for some years in the early days of the Republic and later changed to *won*, as it is called today.

10. U.S. economic grant aid, except for agricultural commodities under Public Law 480, was terminated in 1968. Loans on special terms continued for several more years. In 1986, US aid to Korea was limited to military education and training ($1.8 million), and loans under the Foreign Military Sales program at commercial interest rates ($228 million in 1985, expected to be less in 1986). Cf. *Handbook on Korea-U.S. Relations* (New York: The Asia Society, 1985), p. 179.

11. *North Korea: A Country Study* (Washington: Foreign Area Studies, The American University, 1981; for sale by U.S. Government Printing Office), p. 153.

12. Donald S. Macdonald, "Korea and the Ballot; The International Dimension in Korean Political Development as Seen in Elections" (unpublished Ph.D. dissertation, The George Washington University, 1978), p. 418; Cole and Lyman, *Korean Development*, pp. 25–26.

13. Kuznets, *Economic Growth and Structure*, p. 46–47.

14. Edward S. Mason et al, *The Economic and Social Modernization of the Republic of Korea*, Studies in the Modernization of the Republic of Korea: 1945-1975, Harvard East Asian Monographs, 92 (Cambridge, Mass.: Council on East Asian Studies, Harvard University, 1980), p. 15.

15. Figures computed by averaging data from Economic Planning Board, Republic of Korea, *P'alsimnyondae Kyongje Chongch'aek ui Chinch'ul Songkwa wa Hyanghu Kwajong* (Results of Economic Policy for the 1980s and Future Agenda) (Seoul, 1985), p. 10.

16. Bank of Korea Quarterly Review, March 1985.

17. Kuznets, *Economic Growth and Structure*, p. 50.

18. Parvez Hasan and D. C. Rao, *Korea: Policy Issues for Long-Term Development; The Report of a Mission Sent to the Republic of Korea by the World Bank* (Baltimore: Published for the World Bank by the Johns Hopkins University Press, 1979).

19. *P'alsimnyondae*, p. 156.

20. *P'alsimnyondae*, p. 10.

21. Mason et al, *Economic and Social Modernization*, pp. 28–29.

22. Han, ed., *Korea in Year 2000: Prospects for Development and Change* (Seoul: Asiatic Research Center, Korea University, 1986), p. 23; Kim Chin-ki (graduate assistant) research; U.S. Embassy, Seoul, Economic Trends Report, May 1986.

23. Statistics are from publications of the Bank of Korea. U.S. Embassy, Seoul, reported that gold and foreign exchange reserves at the end of 1985 totalled $7.7 billion.

24. U.S. Embassy, Seoul, Korea, Economic Trends Report, May 1986.

25. *Korea Business World3* (No. 5, May 1987), pp. 122–23.

26. Mason, *Economic and Social Modernization*, p. 18.

27. Additionally, industry has been expected to provide high-level positions for retiring military personnel; the economic impact of this arrangement is probably not great, but it draws criticism.

28. *Fortune*, Aug. 4, 1986, pp. 180–197, includes the following ten Korean firms in its listing of the five hundred largest international corporations according to gross sales: Samsung (No. 38), Hyundai (No. 39), Lucky-Goldstar (No. 43), Daewoo (No.

48), Sunkyong (No. 62), Ssangyong (No. 139), Korea Explosives (No. 185), Hyosung (No. 216), Pohang Iron & Steel (No. 209), Doosan (No. 413).

29. Calculated from *Korean Statistical Yearbook 1985*, p. 158.

30. Figure from Han, ed., *Korea in Year 2000*, p. 5.

31. cf *Business Korea*, March 1986, p. 9.

32. Brunei, Indonesia, Malaysia, the Philippines, Singapore, and Thailand constitute the Association of Southeast Asian Nations (ASEAN).

33. *Korea Times*, June 3, 1986.

34. *Far Eastern Economic Review*, March 6, 1986, pp. 83–84, citing statistics of the US Arms Control and Disarmament Agency.

35. Calculated on the basis of 5.68 million tons produced on 1.23 million hectares of land planted to rice (including double-cropping). *Korea Statistical Yearbook, 1985*, National Bureau of Statistics, Economic Planning Board, pp. 118, 124. The comparison with imported rice cost was supplied by the US Embassy, Seoul.

36. *Korea Herald*, Jan. 29, 1986, quoting the Ministry of Agriculture and Forestry; *Korea Times*, Apr. 11, 1986.

37. *Korea Times*, March 6, 1986, citing ROK Government sources.

38. *Korea Herald*, Jan. 29, 1986; *Korea Times* editorial, May 28, 1986.

39. According to a Bank of Korea survey of 1,345 domestic manufacturing firms, the average manufacturing worker's annual wages rose from 3,692,000 won in 1984 to 3,969,000 in 1985, an increase of 7.5 percent. The worker's product value rose from 35,841,000 to 38,098,000 won, or 6.3 percent. Labor costs took 49.1 percent of value added in 1984, and 48.3 percent in 1985. *Korea Times*, May 25, 1986.

40. The ratios given are for goods actually traded. Ratios based on the total list of commodities are even higher—88 percent and 21 percent, respectively. *P'alsimnyondae*, p. 35.

41. Suh, Sang-mok, "Korea's Sixth Five-Year Plan: A 'Second Economic Take-Off,' " *Korea's Economy* (Korea Economic Institute, Washington, DC) 3 (No. 2, April 1987), p. 12.

42. *P'alsimnyondae*, p. 55.

43. Cf. Young Soo-gil, "A Global Perspective on the Korean Economy in the Year 2000," in Han, ed., *Korea in Year 2000*, p. 28.

44. A final English version of the Sixth Five-Year Plan has not been published, but the main points are summarized in December 1986 issues of *The Korea Herald* and in Suh, "Korea's Sixth Five-Year Plan."

45. Suh, "Korea's Sixth Five-Year Plan," p. 15.

46. For a discussion of the philosophy of north Korean economic development, see Ellen Brun and Jacques Hirsch, *Socialist Korea: A Case Study in the Strategy of Economic Development* (New York: Monthly Review Press, 1977).

47. Joseph Chung, writing in the mid-1970s, stated that there are 22 farms, on the average, per county, each with 6,300 households and 10,000 *chongbo* (about 11,000 hectares or 27,000 acres) of land. Joseph Sang-hoon Chung, *The North Korean Economy; Structure and Development* (Stanford, CA: Hoover Institution Press, 1974).

48. Cf. U.S. Central Intelligence Agency, *Korea: The Economic Race between the North and South* (Washington, D.C.: U.S. Government Printing Office, 1978).

49. *Korea: The Economic Race between the North and South.*

50. National Unification Board, Republic of Korea, *A Comparative Study of South and North Korea* (Seoul, 1982).

51. The term "repatriation" was applied to this movement at the time; but many of the people involved came originally from south Korea.

52. *World Development Report 1986* (Baltimore: published for the World Bank by The Johns Hopkins University Press, 1986), p. 228.

53. The U.S. Central Intelligence Agency's *World Factbook* for 1987 gives an exchange rate of 2 north Korean won per U.S. dollar as of 1984. However, other publications give a higher valuation to the won, ranging up to nearly one-to-one.

54. *Korean Newsletter,* Embassy of the Republic of Korea, Washington, DC, March 1986, p. 6; *World Development Report,* p. 152.

55. *Daily Report—Asia-Pacific,* January 15,1986, p. D15.

56. *Daily Report—Asia-Pacific,* April 23,1987.

57. Lee, Hong-youn, "Structure and Prospect of North Korean Trade," *Vantage Point* (Seoul). September 1981, p. 5.

58. *Daily Report—Asia-Pacific,* Foreign Broadcast Information Service, Dec. 31, 1980, pp. D10–D20.

59. For Kim Il Sung's December 30, 1987 policy speech, see *Daily Report— Asia-Pacific,* January 2, 1987. For commentary on it in North Korean publications, see *Daily Report,* January 14, 1987. For Li Kun Mo's report of the Third Seven Year Plan, see *Daily Report,* April 23, 1987; also commentary by *Nodong Sinmun* and Pyongyang Radio, reported in *Daily Report,* April 23, 1987. President Kim officially promulgated the Third Seven Year Plan on April 23 (*Daily Report,* May 4, 1987.

7 KOREAN NATIONAL SECURITY AND FOREIGN RELATIONS

Introduction

The Korean peninsula is surrounded by three of the most powerful states in the world: the Soviet Union, China, and Japan. These three states are traditional rivals. Each of them, because of geography, fears that Korea may be used by the others against it. Since 1945, the United States has become a fourth major player. Although geographically distant, the United States has become deeply concerned about Northeast Asia for reasons of its own national security and prosperity. Thus, Korea faces the contentious presence of these four great powers as a factor in its national destiny and its foreign policy.

For the past forty years, however, Korea's view of the larger geopolitical picture has been overshadowed by the confrontation on the peninsula. The two Korean states have been, and continue to be, each other's chief security

FIGURE 7.1 A typical scene at the Demilitarized Zone dividing Korea (photo courtesy of Korea Overseas Information Service)

threat. The Korean War tragically demonstrated this fact. Technically, the Korean War has never ended; the Armistice Agreement of 1953 is the longest cease-fire in history, and it is still only a suspension of hostilities. Taking Korea as a whole, more than one of every seven men between twenty and forty-five years old is in full-time active military service in the two massive armies facing each other across the Demilitarized Zone (Fig. 7.1) that separates them. Almost 6 percent of south Korea's gross national product, and up to 20 percent or more of north Korea's—around 9 percent of the whole peninsula's product—are devoted to military preparedness.

The foreign relations of both Korean states are dominated by this situation. Rivalry between them for international recognition has been a principal theme for both. Despite some north-south dialogue from time to time, each state regards the other as illegitimate (although the south, unlike the north, says it will accept the reality of a separate independent state and has proposed concurrent United Nations membership for both). Each of the two seeks international support for its security. The competitive concerns of the two separate states prevent attention to the larger and longer-range problems of the peninsula and people as a whole.

At the same time, however, both Korean states are committed to reunification, which is a universal aspiration of the people in both north and south. In the Korean historical perspective, even forty years of division are only 3 percent of the nation's life since unification in A.D. 668. Unification is not a short-term likelihood but is probable in the longer run. Its eventual attainment will bring Korea face-to-face once again with the larger realities of Korea's geopolitical situation. (The unification problem is discussed in Chapter 8.)

Meanwhile, both Korean states need relations with other countries in meeting popular aspirations for economic and social progress. South Korea, especially, with almost no natural resources beyond land and people, must look to the world for its raw materials and for export earnings to pay for them. Both Koreas need advanced technology and foreign investment capital, although north Korea, particularly, has encountered both foreign and domestic obstacles in getting them.

The two Koreas are also in intense international competition for legitimacy, prestige, and support. The Korean people, especially in the south, are motivated by their recent history to want not only national independence, but also national prestige. Popular perception of the Korean governments' standing in the world is therefore a factor in domestic stability. International perception of each Korean state is also a contributing factor to national security, since the perception affects international attitudes in the event of renewed hostilities.

Current Korean attitudes toward relations with other states are strongly conditioned by two historical traditions: the "siege mentality" that has resulted from repeated invasions throughout recorded history; and the special relationship with China, which was the principal basis for Korea's national security for many centuries. A brief review of the Chinese relationship is therefore in order.

As an agricultural state at subsistence level, Korea was essentially self-sufficient during most of its history. National security and the security of the ruling dynasty were its only foreign policy concerns. To meet these concerns, Korea accepted a "younger-brother" relationship to China, which until the nineteenth century was by far the dominant power of the region. China was not only Korea's protector but also its political and cultural "older brother," mentor, and ultimate source of the ruling dynasty's legitimacy. In a family-style East Asian international order, China was at the center or summit, and all other nations at various inferior levels; they were autonomous but tributary states.

The Chinese provided key support to the Koreans in driving out the sixteenth-century Japanese invaders. Thereafter, Korea closed its borders against all other powers and put all its security eggs in the Chinese basket— with virtually no military power of its own—until the decline of Chinese power was made manifest by China's defeat in the Sino-Japanese War in 1895. In thus becoming a "hermit nation," Korea was following the same course as China and Japan, which also had policies of exclusion.

After the Japanese "opened" Korea with the Kanghwa Treaty of 1876, the nation was wrenched out of its attempted self-isolation. After thirty years of imperialist rivalry, the Russo-Japanese War of 1904 left Korea in Japanese hands. Thus three centuries of self-imposed Korean isolation were followed by thirty years of traumatic exposure to the outside world, and then by forty years of national eclipse as a Japanese colony. During the colonial period, Korean nationalists (mostly in exile) were split into two ideological camps by the influence of the Russian Revolution. In consequence, the Cold War entered Korean politics (as it did in China) even before it began elsewhere.

The Japanese defeat in 1945 left Korea divided into U.S. and Soviet zones of occupation. Reinforced by the ideological division between radical and conservative Korean nationalists, the split became permanent. Given Korea's history, it was natural for Koreans in the two new Korean states to transfer to the Soviet Union and to the United States, respectively, the same younger-brother relationship formerly given to China, rather than to unite in opposition to both. However, as indicated in Chapter 2, both states have moved since the Korean War toward a position of greater self-reliance and independence of action—sooner and faster in the Democratic People's Republic of Korea in the north than in the Republic of Korea in the south.

Foreign Relations of the
Republic of Korea (South Korea)

National security, economic progress and trade, and enhancement of legitimacy and prestige are the basic themes of south Korean foreign policy. These themes are interrelated. Security is essential for economic progress; economic progress is now the primary basis for Korea's improving international reputation; and prestige enhances both security and prosperity.

In general, the Republic's foreign policy is characterized by caution, preservation of established relationships, and incremental improvement, rather than innovation; the prospect of sudden shifts in the policies of other countries, particularly the United States (as in President Jimmy Carter's troop withdrawal initiative of 1977) is a grave concern.

National Security Policy

Basic Policy Themes. In addition to maintaining its own powerful military and internal security forces, the security policy of the Republic centers on keeping a special relationship with the United States. South Korean dependence upon the United States for security began with the occupation in 1945 and was almost total during the Korean War. Today, however it is as much psychological as military. The suffering imposed by the war is a vivid personal memory for half the south Korean population, and the possibility of its renewal is a very real apprehension. U.S. ground combat forces stationed in Korea are a significant but marginal increment to Korea's own military capabilities. Of much greater significance is the reassurance they provide. Their presence demonstrates to both the south Koreans and their enemy that the United States is committed to the Republic's defense, thus providing a major deterrent to north Korean attack; and it ensures that the United States would not opt out of actual hostilities. U.S. air, naval, and logistic support are of much more military importance, but their actual commitment would be less assured in the event of attack if U.S. ground forces were not in place.

Such reassurance is particularly important to south Korea for two reasons. First, the certainty of prompt U.S. military support—especially air support— is a key factor in the credibility of the "forward defense strategy" adopted in 1973, under which a north Korean attack would be stopped north of the city of Seoul.[1] Second, south Korea has good historical reason to doubt the permanent reliability of its U.S. ally. As the Koreans see it, the United States violated its commitment to provide good offices under Article I of the Korea-U.S. treaty of 1882 in accepting Japanese hegemony in 1905 (the United States was the first nation to withdraw its legation from Korea). Again, the United States ignored Korean nationalists' appeals for self-determination in 1919, even though it was President Woodrow Wilson who championed the self-determination doctrine.

Many Koreans blame the United States for the division of the country in 1945 (a complicated issue which is discussed in Chapter 8). In Korean eyes, U.S. disengagement from the Republic after its independence encouraged the north Korean attack in 1950. The Americans refused to believe that north Korea would invade the south. Equally concerned about preventing a southern attack on the north, the United States did not provide adequate equipment and training for defense; it denied the Republic an air force; and it withdrew its remaining troops in 1949 over Korean protest. Secretary of State Dean Acheson's 1950 speech, seemingly defining the U.S. defense perimeter in the western Pacific to exclude Korea, coupled with U.S. preoccupation in Europe (the Berlin Blockade was then at its height), probably encouraged Kim Il Sung to believe an easy north Korean victory over the south was within his grasp. Although U.S. forces were the key to the Republic's survival in the Korean War, a renewal of such support was put in doubt by the Vietnam experience and subsequent U.S. policies.

The presence of forty thousand armed foreigners on Korean soil, while considered necessary for security, creates both foreign and domestic policy problems for south Korea. Unlike north Korea (from which the last foreign troops were withdrawn in 1958), the Republic has been unable to gain full membership in Third World councils such as the Non-Aligned Movement. Pyongyang never tires of lashing the south Koreans as puppets of neo-colonialist masters. Within the country, the visibility, boisterous behavior, and occasional crime of U.S. soldiers reinforce nationalist charges of "American imperialism" and cries of "Yankee go home" from radicals. It is a testimony to good management by Korean and U.S. authorities, and to long-established Korean-U.S. friendship, that domestic criticism has thus far been limited to a small minority, while Korean public attitudes have thus far remained generally friendly toward the United States.

Because of uncertainty (dormant in the mid-1980s as a result of firm pledges by the United States) of future U.S. support, as well as nationalist sentiment for self-reliance, the Republic has sought to dilute its dependence on the United States. It has increased its own armaments manufacturing capability, increased the munitions reserve stockpiles within the country, and procured some weapons systems from non-U.S. (chiefly French, Italian, and British) sources. These moves, however, have not greatly reduced south Korea's dependence upon the United States. The Republic has also sought to export its own arms manufactures to other countries, both to utilize its production capacity and to increase foreign trade earnings; but its ability to do so is limited by U.S. license restrictions. In the mid-1970s, at the height of its worry about U.S. reliability, south Korea apparently considered going nuclear with French assistance, but decided against it, to the relief of the United States. (The Republic of Korea is a signatory of the Non-Proliferation Treaty and subscribes to the full-scope safeguards of the Treaty, as they apply to its nuclear plants. In 1985, north Korea announced its accession to the Treaty.)

The Republic considers that its military strength contributes to the security of Japan because that strength denies the peninsula to Communist forces. (South Korean briefing officers sometimes assert that their forces "tie down" 50 Soviet divisions stationed in the Far East, although this goes beyond most observers' view.) South Korea used this argument in seeking major economic assistance from Japan in the early 1980's, although the Japanese refused to acknowledge its merit. However, Korea does not want to accept Japanese forces as a factor in its own security. Because of past experience with Japanese aggression, the Republic does not favor strengthening of Japanese military capability. South Korean forces nevertheless cooperate in arrangements with U.S. and Japanese forces for radar warning and communications, and there is limited consultation between Korean and Japanese military leaders.

In theory, cooperative military arrangements with other states in the region would offer Korea an alternative to dependence upon the United States.

Ever since President Rhee vainly tried to promote a "Northeast Asia Treaty Organization" in the late 1940s, the Republic has been interested in promoting closer regional cooperation. The Association of Pacific Nations (ASPAC) in the 1960s and 1970s was another Korean initiative. However, the Republic does not want security arrangements to include Japan, its traditional enemy. It has no relations with the People's Republic of China or the Soviet Union, both of which have mutual defense treaties with north Korea. Other regional nations are too small, too distant, or too disinterested.

The nations that contributed troops to the United Nations action in 1950–1953 are still signatories to the July 27, 1953, Declaration of the Sixteen, which stated that if there should be a renewal of hostilities, they would be prompt to resist. In practice, however, it is doubtful that all of them would involve themselves. Ethiopia, now a Marxist state with ties to the Soviet Union, would be an extreme example.[2]

The Security Threat. The threat faced by the Republic is a very real and serious one, notwithstanding its exploitation for domestic political purposes. North Korea has made no secret of its hostility toward the south Korean regime and the United States, complaining constantly of U.S.-Japanese–south Korean aggressive schemes. Since the early 1960s, north Korean military power has been greatly increased. As Table 7.1 shows, north Korea has larger forces and more weapons and equipment than the south, and these appear to be offensively deployed. At least three north Korean underground tunnels have been found beneath the Demilitarized Zone, large enough for division-sized forces to invade the south, and as many as sixteen more are suspected.

It is unlikely that the north Koreans could successfully repeat their lightning sweep of June 1950 through the peninsula. They would suffer a terrible cost in south Korean and U.S. air attack if they tried, to say nothing of the ground force casualties they would suffer. However, it is quite possible that the north Koreans, if they detected weakness in the south Korean or U.S. position, might try a blitzkrieg aimed at capturing the Republic's territory north of the Han River within a few days time. To do so would require an advance of only thirty to thirty-five miles in the western sector of their line. If they were successful, they would control a quarter of south Korea's population and nearly half its economic capacity and would have a greatly strengthened hand in gaining international acquiescence for unification on their own terms. It is for this reason that the deterrence afforded by the U.S. presence is considered so vital.

The north Koreans have launched thousands of infiltration operations against the south since 1953, through the Demilitarized Zone and along the seacoast. Highly trained north Korean special warfare troops continue armed infiltrations into the south; some of these are detected and many probably are not. Such operations are aimed at disturbing authority and public order,

TABLE 7.1 Comparative Military Strength and Equipment
of North and South Korea, January 1986
(including US Forces Deployed in Korea)

	North Korea	South Korea	United States
Personnel			
Ground force	785,000	500,000	27,000
Air	55,000	30,000	10,000
Naval	38,000	20,000	300
Reserves	5,000,000	3,000,000	0
Weapons and equipment			
Tanks	3,500+	1,200	150
Armored personnel carriers	1,700	600	100
Towed artillery	3,300	2,600	40
Self-propelled artillery	2,000	80	40
Anti-aircraft artillery	10,000	1,300	80
Surface-to-air missiles	n/a	n/a	n/a
Total aircraft	800-1,100	n/a	n/a
Jet fighters[a]	350-650	400+	100+
Bombers	65-85	0	0
Transport aircraft	100-250	n/a	n/a
Helicopters	260	300	n/a
Total ships	350-490+	140	0
Destroyers	0	10	
Patrol frigates	6-8	10[b]	
Amphibious craft	100-110	10	
Missile attack (or patrol) boats	18-35	10	
Patrol ships/boats	n/a	70	
Submarines	6-8	0	
Torpedo boats	175	0	
Midget submarines	35	0	
Mine warfare vessels	n/a	10	
Auxiliary ships	n/a	20	

[a]North Korea: 480 MiG 15, 17, 19; 160 MiG 21; 20+ MiG 23.
    South Korea: 65 F-4; 50 F-86; 250 F-5; 20 OA/A-37; 8 RF-5
    United States: 24 F-4; 48 F-16; 13 OA/A-37; 24 A-10; 5 RF-4

[b]APD/APC

Source: Adapted from Public Affairs Background pamphlet, Headquarters, United Nations Command/Combined Forces Command/ United
States Forces Korea/Eighth United States Army, APO San Francisco
CA 96301: "Korea: A Military Balance" as of January 1986. 9 pp.,
offset.

planting long-term agents for subversion and espionage, and promoting uprisings. These objectives are consistent with the apparent north Korean belief that the south Korean people are against their own government and will, if offered the chance, overthrow it in favor of unification with the north. Should such an uprising occur, in this view, the north Korean armed forces could legitimately support it.

Most notorious among the many north Korean forays against south Korea (aside from the 1976 ax murders of two U.S. Army officers in the Joint Security Area) were the attempted assassination of the President in January 1968 and the landing of 120 provocateurs on the eastern seacoast in October 1968. These and other attempts have so far been unsuccessful because of the effectiveness of the south Korean security forces and the alertness of the south Korean population, very few of whom have been willing to cooperate with northern agents.

Most recently, north Korea tried to assassinate south Korean President Chun Doo Hwan during a wreath-laying ceremony at the Aung San mausoleum in Rangoon, Burma, in October 1983. A traffic delay saved him, but seventeen south Koreans, including four cabinet ministers, were killed, as well as four Burmese.

Armed Forces

The core of the national security establishment of the Republic of Korea consists of somewhat over 600,000 full-time military personnel in three uniformed services—each commanded by its own chief of staff—and a Chairman of the Joint Chiefs of Staff as coordinator, under the Ministry of National Defense. The President is commander-in-chief of the armed forces; he is advised by a National Security Council consisting of himself, the Prime Minister, Deputy Prime Minister, ministers of Foreign Affairs, National Defense, Home Affairs, and Finance, and the Director of the Agency for National Security Planning (the national intelligence agency).

The Army, by far the most important of the three services, consists of three armies and the Capital Defense Command, over twenty regular divisions (including one mechanized division), eight reserve divisions (each of which has a professional cadre), and various specialized units, including Special Forces. (There are also two Marine Corps divisions.) The First and Third armies have frontline defense responsibilities, on the east and west respectively; the Second Army is for training, logistics, and rear-area defense. An unpublished number of Korean Army divisions are assigned to the Combined ROK-U.S. Field Army, which guards the principal invasion corridor. South Korean ground forces are equipped with M-48 tanks, armored personnel carriers, artillery, missiles, and helicopters; their strength and armament are numerically less than those of north Korea, although both quantity and quality of equipment are increasing. Table 7.1 contains statistics on strength and equipment.

The primary Air Force missions are close combat support for the Army and defense against enemy aircraft and submarines. The Air Force has a strength of about 30,000, organized into three commands for combat, logistics, and training. The ROK Air Force combat capability is integrated with that of the U.S. Air Force in the Air Component Command of the Combined Forces Command. Korean aircraft include over 400 tactical fighters, many of them in process of replacement with more modern craft (such as F-16s); there are 250 F-5 fighters (being produced in Korea) and 65 F-4s. Armament includes Sidewinder and Sparrow air-to-air missiles and Maverick anti-submarine missiles. The Air Force, with over 100 squadrons, also has cargo aircraft, trainers, and combat helicopters.

The Navy is responsible for coastal defense, particularly the countering of north Korean maritime infiltration. Its 49,000 personnel are divided almost equally between sea operations and the two divisions plus one brigade of the Marine Corps. There are naval reserves of 25,000 and Marine reserves of 24,000 (one division and two brigades). There is a total of 140 ships, ranging from 10 destroyers to 70 patrol ships (see Table 7.1).

The Republic has universal conscription of males from eighteen to thirty years old, who serve twenty-four to thirty months in the Army or volunteer for three years in any of the three services. College students are required to undergo military training, whether or not they participate in the reserve officers' training program.

Upon completion of military service, men enter reserve status in the Homeland Reserve Forces, with periodic call-up and training until they are thirty-five. There are eight reserve divisions, with field grade positions held by regular army officers. Total strength is approaching the goal of three million. Since 1975, a paramilitary Civil Defense Corps has been organized in all communities and places of employment to protect lives and property in case of disaster or attack. Under the jurisdiction of the Ministry of Home Affairs, it has about two million members. All males from seventeen to fifty are liable for service, unless they are in other security forces.[3]

Other Security Agencies. Internal security in peacetime is the responsibility of the Ministries of Home Affairs and Justice and the Agency for National Security Planning (ANSP). In addition to the ANSP, security forces comprise the National Police (including the combat police), prosecutors in the Ministry of Justice and their investigative staff (judicial police). The Defense Ministry's Defense Security Command has internal security responsibilities that extend beyond the armed forces. The President has a security force directly responsible to him for protection of his person and office.

United Nations Command, Combined Forces
Command, and U.S. Forces Korea

About 40 percent of all uniformed military forces of the Republic of
Korea are under the "operational control" of the senior U.S. military
commander in Korea, as Commander-in-Chief, Combined Forces Command
(CFC). Most, but not all, south Korean combat units north of the Han River
are within such operational control. This means that their deployment to
meet an external armed attack and their employment in combat are subject
to his orders (or, if he is incapacitated, to those of his Korean deputy, also
a four-star general). The senior U.S.commander is concurrently Commander-
in-Chief, United Nations Command (UNC), and Commander, United States
Forces Korea (USFK). He is also Commanding General of the United States
Eighth Army, the ground component of USFK.

The United Nations Command was established pursuant to a United
Nations Security Council resolution in July 1950. The resolution invited UN
members to contribute forces to help repel north Korean aggression and
established an umbrella organization for such forces. The United States was
made executive agent. A U.S. military officer (initially, General Douglas
MacArthur) therefore became Commander-in-Chief of the UNC (CINCUNC).
Sixteen UN member nations, including the United States, contributed forces.
The Republic of Korea itself was not a member of the United Nations; but
Korea's President Rhee, by a letter of July 14, 1950, gave operational control
of ROK forces to General MacArthur. This arrangement was confirmed in
an annex to the ROK-U.S. Mutual Defense Treaty of 1953 (ratified in 1954).
However, the non-U.S. UN presence rapidly dwindled after the Armistice,
and by the early 1970s consisted of a symbolic Honor Guard with members
from the Republic of Korea, Philippines, Thailand, United Kingdom, and
United States. (Representatives of these countries, plus Australia, Canada,
France, and New Zealand, were members of the United Nations side of the
Military Armistice Commission in 1986. The other original contributor nations
were Belgium, Colombia, Ethiopia, Greece, Luxembourg, The Netherlands,
Turkey, and South Africa.)

In 1985, the only current responsibility of the UNC was to maintain the
Armistice Agreement. The agreement provides for enforcement by a Military
Armistice Commission (MAC) composed of five representatives from each
side (the United Nations Command and the Korean People's Army/Chinese
People's Volunteers), a Secretary for each side, and staff. Although the
Republic of Korea is not a signatory, an ROK military officer sits with the
UNC side. By the end of 1985, the MAC had held 431 plenary meetings,
most of which were without substance; most MAC business is done at staff
level. The Armistice Agreement also provided for a Neutral Nations Super-

visory Commission (NNSC) to oversee compliance with troop and equipment limitations, but less than two years after the Armistice the NNSC was reduced to a largely symbolic mission. Representatives of Czechoslovakia, Poland, Sweden, and Switzerland make up the NNSC, which, like the staff of the MAC, is stationed within the Joint Security Area.

The Military Armistice Commission meets in a small Joint Security Area at Panmunjom (the site of a small village destroyed by the war) within the so-called Demilitarized Zone (DMZ) that separates the armies of the two sides. (Over the years, both sides have moved military installations into the DMZ, notwithstanding the armistice provisions.) A small complement of US and south Korean troops, under the United Nations Command, is responsible for security within the Joint Security Area; the north Korean and Chinese side has a similar security force.

Since the Republic of Korea never signed the armistice agreement (because of President Rhee's insistence on military reunification), the UNC was an awkward umbrella for operational control of south Korean armed forces and gave insufficient recognition to the preponderance of ROK military power in the defense of the south. This disparity was highlighted by U.S. withdrawal of one of its two divisions in Korea in 1971. Accordingly, the Republic of Korea and the United States agreed to establish a Combined Forces Command, comprising the combat forces of both countries, with a U.S. general as commander and a Korean as deputy (both of four-star rank). Established in 1978 as a means of carrying out the Mutual Defense Treaty of 1953, this is the mechanism through which operational control is exercised.

Operational control, as it applies in Korea, is a widely misunderstood term. The Combined Forces Command is responsible to the national command authorities of the Republic of Korea and the United States for Korea's external security. It has operational control over forces committed to it for that purpose. The number of forces so committed, both Korean and U.S., differs according to the level of defense readiness—in general, the higher the level (as the threat grows more serious or imminent), the more forces are committed.

Operational control does not extend to internal security matters, over which the Republic has sovereign jurisdiction, nor to administrative matters such as recruitment, training, procedures, or discipline. Moreover, operational control applies only to forces explicitly placed under such control by Korea. The Capital Security Command, for example, is not so placed. The Special Warfare Command (unconventional warfare forces) comes under CFC control at a designated level of alert status. The Second Army is not under U.S. operational control nor are any army units stationed south of Seoul.

If the Republic of Korea decides to withdraw a unit of its armed forces from CFC operational control, it does not require CFC permission to do so, but must give notification of the withdrawal. The Commander-in-Chief of CFC may object to the withdrawal, but only on the basis that the unit is urgently needed for the defense of the Republic against external attack. There has been no instance since 1952 of refusal to release ROK forces for internal purposes; forces employed in the two assertions of military control (1961 and 1979) were unilaterally withdrawn.

In the eyes of the Korean public and of many in the United States, however, the United States is involved in any deployment or use of military forces. It is for this reason that the United States is blamed for the harsh military action against the Kwangju revolt on May 18, 1980, even though the Special Forces that carried it out were not under CFC operational control at the defense readiness level then in effect. The forces which eventually contained the uprising a week later were withdrawn from operational control by the Korean government, after notification to the Combined Forces commander.

The Combined Forces Command has three major subordinate commands for ground, air, and naval components. The Commander-in-Chief, CFC, is concurrently commander of the ground component; the air component is commanded by a U.S. Air Force lieutenant general. The naval component is commanded by a Korean Navy vice admiral. Two additional components are the Combined Unconventional Warfare Task Force and Marine Forces Korea.

The main U.S. ground combat force in Korea is an infantry division (as of 1986, the 2d Division), with an authorized strength of about 17,000; about 2,500 of its positions are filled by Korean soldiers as Korean Augmentation to the U.S. Army (KATUSA). The U.S. division is encamped a few miles behind the front line, as reserve force for the Combined ROK-U.S. Field Army, that defends the sector of the Demilitarized Zone which faces the traditional principal north-south invasion corridor. This Army is commanded by a U.S. lieutenant general, with a Korean Army deputy. The Division's weapons and equipment, considerably more sophisticated than those of the Korean forces, are summarized in Table 7.1.

Other U.S. forces in Korea (as of mid-1986) include six squadrons of fighter aircraft in the 7th Air Force, and a variety of special combat and logistical units. There are no U.S. naval forces committed to the CFC, but there is a naval liaison unit at CFC headquarters. Joint Korean-U.S. military maneuvers are conducted from time to time to assure the effectiveness of U.S. support. Since the mid-1970s, there has been an annual exercise in early spring called "Team Spirit," which in the mid-1980s typically involved over 200,000 military personnel from both countries in simulated defense against northern attack.

Joint ROK-U.S. security responsibilities are coordinated in the annual Security Consultative Meeting (SCM), specified in the Mutual Defense Treaty of 1953. The ROK Minister of Defense and U.S. Secretary of Defense head the two delegations, meeting alternately in Seoul and Washington. The nineteenth such meeting was held in Washington in April 1987. Under the SCM is a Military Committee, headed by the two chairmen of the respective Joint Chiefs of Staff, which meets in plenary session once a year in conjunction with the SCM, and at other times when necessary; it has daily oversight authority on matters of ROK-US defense relations.

The rights and responsibilities of U.S. military personnel in Korea, and of the U.S. civilians who support them, are specified in a Status of Forces Agreement signed in 1965. Under the Agreement, many offenses committed by U.S. personnel while on official duty are acted on by U.S. authorities, and Korean authorities may transfer American suspects to U.S. jurisdiction. Serious crimes committed by U.S. personnel, however, are judged in Korean courts. Other matters covered by the Agreement include customs procedures, tax exemptions, vehicles, property, local employee relations. Problems arising under the Agreement are handled by a joint committee of representatives of the Korean government and U.S. Forces Korea; but in recent years this body has had to meet only three or four times a year, since problems have been relatively few. Legal matters are handled between the Korean Ministry of Justice and the USFK Judge Advocate General.

Foreign Economic Policy

South Korea's continued economic progress depends heavily on the international environment. Imports and exports each amount to over one-third of gross national product; exports have risen a thousandfold from the beginning of the Korean export-led economic take-off in the 1960s (at current prices, from US$30 million in 1960 to $30 billion in 1985). Since the country is densely populated and lacking in most essential natural resources, it depends upon imports, which must be paid for through export. Such vital materials as oil, coal, iron ore, and aluminum must be wholly or largely imported. Imports make up the grain deficit.

As Korea enters the ranks of industrial nations, it must import technology and know-how to be competitive in high-technology production. Its past industrial growth has been based largely on foreign capital borrowing, repayment and interest for which must come from export earnings; and the need for foreign sources of capital will continue. Korea also needs export markets to meet its own people'e expectations, as well, because it can produce better goods more cheaply when markets abroad increase the volume of its production beyond domestic demand. Moreover, a rising standard of living brings greater demand for import of goods not made in Korea. All of these factors make the Korean domestic economy highly vulnerable to international fluctuations.

Continued economic growth is an essential element in political stability. Because the government of the Republic has twice been taken over by military leaders on the basis of force rather than constitutional process, it lacks popular legitimacy. The principal basis for its acceptance is its demonstrated capacity to meet the material needs and aspirations of the people. Moreover, economic growth is essential to absorb the large numbers of young people coming into the labor market each year, including ever-increasing numbers of women who want jobs outside their homes.

South Korea therefore has a large stake in maintaining an international climate favorable for its trade and investment. But this stake is increasingly hard to defend. Protectionist barriers are mounting in the industrial countries that have been the nation's principal financial supporters and trading partners, especially the United States and Japan. Moreover, the Korean government confronts domestic protectionist pressures of its own, as it seeks to respond to international demands for better access. It also confronts nationalistic demands for reducing what a radical minority perceives to be U.S. neo-imperialist domination of the Korean economy.

At present, south Korean foreign economic policy contains the following elements:

- vigorous promotion of Korean products and services abroad, by both officials and private traders, coupled with emphasis on quality and cost controls;
- diplomatic initiatives against protectionist policies and actions of other countries, including support of international free trade agreements and practices, and the hiring of professional lobbyists in the United States to explain Korea's case to American government officials and legislators;
- gradual liberalization of foreign access to Korean markets for goods and services, and extension of legal protection on such items as intellectual property and electronic software;
- participation in multinational commodity agreements;
- renewed attention to import substitution in areas such as machine parts that are now well within Korean industrial competence;
- promotion of high-technology export industries as a means of sustaining exports;
- induction of foreign capital investment and technology through joint ventures and, in selected cases, foreign-owned firms;
- negotiation of foreign investment loans from governments, international organizations, and banks, on the most favorable possible terms, both for continued economic expansion and for management of the existing foreign debt portfolio;
- continued controls on wage levels to hold production costs down;
- promotion of new and expanded markets in Europe, the Third World, and China;

- special tax and financial assistance to exporters with a proven record (a past practice that is being phased out).

As noted in Chapter 6, the Economic Planning Board is the central economic policy-making and coordinating organ. However, negotiations with foreign countries on trade matters are the responsibility of the ministries of Foreign Affairs and of Commerce and International Trade. In financial areas, the Ministry of Finance handles this function. Other ministries play supporting roles.

In the case of the United States, Japan, and some other countries, there are annual joint meetings of economic ministers, in addition to negotiations on specific problems. The Republic of Korea is represented in the World Bank, International Monetary Fund, and other international organizations, including the General Agreement on Tariffs and Trade (GATT). Korean diplomatic establishments overseas have attachés specializing in commerce, finance, and agriculture, drawn from the corresponding ministries.

Government activities are complemented by business groups, particularly the Korean Traders' Association (composed of selected large Korean trading firms). A Korea–United States Economic Council has both Korean and U.S. firms as members; similar organizations exist for other countries. These and other groups work closely with the Korean government in promoting effective international trade relations.

General Diplomacy

South Korea's quest for international recognition supports its security and economic concerns. Beyond those concerns the Republic is in continuing competition with north Korea for legitimacy as representative of the sixty million Korean people; for promoting its own approach to national reunification; and for enhancement of national prestige.

The United States. The United States remains the central concern of Korean diplomacy because of the U.S. role in Korean national security and importance as a market and source of investment capital. Korea seeks to maximize U.S. support for the retention of U.S. troops in Korea and for armaments sales on preferential credit under the Foreign Military Sales (FMS) program (under which south Korea received no allocation in 1987). The Republic also endeavors to hold down U.S. protectionist moves against Korean exports, or reductions in benefit under the Generalized System of Preferences (GSP). Since for historical reasons the Republic wants to avoid dependence on Japan and avoid Japanese economic or other manipulation, it needs the United States as counterweight.

Beyond these considerations, the United States is of great importance to the Korean self-image. Despite growing anti-American feeling among a minority of Korean intellectuals and students, the United States continues to be a cultural and political model. Although the Republic is becoming increasingly self-confident and independent in the conduct of its foreign affairs, some vestige of the old relationship with China still clings to the relationship with the United States.

It should be recalled that during the administration of President Rhee (1948–1960), Korea's foreign policy was almost exclusively concerned with maximizing its benefits through its special relationship with the United States. The United States was the Republic's principal source of international support—diplomatic, economic, and military; concessionary economic assistance continued into the 1970s (although most grant aid ceased in 1968); and an U.S. presence is still integral to the Republic's defense, as explained above. Korean concern over the possible loss of American security support, and sensitivity to American criticism of the Korean domestic political situation, led to the so-called Koreagate crisis of the mid-1970s, involving Korean attempts to influence members of the U.S. Congress by favors and cash payments.[4]

American official views and public opinions are given great attention in Korea, and the amount of influence over Korean domestic affairs commonly attributed to the United States is far out of proportion to reality. Such misperceptions can lead Korean politicians to try mobilizing this or that segment of U.S. opinion for their cause, neglecting the political realities of Korean-U.S. relations. Such attempts create difficulties for the overall bilateral relationship. Alternatively, Korean dissidents can blame the United States for domestic political problems.

In formal terms, the Republic of Korea is linked with the United States by a Mutual Defense Treaty, signed in 1953 and ratified the following year; a Treaty of Friendship. Commerce, and Navigation, concluded in 1956; and numerous other treaties and agreements on specific aspects of Korean-U.S. relations. As of the mid-1980s, there were annual bilateral conferences at cabinet level on security, on economic and trade matters, and on foreign relations. Each state is represented by a large embassy in the other's capital.[5]

Japan. The Republic's relations with Japan are based on necessity rather than choice. Japan is a traditional enemy, and the emotions created by forty years of harsh occupation still affect the two countries' relations. However, Japan is a permanent neighbor and an important member of the non-Communist world, and Japan's support for the Korean cause is important. The forty-year Japanese administration left a legacy of Japanese methods, equipment, and trade ties that still favor Japan as a market (despite Japanese restrictions and a severely adverse trade balance) and as a source of investment, know-how, and equipment. Japanese capital, in particular, has been important for Korea's economic development as U.S. aid phased out. For these reasons, south Korea after many years of negotiations normalized its relations with Japan in the Korea-Japan Basic Treaty of 1965, despite popular outcry and demonstrations in both countries. Annexed agreements cover specific aspects of relations such as fishing rights and the special status of the 700,000 Korean residents in Japan. Each state established an embassy in the other's capital.

Since normalization, relations between the two countries have fluctuated between near-cordiality and distrust. A low point was the abduction of south Korean opposition leader Kim Dae Jung by south Korean security agents from his room in a Tokyo hotel in 1973, an act that caused great outcry among Japanese press and public. In contrast, in 1983, Japan responded to Korean requests for assistance by pledging U.S. $4 billion in government and private credits for Korean economic growth. In 1986, south Korean President Chun Doo Hwan made a state visit to Japan, calling on both Emperor and Prime Minister and receiving expressions of regret for the Japanese occupation of Korea. Treatment of the Korean minority of 700,000 in Japan has caused diplomatic problems between the two countries—most recently over the Japanese policy of fingerprinting aliens. The continuing trade imbalance is a source of controversy. Nonetheless, the long-term trend is toward improvement of relations that have been advantageous to both sides.

A continuing source of difficulty is Japanese policy toward north Korea: Although Japan does not recognize the Democratic People's Republic of Korea, it permits private economic and social contacts of considerable magnitude, such as the emigration of 100,000 Korean residents in Japan to north Korea under Red Cross auspices beginning in 1959 (a flow that practically ceased within a very few years) and the conclusion of a fishing agreement between Japanese and north Korean "private" groups.

The United Nations. The United Nations, once of great significance in the Republic's international affairs, has receded in importance over the years. The Republic came into being through elections observed by a United Nations commission in May 1948 and was recognized as the only duly constituted government in (not of) the peninsula by a UN General Assembly resolution in January 1949.[6] UN Security Council resolutions called for assistance to the Republic in defending against north Korean attack in 1950 and established the United Nations Command to lead the defense. UN commissions, composed of seven UN member nations, resided in Seoul from 1948 until 1973. From 1950, the group was known as the United Nations Commission for the Unification and Rehabilitation of Korea (UNCURK). Although the UN representatives could do nothing to further the cause of reunification, they regularly observed south Korean elections and political developments, and reported annually to the UN General Assembly.[7]

For several years after the Korean War, the United Nations was the principal forum for international concern with the peninsula. The "Korean

Question" was debated annually until 1975, and until that year resulted in General Assembly resolutions favoring the south. North Korea accordingly sought to undermine international support of the south and to increase its own. As many new countries with radical and anti-imperialist attitudes gained their independence, the north made considerable headway among them for recognition. Beginning with the World Health Organization in 1973, the Democratic People's Republic of Korea was admitted to most of the UN specialized organizations and gained UN observer status on a par with the Republic of Korea. In 1973, UNCURK was abolished. In 1975, two conflicting UN resolutions were passed favoring each of the Koreas, one of them calling for the withdrawal of U.S.troops. Since then, there has been no further UN debate on the "Korean Question."

The Republic of Korea is a member of all United Nations specialized agencies except the International Labour Organisation and, as already noted, has observer status with the UN itself. It is a member of the World Bank and International Monetary Fund (IMF) (whose annual meeting it hosted in 1985). It participates in the Asian Development Bank. The United Nations Development Programme has a small resident staff in Seoul to manage technical assistance programs.

Other Countries. Since the end of the Rhee regime in 1960, south Korea has increasingly turned its attention to the world as a whole, to diversify its markets and its sources of security and support. Its major targets are Western Europe, the Middle East, and the Pacific Basin, but it also promotes relations with the Third World generally. On the basis of its remarkable record of economic progress and through its diplomatic skills, the Republic has gained formal recognition from 125 states out of a total of about 165 in the world (compared with 101 for north Korea) as of early 1986. The attempted assassination of President Chun in Rangoon gave the country a boost in the competition for recognition, since Burma, a nation with impeccable non-aligned credentials, officially found north Korea responsible for the act. South Korea maintains resident embassies in over 80 states and hosts resident embassies of nearly 50 states in Seoul.[8]

As levers in promoting its international relations, the Republic makes good use of official visits and international conferences. In 1984, a fairly typical year, thirteen chiefs of state or heads of government visited the Republic of Korea. There was a total of forty-three such visits from January, 1981, to June, 1985. The total number of foreign ministerial visits was far greater. Senior Korean leaders visited foreign capitals in comparable numbers. President Chun visited the United States in 1981 and 1984, Southeast Asia in 1981, African states in 1982, and Western European states in 1986. His visit to Asian nations in 1983 was cut short by the assassination attempt in Rangoon.[9]

A number of recent major international conferences have been held in Seoul, including that of the Interparliamentary Union (IPU) in 1983—a meeting that north Korea exerted great but unsuccessful effort to move elsewhere. In 1985, the Republic successfully hosted the large annual conclave of the World Bank and International Monetary Fund, as noted above. Through international conference participation, south Korean representatives have entered the Soviet Union, China, and Eastern European countries, although these states do not recognize the Republic. Invited foreign visitors see at first hand the advanced state of the south Korean economy; such people are often taken on tours of modern industrial plants, scenic attractions, and the truce headquarters at Panmunjom.

The Republic also participates vigorously in non-governmental conferences, of which a growing number are being held in Seoul. In 1986, it was host to the Association of National Olympic Committees, attended by representatives of 152 nations (including the Soviet Union and Eastern Europe), and the Asian Games. Its greatest international triumph will come in 1988, when it hosts the Summer Olympics, with over 150 national teams and half a million participants and spectators. Massive preparations for this event have been in progress for several years. A great deal of financial and psychic capital has been invested in the Olympics by the entire Korean people (including some who have criticized the outlay on the basis that the money should be spent to alleviate poverty). In 1989, the Republic will host the annual world convention of Rotary International, a major businesspersons' service organization with over 22,000 clubs and 1 million members in 160 countries.[10]

Relations with Third World countries have also been promoted through modest technical assistance programs—some of them centered around south Korea's New Community Movement—and provision of doctors and nurses. In 1985, south Korea invited ninety-three farming experts from thirty-six countries for training in rice farming, silk culture, farm machinery, and rural extension programs.

Foreign Relations of North Korea
(Democratic People's Republic of Korea)

Security Policy

The Threat. North Korea's official view of its security situation is a bleak one. In this view, expressed almost daily in domestic and foreign propaganda, a triangular alliance of the United States, Japan, and south Korea is conspiring to repeat what north Korea claims to have been the aggression of 1950 against the peace-loving people of the Democratic Republic (the DPRK still maintains that the United States and south Korea started the Korean War and that the north Korean attack was a defensive action.) North Korea therefore holds that it must maintain a high state of readiness to repel this aggression. At the same time, the north repeatedly asserts its commitment to peaceful means of reunification.

Allegations of American and south Korean aggressive schemes, and of what north Korea terms the U.S.-Japan–south Korea triangular alliance, are strongest during the annual joint Korean-American "Team Spirit" exercise and during the north's yearly Anti-American Struggle Month. Frequently, charges of aggressive U.S. and south Korean intent are supported by accounts of spy plane overflights or south Korean military incursions—often surfaced in Military Armistice Commission meetings and then played through the mass media.

The defensive theme and pledges of peaceful unification have been uppermost in north Korean statements of recent years. Nevertheless, up to 65 percent of the north's military strength is deployed within a few miles of the Demilitarized Zone. Kim Il Sung in 1970 called for "revolutionary violence" and "mass struggle against fascism" in south Korea. The might of the north Korean Army has been said to be poised to strike the "main blow" against the imperialist lackeys in the south in support of popular revolution when it comes.[11] Infiltration attempts continue, suggesting that the DPRK remains committed to the "liberation" of the south.

Military Buildup. In 1962, as the Soviet Union was withdrawing its support, north Korea decided to give equal emphasis to military buildup and economic development. The delay in achieving the targets of the First Seven Year Plan (1961–1967) was publicly attributed to this policy. Nevertheless, 15 to 20 percent of the national product (even more, according to some calculations) continues to go to defense. More than the south, north Korea has built up its armaments industry for self-sufficiency. This industry is believed capable of supplying most of north Korea's weapons needs except for highly sophisticated systems and high-performance aircraft that it purchases from the Soviet Union. In the mid-1970s, south Korean and U.S. intelligence established that north Korea had also greatly increased the numbers of its regular military forces.

The DPRK does a booming business in supplying weaponry, along with military training and advice, to Third World countries and national liberation movements. North Korean weapons and advisory or training personnel have been reported in several African and radical Middle Eastern countries—a division of Zimbabwe troops was trained and equipped by north Koreans— and among Tamil separatists in Sri Lanka, for example. North Korea reportedly was selling considerable quantities of arms to Iran in the 1980s for its war with Iraq.

At the same time, north Korea cultivates relations with its two giant Communist allies, both for support of its military posture and for armament supply. Exchanges of visits by senior military officials with China have been frequent in recent years; and the Chinese continue to be represented on the Military Armistice Commission (although they were absent from it during their Cultural Revolution in the latter 1960s). The Soviet Union is the main source of advanced weaponry, since north Korea's industry is probably ahead of China's in most fields other than nuclear weapons (which north Korea does not have).

After Kim Il Sung's falling out with Soviet leader Khrushchev in 1962, the Soviets withdrew their advisers and refused to upgrade north Korean armaments; but relations have improved in recent years, especially since the visit of Kim Il Sung to the Soviet Union in 1984. The Soviets started supplying MiG-23 aircraft the following year. In return, they have enjoyed overflight rights, and gained access to north Korean ports for naval use. So far as is known, there are no large-scale joint military exercises with either China or the Soviet Union, although there may have been a joint naval exercise in 1986. Given north Korea's official commitment to self-reliance and non-alignment (notwithstanding mutual defense treaties with both China and the Soviet Union), such maneuvers would be ideologically difficult to justify, even if the allies were willing to join them.

Despite their continued public support of north Korean policy positions, it does not appear that either the Soviet Union or China would welcome renewed hostilities in the Korean peninsula. China, in particular, is believed be counseling north Korean moderation. However, north Korea may believe that if it were to reopen the war with the south, its allies would have no choice but to support it. Moreover, north Korea is thought to have enough stockpiles and productive capacity to support a war with its own resources for up to three months, by which time its allies might feel obliged to provide assistance.

Armed Forces

By Western estimates, north Korea is believed to have a total of over 800,000 full-time military personnel, 700,000 of whom are in the ground forces.[12] Since north Korea's total population is about half the south's, this number represents a massive human commitment to military readiness— about 4 percent of the people. Another 2 percent are in the reserve forces, and 11 percent in the Worker and Peasant Red Guard, a paramilitary force that performs the same functions as both the Homeland Reserve Forces and Civil Defense Corps of the south.

Unlike south Korea, the DPRK includes naval and air forces within the Korean People's Army (KPA). The KPA is controlled both by the Korean Workers' Party, through its Military Committee (chaired by President Kim Il Sung), and by the state, through a Military Commission of the Central

People's Committee (also chaired by Kim Il Sung). The two bodies have overlapping membership; the Minister of the People's Armed Forces, a Marshal of the KPA, is a member of both.

Under a Chief of General Staff, with sixteen functional staff bureaus (including a Political Bureau), there are an estimated eight corps, forty-three divisions (including two tank, three motorized, and three artillery divisions) of about 11,000 personnel each (smaller than south Korean divisions). There are six service arms: missile, armored, artillery, naval, air force, and special forces. The special forces, believed to number as many as 80,000—sometimes estimated to be over 100,000—make frequent forays into south Korea, mostly as individuals and small groups, for intelligence, subversion, and support of revolutionary movements; 3 of their officers planted the explosives in the Rangoon assassination attempt of 1983. As in other north Korean government organizations, there is a parallel hierarchy of Party committees and officials in military units at all levels, which oversees ideological training and propaganda. Twenty percent of platoon members are Korean Workers' Party members; the rest are members of the Socialist Working Youth League.

The Army Ready Reserve consists of 260,000 persons—army veterans less than thirty-five years old—in twenty-three divisions, which could be mobilized within a month. A Workers' and Peasants' Red Militia of 1.5 million consists of men eighteen to forty and women eighteen to thirty years old who are not otherwise committed to security functions, including students. Organized territorially and by workplace, they receive 200 hours of training per year. The 700,000 Red Youth Guards include high-school students over fourteen; army conscription begins at age sixteen. [13]

Major items of north Korean weapons and equipment, as estimated by Western sources, are listed in Table 7.1. As noted in discussing the security threat to south Korea, the north is far superior in quantitative terms (more and better tanks, twice the quantity of artillery, several times the number of anti-aircraft weapons, nearly twice as many aircraft—including seventy-two Hughes helicopters illegally acquired from the United States). Much of the north's weaponry is underground or in concrete revetments.[14]

Foreign Economic Relations

North Korea's foreign economic policy has two basic themes: self-reliance (*juche*) and support for economic development. Kim Il Sung has publicly stated that necessary trade with non-imperialist countries is consistent with the *juche* doctrine; and in his speech to the Sixth Party Congress in 1980, he called for quadrupling foreign trade during the 1980s. However, north Korea's international trade is a much smaller proportion of its national product than is that of south Korea; in 1979, exports and imports each amounted to about 13 percent of national product, compared with over 30 percent each for the south.[15] In 1985, north Korean trade with China, one of its principal partners, is believed to have been less than south Korean China trade (mostly through Hong Kong), although China does not recognize the south. Like south Korea, the north is totally dependent upon outside sources for petroleum, which makes up 15 percent of imports from the Soviet Union and more of those from China.

North Korean authorities emphasize to foreign visitors the extent to which its industrial plants and machinery are domestically produced. However, technology and technical assistance from Communist countries have been important in north Korea's rehabilitation and growth. The Soviet Union has helped in the construction of a number of plants on an output-sharing basis; in the 1980–1985 period, sixteen projects were completed or in progress on this basis, with the help of teams of Soviet technicians. The Soviets are assisting in construction of north Korea's first nuclear plant, now under way. The Chinese assisted in building hydroelectric projects along the Yalu River boundary, from which they also received power. The DPRK joined the United Nations Development Programme in 1979; since then a resident mission has helped in developing ports, railroads, and electronic industry.

In 1972, north Korea undertook an accelerated program of importing Western technology in the form of complete plants from Japan and industrial European countries, to be paid for through loans. That was the year in which senior north Korean officials secretly visited the south, in the negotiations which led to the north-south Joint Statement. They may have been concerned at the rapid pace of south Korean progress and thus motivated to turn to the West for improved technology. This strategy backfired because the oil crisis of 1973 hurt the north Korean economy and because the planners miscalculated the difficulties and the time lag in generating exports to pay off the loans. North Korea defaulted on its payments and has been struggling with rescheduling arrangements ever since. Its international credit is therefore poor, and its hard-currency earnings remain low.

As a new approach to the problem of technology transfer, north Korea enacted a joint venture law in 1984 under which foreign enterprises could do business. (China had adopted the same policy some years previously.) There was little Western enthusiasm, however. As noted in Chapter 6, joint ventures thus far appear to be relatively small in both scale and numbers.

General Diplomacy

North Korean foreign policy, like that of the south, aims to maintain the support of its allies and friends for its defense, for its claim to be the only true government of all Korea, and for its position on reunification; and to gain the widest possible support for its position among all nations. The

DPRK seeks legitimacy and respect, not only to strengthen national security and domestic stability, but also from the elemental desire for world status and prestige.

The Democratic People's Republic of Korea was formally recognized by 101 states in 1985, or two dozen less than south Korea. (Reaction to the Rangoon bombing resulted in a reduction from the maximum of 108 that had been reached in 1982). Approximately 90 states recognized both Koreas; apart from the Scandinavian countries and Austria, no major Western state recognized the north, while all recognized the south. The converse was true for the major Communist states.

Within the Communist Orbit. There is constant interchange between north Korea and other states on government, party, and other organizational levels within the Communist orbit. Visits by delegations of the various countries are frequent, and north Korea participates in and hosts international Communist gatherings. However, the DPRK is not a member of either the international Communist economic organization, the Council for Mutual Economic Assistance (CEMA), or the military Warsaw Pact grouping.

Until the Korean War, the relations of the Democratic People's Republic of Korea (north Korea) with the Soviet Union were as close and dominant as those of the south with the United States, or perhaps more so. Since north Korea had gained its independence in defiance of the United Nations, it lacked legitimacy in the non-Communist world.

After north Korea was defeated in its attack on the south in 1950, it was China, rather than the Soviet Union, that came to the rescue, and prevented the extinction of the Democratic People's Republic of Korea as a state. Following the armistice in 1953, north Korea received assistance from both China and the Soviet Union in rebuilding its shattered armed forces and economy. Chinese troops remained in the country until 1958; and in 1961, north Korea signed treaties with both its allies which pledged their military support. At about the same time, the Sino-Soviet split came into the open.

North Korea has accordingly been able to play one side against the other and preserve a considerable measure of policy independence, while maintaining relations and receiving support from both, with periodic movements to one side or the other. A low point in relations with Moscow came during the Khrushchev era (1955–1963), and with China during the Great Proletarian Cultural Revolution (1966–1971). There are indications that Kim Il Sung's aggressive posture toward the United States and south Korea and his decision to name his son, Kim Jong Il, as his successor have caused strains in relations with both allies.

Kim Il Sung's 1984 visit to Moscow was his first in twenty years. It began a trend toward closer relations with the Soviet Union, after years of relative coolness. Soviet Vice Premier Geidar Aliyev, who visited north Korea the following year, was the first official of that rank to do so for many years; and the twenty-fifth anniversary of the north Korean-Soviet Treaty of Mutual Assistance was celebrated with great fanfare in 1986. At the same time, however, north Korea has maintained its relationship with China, with which on the whole it is probably more comfortable for reasons of history, culture, and proximity.

Relations with Japan. Outside the Communist world, chief north Korean diplomatic targets are Japan and Third World countries. Toward Japan, north Korea is ambivalent. On the one hand, Koreans in the north share the dislike of all Koreans for the Japanese and their forty-year occupation, and Kim Il Sung's personality cult is based in large part upon his image as a leader in the anti-Japanese struggle. On the other hand, Japan is a potential source of economic support, and official Japanese recognition of the north would be a great political gain.

In dealing with Japan, the DPRK has the levers of its strategic geographic position, its support from the Japanese Socialist party and some intellectuals, the large Korean resident minority in Japan, and the ties and attitudes remaining from the colonial period, as well as Japanese business desires for trade. For many years, the DPRK had total support from the Japanese Socialist Party, much more radical than its European counterparts. Although a minority party, the Socialists had a large popular following and some political power because of their obstructionist capabilities in the Japanese legislature and on the streets. Up until 1985, the Socialists had still not recognized the legitimacy of the government in the south, although the Party was apparently moderating its political views on this and other subjects. A principal stumbling block in the negotiations for normalization of relations between Japan and south Korea in the 1960s was the Socialist contention that the south could not negotiate on behalf of all Korea.

Since normalization, Japan has refused diplomatic recognition to north Korea, but has permitted varying levels of private cooperation, such as a treaty on fishing rights negotiated by a private Japanese fisheries group. As already noted, the volume of trade between Japan and north Korea has grown rapidly since the late 1960s, although it suffered a setback in the 1970s. Japan refused to allow official visits of north Koreans to Japan, but there have been exchanges of visits by members of the two parliaments under the auspices of a joint friendship organization.

The United States. As might be expected, north Korea has been strongly anti-American in both domestic and foreign policy since 1948, and particularly since the Korean War. The DPRK has repeatedly expressed its apprehension of renewed U.S. aggression. It has sponsored "Anti-American Struggle Month" from June 25 to July 27 in each recent year[16] in as many countries as it can reach, and visitors to north Korea are routinely taken to a museum exhibiting U.S. war damage and "atrocities." The meetings of the Military

Armistice Commission at Panmunjom have been dominated by north Korean allegations of aggressive designs by the United States and its south Korean "puppet," both allegedly linked with Japan in an aggressive triangular alliance.

The height of north Korean anti-Americanism came in the late 1960's, when the United States was embroiled in Vietnam. This was also a period of heightened subversion against south Korea, including the attempted assassination of President Park Chung Hee in January 1969. Two days later, the north Koreans captured a U.S. naval intelligence vessel, the USS *Pueblo*, and held it and its crew for eleven months, finally extracting a statement of guilt and apology from the United States (disavowed while it was being made) to secure the release of the crew.

The following year, the north Koreans shot down an unarmed U.S. EC-121 reconnaissance aircraft over the East Sea (Sea of Japan), with the loss of its entire thirty-one-man crew. The latter action apparently embarrassed north Korea's allies; the Soviets offered assistance in searching for survivors. The north has since shot at reconnaissance aircraft over or near its territory (the most recent such reported incident was in 1984) and has downed U.S. Army helicopters that strayed over north Korean territory.

The harshest actions against the United States since the late 1960s were the senseless "ax murders" at Panmunjom in August 1976, which took two U.S. Army officers' lives; and a firefight at Panmunjom in November, 1984, triggered by the successful defection of a young Soviet visitor, which killed a Korean guard and wounded an American soldier. (The 1976 incident started with an attempt by a small detachment of U.S. soldiers to prune a tree that obstructed the view from a UN Command observation post in the Joint Security Area within the Demilitarized Zone—an area then open to both sides. For reasons not clearly understood, a group of north Korean soldiers set upon the group and killed two officers with axes in a brutal beating. In the 1984 incident, a Soviet citizen touring the northern side of the Joint Security Area suddenly broke and ran to the southern side; he was pursued by north Korean troops, shooting as they went. UN Command forces fired back. There were casualties on both sides, but the Soviet made good his escape and was given asylum.)

Nevertheless, north Korea since the 1960s has continually but unsuccessfully sought direct diplomatic talks with the United States, both through propaganda and by contacts through third countries. Its stated purpose has been to lower tensions and reach a peace treaty to end the Korean War. It may also have had in mind that whether or not such talks had any practical result, they might yield, as a by-product, the increase of north Korean international stature and furtherance of its own policies. In 1984, north Korea dropped its objection to the inclusion of south Korea in such talks, proposing trilateral discussions. This proposal, somewhat like a suggestion by President Carter in 1979, has been frequently repeated by the north, but has been rejected by both south Korea and the United States. North Korea has also cultivated people-to-people relations with ethnic Koreans in the United States and a limited number of journalists. Over 700 Korean-Americans visited the north in 1985 and 1986 to meet family members, returning with pictures and favorable reports of conditions.

The United States, still officially committed to the UN "police action" to repel north Korean aggression, has maintained a near-total embargo of trade and relations. The U.S. position is that solution of the "Korean question" is up to the Koreans themselves. In the 1970s, the United States suggested four-way talks, including China, or six-way talks, including the Soviet Union and Japan. North Korea has rejected such proposals (see Chapter 8). Very recently, the United States slightly relaxed its ban on diplomatic contacts with the north and held out the possibility of limited trade in commodities such as medical supplies. This policy was suspended after the bombing of a south Korean civil aircraft in December 1987 was traced to north Korean agents.

Other Non-Communist Countries. In its approach to the Third World, the DPRK capitalizes upon its own revolutionary tradition, upon its doctrine of self-reliance, and upon its anti-American and anti-imperialist record. North Korea has been a leading radical and anti-American member of the Non-Aligned Movement, in spite of its mutual defense treaties with China and the Soviet Union; it has claimed special ideological leadership in national development and has supported "wars of national liberation" with weapons, training, and in some cases small combat units. North Korean security assistance has been welcomed in a number of African nations.

Until the 1970s, the DPRK could also point to its rapid economic progress as a model for other developing countries; but in recent years, as its foreign debt problems mounted and its economic progress stagnated, it has lost this advantage to its southern adversary. Its radicalism has been less effective than south Korea's economic progress and diplomatic skill.

The principal tools of North Korean diplomacy have been visits, international conferences, propaganda, military assistance (training and weapons), and trade. A steady stream of senior government officials and political and social figures—especially those from the more radical African and Middle Eastern states and chiefly from the smaller ones—has come to Pyongyang to be wined and dined, taken on standard tours of industry, agriculture, and scenery, and invited to make statements supporting DPRK policies and accomplishments. Prince Norodom Sihanouk, former ruler of Kampuchea (Cambodia), has taken up residence in a palace built for him outside Pyongyang and spends several months there each year. A relatively small number of senior north Korean officials have travelled extensively among Third World countries. The DPRK has promoted bilateral friendship societies and groups for the study of the *juche* idea, not only in the Third World but also in some European countries.

In Europe, north Korea appeals to the left-leaning minority and has found some support, particularly in Scandinavia, which has been somewhat more neutral toward the two Korean states than the rest of the industrialized world. France—notwithstanding its participation in the military defense of south Korea during the war—has seemed at several times on the verge of recognition.

North Korea's diplomacy has also focused on the United Nations. The DPRK opposed the UN actions that had brought the Republic of Korea into being in the south. Its attempts to achieve UN membership, like those of the south, were rebuffed. Following the Korean War, north Korea held that the UN itself was a co-belligerent, and the UN, for its part, refused to give the North any voice in UN proceedings.

As the character of UN membership began to change, support for the north increased yearly. The DPRK, admitted to the World Health Organization in 1973, entered most other UN specialized agencies thereafter. In 1975, the Assembly adopted a pro-north Korean resolution, calling for withdrawal of American troops from Korea, although it also adopted a pro-south Korean resolution, calling among other things for dialogue between the two Korean states. Although the UN has not since debated the Korean question, north and south still compete in getting statements on Korea included in the speeches of national delegates at UN General Assembly sessions.

Misbehavior by DPRK representatives abroad has damaged North Korea's international image. The government apparently expects its missions abroad to support themselves and even to return money to Pyongyang. In recent years, north Korean diplomats in Scandinavian capitals, Rome, New Delhi, Kathmandu, and elsewhere have been found involved in smuggling of drugs, gold, watches, and pornographic movies. They have sought to bribe international organization officials in Finland and rioted on soccer fields in India. Recently, the lurid revelations of a noted south Korean movie producer-actress couple, Shin Sang-ok and Choi Un-hi, who sought asylum in the U.S. Embassy in Vienna in 1986 and said they had been kidnapped from Hong Kong to north Korea on orders of Kim Il Sung's son, Kim Jong Il, have added to north Korean embarrassments. (The couple is now back in south Korea.)

Overseas Korean Residents
as a Foreign-Policy Factor

In addition to the 60 million Koreans living on their native peninsula, there are approximately 4 million in other countries. Of this number, 1.7 million live in China–the majority of them in Manchurian provinces bordering

Korea. The United States has about 1 million (about a quarter of them in the Los Angeles area), many of whom have taken U. S. citizenship. Seven hundred thousand Koreans live in Japan. Approximately 400,000 live in the Soviet Union, many of them in the Republic of Kazakhistan, to which they were moved from the Maritime Provinces adjoining Korea during the buildup of Japanese-Soviet tensions in the 1930s. Small but significant Korean colonies are in Brazil and other South American countries, and smaller numbers live in Europe. At the height of south Korean construction activity in the Middle East, there were about 200,000 Korean workers there; the number was greatly reduced in the 1980s. Almost all these workers return home as their work terms expire or their jobs terminate. Additionally, many thousands of Koreans go abroad for university study, chiefly to the United States, Japan, and Western Europe from the south, and to the Soviet Union and Eastern Europe from the north.[17]

The chief concerns of south Korea with ethnic Koreans abroad are to keep them from becoming an embarrassment to relations with the host countries, win their support for the government in Seoul, and prevent their being used for north Korean espionage, propaganda, and subversion. South Korean government policy is to promote emigration, especially to South America, as a means of dealing with the very high density of population at home. (Until the present, emigration to the United States has not needed encouragement.) Diplomatic and consular officials of the Republic of Korea keep in touch with the affairs of the Korean communities abroad. Cooperation and modest support are given to organizations and to schools for Korean children in the larger expatriate communities. Through information and contact, Korean officials endeavor to blunt the criticism of the south Korean government, which has long prevailed among overseas Koreans.

In cooperation with host country authorities, a watch for subversive activity is kept by south Korean security agents overseas. The concern is not unfounded. In 1974, a Korean student resident in Japan, apparently acting as a north Korean agent, shot at President Park on the stage of the principal theater in Seoul, but missed the President and killed his wife. South Korean security authorities apprehend numbers of Koreans from Japan each year for involvement in espionage and subversive activity. In the mid-1970s, concern for north Korean recruitment among Koreans in Germany led to an aggressive anti-espionage campaign by south Korean authorities operating abroad that caused considerable tension in Korean-West German relations. To some extent, the same was true in the United States during the same period.

North Korea has apparently concentrated its attention on the large Korean minority in Japan, although south Korea has charged that north Korea has recruited Koreans in Europe and the United States for espionage, as above noted.

The Korean community in Japan—a survival from Korea's time as a Japanese colony—is largely composed of people in the lower part of the socioeconomic spectrum, who suffer from prejudicial attitudes of the Japanese as well as from unemployment and depressed living standards. Yet there are some Korean residents who have prospered; among these are substantial investors in enterprises in both north and south Korea. Some Koreans have taken Japanese citizenship, but the majority have not.

A series of difficult problems has arisen as to the legal status of the Koreans in Japan as Korean nationals, their eligibility for Japanese welfare benefits, and their control as aliens by the Japanese authorities. In the 1980s, concern focused on a Japanese requirement that all resident aliens be fingerprinted—a requirement strongly resisted by the Koreans.

Prior to the 1965 normalization of relations between south Korea and Japan, north Korea had clear majority support among the 700,000 Koreans in Japan, for whom it provided education, organization, and propaganda through an organization known by the Japanese acronym *Chosoren*. In 1959, numbers of them started moving to north Korea as repatriates under auspices of the Red Cross societies, and before the program petered out, over 100,000 had been repatriated. This was important to north Korea as a source of needed labor and as a propaganda triumph; the Japanese welcomed the move because it lessened the troublesome burden of the Korean community. Following normalization of relations with south Korea in 1965, however, the north's ascendency among Korean residents has been aggressively challenged by south Korean representatives, with considerable success. A rival pro-south residents' association (*Mindan*) has gained support about equal to the north's.[18]

A large proportion of the Koreans in China are concentrated in an autonomous district along the Yalu River in Manchuria. Since the end of the Cultural Revolution, they have won the right to govern themselves, maintain their own schools and newspapers, and use the Korean language, although they are Chinese citizens. Many of them came originally from south Korea, and recent visitors to the area report that they are more interested in south than in north Korean affairs.

In the United States, most members of the Korean community are educated, highly qualified professional and technical people. The Korean residents as a whole have been economically successful and socially self-controlled. Although their critical attitude toward the government of their homeland has sometimes embarrassed its representatives, it has not been a major problem in the two states' relations. Like many ethnic groups in the United States, the Koreans have come under occasional attack by other groups. Korean businesspeople, especially in the inner cities, have been shot and their stores firebombed. This is not a uniquely Korean problem, however; and the presence of Koreans at various levels in professional and business life throughout the United States demonstrates their capability and the degree (even if not total) of their acceptance by the U.S. public.[19]

Notes

1. Cf. Larry Niksch, "North Korea" and "South Korea" in *Fighting Armies; Non-Aligned, Third World, and Other Ground Armies; A Combat Assessment,* Richard A. Gabriel, editor (Westport, Ct.: Greenwood Press, 1983), pp. 103–152.

2. The sixteen signatory nations (which also signed the Armistice Agreement) were Australia, Belgium, Canada, Colombia, France, Ethiopia, Greece, Luxembourg, Netherlands, New Zealand, Philippines, Thailand, Turkey, Republic of South Africa, United Kingdom, United States.

3. *South Korea: A Country Study* (Washington, DC: U.S. Government Printing Office, 1981); *The Military Balance 1981–1982* (London: International Institute of Strategic Studies, 1982) (regarding composition and missions of ROK armed forces).

4. For an account of the "Koreagate" affair, see the report of the Subcommittee on International Organizations, U.S. House of Representatives, 95th Congress, 2d session, *Investigation of Korean-American Relations,* Oct. 31, 1978.

5. A useful reference work on U.S.-Korean relations is the *Handbook on Korean-U.S. Relations* published by the Asia Society, New York (1985).

6. UN General Assembly Resolution, December 1, 1948. For a discussion of United Nations role in Korea, see Leland M. Goodrich, *Korea: A Study of U.S. Policy in the United Nations* (New York: Council on Foreign Relations, 1956).

7. Following referral of the Korean question to the United Nations in 1947, a temporary commission was established to observe elections. After the elections were held in 1948, a new successor commission, the United Nations Commission on Korea (UNCOK) was established, stationed in south Korea. During the Korean War, this commission was replaced by UNCURK, composed of seven states-members: Australia, Chile, The Netherlands, Pakistan, the Philippines, Thailand, and Turkey. The commissions reported annually to the UN General Assembly; the reports are available as UN documents. Also established in 1950 was the United Nations Korea Reconstruction Agency (UNKRA), composed of UN Secretariat personnel under a Director-General, which dispensed $500 million in international development assistance. It was abolished in 1958.

8. Cf. *Korea Annual 1985* (Seoul: Yonhap News Agency, 1985), pp. 379–385.

9. *Korea Annual 1985,* p. 61.

10. Figures provided by Rotary Korea office, Seoul, as of May 1986. Rotary has proved very popular in Korea, as in Japan. From one club started during the Japanese period and revived in the mid-1950s, Rotary in south Korea has grown to 467 clubs with 17,461 members (as of April 1986).

11. Niksch in *Fighting Armies,* p. 115.

12. North Korea does not give statistics on military strength and equipment, and non-Communist estimates are classified. U.S.officials in South Korea put the total full-time military strength of north Korea at 840,000 men in mid-1986.

13. Niksch in *Fighting Armies,* pp. 113–114.

14. Information provided by U.S. Forces Korea.

15. Figure calculated on basis of 1980 north Korean national budget of $9.5 billion, assumed to be 80 percent of national income, and exports and imports of approximately $1.5 billion in 1979. cf *North Korea: A Country Study*, pp. xiv, 155.

16. June 25 is the anniversary of the 1950 outbreak of the Korean War, for which north Korea blames the United States; July 27 is the date in 1953 on which the Armistice Agreement was signed.

17. On Koreans overseas, see Chae-Jin Lee, *China's Korean Minority: The Politics of Ethnic Education* (Boulder, Colo.: Westview Press, 1986); George and Herta Ginsburgs, "A Statistical Profile of the Korean Community in the Soviet Union," *Asian Survey* 17 (No. 10, Oct. 1977):952–956; Richard H. Mitchell, *The Korean Minority in Japan* (Berkeley: University of California Press, 1967); *The Korean Diaspora: Historical and Sociological Studies of Korean Immigration and Assimilation in North America*, Hyung-chan Kim, editor (Santa Barbara, Cal.: ABC-Clio, 1977).

18. Statements about the Korean minority in Japan are based on Mitchell, *The Korean Minority in Japan*; my own professional experience and observation; and discussion with U.S. and south Korean government officers.

8 THE PROBLEM OF KOREAN REUNIFICATION

Introduction

To begin the discussion of Korean reunification, it bears repeating once again that the Korean people have been a unified nation since A.D.668, when Silla, one of the three early Korean kingdoms on the peninsula, conquered the other two. (To be precise, Silla unified Korea south of the peninsula's narrow waist; north of Pyongyang, a separate kingdom of Parhae, part Korean, part Khitan, existed for three centuries. The present boundaries were established during the Koryo Dynasty [936–1392].) Koreans have thus been divided only 3 percent of their national lifetime—or 6 percent, if the fifty years or so of division at the end of the Silla Dynasty are counted.

Given the common aspiration of the Korean people for reunification and its many objective advantages, it is reasonable to expect that Korea will be reunified someday. The questions are how and when, even more than whether, it will be accomplished. Nevertheless, the obstacles are formidable, and the trend since 1945 has mostly been away from reunification, rather than toward it.

Why Korea Was Divided

Korea's strategic location in East Asia has made it the object of great-power rivalries for centuries, and particularly in the past hundred years. After Japan defeated China in 1895, Japan and Russia struggled for hegemony in Manchuria and Korea. In 1896, Russia proposed that the two countries divide Korea into spheres of influence at the 38th parallel; Japan refused. In 1904, Japan proposed a similar division at the 39th parallel; Russia refused. The Russo-Japanese War was fought to settle the two countries' rivalries in Korea and Manchuria. Japan won, gaining total control of Korea. This control was unchallenged (except by the Koreans) until Japan went to war with the United States in 1941.

At the Tehran Conference of 1943 among Soviet, British, and U.S. leaders, US President Roosevelt proposed an international trusteeship over Korea. This proposal followed the Cairo Declaration of a few days earlier, promising that the Korean people should "in due course become free and independent." Roosevelt initially thought in terms of a forty-year trusteeship period, having in mind the Philippine precedent. Stalin was not enthusiastic about trusteeship, but acquiesced in it, while insisting that it be as short as possible.

At Potsdam, in July 1945, the Allies stated that Japan would be stripped of all territories annexed since 1895, including Korea. Also at Potsdam, the Soviet Union—up until then not a belligerent in the Pacific—was encouraged to enter the war against Japan. Up to that time, no detailed plans had been made for Korea; all attention was fixed on the defeat and postwar occupation of Japan. The Soviet Union declared war on Japan on August 8, and its forces engaged Japanese forces in Korea the next day. The impending Japanese surrender up to a year earlier than had been anticipated by the United States (the surrender coming partly as a result of the atomic bombing of Hiroshima and Nagasaki) necessitated immediate decision on Korea.

To forestall total Soviet control of Korea, the U.S. authorities proposed that U. S. forces occupy the peninsula south of the 38th parallel, to take the surrender of the Japanese armed forces there, and that the Soviets do the same north of the 38th parallel. The Soviets accepted the arrangement, and abided by it.[1]

The final form of the trusteeship proposal was worked out at the meeting of foreign ministers in Moscow in December 1945. The United States, the Soviet Union, Great Britain, and China would exercise the trusteeship for five years; a transitional Korean administration would be formed by consultation between the two occupying powers, which would consult the Korean people in the process.

Public announcement of the Moscow agreement evoked wide and intense resentment throughout the peninsula among the Koreans, who were largely taken by surprise although the idea had been expressed by a U.S. diplomat the previous September in a New York speech. They viewed the idea as a trick to deny them their independence. The overwhelmingly hostile Korean reaction helped to destroy any possibility that the proposal would be carried out. Instead, it became a Soviet tool in subsequent fruitless US-Soviet negotiations for a united transitional regime.

Following the Moscow Declaration, the Soviets prevailed on their partisans in both north and south to support trusteeship, while in the south the U.S. faced a general strike by the military government's Korean employees and nationwide demonstrations. By acting as they did, the Soviets laid the basis for excluding from consultation with the Joint Commission any Korean who did not support trusteeship, which meant in effect that only Koreans who supported the Soviet point of view would be consulted. Meanwhile, Dr. Syngman Rhee, the conservative Korean nationalist who had returned from forty years of exile in the United States, pushed for a separate anti-Communist state in the south. The original temporary division, intended by the United States to avoid Soviet domination of the entire peninsula, thus became permanent.

The much-criticized trusteeship proposal, viewed in retrospect, had been a rational device. It might have protected Korea from the rival ambitions of surrounding powers while the nation developed its own political structure. However, the principal actors, the United States and the Soviet Union, distrusted each other, and the Koreans, unprepared for the idea, rejected it (except for those whom the Soviets persuaded to change their minds). It was therefore never tried.

The first conference between representatives of the U.S. and Russian military commands was held in January 1946. It resulted in minor arrangements for exchange of mail, railroad communication, and the like, but the demands and refusals of the two sides fueled mutual distrust. A formal conference of the USSR-U.S. Joint Commission, as provided in the Moscow Declaration, began in March 1946 and ended without result in August 1947. A U.S. attempt at unification under UN auspices failed, and the temporary division of Korea became permanent.

The damage done to Korea by international rivalries, culminating in its division, was reinforced by internal weakness and age-long factionalism. A thousand years ago, as the Silla Dynasty grew feeble and rent with internal dissention, rival leaders set up their own states of Latter Koguryo and Latter Paekche. In its closing years, Silla controlled little more than the capital city of Kyongju. Reunification was accomplished by Wang Kon, founder of the Koryo Dynasty, with a mixture of force and wise diplomacy. Koryo and the succeeding Choson (Yi) Dynasty ruled a united country for a millennium, although Koryo was weakened by the Mongol invasion and Choson by the Japanese.

A century ago, the aging Choson Dynasty, weak and torn with internal dissension, faced challenges far greater than Silla or Koryo could have imagined. Western nations were establishing imperialist hegemony over Asia, based on military and material superiority, and Japan was following suit. China, Korea's long-time mentor, was also in decline. Korea's only response was self-isolation, dependence on China, and, later, alliances of contending Korean factions with contending foreign powers. Korea fell to Japan and for forty years was denied opportunity to move into the modern world under its own leaders. Thus, the Koreans were still weak and divided when the Japanese rule ended. During that period, Korean nationalists were split by both ideology and factional loyalty. Because of this dissension, Korean leaders reinforced the division of the country by the United States and the Soviet Union, rather than resisting it.

Rival foreign ideologies are another cause of Korea's division. After Korea was annexed by Japan in 1910, nationalists—mostly in exile—continued to work for Korean independence. At first they embraced capitalism and liberal democratic ideals and sought Western support; but none was forthcoming. After the Bolshevik Revolution of 1917, some nationalists began to look to Russia and communism to support their struggle. Thereafter, the nationalist leadership was divided by the conflict between the two ideologies of liberal capitalist democracy, preferred by the propertied conservatives, and Marxist socialism or communism, preferred by some of the intellectuals and many of the impoverished peasantry and workers.

The ideological split was reinforced by the experience of the Japanese occupation itself. Because the Japanese regime was capitalist in form, some of the hatred of Japanese domination seems to have extended to Western capitalism. There was considerable Marxist thinking among Japanese intellectuals, which influenced some of the young Koreans who studied in Japanese universities. Such views emerged at the end of World War II. Moreover, the Soviet Union, which has a common border with Korea and Manchuria, was able to give the nationalist cause a modicum of support and thus added to the favorable image of communism. The Western European countries and the United States did nothing for Korea, except for moral support at the time of the 1919 independence uprising.

All these factors—great-power rivalry, Korean weakness and internal dissension, and ideological conflict—reinforced one another and interacted with Korean nationalism. The Korean people themselves objected violently to continued outside control in the form of trusteeship. The political orientation of the two halves of Korea was already differentiated by the influence of the two occupying powers. The United States refused to recognize the left-oriented People's Republic of Korea, declared two days before the arrival of U.S. occupation forces in early September 1945. Instead, the United States looked largely to conservative leaders for support in organizing a military government under direct U.S. control. In contrast, the Soviet authorities used local organizations of the People's Republic as a basis for organizing the north on Communist lines.

An independent government was finally established in the south through UN-observed elections in 1948. The Soviet Union and Eastern European states recognized a separate Communist state in the north. Thus the ideological and territorial divisions came together and reinforced each other. Additional reinforcement of both factors came from the suffering and bitterness of the ensuing Korean War.

Still another factor in the continued division of Korea comes from the division itself. The existence of two separate states for nearly forty years has entrenched two governments in sovereign power, each of which claims to be the only legitimate government of all Korea. Unification would require that one government absorb the other, or that both yield to a third. There are few cases in human history in which a political leader or power structure has voluntarily subordinated itself to another. Additionally, each Korean state has developed a wholly different organization. Although the common cultural heritage appears to persist on both sides of the Demilitarized Zone, differences will inevitably grow. Already some of the words in the language have different meanings in north and south. The longer the division persists, the greater the barrier to reunification that this cultural difference will create.

The Case for Korean Unification

From the standpoint of Korea's interests as a whole nation, the objective advantages of reunification are enormous. A united Korea, with sixty million people—three times the population of north Korea, or 50 percent more than south Korea—would be an impressive medium-sized state. With a considerable natural resource base and an internal market bigger than many industrialized countries, it would enjoy a considerable measure of economic independence. It would have defensible natural boundaries. It would be freed from at least part of the enormous present military burden and from the threat of subversion and attack within the peninsula. It would be freed from the trauma of divided families. With the military competence both Koreas have demonstrated, the reunited nation would be able to inflict heavy damage on its neighbors in the event of attack. Thus, with judicious diplomacy,

Korea could look forward to a reasonably secure future as a proud and prosperous country, notwithstanding the enormous power of its neighbors.

However, there are massive obstacles to unification. All the causes of division already noted still have their effect, although Korea's weakness is now a function of its territorial division, rather than lack of energy or ability. Great-power rivalry and the ideological division continue in full force, and every passing year adds to the firm entrenchment of the two rival political regimes. The mutual distrust of these regimes is so high that even the thought of reunification in the present seems ridiculous. The huge military establishments on both sides have already been discussed.

At present, great-power rivalries largely coincide with the rivalry of the two Korean states. The Soviet Union backs Communist north Korea, while the United States backs the anti-Communist south. Communist China is the north's ally, while non-Communist Japan is politically and economically close to the south. However, the picture has been complicated in recent years by the Sino-Soviet split, by the China-U.S. rapprochement, and by Japan's policy of "non-governmental" dealings with the north.

Neither China nor the Soviet Union wants north Korea to gravitate into the other's orbit, given the peninsula's strategic location. Both China and the Soviet Union would resist any change in the north's political or ideological orientation, although neither seems prepared to support a renewal of hostilities to extend the Communist hold over the whole peninsula. Japan considers Korea important to its own security and would oppose the communization of the whole country. The United States wants to maintain the stability of the region because of its strategic and economic interests; it wants to contain Soviet expansion into the region; and it wants democracy maintained, if not expanded. The U.S. troop presence in Korea deters an attempt to reunify the peninsula by force; it also offers the United States a strategic foothold on the Asian mainland.

Although the present situation in Korea is not completely to the liking of any of the surrounding powers, all of them apparently believe that the known risks and problems of the present are preferable to the unknown risks of change. Thus, although all the powers pay lip service to the idea of unification, they do so in accordance with their respective national policies and interests. No outside power is likely to push for reunification, in the light of the risks of renewed conflict. If there should be renewed hostilities in Korea short of a larger international conflict, the likely result would be to maintain the status quo. In the writer's view, reunification will come only through the initiative of the Koreans themselves, based on the recognition in both north and south of its long-range advantages for the Korean nation, and accompanied by appropriate international guarantees.

Unification Policies and Initiatives

Basic Policies

The following general propositions characterize the whole history of Korean unification initiatives:

- Both Koreas are strongly committed to reunification. All their allies support unification in public, but attach little priority to it in private.
- Both Koreas are publicly committed to unification only by peaceful means. However, both Koreas have been more willing to use force than their great-power allies, except that the Soviet Union and China, consistent with their revolutionary ideologies, have been more supportive than the United States (particularly in the north Korean aggression of 1950).
- Both Koreas call for settlement of the unification problem by the Korean people themselves. The Soviet Union and China support this position. The United States has never disavowed its 1953 position that unification should be accomplished by UN-observed elections throughout Korea for representatives to determine the government of a unified state; but since the mid-1970s the United States, also, has supported the principle of unification by the Korean people themselves.
- South Korea and the United States since the mid-1970's have advocated an international conference including both Koreas, China, the United States, and possibly the Soviet Union and Japan, to discuss unification. North Korea wants negotiation directly with the United States to arrange a peace treaty and withdrawal of U.S. troops but since 1984 has proposed that south Korea join such a conference. China supports the north Korean position; the Soviet Union has kept silent on it. The United States, although President Carter made a somewhat similar suggestion for a three-way conference in 1979, has since supported south Korea's opposition to it.
- North Korea has envisaged a people's revolution in the south, perhaps assisted in the critical stage by the north Korean armed forces, as the stepping-stone to unification. At times, it has sought to promote the revolution with its own agents and strategies. South Korean policies have no revolutionary component.
- South Korea's approaches to peaceful unification are based on gradual, step-by-step programs of specific cooperative action, through direct contact between north and south, building up to eventual political union. North Korea has stressed major top-level meetings and "grand conferences" as the point of departure.

- South Korea favors elections and decision-making on the basis of one person, one vote, which would give it a two-to-one advantage over the north. Nevertheless, equality with the north was one implicit point in the south's 1982 proposal. North Korea, for its part, advocates negotiation on the basis of equality. Probably for this reason, north Korea has redefined its political subdivisions so that it has the same number of provinces and special cities as the south.
- North Korea, since the Korean War, has demanded the withdrawal of U.S. forces, usually as a precondition for negotiations on unification. South Korea, which holds that U.S. forces are present in accordance with its Mutual Defense Treaty with the United States, wants them to remain in place until enforceable agreements are reached.
- Despite some contact between the two sides, and one joint policy statement in 1972, each Korean state regards itself as the only legitimate government of Korea and usually refers to the other in derogatory terms. South Korea has five north Korean provincial offices in its governmental structure; north Korea has south Korean representatives in its legislature. However, whereas north Korea insists that Korea can be admitted to the United Nations only as a unified entity, South Korea advocates immediate membership of both Koreas, on the German model.
- The United States does not want to see Korean unification under Communist auspices; the Soviet Union and China would not accept unification that appeared to "roll back" Communism. Thus, although all three powers support unification along the lines of their respective Korean allies, they implicitly support the divided status quo. All three are apparently opposed to a military solution to the problem. Some authors believe that China, in particular, deterred Kim Il Sung from such a solution in the 1960s.

Overview of Unification Efforts Since 1945

First Phase: Early U.S. Initiatives. The temporary division of Korea in 1945, proposed by the United States and accepted by the Soviet Union, was not initially viewed by either of them as a political division of the country. At the end of World War II, Korea was legally Japanese territory, although its people were anti-Japanese. The military occupation was a means of filling the power vacuum left by the Japanese defeat until a Korean administration could be formed. The situation was somewhat similar to that of Austria, which also had Soviet and U.S. (as well as French and British) occupation zones; it was unlike that of Germany, which was occupied for political as well as military control of a defeated enemy.

The U.S. international trusteeship proposal was intended to bring a united Korean administration into being. It failed, without even being tried, because the Koreans objected to it; because each of the occupying powers wanted to ensure that the future Korean government would be politically and ideologically acceptable, but had incompatible standards of acceptability; and because the ideologically and factionally divided Korean nationalists could not agree on a formula of their own.

Second Phase: United Nations Involvement. Already resolved to take its troops out of Korea, the United States in 1947 sought to solve the "Korean question" by referring it to the United Nations. The Soviet Union opposed referral to the United Nations, on the basis that Article 104 of the Charter excluded from UN jurisdiction issues arising out of World War II. This position had some legal validity, although the uncompromising Soviet stand did not win any friends. The United States had such overwhelming UN support at the time that the question was taken up anyway. The Soviet Union then submitted, in the General Assembly, its own draft resolution, which was turned around by U.S. amendments and eventually passed. The Assembly resolution, as passed, anticipated that a UN Commission would undertake consultations throughout Korea on the shape of a new Korean government. Refusal of the north Korean authorities to admit the UN commission ended all hopes that a unified Korean regime could be brought into being through peaceful negotiation. (The Soviet Union consistently referred U.S. and other authorities to the north Korean administration the Soviets had set up, although they actually held the final power until September 1948.) As already noted, separate independent states were established in the two halves of Korea, and the occupying powers withdrew their military forces.

Third Phase: Unification by Force. After military mutiny and widespread guerrilla action in the south had failed to dislodge the UN-recognized Republic of Korea, north Korea and the Soviet Union sought unification through a quick military victory over the south. They counted upon a strong north Korean military buildup, U.S. indifference, and south Korean unreadiness. Had the United States not reversed its policies and provided massive military support under the United Nations umbrella, the attack would probably have resulted in reunification of Korea as a Communist state. Its failure led to a brief United Nations attempt to occupy north Korea and set the clock back to 1947; but the Chinese intervention eventually resulted in restoration of the pre–Korean War situation. (It is worth noting that the United States in the fall of 1950, briefly adopted a policy of supporting neutral status for a unified Korea.)

Fourth Phase: Return to the United Nations. Pursuant to a clause in the 1953 Armistice Agreement calling for a political conference, representatives of nations on both sides of the Korean War met in Geneva in 1954 to discuss Korea's future. The United States, supported by the other fifteen nations of the United Nations Command, called for elections under United

Nations observation throughout Korea, in proportion to population (north Korea having at that time less than half the population of the south) to set up a conference that would decide Korea's government. South Korea's representative presented a thirteen-point unification plan, which also called for elections but upheld the legitimacy of the Republic established in 1948 as the government of all Korea.[2]

The north Koreans, supported by the Chinese and Soviets, maintained that the United Nations was itself a belligerent in the war and that the solution to the Korean question should be left to the Koreans themselves (implicitly calling for equal status of the two Korean states). They proposed that foreign troops should be first withdrawn from Korea. Free elections would then be held without foreign interference throughout Korea for representatives to a national conference, in which the two sides would be equally represented, to work out a unified administration.

The Geneva Conference broke up in disagreement, but the proposal for elections throughout Korea under UN observation became part of the subsequent UN General Assembly resolution that year. Symptomatic of the small practical value attached to this plan, it was not spelled out in the resolution—simply incorporated by reference. The UN General Assembly debated the Korean question yearly until 1975; it has not done so since. The UN role in Korean unification has virtually ceased, except as it is involved in proposals for Korean membership and in the activities of the residual United Nations Command. However, UN secretaries general in recent years have talked separately with the two Korean governments in efforts to promote dialogue betweem them.

Fifth Phase: North Korean Propaganda and Subversive Initiatives. The north Korean unification formula proposed at the Geneva Conference, with variations, underlay north Korean proposals for the rest of the 1950s. Meanwhile, the north denied the legitimacy of the Republic of Korea, heaped abuse on it as an imperialist puppet, endeavored to subvert it through its own agents, and called for popular revolution against it. After their Army was defeated, thousands of north Korean soldiers melted into the south Korean hills. For nearly two years after the armistice, they continued to fight as guerrillas, based in the rugged mountain chain in south-central Korea. The Republic's combat teams, according to one report, killed approximately 82,000 guerrillas in subduing the insurgency.[3]

In 1954—at the same time the guerrillas were fighting—north Korea proposed a joint conference of representatives of north and south to negotiate unification. It proposed a non-aggression pact in 1955; an international conference to solve the Korean question, and mutual reductions of forces to 100,000 each, both in 1957. In this period, north Korea also advocated economic and cultural exchanges between the two Koreas. At the time, the north was the more dynamic economy and stable polity and maintained the propaganda initiative in the international arena. The south did not respond; official policy until 1960 under Syngman Rhee was *pukchin t'ongil* (march north for unification), with no compromises.

Sixth Phase: Confederal Republic and People's Revolution. The political upheaval of April 1960 in south Korea stimulated a new north Korean proposal. On August 14, 1960, north Korean President Kim Il Sung proposed formation of a Confederal Republic of Koryo, which would preserve the separate systems and international relations of the two states, on a basis of equality, but would set up a Supreme National Committee to handle certain matters in common. This idea, put forward again in somewhat modified and more detailed form in 1980, remains a central north Korean theme, along with proposals for a "grand national conference" of equal representation from both sides to bring it into being.

The new 1960 initiative may have been motivated by north Korean anticipation of increasing instability in the south. However, the military coup d'état of 1961 seems to have disappointed these hopes. North Korea then started its military buildup and, as the United States became bogged down in Vietnam, sought to take advantage of the situation to destabilize the south. Its military adventures during this period were described in the previous chapter.

Seventh Phase: North-South Contact After the "Nixon Shock." The U.S. withdrawal from Vietnam, the Guam Doctrine on non-employment of U.S. forces, and the U.S. opening to China as well as U.S. moves toward détente with the Soviet Union, all worried both north and south Korean leaders. In 1971, the north accepted a south Korean proposal for talks between the two sides' Red Cross societies on the plight of divided families. Concurrently, secret contacts between the two sides led to a surprise Joint Declaration of July 4, 1972, in which north and south pledged themselves to (1) peaceful unification, (2) no foreign interference, (3) independence. (These are frequently cited by north Korea as the Three Grand Principles of National Unification. North and south soon disagreed as to whether "independence" excludes the U.S. troop presence.) The two sides agreed not to insult each other, to set up a South-North Coordinating Committee (SNCC) with five members on each side, to discuss unification measures, and to establish a telephone "hot line" between Seoul and Pyongyang.

Preliminary negotiations went forward at both the SNCC and Red Cross levels, and one Red Cross plenary north-south meeting was held in August 1972. The first conference of SNCC co-chairmen opened at Panmunjom the following October. Neither conference reached significant agreement. Talks at both levels petered out by 1973, following the establishment of the strongly authoritarian *yusin* regime in the south in late 1972. The north Koreans from 1976 ceased to acknowledge test calls on the hot line and reverted to belligerent propaganda.

In the following years, south Korea took the initiative in proposing a non-aggression agreement (January 1974) and an economic consultative organization for inter-Korean cooperation (June 1978). In his New Year address in January 1979, south Korean President Park proposed a meeting of south and north Korean authorities at any time, any place, and any level. In its turn, north Korea called for negotiation of a peace treaty with the United States (March 1974) and in January 1976 sent letters to selected prominent persons in the south, proposing a political conference. None of the proposals bore fruit.

The assassination of President Park Chung Hee in October 1979, and the convening in 1980 of the first north Korean party congress in ten years, stimulated a north Korean elaboration of its earlier proposal for a Confederal Republic of Koryo, with a Ten Point Plan for the confederation to promote north-south interchange and cooperation. Under the October 1980 proposal, the confederation would have a confederal assembly, a standing committee of which would "discuss and decide on political affairs, national defense problems, foreign affairs, and other matters of common concern." There would be a "combined national army" in addition to regional forces. Each half of Korea would keep its own political and economic system and its treaty arrangements.

North Korea also proposed that the prime ministers of the two sides should meet. Several preliminary talks were held in the Joint Security Area at Panmunjom between working-level representatives of both sides, but no definite agreement was reached. The north broke off contact following establishment of the Fifth Republic in the south in late 1980.

In January 1981, south Korean President Chun proposed an exchange of visits by the "highest authorities" of the two Koreas. He reiterated this proposal in June, calling also for opening up the two societies. In January 1982, he proposed the adoption of a constitution for a unified Korea and a new formula for national reconciliation and unification. This was followed by a south Korean list of twenty pilot projects to facilitate reconciliation and mutual trust, announced in February 1982, and a proposal for cabinet-level inter-Korean talks. (The twenty pilot projects, relating to economic, cultural, and military matters, ranged from opening a highway between Seoul and Pyongyang and setting up a joint tourist zone in east-central Korea to removing military facilities from the Demilitarized Zone and discussion of arms control measures.[4])

The January 1982 proposal, in effect a counter to the north Koreans' confederation scheme, was the most detailed and realistic that the south Korean government had put forward. It moved quite a distance in bringing north and south Korean approaches into harmony; for example, it implicitly accepted equal status of the two halves. It was based, however, on the evolutionary approach through smaller confidence-building steps to larger ones, in contrast to the north Korean proposal for unification by a sort of once-and-for-all leap of faith. Unsurprisingly, the north was not impressed.[5]

Recent Developments:
Renewed North-South Conferences

After working-level meetings ceased in 1980, both sides renewed their confrontation tactics and mutually hostile propaganda barrages. The north put forward its proposal for three-way talks among both Koreas and the United States soon after its agents endeavored to blow up the south Korean president and his party in Rangoon in October 1983. Coming hardly a month after the Soviet Union had shot down a Korean passenger airliner, the Rangoon incident poisoned the atmosphere against the idea, even if it was worthy of consideration. (President Carter had made a somewhat similar suggestion in 1979.)

Despite the hostility it had engendered, north Korea proposed in the spring of 1984 that representatives of the two sides discuss the formation of a joint Korean team for that year's Summer Olympics in Los Angeles. South Korea had made such a proposal in 1981, which the north had previously ignored. It was obviously too late to make such arrangements. Nevertheless, representatives of the two Olympic committees held two meetings to discuss the idea of a joint team for subsequent events—in particular, the 1986 Asian Games and the 1988 Summer Olympics, both to be held in Seoul. The talks were inconclusive. In an effort to move them forward, the chairman of the International Olympic Committee invited representatives of both sides to meet with him in Lausanne, Switzerland, but without tangible result.

Frustrated in its attempts to obstruct the holding of the 1988 Olympics in Seoul, the north in 1985 demanded to be co-host for the games, half of which would be held in Pyongyang. The International Olympic Committee (IOC) charter does not allow co-hosting. South Korea suggested that some preliminary games be held in Pyongyang, but this did not satisfy the north, which stuck to its co-host demand. Several talks on this subject, sponsored by the IOC, were held with north and south in Lausanne. The IOC proposed, with south Korean agreement, that two of the 1988 games (fencing and archery) and one of the preliminary soccer matches be held in Pyongyang and that a long-distance cycling race begin there. Although the IOC eventually offered five games, with the acquiescence of south Korea, the north continued to demand that more of the games be held in Pyongyang but moved back and forth on its bid to be co-host. Discussions were continuing in 1987 but with little hope of agreement.

In August, 1984, continuing the series of offers each side had made the other over the years, south Korean President Chun proposed south-north

FIGURE 8.1 Meeting of representatives of north and south Korea (photo courtesy of Korea Overseas Information Service)

economic exchanges and offered to supply commodities to the north Korean people. North Korea did not accept; but in September it offered to supply relief goods to the victims of a severe flood in the Seoul area. For the first time in Korea's postwar history, south Korea accepted. The north fulfilled its promise to the letter, delivering 7,200 metric tons (7,900 U.S. short tons) of rice, 100,000 metric tons (110,000 U.S. tons) of cement, 500,000 meters (547,000 yards) of textiles, and 759 cartons of medicine by truck and ship to Panmunjom and designated south Korean destinations.

Following this unprecedented event, contacts between the Red Cross societies of both sides resumed. Full-dress plenary meetings were held in Seoul and Pyongyang, leading to visits by fifty separated family members of each side, in September 1985, to meet relatives in the capital city of the other side. At north Korean insistence, cultural troupes journeyed with the family members, and gave performances. Teams of reporters covered the visits. Not all visitors met their families, and the reunions had heavy propaganda overtones. Nevertheless, the exchange was universally considered to have historic significance.

Following up on an earlier south Korean proposal, discussions on economic cooperation also began in November 1984 between the two sides. Both sides designated government officials as representatives, thus implicitly acknowledging each other's government (Fig. 8.1). The south advanced several specific proposals for exchange of commodities, reopening of rail links, and others. The north, however, concentrated on organization of an overall coordinating mechanism as a first step—an extension into the economic field of its usual philosophy of high-level, general agreement first.

The south reluctantly agreed to much of the north's concept, accepting formation of a committee at the deputy prime minister level; but actual economic exchange continued to elude agreement.

Also in 1984, north Korea proposed a meeting of the two sides' legislatures. Representatives of the two assemblies met several times—first at staff level, then between assembly members—to consider topics for discussion. The north wanted the joint conference to consider a non-aggression declaration. The south, pointing out that this was the business of the executive branch, counter-proposed discussion of a confederal constitution for a united Korea.

Talks in all four areas—sports, Red Cross, economic, and parliamentary— were suspended by the north when a Soviet visitor at Panmunjom dashed across the Joint Security Area to the southern side in October 1984. The north again suspended talks during the annual joint ROK-U.S. Team Spirit exercise in both early 1985 and early 1986. By mid-1986, only the sports talks were continuing; north Korea turned down suggestions for resumption of economic talks. Nevertheless, it was still hoped that some small agreements, such as more family visits and perhaps minor economic exchanges, would eventually materialize.

Motives for the northern show of peaceful cooperation, and for its subsequent suspension, could only be surmised. It might be intended, once again, to mask preparations for military or subversive action, as in 1950 and 1983. It might also be intended to improve north Korea's international image, which had suffered in recent years not only from the opprobrium of the Rangoon bombing and misconduct of north Korean diplomats but, more importantly, from its economic difficulties and defaulted loans. Some connection with the north Korean political succession problem was possible. Whether there was a deeper significance, such as a desire to lessen the tension on the peninsula and thus ameliorate the heavy military burden, could only be determined in the light of future developments.

Unification Prospects

Considering the universal Korean desire for reunification, with its clear political, economic, and military advantages, and the risks and costs of the present military confrontation, I believe that Korea will eventually be reunified. However, reunification will not come about except by the united effort of the Korean people themselves. In the absence of a strong push by the Koreans, no single outside power or combination of powers will work to change the status quo except to gain a strategic advantage for themselves (such as the Soviet Union's support of the north Korean attack in 1950). Any outside power's attempt to gain such an advantage would be resisted by other powers.

Real Korean moves toward unification, as distinguished from propaganda initiatives or cosmetic gestures, are inhibited primarily by suspicion, ideology, inertia, power and status concerns, and fear of jeopardizing relations with outside powers.

Suspicion is a traditional part of Korean political attitudes; it is rooted in history and culture. In north-south relations, suspicion is enormously magnified by the history of the Korean War, north Korean attempts at subversion and sabotage over the years—climaxed by the 1968 and 1983 assassination attempts—and the belligerent and vituperative posture of each Korea toward the other. Each leadership group assumes (correctly, in all probability) that the other side intends to overthrow it if possible, and responds in kind. There is little early prospect for change, although over time, with continuing contact and small-scale agreement, and if military tensions are lessened, the suspicion may abate. South Korea's emphasis on small-scale agreements and confidence-building measures is a recognition of this problem.

North Korea's 1980 proposal for a Confederal Republic of Koryo, in which north and south would retain their respective political and economic systems, is an attempt to finesse the clash of ideologies. The south's 1982 proposal for discussion of a confederal constitution is somewhat parallel. The idea probably should not be ruled out as an eventual intermediate step, particularly since the status of Hong Kong in China is to be based on a similar concept. South Korea's more modest and practical proposals, for simultaneous admission of both Koreas into the United Nations and cross-recognition by the allies of each side, have thus far met with total north Korean rejection; but the example of East and West German UN membership and special economic relations may eventually prevail. Closer contact and understanding between the two halves of Korea might result; and these, in turn, would facilitate reunification.

Complete political reunification of Korea will not automatically result from a Confederal Republic or from the German "two states, one nation" model. It can come only with the crumbling of north Korea's intense Communist (or *juche*) ideology, which will take a long time. The alternative—acceptance of north Korean *juche* doctrine in its present dogmatic form by forty million south Korean people—is inconceivable to me. Also necessary for unification is the recognition by political leaders on both sides that the national benefit from unification outweighs the risks to stability and to personal power positions. Some sort of compromise along Austrian lines might then be achieved.

There is no way to document the interrelated problems of inertia and power-status concerns; but their importance is obvious. Presidents Syngman Rhee and Park Chung Hee of south Korea both hung onto power until one was ruined and the other assassinated. They did so not only out of pride, conviction, and enjoyment of office, but also because their supporters needed them for their own prosperity and survival. Korean and world history is full of similar examples. Neither of the two Korean power hierarchies wants to concede first place to the other, even if it could be assured of fair treatment, and even if the ideological differences could be removed. The pressure for reunification will have to be much stronger, and probably will have to be coupled with some kind of internal crisis, to induce such a concession. Yet when the concession comes, the person or group that makes it can become national heroes.

The final and most dangerous problem is the attitude of outside powers. Given its sensitive strategic location, any move toward change in the Korean peninsula will be viewed by each of the powers with deep suspicion as a ploy on the part of one or more of the others. It will also be viewed with suspicion by the Korean people as a new example of *sadaejuui* (subservience to power). Any move toward change, therefore, will have to be worked out through skilled and subtle diplomacy and full consultation, both internationally and domestically. Moreover, the results of the change cannot appear to be seriously disadvantageous to the interests of any outside power.

North Korea is allied with the Soviet Union and China. Presumably, the "Brezhnev doctrine," under which the Soviet Union asserts its right to resist any attempted roll-back of communism, applies to Korea as well as to Czechoslovakia. South Korea is equally or more firmly allied with the United States. The United States has made no blanket claim of ideological jurisdiction, but its interests, both worldwide and in the region, would be hurt if all Korea went Communist. China and Japan have been less ideologically assertive, but neither of them would welcome a shift in alignment, particularly if it produced a reunited Korea allied with the Communist powers (for Japan) or with the United States (for China).

If a Democratic Confederal Republic of Koryo, however loosely constituted, were to have armed forces under confederal control as north Korea has proposed, it would introduce a brand-new and unpredictable dimension in the present military balance of East Asia, particularly if U.S. forces were withdrawn, as north Korea wants. This part of the north Korean initiative is therefore patently unrealistic and adds further doubt to the sincerity of the idea in its entirety. But an even greater problem is involved in any reunification scheme: The united Korean state would control the armed forces, and the outside powers would want to know whose side these forces were on.

Since Korea's historical experience and geopolitical location demonstrate the need for a significant defensive capability, the country cannot be demilitarized. Therefore its military forces will be a significant factor in the regional military balance, even if the present confrontation along the Military Demarcation Line can be ended. It follows that the achievement of a united

Korea will have to be accompanied by a credible international arrangement giving other powers assurance that neither the Korean armed forces, nor the schemes of any of the interested outside powers, will upset the balance or trigger hostilities. The examples of Switzerland, Austria, Sweden, and Finland all offer material for study that could inform Korea's future.

This brief analysis of Korea's reunification problem demonstrates again what most informed people recognize: the great difficulty of finding a workable solution. However, Korea since World War II has demonstrated its capacity to solve many problems, sometimes when solutions seemed impossible. No matter how difficult reunification may be, it is not impossible. Its potential contribution to the stability of East Asia, and the desire of the Korean people for it will probably bring about its eventual achievement.

Notes

1. On the decision to divide the zones of occupation at the 38th parallel, see Michael Sandusky, *America's Parallel* (Alexandria, Va.: Old Dominion Press, 1985).

2. *The Korean Problem at the Geneva Conference, April 26–June 15, 1954*, International Organization and Conference Series II, Far Eastern, U.S. Department of State (Washington, D. C.: U.S. Government Printing Office, 1954).

3. Report of Dr. Paul Crane, who as a U.S. Army medical officer was involved in the operation.

4. *Korea Herald*, February 2, 1982, cited in *Korea and World Affairs* 6 (No. 1, Spring 1982):198–200.

5. For an analysis of the south Korean 1982 unification proposal, see Yong Sun Yim, "The Significance of the January 22 Unification Proposal," *Korea and World Affairs* 6 (No. 1, Spring 1982):19–38.

APPENDIX A: GLOSSARY

A-ak. Formal Confucian court music, preserved in Korea in its traditional Chinese form.

Ajon. Locally appointed functionaries of the Choson Dynasty, who were often at their posts for life, thus providing continuity and linkage to the central government, as well as a liaison service with the agricultural villages.

Armistice. After two years of protracted cease-fire negotiations, an armistice was signed July 27, 1953, between representatives of the two opposing military commands (United Nations Command and Korean People's Army/Chinese People's Volunteers). Both sides agreed to withdraw their forces behind a Demilitarized Zone that extended two kilometers on either side of a Military Demarcation Line marking the approximate positions of the two armies, slightly north of the original 38th parallel division between north and south Korea. Prisoners were exchanged and a Military Armistice Commission established to enforce the truce.

Cadre. Key officials of the Democratic People's Republic of Korea, usually core members of the Korean Workers' party, who ensure that party policies are effectively carried out.

Chaebol. Large south Korean business conglomerates, engaged through their component units in many lines of industry, which have played key roles in the export drive of the Republic of Korea from the mid-1960s.

Chajusong. Concept of standing for oneself; an inherent part of north Korea's *juche* philosophy.

Changgi. A Korean version of chess.

Chollima (thousand-league horse). Term used for the economic campaign in north Korea in the late 1950s, which brought temporary rapid progress at the price of lowered quality and worker exhaustion.

Ch'ondogyo (religion of the heavenly way). Name of a native Korean religion established in the nineteenth century in reaction to western influence and dynastic decay. Under the name *tonghak* (Eastern learning) it inspired the revolt which triggered the Sino-Japanese War in 1894.

Choson. (1) An early Korean state in southern Manchuria or north Korea (Ancient Choson), extinguished by China in 108 B.C. (2) The name of Korea during the Choson (Yi) Dynasty (1392–1910); also used of the reigning dynasty.

Chungin. A small intermediate social class of petty officials below the *yangban* aristocracy, but above the common people, during the Choson Dynasty.

Committee to Promote a Democratic Constitution. Umbrella group for non-party opposition activists that played a leading role in calling for constitutional amendment in 1987.

Demilitarized Zone (DMZ). A strip 4 kilometers (2.5 miles) wide and 240 kilometers (150 miles) long that separates the armed forces of the two sides in Korea. A Military Demarcation Line runs in its center. Under the Armistice Agreement, no military forces or equipment are to be deployed in the DMZ, other than security patrols. In fact, the DMZ has become militarized on both sides.

Democratic centralism. A principle of north Korea's governing ideology under which all suggestions and criticisms of the people are conveyed to the decision-making center of the Korean Workers' party, but once the decisions are made, all party members and citizens are obligated to carry them out regardless of their previous attitude.

Democratic Confederal Republic of Koryo. The name for a reunified Korea proposed by north Korea in its reunification initiatives.

Democratic Justice party (DJP). The political party organized in 1981 by the supporters of south Korean President Chun Doo Hwan to mobilize political support for his administration. (In Korean: *minju chonguidang*, or *minjongdang*.)

Democratic Korea party. From 1981 to 1985, the principal opposition party in the Republic of Korea; subsequently reduced to minor-party status. (In Korean: *minju han'guktang*.)

Han'gul. The phonetic Korean alphabet created by King Sejong in the fifteenth century and in general use today—often mixed with Chinese characters called *hanja*.

Hwan'gap. A great social occasion marking a man's sixtieth birthday.

Hwarang. A society of young warriors in the Silla Dynasty (18 B.C.–A.D. 936) with a code of conduct reminiscent of Japanese *bushido* or European chivalry.

Hwarangdo. (1) The code of the *hwarang*. (2) A system of fighting similar to *taegwondo*, but making use of the sword and other weapons.

Hyangga. Sung or chanted poems of the Silla period.

Ibul. Quilt to cover the body for sleeping on the floor, used together with a sleeping pad (*yo*).

Joint Security Area (JSA). A circular area within the Demilitarized Zone at Panmunjom within which both sides of the Military Armistice Commission meet and have their offices.

Juche. (1) Self-reliance. (2) (*juche sasang*) Kim Il Sung's version of Communist ideology as applied to national development, emphasizing self-reliance and the supremacy of man over his environment.

Kasa. A brief form of prose-poetry that emerged in the late sixteenth century, usually based on the beauties of nature.

Khitan. A warlike, nomadic people from the Tungus Valley area of eastern Siberia, probably related to the Koreans, who harassed both China and Korea over the centuries and for two centuries ruled north China as the Liao Dynasty.

Kimch'i. A spicy national dish made from pickled and peppered cabbage and other vegetables, vaguely similar to sauerkraut but much spicier.

Kisaeng. Professional woman entertainer of men at social occasions, who can make intelligent conversation, recite and even compose poetry, sing, dance, and play musical instruments.

Koguryo. A kingdom constituted by nomadic peoples that dominated much of the northern part of the Korean peninsula as well as Manchuria, which thrived from the first to the seventh centuries A.D. It was extinguished by Silla in the unification of the peninsula in 668 A.D.

Korea National party (KNP). A minor south Korean political party, organized in 1981 by former members of the government party in the Park administration (1963–1979), that often took positions between government and opposition. (In Korean: *han'guk kungmindang.*) In late 1979 the KNP became the New Democratic Republican party (NDRP, *sin minju konghwadang*).

Koryo. Dynasty founded by Wang Kon in A.D. 936 after overthrowing the Silla Dynasty; endured until 1392. The Western name for Korea is derived from Koryo.

Ku. Subdivision (ward) of a city (also used as a suffix and sometimes spelled *-gu*); for example, Yongsan-gu, a ward of the capital city of Seoul where the US Forces Korea (USFK) headquarters is located.

Kun. Subdivision (county) of a province (also used as a suffix and sometimes spelled (-*gun*).

Kut. A shamanistic ceremony performed by an adept (*mudang*) with costume, song, and dance, to invoke or exorcise spirits.

Kye. (1) A traditional mutual assistance group common in agricultural villages, typically composed of men in the same age group. (2) In recent times, a group of people, often women, who pool their savings for profitable investment.

Makkoli. A milky, winelike farmers' and workers' drink, brewed from rice, traditional and still popular.

Military Armistice Commission. A body established by the Armistice Agreement of 1953, composed of five representatives of each opposing side, to enforce the provisions of the agreement. Each side also has a secretary, duty officer, and staff.

Minmint'u. A radical, extra-legal student group that endeavors to coordinate student opposition to government policies it deems unjust, including lack of student freedom, unjust distribution of wealth and income, and harsh labor conditions.

Mintongnyon. Another extra-legal radical student umbrella group, organized in early 1987 to lead a struggle for democratization, freedom, and workers' rights.

Mudang. A shamanistic adept, usually female, who is versed in the ancient beliefs about good and evil spirits, is in communication with them, and is sometimes possessed by them in the course of shamanistic ceremony (*kut*).

Myon. Rural township, subdivision of a *kun* (county).

Nangnang. A Chinese military commandery, or colony, established in 108 B.C. in southern Manchuria or northern Korea during the Chinese Han Dynasty (208 B.C.–A.D. 220). Nangnang fell to the Korean state of Koguryo in A.D. 313.

New Korea Democratic party (NKDP). Political party established in early 1985, which attained the status of major opposition by winning sixty seats in the legislative elections that year, but was reduced to minor-party status by the departure of its principal organizers in April 1987 (in Korean: *sinhan minjudang*).

Nongak. Traditional folk music played by amateur farmer-musicians, often accompanied by group dancing.

Ondol. Unique Korean house-heating system whereby hot flue gases from the kitchen fire provide heat by passing through serpentine channels among stones under the floors before escaping through a chimney.

Paduk. A popular and intellectually challenging Korean board game (called *go* in Japan), somewhat similar to checkers but more complex.

Paekche. Kingdom established in southwest Korea, which flourished in the fourth to seventh centuries A.D. and had ties to both China and Japan. It was defeated and incorporated into the united Silla kingdom in A.D. 668.

P'ansori. A form of folktale with song, performed solo to the accompaniment of a barrel drum. Developed during the Choson Dynasty, its often humorous repertoire ridicules the life of the aristocracy and priesthood and extols the traditional Confucian virtues.

Parhae. Kingdom in northeastern Korea and southern Manchuria, including both Korean and Tungusic people, which was formed after the fall of Koguryo to Silla in the late seventh century A.D. and endured until conquered by the Khitan in 926. Its territories south of the Yalu and Tumen rivers (which form the present Korean border) were incorporated into Korea by the early Koryo kings.

Peace and Democracy party. South Korean political party formed by opposition leader Kim Dae Jung and his supporters in November 1987, after they split from the Reunification Democratic party. (In Korean: *p'yonghwa minjudang,* or *p'yongmindang.*)

Pukchin t'ongil. A slogan ("advance north for unification") commonly voiced during President Rhee's administration in south Korea (1948–1960) expressing his desire for reunification of Korea by extending the Republic's jurisdiction—by force, if necessary.

Reunification Democratic party. Political party formed on May 1, 1987, by supporters of opposition leaders Kim Young Sam and Kim Dae Jung, who bolted the New Korea Democratic Party and became the main opposition. The new party was split in two with the departure of Kim Dae Jung and his supporters in late 1987. (In Korean: *t'ongil minjudang,* or *t'ongmindang.*)

Ri. Village within a township (*myon*); the smallest rural Korean political unit.

Ri (also romanized as *li*). A traditional Korean unit of distance, equivalent to about one-half kilometer (one-third of a mile).

Sadaejuui. The principle of respect for (or subservience to) power (or greatness) that characterized Korean attitudes toward China during the Choson Dynasty. Then a reflection of Confucian morality, the term is now one of opprobrium applied to people who dance to the foreigner's tune.

Saemaul undong (New Community Movement). A nationwide movement launched in 1971 by south Korean President Park Chung Hee to mobilize villagers for their own mutual benefit to improve their quality of life. Villagers were encouraged to band together for group action on public works such as housing, roads, irrigation, and community facilities, as part of a nationwide organization.

Sarangbang. A special room in well-to-do homes where men met and entertained.

Security Consultative Meeting (SCM). Annual meeting of high defense officials of the Republic of Korea (headed by the Minister of National Defense) and the United States (headed by the Secretary of Defense) to review security matters of mutual concern. The meetings are held alternately in the two countries.

Sejong. Fourth king of the Choson Dynasty. His reign, 1418–1450, is regarded as the high point of the dynasty, and he is considered the father of the Korean phonetic alphabet, *han'gul.*

Si. Korean term for a city (generally 50,000 population or more); also used as a suffix, as in Suwon-si, city of Suwon. Seoul, the capital, is termed "special city" (*t'ukpyol si*); the cities of Pusan, Taegu, Inch'on, and Kwangju are also referred to as special cities in English but are termed *chikhwal si* (directly administered city) in Korean. All five are administratively equal to provinces. Other cities are equivalent to counties.

Sijo. A form of philosophic poetry, written in pure Korean rather than Chinese, that became a major form of literary expression during the Choson Dynasty.

Silla. Located in the southeastern part of the peninsula, Silla grew to prominence in the fourth and fifth centuries A.D. as one of Korea's "three kingdoms." By A.D. 668 Silla had conquered the other two kingdoms and ruled over most of the peninsula until A.D. 936.

Sirhak. A movement by young Confucian scholars in the eighteenth century to reform the rigid prevailing neo-Confucian philosophy. The Korean word means "practical learning."

Soju. A cheap, strong liquor distilled from rice that is popular among Korean farmers and workers.

Songgyun'gwan. The highest-level educational institution of the Choson Dynasty, a Confucian university. Songgyun'gwan still operates on its original site as a modern liberal arts university, but retains some of its Confucian heritage.

South-North Coordinating Committee (SNCC). Established by the Joint North-South Declaration of July 4, 1972, the Committee consists of five representatives each of north and south Korea who are theoretically charged with the negotiation of steps toward reunification. In practice, however, the Committee has seldom met except for sporadic exploratory working-level sessions.

Sowon. Academies for the instruction of young people organized by scholars and ex-officials, particularly those out of favor, during the Choson Dynasty. The *sowon* often served as headquarters for factions vying for political power; for this reason, most of them were abolished in the mid-nineteenth century.

Ssirum. Korean version of wrestling by men with large, heavy bodies; somewhat similar to Japanese *sumo.*

Suzerainty. Control exercised by one state over another's foreign affairs without destroying the latter's identity. As Korea's suzerain during the Choson Dynasty, China controlled Korea's foreign relations but in general did not interfere in its internal affairs.

T'aegwondo. A Korean martial art, famous worldwide. It emphasizes mental discipline and quick foot and fist movements, performed in a controlled manner carefully practiced in advance.

T'aejo. Reign name (meaning "great progenitor") of Yi Song-gye, a military leader who overthrew the Koryo Dynasty and founded his own Choson Dynasty in 1392. T'aejo cultivated good relations with Ming Dynasty China to reinforce his own legitimacy and modelled his government and political philosophy after that of China.

Taejonggyo. Religion of recent origin organized around the worship of Tan'gun, mythical founder of Korea.

Tan'gun. The mythical founder of the Korean nation in 2333 B.C., a man born of a bear at the bidding of a god.

Team Spirit. Annual large-scale Korean-U.S. joint military exercises conducted in early spring to verify the ability of the Combined Forces Command to stop a north Korean attack. In recent years the exercise has involved 200,000 or more troops of both countries and naval and air units as well as ground forces.

Three Kingdoms Period. A period of three or more centuries when three Korean states co-existed in the Korean peninsula—Koguryo, Paekche, and Silla. Silla unified much of the peninsula by conquering the other two kingdoms in A.D. 668, although the northeastern portion of the peninsula was controlled by a separate state of Parhae.

Three Revolutions. A campaign launched in the early 1970s, under the leadership of north Korean president Kim Il Sung's son, Kim Jong Il, to encourage innovation and eliminate the barriers of bureaucratic immobilism. The three revolutions are technological, ideological, and cultural.

To. Province, the major territorial division of Korea (often written -*do* and used as a suffix). During most of the Choson Dynasty, there were eight Korean provinces; five of these were divided in two in 1895, for a total of 13. North Korea has further subdivided the five provinces in its territory, for a total of nine, equal to south Korea. In addition, each Korean state has four special cities with status equal to provinces; south Korea added a fifth (Kwangju) in 1987.

Tong. Precinct; subdivision of a city ward (often written -*do* and used as a suffix).

Tonghak. A religious movement of the mid-nineteenth century that was a cause of the Sino-Japanese War. See under Ch'ondogyo.

T'ongilgyo. The Unification Church of the Rev. Sun Myung Moon (Mun Son-myong), an offshoot of Christianity, which has gained many converts in the United States, Japan, and other countries.

Uibyongdae. Volunteer bands who fought the Japanese invaders of the late sixteenth century, and again in the early twentieth century.

Up. Urban township or borough, subdivision of a county on the same level as a *myon*; often used as a suffix.

Won. The Korean monetary unit. The south Korean won is worth slightly over one-tenth of a U.S. cent; the exchange rate varies, but in early 1987 was around 850 won per dollar. There is no real exchange rate between the north Korean won and the dollar, but it is worth several hundred times the value of its south Korean counterpart.

Yangban. Scholar-officials who constituted the aristocratic or noble class of the Choson Dynasty. The majority were selected through an examination system based on the Chinese classics.

Yi Dynasty. Another term for the Choson Dynasty (1392–1910), derived from the family name of its founder, Yi Song-gye. Korean historians now prefer the term Choson for this period.

Yo. A pad, or thin mattress, placed on the floor for sleeping.

Yut. A traditional game for young and old, played with four sticks tossed in the air.

APPENDIX B: THE KOREAN LANGUAGE AND ITS ROMANIZATION

General Description

Korean is a language common to all 60 million inhabitants of the Korean peninsula and is an important element of Korean national identity. It is similar in structure to Japanese, Mongolian, Turkish, Hungarian, and Finnish, with which it is sometimes grouped in a Ural-Altaic family of languages. However, its phonetic structure is unique. Korean differs from the other Ural-Altaic languages even more than English differs from, let us say, Hindi, although both are Indo-European languages.

The Korean language is called agglutinative—that is, syllables are added to verbs, adjectives, and nouns to show relationships of time, place, subject to object, and social position of speaker, hearer, and person spoken about. Word order in a sentence typically puts the subject first, followed by the object, with the verb at the end. Modifiers, or adjectives, behave somewhat like verbs and can take the place of verbs. Particles (usually single syllables) known as postpositions follow nouns in somewhat the same way as English prepositions precede nouns. These differences in structure make translation from Korean to English, or vice versa, rather difficult.

The polysyllabic, agglutinative character of Korean makes it totally unlike Chinese, which is basically monosyllabic and without word inflection. Also unlike Chinese, but like English, "tones" or variations in pitch, play no part in the meaning of individual words in Korean, but do convey feeling and complement grammatical structure, distinguishing questions, statements, and commands.

Phonetically, Korean differs sharply from English in that the meaning of its consonants differs according to whether they are aspirated or unaspirated (that is, whether their articulation is, or is not, accompanied by a puff of breath). It does not matter, in Korean, whether a consonant is voiced (like the English "b" or "d") or unvoiced (like the English "p" or "t"); voicing depends on the position of a consonant in a word or phrase. This pattern is the reverse of English, which aspirates some consonants and not others without effect on meaning. Additionally, a group of Korean consonants is distinguished by an almost explosive tenseness in pronunciation, somewhat like the French "p." The Korean alphabet distinguishes fourteen consonants; at least one Korean scholar has identified twenty-four different consonantal sounds.

The Korean Writing System

Until the fifteenth century, Korea had no writing system of its own. Records were kept in Chinese or by using the pronunciation of Chinese characters to represent Korean sounds. A set of abbreviated Chinese characters, called *idu,* was developed for this purpose. The great King Sejong convened a committee of scholars who developed the phonetic alphabet now known as *han'gul.* The new alphabet was proclaimed in 1446, but despite its obvious advantages it was not generally accepted by the Korean scholarly community until the twentieth century; the official records of the Choson Dynasty (1392–1910) were kept in classical Chinese. A page from the original fifteenth-century instructions for the use of *han'gul,* intermixed with Chinese characters, is shown in Figure B.1; there has been considerable change in spelling and pronunciation since then but not much change in the manner of writing the characters. The modern *han'gul* characters, with their roman letter equivalents, are shown in Table B.1.

Han'gul is almost always written in syllabic groups, with the initial consonant at the left or top, the vowel to the right, center, or bottom, and the final consonant, if any, underneath. If there is no initial consonant, this fact is signalled with a separate character—the same one used for the "ng" sound. If there is no final consonant, it is simply omitted.

The use of syllabic groups makes it easy to combine the phonetic script with Chinese characters. Literate Koreans in the south still use Chinese characters for words derived from Chinese (which make up about half the listings in Korean dictionaries), and the schools teach a standard list of 1,900 such characters. In north Korea, the use of Chinese characters was abolished many years ago. This was an understandable gesture of nationalist assertion, and it simplified the reading and writing of Korean for the general public; but it also added to north Korea's isolation from its neighbors.

Traditionally, Korean (like Chinese) was written from top to bottom of the page, and right to left; the pages of a book were therefore in the reverse order to English. Today, both the traditional style and the Western style (horizontally, left to right) are used—the latter particularly in scholarly works where quotations from Western languages are interspersed in the text. Most publications are printed, but calligraphy is still an honored art form in Korea. It is common for noted persons to write short poems or epigrams—usually in Chinese characters, but sometimes in *han'gul*—for presentation to their followers and friends. The signboard on the Kwanghwamun, the gate in front of the old capitol building in Seoul (now a national museum), was inscribed in *han'gul* by the late President Park Chung Hee; it is one of the few examples of such inscriptions which reads in the modern manner, from left to right.

Romanization—Writing Korean in Roman Letters

The spelling of Korean in the Latin alphabet for English speakers is made very difficult by differences in the phonetic systems of the two languages, which also make the Korean language difficult for English speakers to learn. After years of experimentation, both the governments of both the Republic of Korea and the United

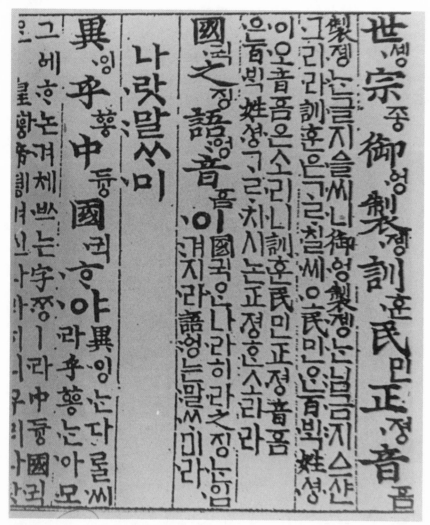

FIGURE B.1 A page of Korean phonetic script from the fifteenth-century document, *Hunmin Chongum,* showing *han'gul* intermingled with Chinese characters (photo by Edward Adams)

States and many Western scholars have come to accept a romanization system devised by George M. McCune and Edwin O. Reischauer in 1938. Scholarly files in the United States, including the index of the Library of Congress and most university libraries, are based on the McCune-Reischauer system of romanization.

The McCune-Reischauer system uses roman letters chosen to represent the English sound most nearly approximating Korean. An apostrophe (') after a consonant shows that it is aspirated ("p'," "t' "), and a double letter ("pp," "tt") indicates a "fortis"

TABLE B.1   Romanization of Korean

	Consonants				Vowels	
han'gul	Roman (according to position)[a]				han'gul	Roman
	Initial	medial	final			
ㄱ	k	g	k		ㅏ	a
ㄴ	n	n	n		ㅑ	ya
ㄷ	t	d	t		ㅓ	ŏ
ㄹ	n, r	1, n, r	1		ㅕ	yŏ
ㅁ	m	m	m		ㅗ	o
ㅂ	p	b	p		ㅛ	yo
ㅅ	s	s	s		ㅜ	u
ㅇ	–	ng	ng		ㅠ	yu
ㅈ	ch	j	ch		ㅡ	ŭ
ㅊ	ch'	ch'	ch'		ㅣ	i
ㅋ	k'	k'	–		ㅐ	ae
ㅌ	t'	t'	t		ㅒ	yae
ㅍ	p'	p'	p		ㅔ	e
ㅎ	h	h	–		ㅖ	ye
ㄲ	kk	kk	kk		ㅘ	wa
ㄸ	tt	tt	tt		ㅙ	wae
ㅃ	pp	pp	–		ㅚ	oe
ㅆ	ss	ss	tt		ㅝ	wŏ
ㅉ	jj	jj	jj		ㅞ	we
					ㅟ	wi
					ㅢ	ui

[a]The chart does not show elisions
and euphonic modifications resulting
from juxtaposition of consonants.

Source: Adapted from Korean Overseas Information Service, Han'gul
(Korean Alphabet and Language), Korea Background Series, Vol. 9
(Seoul, n.d.), pp. 56-58.

or explosive pronunciation. In general, an unaspirated consonant is voiced in Korean when it occurs in the middle of a word and is therefore romanized in the McCune-Reischauer system with its approximate English voiced equivalent (*b, d,* etc.).

Most of the vowels in Korean have approximate—but not precise—English counterparts. Two of them, which lack even approximate English equivalents, are spelled in the McCune-Reischauer system with a diacritical mark: "ŏ," a sound between the English "o" in "oh" and "u" in "uh"; and "ŭ," a sound like the French "u." In this book, the diacritical marks have been omitted for simplicity, so that the proper distinction in pronunciation between "o" and "ŏ," "u" and "ŭ," is lost. For purposes of managing the few Korean terms that appear in common U.S. use, the loss is not serious, but the reader should be aware of it. In *han'gul,* ten vowel symbols are distinguished, but they are used in combination to represent additional sounds.

Table B.1 shows the *han'gul* characters for the Korean consonants and vowels and their roman equivalents according to the McCune-Reischauer system. One special feature of the McCune-Reischauer system must be noted: the additional use of the apostrophe (') to separate "n" and "g" in cases where they are not to be pronounced together. In Korean, there is a separate single symbol for the nasal "ng" sound (as in the English word "sing"); but when this sound is romanized as "ng," it cannot be distinguished from two successive syllables, one with a final "n" and the other with an initial "g." Accordingly, whenever the two romanized consonants appear together *without* an apostrophe, they are pronounced together as "ng"; when separated ("n'g"), they are pronounced separately. Thus, the Han River, *han'gang,* has a separate "n" and "g," while "Eastern Sea" or "Oriental," *tongyang,* has an "ng" sound.

Unfortunately, there has been a great deal of romanization of Korean that does not follow the McCune-Reischauer system. Before that system was devised, writers used their own phonetic interpretations. The nineteenth-century French Catholic missionaries devised a romanization system (from which the present spelling of the capital city, Seoul, is derived). The U.S. Military Government had its own system. The south Korean Ministry of Education established a system that was followed for a decade. Individual Koreans spell their own names according to their own preferences (for example, the former south Korean National Assembly Chairman, whose name would be Sin Ik-hui in McCune-Reischauer, styled himself P. H. Shinicky; people with the family name spelled Yi in McCune-Reischauer use Lee, Rhee, Rii, Leigh).In this book, the McCune-Reischauer system is used except for proper names commonly romanized otherwise.

I have not seen any written rules for the north Korean system of romanization. However, north Korean English-language materials suggest that unaspirated consonants are represented by their voiced English equivalents and aspirated consonants are represented by the unvoiced equivalents, instead of using apostrophes. The south Korean Ministry of Education's former system employed somewhat the same principle. Some Koreans believe that this method is better than McCune-Reischauer, because to their ears it seems to make English speakers pronounce the consonants better. (The pinyin romanization system of Chinese adopted by the People's Republic of China to replace the missionary-devised Wade-Giles system also uses voiced English equivalents for unaspirated consonants, and unvoiced equivalents for aspirated ones, rather than the Wade-Giles apostrophes.)North Korean romanizations, insofar as they are known, have been used for north Korean names in this book.Thus, Kim Il Sung's son's name is spelled Kim Jong Il, rather than the McCune-Reischauer Kim Chong-il; the capital city is Pyongyang, rather than P'yongyang, in post-1945 references.

APPENDIX C:
KOREAN STUDIES READING LIST

The following is a representative selection of English-language materials considered suitable for undergraduate college or high-school study. Specialized scholarly works and children's books on Korea, of which there are a growing number, are not listed.

General Overview

Bartz, Patricia. *South Korea.* New York: Oxford, England: Clarendon Press, 1972. 203 pp. The only recent geographical study of Korea; also contains a brief, although now somewhat outdated, summary of Korean history and government.

Cumings, Bruce. *The Two Koreas.* New York: Foreign Policy Association, 1984. 80 pp., paper. Brief, readable description of both Korean states, objectively and clearly written, with some historical background. Prof. Cumings, of the University of Washington, is a highly qualified scholar of Korea. (Available from the Foreign Policy Association, 205 Lexington Avenue, New York, NY 10016.)

"Democratic Peoples Republic of Korea (North Korea)." *Background Notes.* U.S. Department of State. Washington, D.C.: U.S. Government Printing Office, 1985. 8 pp. Useful quick-reference summary, one of a worldwide series of the Department of State.

Focus on Asian Studies: Korea. New York: The Asia Society, 1986. 84 pp. Illustrated essays, brief readings, and references on various aspects of Korea, for use by teachers and students at high-school level. (Available from the Asia Society, 725 Park Ave., New York, N.Y. 10021.)

"Republic of Korea (South Korea)." *Background Notes.* U.S. Department of State. Washington, D.C.: U.S. Government Printing Office, 1987. 8 pp. Useful quick-reference summary of Korean geography, history, politics, economics; one of a worldwide series published by the Department of State.

Sixteen Lessons About Korea. San Francisco, CA: World Affairs Council of Northern California, 1986. Material developed by teachers who participated in a 1985 Korea travel/study program; most designed for elementary levels, covering kites, masks, folktales, games. (For information write to the Council at 312 Sutter St., San Francisco, CA 94108.)

Two Koreas—One Future. Sullivan, John, and Foss, Roberta, editors. Philadelphia: American Friends Service Committee, 1987. 200 pp. Survey of Korea from a standpoint somewhat critical of U.S. and south Korean policies.

History

Fairbank, John K., Reischauer, Edwin O., and Craig, Albert M. *East Asia: Tradition and Transformation.* Cambridge, Mass.: Houghton Mifflin Co., 1973. 969 pp. This excellent survey of East Asian history from early times to the present has two chapters on the history of traditional Korea (Chapters 11 and 12, pp. 277–323), and sections of two others (Chapter 20, pp. 609–18, and Chapter 27, pp. 878–86) on Korea since the mid-nineteenth century.

Goulden, Joseph C. *Korea; The Untold Story of the War.* New York: Times Books, 1982. 690 pp. Thorough description of the war from the U.S. point of view, with emphasis on personalities and politics. Like other American histories of the war, it gives insufficient attention to the south Korean forces involved.

Han, Woo-keun. *The History of Korea.* Translated by Lee Kyung-shik, edited by Grafton K. Mintz. Honolulu: East-West Center Press, 1971. 546 pp. Now republished in paperback, this is perhaps the most readable of several good English-language histories. Unfortunately, like the others, it has little to say about Korea since 1910.

Kim, Joungwon Alexander. *Divided Korea; the Politics of Development, 1945–1972.* Cambridge, Mass.: East Asian Research Center, Harvard University (distributed by Harvard University Press), 1975. 300 pp. The best single source for the political history of Korea since liberation in 1945.

Korean History. Focus on Korea, vol. 2. Seoul: Seoul International Publishing House, 1986. 111 pp., illustrated, indexed; high school level.

Lee, Chong-sik. *The Korean Workers' Party: A Short History.* Stanford, Cal.: Hoover Institution Press, 1978. 200 pp., paper. Excellent summary of North Korean history since 1945, told through the evolution of the dominant Communist party.

Society and Culture

Brandt, Vincent S.R. *South Korean Society in Transition.* Elkins Park, Pa.: Philip Jaisohn Memorial Foundation, 1983. 50 pp. Well-written explanation of current Korean social problems, in a brief paperback pamphlet available from the Foundation (60 East Township Line Road, Elkins Park, Pa.). Dr. Brandt, a social anthropologist, is one of the few recognized U.S. authorities on Korean society.

Clark, Donald N. *Christianity in Modern Korea.* Asia Society monograph. Lanham, MD: University Press of America, 1986. 86 pp. Useful survey of the background and present position of Korean Christianity, the faith of a quarter of the south Korean population.

Covell, Jon Carter. *Korea's Cultural Roots.* Fifth edition. Seoul: Hollym International Publishing Co., 1983. 175 pp. Brief, lively, illustrated discussion of the main religious and philosophical strands in Korea's heritage.

Crane, Paul S. *Korean Patterns.* Seoul: Hollym Publishing Co., 1967. Insights on Korean society by a long-time medical missionary in Korea. Written nearly twenty years ago, it does not fully reflect today's social tensions but is a valuable guide to the wellsprings of Korean behavior.

Kalton, Michael. *Korean Ideas and Values.* Elkins Park, Pa.: Philip Jaisohn Memorial
  Foundation, 1979. 21 pp. Concise explanation of basic Korean social values, in
  a brief pamphlet. Available from the Foundation.
Morse, Ronald A., ed. *Wild Asters: Explorations in Korean Thought.* Lanham, MD:
  University Press of America, 1987. 150 pp. Thought-provoking discussions of
  various aspects of Korean psychology and society, based on a lecture series at
  the Woodrow Wilson International Center for Scholars.

Arts and Literature

Lee, Peter H., compiler. *Anthology of Korean Literature; from Early Times to the
  Nineteenth Century.* Honolulu: University of Hawaii Press, 1981. 448 pp., paper.
  Good selections to give the flavor of Korean writing, with introductory explanations.
McCune, Evelyn. *The Arts of Korea: An Illustrated History.* Rutland, Vermont: Charles
  E. Tuttle Co., 1962. 452 pp., bibliography, index. For the general reader, this is
  still the best short survey of Korean art, although there are more scholarly and
  more recent works.
Schultz, Edward J. *The History and Culture of Korea.* Six sound and color filmstrips
  with text and guide. Honolulu: University of Hawaii Press, 1985. Suitable for
  secondary and adult audiences.
So, Chong-ju. *Unforgettable Things.* Poems translated by David McCann. Seoul and
  New York: Si-sa-yong-o-sa, 1986. 158 pp. So Chong-ju is one of Korea's foremost
  contemporary poets, and has been mentioned as a possible nominee for a Nobel
  prize. David McCann is a U.S. authority on Korean literature.

Politics

An, Tai Sung. *North Korea: A Political Handbook.* Wilmington, Del.: Scholarly
  Resources, Inc., 1983. 294 pp. The most recent book available exclusively on
  North Korea.
Han, Sungjoo. *The Failure of Democracy in South Korea.* Berkeley: University of
  California Press, 1975. 250 pp. Scholarly study of the reasons for the failure of
  South Korea's brief experiment with full parliamentary democracy in 1960–1961.
Human Rights in Korea. New York: Asia Watch, 1987. 364 pp. Report of the human
  rights situation in Korea by a humanitarian group dedicated to observation of
  human rights violations worldwide.
Journey to North Korea. Kim, Eugene C.I., and Koh, B.C., editors. Berkeley: University
  of California Press, 1983. 152 pp. Accounts by several scholars of their observations
  during a visit to north Korea.
Kihl, Young Hwan. *Politics and Policies in Divided Korea; Regimes in Contest.* Boulder,
  Colorado: Westview Press, 1984. 307 pp. A critical scholarly survey of Korean
  politics, both north and south; thoughtful, but not light reading.
McCormack, Gavin and Selden, Mark, editors. *Korea North and South: The Deepening
  Crisis.* New York: Monthly Review Press, 1978. 300 pp. The revisionist viewpoint,
  very critical of the United States and south Korea.

"A Stern, Steady Crackdown"; Legal Process and Human Rights in South Korea.
New York: Asia Watch, May 1987. 133 pp.

Foreign Relations, National Security, Unification

Clough, Ralph N. *Embattled Korea: The Rivalry for International Support.* Boulder,
Colo: Westview Press, 1987. 401 pp. Valuable survey of north and south Korean
international relations, from the standpoint of their rivalry for international support
and their differing positions on reunification.

Koh, Byung Chul. *The Foreign Policy Systems of North and South Korea.* Berkeley:
University of California Press, 1984. 274 pp. Good description of how and why
foreign policy is made in the two Koreas. A scholarly book, but intelligible to
the intelligent general reader.

Korean Politics in Transition. Edward Reynolds Wright, editor. Seattle: Published for
the Royal Asiatic Society, Korea Branch, by the University of Washington Press,
1975. 399 pp. Now unfortunately out of print, this book contains insights into
Korean affairs that are still very useful.

Ku, Yong-nok. and Han, Sungjoo, editors. *The Foreign Policy of the Republic of
Korea.* New York: Columbia University Press, 1985. 300 pp. Well-written, cogent
essays analyzing Korean foreign relations.

South-North Dialogue in Korea. Seoul: International Cultural Society of Korea, 1984.
100 pp. Pamphlet summarizing the problem of reunifying Korea and current
diplomatic activity regarding the problem, written from the south Korean government's point of view. Available from Republic of Korea (south Korea) government
information offices overseas.

Economics

Brun, Ellen, and Hirsch, Jacques. *Socialist Korea: A Case Study in the Strategy of
Economic Development.* New York: Monthly Review Press, 1977. 432 pp. Written
from a viewpoint favorable to Communist north Korea, this book is useful for
those who want to understand the arguments in favor of that country's centrally-
directed economic system. It gives little hint, however, of the serious problems
that have plagued that system since the early 1970s.

Kuznets, Paul W. *Economic Growth and Structure in the Republic of Korea.* New
Haven, Ct.: Yale University Press, 1977. 238 pp. Scholarly discussion of south
Korea's economic development since the Korean War.

Mason, Edward S., et al. *The Economic and Social Modernization of the Republic
of Korea.* Cambridge, Mass.: Harvard University Press, 1980. 500 pp. Summary
of a comprehensive study by Harvard University's Center for Economic Development
and the Korea Development Institute in south Korea of the reasons for Korea's
economic success.

From Patron to Partner: The Development of U.S.-Korean Business and Trade Relations.
Moskowitz, Karl, editor. Lexington, Mass.: Lexington Books, 1984. 234 pp. Essays
by Korean and U.S. authorities discussing the evolution of the Korea-U.S. economic
relationship and its current problems.

Current Sources of Information on Korea

Daily Newspapers

Two daily English-language newspapers (8 pages, tabloid size) are published in south Korea: The *Korea Times* and the *Korea Herald*. They are similar in coverage, although the *Times* is published by the privately owned Korean daily *Hankook Ilbo*, while the *Herald* is published by the government-owned *Seoul Sinmun*. The *Herald* has a New York edition. U.S. newspapers do not give much coverage to Korean affairs except in times of crisis or disaster.

Weeklies

To keep up with Korean political and economic affairs, the best single source is probably the *Far Eastern Economic Review*, a weekly newsmagazine published in Hong Kong. The *Asian Wall Street Journal*, also published in Hong Kong, has a weekly edition.

For general coverage of the current South Korean scene, the best English-language publication is *Korea Newsreview*, a weekly published by the government-subsidized International Cultural Society of Korea in Seoul. News bulletins and pamphlets on current topics are often available from Korean information offices attached to diplomatic and consular missions; these, of course, tend to reflect the official view.

Weekly Report of the North American Coalition for Human Rights in Korea (Korean title: *Ingwon Sosik*, Human Rights News). Report by a Christian action group based in Washington, D.C., of current events in Korea relating to political oppression and human rights abuses. There are also periodic *Update* bulletins. (For information, write to the Coalition at 110 Maryland Avenue, N.E., Washington, DC 20002.)

For north Korea, there are English-language publications sponsored by the north Korean government, but they are not generally available in the United States, and are heavy on propaganda. An alternative is the daily and weekly Asia-Pacific reports summarizing radio and newspaper stories, published by Foreign Broadcast Information Service, a U.S. Government operation attached to the Department of Commerce. These are available in metropolitan and large university libraries. The south Korean government also publishes useful materials on north Korea, although some of them have heavy propaganda overtones.

Monthlies and Quarterlies

Asian Survey, a monthly published by the University of California, containing articles covering all of East and South Asia. The January and February issues each year summarize the previous year's developments in separate articles on all Asian countries, including north and south Korea.

Bulletin of Korean and Korean-American Studies, quarterly published by Dr. Hesung Koh, Human Relations Area Files, New Haven, Connecticut. Articles and source materials useful for the teaching of Korea.

Journal of Northeast Asian Studies, quarterly published at the Institute for Sino-
Soviet Studies, The George Washington University, Washington, D.C. Concentrates
on China, Japan, and Korea.

Korea and World Affairs. Quarterly journal of the Research Center for Peace and
Unification of Korea; has a good collection of articles on foreign affairs by
recognized Korean and foreign scholars.

Korea Journal, monthly publication of the Korean Commission for UNESCO, Seoul.
Articles on all aspects of Korean national life, with emphasis on history and
culture. Highly recommended.

Korean Culture, quarterly published in Los Angeles under South Korean government
subsidy and distributed free to teachers and others on request. Focusing on
Korean art and culture, it is well written and illustrated with color reproductions.

Mid-Atlantic Bulletin of Korean Studies. Published three times a year at the Asian
Studies Program, School of Foreign Service, Georgetown University. Reports recent
publications and events relating to Korean studies.

Monthly Review of Korean Affairs, a publication of the Council for Democracy in
Korea, Arlington, Virginia; sharply critical of the south Korean government. Usually
bimonthly.

Transactions of the Korea Branch, Royal Asiatic Society (KBRAS). Yearly journal of
the Korea Branch in Seoul. (KBRAS also publishes a quarterly newsletter for
members, publishes and sells books on Korea, and conducts tours.)

Reference Materials

Handbook of Korea. 6th edition. Seoul: Korean Overseas Information Service, Ministry
of Culture and Information, 1987. 549 pp. Excellent reference on all aspects of
south Korea, including a brief historical summary. Readably written and profusely
illustrated in color. (Limited free distribution has been made to institutions by
the Ministry's overseas representatives at embassies and consulates.)

Korea Annual. Seoul: Yonhap News Agency, yearly. About 675 pp. Compendium of
current facts on Korea.

North Korea: A Country Study. Frederica M. Bunge, ed. Foreign Area Studies, The
American University. Third edition. Washington, D.C.: U.S. Government Printing
Office, 1981. 300 pp. One of a series of country volumes commissioned by the
U.S. Army for training and reference purposes, written by competent civilian
specialists. Very useful, readable reference.

South Korea: A Country Study. Frederica M. Bunge, ed. Foreign Area Studies, The
American University. 3d ed. Washington, D.C.: U.S. Government Printing Office,
1982. 300 pp. Companion volume to the one immediately above.

BIBLIOGRAPHY

Books

Acheson, Dean. *The Korean War.* New York: Norton, 1971.

An, Tai Sung. *North Korea In Transition: From Dictatorship to Dynasty.* Contributions in Political Science, No. 95. Westport, Ct.: Greenwood Press, 1983.

Apter, David. *The Politics of Modernization.* Chicago: The University of Chicago Press, 1965.

Bartz, Patricia. *South Korea.* New York: Oxford University Press, 1972.

Berger, Carl. *The Korea Knot, A Military-Political History.* Revised edition. Philadelphia: University of Pennsylvania Press, 1965.

Brandt, Vincent S.R. *A Korean Village; Between Farm and Sea.* Harvard East Asian Series 65. Cambridge: Harvard University Press, 1971.

————. *South Korean Society In Transition.* Philip Jaisohn Memorial Paper No. 12. Elkins Park, Pa.: Philip Jaisohn Memorial Foundation, 1983.

Brandt, Vincent S.R., and Cheong, Ji Woon. *Planning from the Bottom up; Community-Based Integrated Rural Development in South Korea.* Essex, Ct.: International Council for Educational Development, 1979.

Brun, Ellen, and Hirsch, Jacques. *Socialist Korea: A Case Study in the Strategy of Economic Development.* New York: Monthly Review Press, 1971.

Carles, W.R. *Life in Corea.* New York: Macmillan & Co., 1894.

Cho, Soon Sung. *Korea in World Politics 1940–1950; An Evaluation of American Responsibility.* Berkeley: University of California Press, 1967.

Choe, Sang-su. *Annual Customs of Korea.* Seoul: Seomun-dang Publishers, 1983.

Chung, Joseph Sang-hoon. *The North Korean Economy; Structure and Development.* Stanford, Cal.: Hoover Institution Press, 1974.

Clark, Allen D. *A History of the Church in Korea.* Revised edition. Seoul: The Christian Literature Society of Korea, 1971.

Clark, Donald N. *Christianity in Modern Korea.* Asia Society monograph. Lanham, MD: University Press of America, 1986.

Cole, David C., and Lyman, Princeton N. *Korean Development: The Interplay of Politics and Economics.* Cambridge: Harvard University Press, 1971.

Conflicts and Harmony in Modern Society. Edited by Yong Sang Cho. Taegu: The Research Institutes for Social Sciences, Keimyung University, 1985.

Conroy, Hilary. *The Japanese Seizure of Korea, 1868–1910: A Study of Realism and Idealism in International Relations.* Philadelphia: University of Pennsylvania Press, 1960.

Contemporary Korean Painting. Berkeley, Cal.: Asian Humanities Press, 1979.

293

Cook, Harold F. *Korea's 1884 Incident; Its Background and Kim Ok-kyun's Elusive Dream.* Seoul: Royal Asiatic Society, Korea Branch, 1972.

Covell, Jon Carter. *Korea's Cultural Roots.* Fifth edition. Seoul: Hollym International Publishing Co., 1983.

Crane, Paul S. *Korean Patterns.* Seoul: Hollym Publishing Co., 1967.

Cumings, Bruce. *The Origins of the Korean War; Liberation and the Emergence of Separate Regimes, 1945–1947.* Princeton: Princeton University Press, 1981.

_____. *The Two Koreas.* New York: Foreign Policy Association, 1984.

deBary, William T., and Haboush, JaHyun Kim, editors. *The Rise of Neo-Confucianism in Korea.* New York: Columbia University Press, 1985.

Fairbank, John K., Reischauer, Edwin O., and Craig, Albert M. *East Asia: Tradition and Transformation.* Cambridge, Mass.: Houghton Mifflin Co., 1973.

Fighting Armies; Non-Aligned, Third World, and Other Ground Armies; A Combat Assessment. Richard A. Gabriel, editor. Westport, Ct.: Greenwood Press, 1983.

Friedrich, Karl J., and associates. *American Experience in Military Government in World War II.* New York: Rinehart, 1948.

Goodrich, Leland. *Korea: A Study of U.S. Policy in the United Nations.* New York: Council on Foreign Relations, 1956.

Goulden, Joseph C. *Korea; The Untold Story of the War.* New York: Times Books, 1982.

Grajdanzev, Andrew. *Modern Korea.* New York: International Secretariat, Institute of Pacific Relations, distributed by John Day Co., 1944.

Grant, Bruce K. *A Guide to Korean Characters; Reading and Writing Hangul and Hanja.* Second revised edition. Elizabeth, N.J.: Hollym International Corp., 1982.

Griffis, W. E. *Corea; The Hermit Nation.* New York: AMS Press, 1971 (reprint of ninth, 1911, edition).

Hahm, Pyong Choon. *The Korean Political Tradition and Law: Essays in Law and Legal History.* Royal Asiatic Society, Korea Branch. Monograph series, No. 1. Seoul: Huimang Ch'ulp'ansa, 1965.

Han, Sungjoo. *The Failure of Democracy in South Korea.* Berkeley: University of California Press, 1975.

Han, Sungjoo, editor. *Korea in the Year 2000: Prospects for Development and Change.* Seoul: Asiatic Research Center, Korea University, 1986.

Han, Woo-keun. *The History of Korea..* Translated by Lee Kyung-shik, edited by Grafton K. Mintz. Seoul: Eul-yoo Publishing Co., 1970.

Hasan, Parvez, and Rao, D. C. *Korea: Policy Issues for Long-Term Development; The Report of a Mission Sent to the Republic of Korea by the World Bank.* Baltimore: Published for the World Bank by the Johns Hopkins University Press, 1979.

Henderson, Gregory. *Korea: The Politics of the Vortex.* Cambridge, Mass.: Harvard University Press, 1968.

Hong, Sung Chick. *The Intellectual and Modernization: A Study of Korean Attitudes.* Seoul: Social Science Research Institute, Korea University, 1967.

Human Rights in Korea. New York: Asia Watch, 1987.

Kalton, Michael. *Korean Ideas and Values.* Philip Jaisohn Memorial Paper No. 7. Elkins Park, Pa.: Philip Jaisohn Memorial Foundation, 1979.

Kihl, Young Hwan. *Politics and Policies in Divided Korea; Regimes in Contest.* Boulder, Colorado: Westview Press, 1984.

Kim, C.I. Eugene, ed. *Journey to North Korea; Personal Perceptions.* Berkeley: Institute of East Asian Studies, University of California, 1983.

Kim, C.I. Eugene, and Chee, Ch'angboh, editors. *Aspects of Social Change in Korea.* Kalamazoo, Mich.: Korea Research and Publication, 1969.

Kim, C.I. Eugene, and Kim, Han-Kyo. *Korea and the Politics of Imperialism, 1876–1910.* Berkeley: University of California Press, 1967.

Kim, Chum-kon. *The Korean War; The First Comprehensive Account of the Historical Background and Development of the Korean War (1950–1953).* Seoul: Kwangmyong Publishing Co., 1973.

Kim, Dae Jung. *Mass-Participatory Economy; A Democratic Alternative for Korea.* Cambridge: Center for International Affairs, Harvard University; Lanham, Md.: University Press of America, 1985.

Kim, Joungwon A. *Divided Korea: The Politics of Development, 1945–1972.* Published by East Asian Research Center, Harvard University, under joint sponsorship with Research Institute on Communist Affairs, Columbia University. Cambridge: Harvard University Press, 1975.

Kim, Kwan Bong. *The Korea-Japan Treaty Crisis and the Instability of the Korean Political System.* New York: Praeger Publishers, 1971.

Kim, Richard E. *Lost Names; Scenes from a Korean Boyhood.* New York: Praeger Publishers, 1970.

Kim, Se-Jin. *The Politics of Military Revolution in Korea.* Chapel Hill: University of North Carolina Press, 1971.

Koh, Byung Chul. *The Foreign Policy Systems of North and South Korea.* Berkeley: University of California Press, 1984.

Korea. Republic. Economic Planning Board. *P'alsimnyondae Kyongje Chongch'aek ui Chinch'ul Songkwa wa Hyanghu Kwajong.* Seoul, 1985.

Korea. Republic. Ministry of Education. *Education in Korea 1985–1986,* Seoul, 1985.

Korea under Japanese Colonial Rule; Studies of the Policy and Techniques of Japanese Colonialism. Andrew C. Nahm, editor. Korea Study Series 2: Proceedings of the Conference on Korea, November 12–14, 1970. Kalamazoo: The Center for Korean Studies, Western Michigan University, 1973.

Ku, Yong-nok, and Han, Sungjoo, editors. *The Foreign Policy of the Republic of Korea.* New York: Columbia University Press, 1985.

Kuznets, Paul W. *Economic Growth and Structure in the Republic of Korea.* New Haven, Ct.: Yale University Press, 1977.

Leckie, Robert. *Conflict: The History of the Korean War, 1950–1953.* New York: Putnam, 1962.

Lee, Chae-Jin. *China's Korean Minority: The Politics of Ethnic Education.* Boulder, Colo.: Westview Press, 1986.

Lee, Chong-Sik. *The Korean Workers' Party: A Short History.* Stanford, Cal.: Hoover Institution Press, 1978.

────── . *The Politics of Korean Nationalism.* Berkeley: University of California Press, 1963.

Lee, Hahn-Been. *Korea: Time, Change, and Administration.* Honolulu: East-West Center Press, 1968.

Lee, Ki-baik. *A New History of Korea*. Translated by Edward W. Wagner. Cambridge, Mass.: Harvard University Press, 1985.

Lee, Peter H., compiler. *Anthology of Korean Literature; from Early Times to the Nineteenth Century*. Honolulu: University of Hawaii Press, 1981.

Mason, Edward S., et al. *The Economic and Social Modernization of the Republic of Korea*. Studies in the Modernization of the Republic of Korea: 1945–1975. Harvard East Asian Monographs, 92. Cambridge, Mass.: Council on East Asian Studies, Harvard University, 1980.

McCormack, Gavin, and Selden, Mark, editors, *Korea North and South: The Deepening Crisis*. New York: Monthly Review Press, 1978.

McCune, Evelyn. *The Arts of Korea: An Illustrated History*. Rutland, Vermont: Charles E. Tuttle Co., 1962.

McCune, George M. *Korea Today*. With the collaboration of Arthur L. Grey, Jr. Issued under the auspices of the International Secretariat of the Institute of Pacific Relations. Cambridge: Harvard University Press, 1950.

McCune, Shannon. *Korea's Heritage: A Regional and Social Geography*. Rutland, Vt.: C. E. Tuttle Co., 1956.

McKenzie, F.A. *Korea's Fight for Freedom*. London, 1920; reprinted, Seoul: Yonsei University Press, 1969.

Mitchell, Richard H. *The Korean Minority in Japan*. Berkeley: University of California Press, 1967.

Moskowitz, Karl, editor. *From Patron to Partner: The Development of U.S.-Korean Business and Trade Relations*. Lexington, Mass.: Lexington Books, 1984.

Nelson, M. Frederick. *Korea and the Old Orders in Eastern Asia*. Baton Rouge: Louisiana State University Press, 1945.

North Korea Today; Strategic and Domestic Issues. Edited by Robert A. Scalapino and Jun-Yop Kim. Korea Research Monograph 8. Center for Korean Studies. Berkeley: Institute of East Asian Studies, University of California, 1983.

Oh, John Kie-chang. *Korea: Democracy on Trial*. New York: Cornell University Press, 1968.

Oliver, Robert T. *Syngman Rhee: The Man Behind the Myth*. New York: Dodd, Mead & Co., 1954; reprinted, Westport, Ct.: Greenwood Press, 1973.

Palais, James B. *Politics and Policy in Traditional Korea*. Cambridge: Harvard University Press, 1975.

Palmer, Spencer J. *Korea and Christianity: The Problem of Identification with Tradition*. Seoul: Hollym Corp., 1967.

Park, Chung Hee. *Our Nation's Path; Ideology of Social Reconstruction*. Seoul: Hollym Corp., 1970.

Park, Ki-hyuk, and Gamble, Sidney D. *The Changing Korean Village*. Seoul: Shinhung Press for the Royal Asiatic Society, Korea Branch, 1975.

Pyun, Y. T. *Korea, My Country*. Seoul: International Cultural Association of Korea, 1949; reprinted, Seoul: Council on Korean Affairs, 1962.

Rees, David. *Korea: The Limited War*. New York: St. Martin's Press, 1964.

Religions in Korea: Beliefs and Cultural Values. Phillips, Earl H., and Yu, Eul-yong, editors. Los Angeles, Cal.: Center for Korean-American and Korean Studies, California State University, 1982.

Sandusky, Michael. *America's Parallel.* Alexandria, Va.: Old Dominion Press, 1985.

Scalapino, Robert A., and Lee, Chong-Sik. *Communism in Korea, Part 1: The Movement.* Berkeley: University of California Press, 1972.

Son, Duk Sung, and Clark, Robert J. *Korean Karate; The Art of Tae Kwon Do.* Englewood Cliffs, N.J.: Prentice-Hall, 1968.

U.S. Central Intelligence Agency. *Directory of Officials of the Democratic People's Republic of Korea.* Washington, D.C., April 1985.

————. *Korea: The Economic Race between the North and South.* Washington, D.C.: U.S. Government Printing Office, 1978.

U.S. Congress. House Committee on Standards of Official Conduct. *Korean Influence Investigation. Hearings.* Part 1, October 19–21, 1977; Part 2, April 3–5, 10, 11, 1978. Washington, D.C.: U.S. Government Printing Office, 1978.

U.S. Department of State. *The Korean Problem at the Geneva Conference, April 26–June 15, 1954.* Publication 5609. Washington: U.S. Government Printing Office, 1954.

Wagner, Edward W. *The Literati Purges: Political Conflict in Early Yi Korea.* Harvard East Asian Monographs, 58. Cambridge, Mass.: East Asian Research Center; distributed by Harvard University Press, 1974.

Weems, Benjamin B. *Reform, Rebellion, and the Heavenly Way.* Association for Asian Studies, Monographs and Papers, No. 15. Tucson: University of Arizona Press for the Association for Asian Studies, 1964.

Wild Asters: Explorations in Korean Thought. Ronald A. Morse, editor. Lanham, MD: University Press of America, 1987.

Wilkinson, William Henry. *The Corean Government; Constitutional Changes, July, 1894, to October, 1895.* Shanghai: Statistical Department of the Inspectorate General, 1897.

Wright, Edward Reynolds, editor. *Korean Politics in Transition.* Seattle: University of Washington Press, 1975.

Yang, Seung Mok. *Korean Etiquette.* Seoul: Ke Rim Corp., 1964.

Yi, Man-gap. *Sociology and Social Change in Korea.* Seoul: Seoul National University Press, 1982.

Articles, Manuscripts, Papers

Baker, Edward, and Stevens, Robert. "The Korean Legal System; Some Initial Observations." Paper presented to 24th meeting of Association for Asian Studies, New York, March 1972.

Brandt, Vincent S.R. "North Korea; Anthropological Speculation." *Korea and World Affairs* 7 (No. 4, Winter 1983):617–28.

Brown, Steven R. "Values, Development, and Character: Appraising Korean Experience." *Korea Fulbright Forum,* (No. 1, Winter 1984), pp. 33–66.

Ch'oe, Yong-ho. "Christian Background in the Early Life of Kim Il-song." *Asian Survey* 26 (No. 10, October 1986):1082–91.

Ginsburgs, George and Herta, "A Statistical Profile of the Korean Community in the Soviet Union." *Asian Survey* 17 (No. 10, October 1977):952–56

"Gist of President Chun Doo Hwan's Special Statement on Constitutional Reform."
    Korea News/Views No. 87-08, Korean Information Office, Washington, D.C., Apr.
    13, 1987. 3 pp., mimeographed.
Kim, Jung-hak. "Ethnological Origins of Korean Nation," *Korea Journal* 3 (No. 6,
    June 1963):5–8.
Kim, Won-yong. "Philosophies and Styles in Korean Art." *Korea Journal* 19 (No. 4,
    April 1979):8.
Lee, Hong-youn. "Structure and Prospect of North Korean Trade." *Vantage Point*
    (Seoul)., September 1981, p. 5.
Lee, Mun-woong. "Family System in North Korea: Continuity and Change." *Korea
    Journal* 18 (No. 3, March 1978):36–43.
Macdonald, Donald S. "Korea and the Ballot: The International Dimension in Korean
    Political Development as Seen in Elections, 1945-1960" (unpublished Ph.D. dis-
    sertation, The George Washington University, 1978).
Shin, Susan. "Tonghak Thought: The Roots of Revolution." *Korea Journal* 19 (No.
    9, September 1979):11–24.
Suh, Sang-mok. "Korea's Sixth Five-Year Plan: A 'Second Economic Take-Off.' "
    Korea's Economy, Korea Economic Institute, Washington, D.C., 3 (No. 2, April
    1987), p. 12.
U.S. Information Service, Seoul. "1985 Human Rights Report for Republic of Korea,"
    Backgrounder, February 19, 1986.
————. "Human Rights Report for Democratic People's Republic of Korea," *Back-
    grounder,* February 21, 1986.
Yim, Yong Sun. "The Significance of the January 22 Unification Proposal." *Korea
    and World Affairs* 6 (No. 1, Spring 1982):19–38.

Newspapers and Periodicals

Asian Survey (University of California, monthly).
Bank of Korea *Quarterly Review* (Seoul).
Business Korea (Seoul, monthly).
Daily Report—Asia-Pacific. Foreign Broadcast Information Service, U.S. Department
    of Commerce, Washington, D.C.
Far Eastern Economic Review (Hong Kong, weekly).
Korea Business World (Seoul).
The Korea Herald (Seoul and New York, daily).
The Korea Times (Seoul, daily).
Korea Journal (Seoul, monthly).
Korea Newsreview (Seoul, weekly).
Weekly Report, North American Coalition for Human Rights in Korea, Washington,
    D.C. (Korean title: *Ingwon Sosik,* Human Rights News).

Reference Materials

Encyclopedia of Asian History, Ainslie T. Embree, Editor in Chief (New York: Charles
    Scribner's Sons, 1987).

Encyclopaedia Britannica, 14th edition, 1973.

Facts on File.

Foreign Relations of the United States. U.S. Department of State, Historical Office, Washington, D.C., various years.

Handbook on Korean-U.S. Relations. New York: The Asia Society, 1985.

Korea Annual. Seoul: Yonhap News Agency, various years.

Korea. Republic. Economic Planning Board. *Social Indicators in Korea, 1985.* Seoul, 1986.

————. National Bureau of Statistics. *Korea Statistical Yearbook, 1985.* Seoul, 1986.

Korea. Republic. Ministry of Culture and Information. Korean Overseas Information Service. *Handbook of Korea.* Sixth edition. Seoul, 1987.

North Korea: A Country Study. Frederica M. Bunge, editor. Foreign Area Studies, The American University. Third edition. Washington, D.C.: U.S. Government Printing Office, 1981.

Political Parties of Asia and the Pacific. Fukui, Haruhiro, editor-in-chief. Westport, Ct.: Greenwood Press, 1985.

South Korea: A Country Study. Frederica M. Bunge, Ed. Foreign Area Studies, The American University. 3d ed. Washington, D.C.: U.S. Government Printing Office, 1982.

U.S. Department of Commerce. Federal Broadcast Information Service. *Asia-Pacific Daily Summary.*

U.S. Embassy, Seoul. *Economic Trends Report.*

INDEX

Acheson, Dean, 50, 227
Agriculture, 8, 64(n14)
  in DPRK, 56, 75, 170, 213–214, 216,
    220(n47)
  modernization of, 74–75
  in ROK, 74–75, 148, 188, 197–199
Aliyev, Geidar, 247–248
Allen, Horace, 42, 102
Amnesty International, 129
Ancestor "worship," 70
Ancient Choson, 27. See also Choson
  Dynasty
ANSP. See Republic of Korea, Agency
  for National Security Planning
Anti-American Struggle Month, 243,
  248
Appenzeller, Henry, 102
Apter, David, 15
Architecture, 76, 99
Aristotle, 83
Armistice Agreement, 4, 21, 52, 224,
  233, 234, 254(n2), 265
Arms industry
  in DPRK, 243
  in ROK, 228
Art, 31, 36, 68, 93–99
Artists. See Yangban aristocracy
ASEAN. See Association of Southeast
  Asian Nations
Asian Development Bank, 241
Asian Games, 242, 269
ASPAC. See Association of Pacific
  Nations
Association of National Olympic
  Committees, 242
Association of Pacific Nations (ASPAC),
  229
Association of Southeast Asian Nations
  (ASEAN), 196

Australia, 206, 233, 254(n2)
Austria, 264, 274
Autocracy, 114

Bank of Korea, 200–201
Belgium, 233, 254(n2)
Brazil, 252
Brezhnev doctrine, 273
Buddha (Gautama), 100
Buddhism, 10, 28, 29–30, 31, 32, 82,
  93, 94–95, 96, 99, 100–101, 103,
  140
Bureaucracy
  in DPRK, 213
  in ROK, 132
Burma, 241

Cairo Declaration, 44, 258
Canada, 206, 233, 254(n2)
Capitalism, 211–212, 260
Carter, Jimmy, 22, 226, 250, 263, 269
Catholicism. See Christianity
Censorship, 98, 138. See also
  Repression
CFC. See Combined Forces Command
Chaebol. See Industrial sectors
Chang, John M. See Chang Myon
Chang Duk Soo, 47–48
Chang Myon, 53, 118, 122, 124, 130,
  187
Chaoxian. See Ancient Choson
Chiang Kai-shek, 43, 44
Children. See Family
China, 10, 23(n1), 37, 60, 78, 81, 239,
  260
  cultural influence of, 11–14, 26, 27,
    29, 30, 31, 32, 34–35, 68, 82, 83,
    93, 95, 96, 99, 115, 225